Writing Public Lives

From Personal Interests to Public Rhetoric

3rd Edition

Christopher Minnix, Carol Nowotny-Young

University of Arizona

HAYDEN
HM
MᶜNEIL

ISBN 978-0-7380-4941-0

Hayden-McNeil Publishing
14903 Pilot Drive
Plymouth, MI 48170
www.hmpublishing.com

HallA 4941-0 W12

Table of Contents

Readings for Rhetorical Analysis

Defining and Envisioning Ourselves

SECTION TWO: CONTROVERSY ANALYSIS

Readings in Controversy

SECTION THREE: PUBLIC ARGUMENT

Readings in Public Argument

SECTION FOUR: REVISION AND REFLECTION

Biographies

Christopher Minnix is Assistant Director of the Writing Program at the University of Arizona. He holds a Ph.D. in Rhetoric, Writing, and Linguistics from the Department of English of the University of Tennessee.

Carol Nowotny-Young is a member of the Writing Program faculty at the University of Arizona and is the course director for English 102, the second-semester course in the first-year sequence.

About the Cover

Cover design winner: Bryce Emily Megdal, University of Arizona 2012

My cover art and weather images pertain to the idea of Citizen Participation in Public Life, Public Life on the University of Arizona Campus, and Public Life in Tucson. The cover photograph was taken from the University of Arizona Football Stadium, facing North. Football is a big attraction in Tucson due to Tucson being a sports town; football games bring thousands of families and local Tucsonans together. Although the crowd consists of people from all over, creating a diverse group, they join together, despite their differences, in a public space to support their Wildcats. In addition, I think most students who attend the University of Arizona, people who are affiliated with the University of Arizona, or residents of Tucson, are aware of Tucson's beautiful and unique weather, particularly its sunsets. I've heard, and can admit as a born and raised Tucsonan, that there's nothing like an Arizona sunset. This is a sincere statement, for there truly is a spectacular quality within a mesmerizing Tucson or Arizona sunset. Its vibrant light and colors, cloud patterns, mountain silhouettes, etc., only emphasize that we should enjoy nature and its richness that surrounds us before it disappears. Besides this, virga is an Arizona weather phenomenon that rarely occurs elsewhere; not many people outside of Tucson, or Arizona, know of the term "virga" (You can refer to pages 193 and 489 to see what virga is!). Therefore, it is a special weather characteristic noticed and appreciated by Arizonans. Hence, included are photographs of Tucson weather at the beginning of the chapters. Thank you!

Titles for Images

Acknowledgments

Writing Public Lives would simply not have been possible without the guidance, support, and encouragement of the University of Arizona's Writing Program and Department of English. We would like to thank Anne-Marie Hall for providing the opportunity to pursue this project and for her expert guidance and generous support. In addition, the administrative staff of the University of Arizona's Writing Program—Monica Vega, Sara Vickery, Penny Gates, and Mitzi Corral—has provided essential administrative support throughout this project.

We would also like to thank the Writing Program faculty—Beth Alvarado, Patrick Baliani, Jo Anne Behling, Barbara Cully, D.R. Ransdell, and Erec Toso—for their support and inspiration during the writing of this book.

It is a rare and delightful situation to work with contributors who possess the acumen and talent of the contributors to *Writing Public Lives*. We are greatly indebted to Angelica Almader, Patrick Baliani, Jessica Burstrem, Erica Cirillo-McCarthy, Adrienne Crump, Marlowe Daly-Galeano, Michelle Faas, Ashley Holmes, Shelly Jackson, Krystal Jenkins, Margaret Jay Jessee, Melissa Koblens, Kristi Kawamoto, Faith Kurtyka, Rachel Lewis, Star Medzerian, Rebecca Richards, Jessica Shumake, Erec Toso, Elise Verzosa, and Maggie Werner.

Writing Public Lives has benefited from the insights of the talented instructors of the University of Arizona's Writing Program since its inception. We would like to thank members of our focus groups—Laura Bivona, Annie Holub, Margaret Jay Jessee, Kara Johnson, Drew Kopp, Mary Woo, Rebecca Richards, and Jacob Witt. The instructors who graciously piloted and assessed

Writing Public Lives in the fall semester of 2009 provided enormously helpful feedback and guidance. We are greatly indebted to Leslie Dupont, Kara Johnson, Regina Kelly, Londie Martin, Robert Matte, and Katie O'Donnell for their insight.

In addition, we are grateful to the instructors and students at the University of Arizona's Writing Program for their responses to two separate surveys.

We would also like to thank Fedora Preston-Haynes and Gustavo Torres for designing and administering a survey of students and instructors who used the pilot version of this textbook. Special thanks to Jennifer Haley-Brown, their instructor, who provided expert guidance during this process.

We are also indebted to Lisa Wess of Hayden-McNeil Publishing for shepherding this project from its conception to the final editing process. Her expertise and encouragement have been vital.

Christopher Minnix would like to also thank his wife, Margaret Jay Jessee, for her brilliant insight and advice on the development of this and many other projects.

Introduction

By Christopher Minnix

This book is about writing to engage the world around you. We begin with a simple proposition: *student writing can make a tangible difference in our society and culture.* This statement isn't merely empty rhetoric, but a fact that is proven year after year on college campuses and in communities across our country. Beginning with this idea, we have tried to create a unique textbook, one that gives you strategies for a wide range of writing situations, some academic and some outside of the university. We want to challenge you to think of your writing as much more than just the answer to an assignment in a class, or one more paper for one more grade. Instead, we would like for you to think about your research and writing as a process of discovery. We hope that you will use this book to pursue those ideas you find engaging.

As you read this book, you will learn a sophisticated set of skills that will ready you to use your writing to make a difference, both in your own academic life and in the lives of those around you. You will also see several striking examples of how students just like yourselves have used their writing to argue for significant changes in their communities. In reading this book, you will be learning about the art of persuasive public communication. This is the art of **rhetoric**. Rhetoric is an art of adapting our messages to persuade our audiences and fulfill our purposes. Because our audiences, purposes, and contexts change, rhetoric is not a list of writing dos and don'ts, but an art of learning how to size up different situations and make effective choices when addressing them.

Let's start by peeking in on three students as they size up their situations and make some important choices about their writing.

A Tale of Three Students: Rhetorical Choices

Anna

Anna stares at a draft of a paper for an elective course on International Politics. Her professor has asked her to choose an aspect from contemporary culture that illustrates a positive or negative effect of globalization. It was a difficult assignment at first, but as Anna researched and brainstormed about the issue she began to develop an idea that she liked: how the banning of American films in several Middle Eastern countries contradicts the idea that globalization is producing a more united world. Having spent the previous summer in the Middle East as part of a study abroad program, Anna is eager to draw upon her own experience in order to support her paper. While abroad, she witnessed many black market sales of American films and heard many arguments about how these films were harmful. The problem is that her assignment states that she is "to write an argumentative essay supported by research" and does not address whether or not she can "use I" or draw upon her personal experience. As she looks at her essay, she thinks of the readings she has done for the class and her previous assignments. Only a few used personal narrative, and these only did so in the introduction. She then thinks of her professor reading the essay, picturing him writing "interesting, but you need to use research to support your argument." She looks back at the paper, glancing at her personal narrative, and contemplates cutting it from her essay.

Parker

Parker stands over a table looking at drafts of an article on the Darfur Genocide for the student newspaper. As a leader of a human rights group on campus, he has been chosen to write an article that explains how students can take action on the genocide by meeting on the campus mall for a Day of Awareness for Darfur. He is wondering if the first draft sounds too formal or "preachy." He feels that it sounds in some ways like a public service announcement: "Over the past six years, over two million people have died in the genocide that has ravaged Darfur in Western Sudan." He thinks that this number helps show how important intervention is, but he wonders if beginning his article in this way will inspire his fellow students to act. It seems, he thinks, like just another news article, more focused on information than activism. The second draft is a bit lean on information, but seems to strike the right emotional tone: "Every day, while we walk across campus listening to our iPods, worried about our grades or relationships, a young man or woman in Darfur walks through a refugee camp wondering if they will eat." Parker looks at each draft, contemplating if he should develop a compromise between the personal and the informative.

Max

Max is staring at an empty status update bar on his favorite social network site. He has been looking at this empty status for about 25 minutes contemplating something funny or ironic to say that would capture his mood and make his friends comment. Nothing interesting has happened on this day; he went to class, bought a set of new ear-buds at the bookstore, and came home to study for a Chemistry exam. Having no event to comment upon, he needs a one-liner to post. He goes through several drafts. "Max finds his love for Ramen Noodles growing cold." Fine, he thinks, but not that funny. "Max needs a life." This one has a ring of truth at the moment, but he is afraid it makes him sound too pathetic. "Max is buzzed on caffeine and bored." This one is neither funny nor interesting. Looking at all of the funny, irreverent posts from his friends, he deletes the last draft of his status update and stares at the blank space some more.

We often find ourselves in situations like Anna, Parker, and Max face, situations where we are staring at a draft or a blank screen wondering if we are making the right choices. This moment is what we will talk about in this book as a **rhetorical situation**, a moment where we are trying to adapt our writing or speech to a specific audience and context in order to fulfill a specific purpose or goal. We encounter these situations not just when we sit down to write, but as part of our everyday lives. Rhetoric, in this sense, can be thought of as touching upon every aspect of human communication.

In Anna's case, she is wrestling with finding the right voice for an academic audience and determining if this audience will accept her own personal experiences in the Middle East as evidence to support her arguments. For some audiences, such as readers of her school's newspaper, this evidence would be effective, but the audience for her research paper requires her to support her arguments with more research than personal experience. Parker is facing almost the opposite dilemma, wondering if his article sounds too academic and if it will fail to show students the importance of acting on this issue or how this issue touches their lives. Max's choices may not seem as important to us at first glance, but the choices that he makes as he updates his status are directly related to his popularity in the social network, and he wants to secure enough responses to his status update to prove this popularity.

Here is one more example taken from my own classroom experience. On the first day of a new course, after going over the syllabus and other materials, I ask my students to think of one or two things that they would recommend to their classmates. It can be anything, from the best new band they have heard recently, the best plate of carne seca in Tucson, the best book they have read or film they have seen. As students think through this, I observe the concentration on their faces and think about how seriously I used to think about this question when one of my favorite graduate school professors began his class this way. One particular recommendation sticks out from several years ago. I pointed to a student sitting in the back row with his baseball hat pulled down right above his eyebrows and asked "What's your recommendation?" He said, suavely, "I recommend mixing certain beverages with Sunny D, if you know what I mean." Ever since then, I have used this example with new classes as an example of how someone responded to a rhetorical situation.

Let's think through my student's reasoning for a second. We might just say that this student is trying to look cool, but if we think about his rhetorical situation there is quite a bit going on. First, he sizes up his **audience**, looking at his classmates and trying to determine if they will relate to his statement. He probably looks at the way they are dressed, the way they are sitting (attentively or in a way that shows they too are too cool for school), and he perhaps thinks about his encounters with other students and the types of things they find funny or cool. He is also thinking through his **context**, or the contemporary circumstances that he and his audience share. He might be thinking about the fact that several of his classmates were talking about a party that they went to before class began, or even how the seriousness of a classroom would make his recommendation all the more shocking and funny. As he thinks through his audience and context, one thing that he is probably anticipating is the reaction of his audience and this reaction serves as his **purpose**, or the goal of his rhetoric.

Rhetorical Analysis and Rhetorical Practice

By watching the choices of Anna, Parker, Max, and the student we might call Sunny D, we can see that rhetoric is an art of choices, one that is less concerned with ironclad or general rules about writing and more concerned with how we adapt that writing for specific audiences, contexts, and purposes. As we explore the various aspects of rhetoric in this book, we will view rhetoric in two important ways:

1. As a method of analyzing the persuasiveness of written and spoken texts. We will refer to this aspect of rhetoric as **rhetorical analysis**.

2. As a practice of persuasive communication for a variety of audiences, purposes, and contexts. We will refer to this aspect of rhetoric as **rhetorical practice**.

These two aspects of rhetoric—analysis and practice—may seem at first like they are completely separate activities, but we shall see that the skills of rhetorical analysis are essential to our effective practice of rhetoric. When we looked in on Anna, Parker, and Max, we watched them making rhetorical choices based upon their analysis of their rhetorical situations.

If we were to analyze what they wrote, we might look at the strategies that they used to persuade their audience. Our focus would be on analyzing and evaluating the persuasiveness of their writing, or how their choices enabled or prevented them from achieving the purposes of their writing. When you practice rhetorical analysis, you will see writers and speakers hit and miss their persuasive goals based upon how well they have sized up their rhetorical situation.

When we move to rhetorical practice, we move from analyzing the persuasiveness of someone else's writing or speech to analyzing our own rhetorical situation. When we analyze these situations we develop strategies for addressing our audience and context and fulfilling our purpose in the most effective way. In this sense, analysis becomes part of our practice. By analyzing the rhetorical choices that others make, we learn about the choices that we make as we use our own rhetoric.

Knowing the choices of other writers and speakers is only a starting point, however. When we use our own rhetoric in writing or in spoken conversation, we often find that our rhetorical situation (audience, context, purpose) might be quite different than those of the texts we have analyzed. This leads us to a final point to consider about rhetoric: **rhetoric is adaptive**.

What does this mean? It means that as writers and speakers we are constantly adapting our rhetoric to new audiences and purposes. This might sound easy. Know the audience and their context, and you can figure out how to achieve your purpose, right? As it turns out, this fundamental process of communication, one we use everyday, is actually more difficult than it appears. Rhetorical situations affect every aspect of our communication, the genre or forms of writing we use, our voice or tone, the arguments we use, the style that we use to develop arguments, the organization of these ideas, even our word choice. All of this is to say that when we think of rhetoric as "adaptive" we are thinking of it as requiring a constant give and take relationship between ourselves and the rhetorical situation we find ourselves in. It also means that as we try to successfully read our rhetorical situation our audience will also be trying to read us. They will attempt to size up our rhetoric from their own social perspective.

This does not mean that our purpose should be to say what our audience wants to hear. We may partially or completely disagree with our audience on an issue. In this case, reading our audience would entail the broad process of analyzing and understanding why the audience holds to the idea or argument that we find objectionable. In doing this, we might attempt to find contradictions between their arguments or the values they attach to them in order to refute their argument. Or, we might compare or contrast their arguments or values with our own in order to find some form of common ground. These are just a few of many options, and we will look at refutation and common ground arguments later in this book. For now, the key thing to keep in mind is that reading our audience entails thinking through the process of how they will read us. Rhetoric provides us with a set of strategies for taking part in this complex and uncertain process.

Rhetoric: It's Not Just for Writing Classes

In the process of using language in your day-to-day life, you analyze or size up a myriad of rhetorical situations and respond to them by adapting your rhetorical practice. Sometimes, like Max, Anna, and Parker, you find yourself thinking more deeply about how to develop an argument that will persuade your audience. Other times, you do this so quickly you don't even realize it.

Here is a real-world example. Watch someone over 40 order a cup of coffee at a coffee house. You may have seen someone that fits this description walk past the sign that gives the prices of *Grande*, *Venti*, and *Tall* and say "I'll have a medium coffee." It's a common enough example, but there are several rhetorical acts going on. First, the person placing the order incorrectly may not know the rhetorical style of the coffee house, or may lack knowledge of the *rhetorical context* of the coffee house. Diction, or word choice, shows that this person is in foreign territory. Second, we have to think about why Italian words like *"Grande"* and *"Venti"* would be used to sell coffee. The coffeehouse itself has made a rhetorical choice in order to link their product to Italy's well-known gourmet or food culture. Small, Medium, and Large sound so boring and pedestrian. *Grande* and *Venti* sound gourmet. Third, the person behind the counter must also make a rhetorical choice about whether or not to simply hand this person a *Grande* coffee or to correct them. This is perhaps the trickiest situation, in that they have to analyze the potential responses of their audience with little to no information about them.

This is just one example of the many ways we use rhetoric in our day-to-day lives and how rhetoric shapes our world. We share examples like these with you throughout this book in hopes that you will see that rhetoric is not just confined to writing courses. This is an important point because while this book gives you excellent strategies for academic writing, or the type of writing you will do at the college level, it does not stop there. Instead, this book will also introduce you to powerful strategies for taking your writing public, or writing for a variety of audiences that exist outside the four walls of your classrooms.

So, what does this all mean for you as a student? It means that in studying rhetoric, you are not learning one way to write in all contexts, but a set of reading, writing, and thinking processes that will allow you to size up and respond to the many communication situations you will find yourself in. In this book, you will learn more than just strategies for academic writing. These are definitely here. But, more importantly, you will learn to use rhetorical analysis to develop a process for analyzing and writing in a variety of different settings and for a variety of different purposes. So, as you read through these chapters and write in your classes, we encourage you to start thinking about how these strategies might apply to your life outside the classroom—your life in your profession, your life in your community.

Prior Theories or Carry-On Baggage

Though each rhetorical situation challenges us to adapt to a new audience, we often show up with what some philosophers of language call **prior theories** about writing. This is not a good or bad thing but a human thing. As people who constantly communicate, we bring our knowledge and experience from our past writing experiences with us, much like we bring our carry-on luggage onto an airplane. These prior theories are simply knowledge that we have accumulated through our experience writing in the past. These experiences are not useless once we move to a new rhetorical situation. In fact, they are one of the starting points of all communication, and the forms of writing we used then served an important function. We run into trouble, however, when we look at our past writing experiences or prior theories as *the* way (or the only way) to write. Remember, rhetoric is adaptive—the situations we find ourselves writing for often have different audiences, contexts, and purposes and challenge us to adapt our writing and thinking in new ways.

So, if you ever find yourself wondering why the way you wrote about an issue in your earlier education (such as Middle School or High School) is not working in your current context, you could be trying to size up a new rhetorical situation with an old theory. This doesn't mean that your previous teachers taught you better or worse writing skills; they taught you a set of skills for the rhetorical situations you were encountering at that specific point. Different situations, however, call for different forms of rhetoric or writing, and these will often change as you move from one field of study to another.

Therefore, when you enter into a new writing situation, you can sometimes feel out of place or even frustrated because your new writing experience doesn't feel like your old experience. This is, of course, a perfectly normal response because you are now writing for different purposes and audiences and often in different contexts and genres. In some cases, you will be asked to write in different disciplines, and sometimes learning to write in these disciplines can make you recognize yourself as an outsider. Moving to a new genre or form of writing or a new context often produces these feelings. We wonder whether or not our audiences will take our voice seriously.

Stay encouraged in these situations. Writing is a learning process that requires us to align our ideas and our expression with the perceived responses of our audience. This means that we will have our misfires along with our successes.

What to Look for as You Read this Book

This book is not a book about rhetoric for its own sake. This means that it is not simply a book where you just learn about rhetoric. Instead, we view rhetoric as a living practice, one that can enable you to think through your processes of communication and assist you in achieving the goals of your writing. This book is broken into four major sections: Rhetorical Analysis, Controversy Analysis, Public Argument, and Revision and Reflection. In the first section, you will learn a variety of strategies for analyzing texts and thinking critically about the choices that authors have made to persuade or move their audiences. The second section of the book will then challenge you to put your skills of analysis into practice by analyzing not just one text, but an ongoing conversation about a social or academic issue. In the third section, you will learn how to use the skills of rhetorical analysis as a starting point for developing your own public argument on a controversy. The fourth and final section then takes you through the process of revising your writing in order to make your writing even more persuasive. Along the way, you will encounter discussions on developing your writing skills and strategies for managing your writing process, making it enjoyable and productive.

We truly hope that your study of rhetoric will be a process of discovering not only strong arguments or helpful writing strategies, but also a process of discovering new perspectives on your world that you will be motivated to share with others long after you have put down this book or left the classroom.

Writing Public Lives

Section One

Rhetorical Analysis

Introduction: What's the Point in Analyzing?

By Christopher Minnix

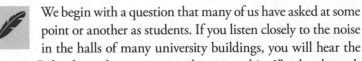 We begin with a question that many of us have asked at some point or another as students. If you listen closely to the noise in the halls of many university buildings, you will hear the question "why do we have to overanalyze everything?" echo through the hallway and out the door. There are, of course, reasons for this response. Learning to look closely at the texts, ideas, and things that shape our world is an intense process, one that requires us to often learn techniques from many different fields of study or disciplines. We often find that there are disagreements about the interpretation of these texts, ideas, and things. If we are used to looking for the "right" answer, we may find these disagreements puzzling. We find that our experience of filling in the right answer for a question, or "knowing the facts," becomes unsettled as we read and watch scholars not only argue about the answers, but the questions themselves. We might, for example, find statistical data on an issue that we feel supports our ideas and never expect that someone would question the methods by which the data was obtained.

The intensive process of learning to think critically about the ideas and arguments that shape our world can lead us to take comfort in the idea that some people "overanalyze everything." I would like to suggest to you that the idea that we "overanalyze" is simply a response to the intensity of learning to analyze, argue, and write in a new and challenging way. We sometimes fall back on this idea when we are frustrated with the difficulties of analysis. Can we look so closely at the details of a text that we miss or lose sight of its most significant points? Absolutely! However, this is true in all fields of study, even the sciences, where analysis of the minutest aspects of a problem or phenomenon is necessary.

We can move beyond feeling as though we are overanalyzing by understanding the stakes of analysis. The stakes are often quite high. Our understanding and perception of the world we live in, our world-view, is often at stake when we are presented with an idea, argument, or text. This might seem a bit dramatic, but by not questioning or analyzing the messages that we are presented with, we may find ourselves adopting or endorsing the viewpoint of these messages unthinkingly. The problem in doing this is that often even the ideas that we might view as "commonsense" are based upon certain understandings of the word with which we might agree or disagree.

Take a look at a common example:

You go to college to get a good job.

This sentence captures an entire view of the world. On one level, most would agree that your experience in college will hopefully lead you to an enjoyable career that provides a stable income. So, we might say, what do we need to analyze? There are actually several important ideas that we are compelled to analyze here. Some might notice that the word "good" is not defined very clearly. Does good mean satisfying or a job that pays around $100,000 per year? Both? Someone might ask, "Does a social-worker or a police officer making $35,000 a year have a 'good job'?" Did they get what they should have out of college? Others might note the logic of the sentence and how it lists a good job as the only reason for attending college. This might lead them to question the philosophy of education in the sentence. In this one sentence, we have a world-view or philosophy of both work and education.

This example illustrates that there is quite a bit at stake in our analysis. By accepting the premises of this statement, we can find ourselves accepting a view of the world with which we may disagree. We might find ourselves agreeing with a set of values about education and work that we find unsettling. This is why learning to critically analyze the ideas, arguments, and texts that shape our world is so important—because part of what is at stake in the process is our own world-view.

This section introduces you to a variety of methods for analyzing the texts and messages that shape our perception of the social world around us. These methods are all part of **rhetorical analysis**: the analysis of the persuasive strategies and purposes of texts. Rhetorical analysis is a particularly important area of study because rhetoric is utilized across every type of human communication and across every field of study. By learning these methods of analysis, you will not only be learning how to analyze texts but also how to size up your own writing situations as well.

The Distinction between Terminology and Analysis

There are several terms in this section of the book that come from the different ways of reading and analyzing texts that you will learn. Before you begin learning about these methods, it is important to understand a very important point.

The goal here is not to memorize terms or definitions. Instead, our goal is to learn to identify and analyze the important strategies of the texts we read and view. We want, in other words, to understand how these texts influence the various audiences that read or view them and we are looking for their patterns of meaning and experience.

This does not mean that the terminology is unimportant, but that you must look at it for what it is: a way of naming certain strategies, ideas, and arguments that we find in texts and writing situations. We are looking for patterns that attempt to persuade. In this sense, *the definitions you encounter here are only starting points*.

What you will see as you read through the following chapters is that each method for analyzing texts doesn't simply give you definitions, but walks you through the process of recognizing and analyzing these terms.

You were introduced to the ideas of rhetoric and rhetorical analysis in the Introduction, but let's step back from the definitions for a moment and think about why we are doing what we are doing. As we said in the introduction to this book, *rhetoric is not just for classrooms*. As you move throughout your day-to-day lives, you encounter texts and take part in networks that shape the way you view the world around you. Studying rhetoric and analyzing texts is a way to understand how the texts we read, see, and watch seek to shape our understanding of the world we live in. In this sense, it doesn't matter if the text is a scientific article, an essay for an English class, or even a webpage for a human rights group that we find while surfing the net. Each text has certain patterns of persuasion or strategies that it uses to persuade us or even move us to identify with its position. Likewise, when you sit down to write you are often drawing upon similar strategies to persuade, even if you don't know what these strategies are called.

So don't lose the forest for the trees in learning these different methods of analysis. Instead, we encourage you to keep coming back to the following questions:

In what ways is the text attempting to persuade me to see the world in a certain way, or to understand an issue or idea in a certain way? What strategies does it use to encourage me to identify with its ideas or vision of the world? Why do I identify? Why am I skeptical?

These are the key questions that all of the methods you will read about in the following chapters help us explore, and you can think of these methods as lenses or perspectives that we use to get to the heart of these important questions.

A Few Key Starting Points

The methods or lenses you encounter in the following chapters may seem very different at first, but they all share a common understanding of texts and writing. We can call this perspective a **rhetorical understanding**. This leads us to three important aspects of rhetorical analysis.

1. Rhetorical analysis means analyzing the strategies texts use to respond to, seek to persuade, and even create their **audiences**.

2. Rhetorical analysis means analyzing how texts are written and read in certain social situations or **contexts** and how both writers and audiences respond to these contexts.

3. Rhetorical analysis means analyzing the various **purposes** that writers are seeking to achieve, and the strategies they use to achieve this purpose.

These basic concepts—audience, context, and purpose—form what we will call the **rhetorical situation**, of a text. You can think of each method of reading in the following chapters as a way to understand how texts respond to different rhetorical situations. These methods of analysis and reading are tools for understanding the rhetorical situations that writers respond to and even create when they take on an issue, develop an idea, solve a problem, or any other writing task.

This doesn't mean that we are just out to understand the "background" of the texts we encounter. Knowing whether a text was written from a specific political or social position or bias, for example, is helpful, but it does not tell us how the text tries to affect its readers. If we only bothered to learn about this background, then reading would just be a process of finding authors who happen to agree or disagree with our opinions and either support or argue against them. Writing, in this sense, would just be a process of writing for audiences we agree with and against audiences we don't.

Our experience with many different types of texts—from speeches to novels to multimedia texts—often defies this type of reading. In this section, we are going to challenge you to go beyond background or simple readings to analyze how texts develop their meaning and argument. This means that we are going to learn not to be satisfied with simply a rough idea of **what a text means**. Instead, we are going to learn how to read texts in a way that helps us understand **how they create their meaning**.

When in Doubt, Remember, It All Comes Back to Audience

You may have noticed an important point as you have read through the introduction to this section: audience is continually present. *Audience is the driving force in rhetoric.* Rhetoric is an art of persuasion: no audience, no one to persuade. That writing should have an audience seems pretty obvious, but audience is a really profound concept when we think about it.

One interesting point is the way we make audiences part of us, or internalize them. If you keep a journal, for example, you might read through the pages and notice the similarities between you as the author and you as the audience of your journal. You might even notice that your writing—even though seemingly private—is written to be read and written as though it is addressed to an audience.

This idea leads us to an interesting point about audience: writers analyze the audiences that they seek to persuade, but since this audience is not often present, they must also create their audiences. We see their perspective on their audience when we read their texts. Let's break down this statement a bit. What we mean here is that writers draw upon the information that they have about their audience in order to create a text that they think will best persuade this audience.

Since audiences are not often made up of people who all have the same attitudes, values, or even information about a topic, writers approximate their audiences when they write. This means that writers sometimes approximate their audiences well and persuade their audiences, but at other times they miss the mark partially or completely.

What Do We Mean by Analysis?

Traditionally, analysis has meant to break something into parts in order to understand how the parts work together to make the object or text work. You probably have some experience doing this with literary texts, analyzing how, for example, **setting** works as a strategy in Mark Twain's *Huckleberry Finn*. In this case, the Mississippi River becomes not only a setting but a metaphor for a journey, one that has been defined as a journey from immaturity to wisdom or even as a journey towards an understanding of the need for racial equality.

If you have learned this type of literary analysis in other classes, you know what it means to look for patterns or strategies that texts use in order to develop their meaning. In rhetorical analysis, we are also looking for patterns and strategies. When we analyze a text, we read it closely and identify those strategies that create or emphasize the meaning of the text. *The process of close reading is similar, but what we look for is a bit different.*

When you read about different methods of analysis, you will learn ways of paying close attention to specific strategies of persuasion. Some of these will be large concepts, such as the way an author uses ideology in their argument, and some may seem a bit smaller to you, such as the way that an author uses metaphor to emphasize their argument. One of the things that you will learn through this process of close reading is that—whether big concept or smaller detail of style—each strategy can play an equally important role in making the text persuasive. When you read and reread the texts you are analyzing, specific strategies will stand out to you. The key part of the interpretive process is formulating your own arguments about why these strategies are so important to the argument or meaning of the text. No interpretation can cover everything, so you will pick and choose the strategies that you feel are most central to the text's argument. For example, when I read Martin Luther King's rhetoric, such as his "I Have a Dream" speech, I find that his style, especially his use of metaphor, is crucial to the way he is able to move his audience to identify with his vision of social justice. So I might use Classical Rhetorical analysis to analyze how he uses metaphors to persuade his audience. My colleague, let's call him Dr. I, might agree that style is important, but might focus his reading of King's speech on the way he uses Christian ideology to challenge those who disagree with him. In this case, neither of us is right or wrong, as long as we can support our interpretations. Each of these aspects of King's speech is vitally important and helps us understand how King responded to the rhetorical situation he faced.

So, you might be asking yourself, does this mean there are no "bad interpretations"? Not really. Think about audience again. Rhetorical analyses are arguments for a specific interpretation or understanding of a text. When we analyze texts we have audiences of our own, audiences who can not only agree or disagree, but can also tell us whether or not an interpretation is plausible or not. So, **as analysts we have our own rhetorical situations**, and this means that we have an audience that we have to persuade. Every classroom is different, but our hope for you is that you have a more diverse audience than just your teacher as you begin to analyze these texts. If so, then you will have the chance to take part in an **interpretive community**, or a group of readers who share a similar set of methods and goals and who debate and think collectively about the persuasiveness of certain interpretations. If you have access to this community, you will clearly see that rhetorical analyses are arguments, as you will have the chance to challenge and be challenged, read and be read. If you do not have this opportunity, seek out someone who might want to talk through your readings of a certain text with you.

Conclusion: So When Do I Use Each Lens or Method?

This is a great question, one that many of you have probably been asking yourselves as you have read through the table of contents or even this introduction. No one method is better than the other; instead, each of the different methods or lenses forms a tool in our analytical toolkit. Instead of seeking to apply each method to every text that you read, we encourage you to think of these lenses or types of analysis as tools that you can use to analyze a certain pattern that you observe in a text.

Start with the text itself. As you read, you will find that certain types of texts lend themselves to various different forms of analysis. Some texts, such as the political speeches, lend themselves to multiple forms of analysis, from classical rhetorical to ideological and cultural analysis. The key is to start by reading the text closely, annotating it and trying to answer our key question: how is this text trying to persuade its audience to identify with its message? By keeping this main question in mind, you will start to see certain strategies emerge and you will be able to choose a method or lens that helps you analyze these strategies.

As you use this book and analyze texts in your class, we hope that you are able to discuss your analysis and writing with your classmates and with other readers of your work. You will find that the aspects of the text that you focus upon are sometimes similar and sometimes very different from those of your classmates, and you will hopefully take part in a dialogue that enriches your understanding of the text you are analyzing.

As you move through each of these methods of reading or analysis, experienced analysts will walk you through the process of using each method. Pay special attention to these parts of the chapters, as they will help you understand how to use these methods to analyze a text that you find compelling. The key here is to remember that learning to analyze is a key part of learning how to size up the rhetorical situations that will call upon you to write.

As you begin, here are a few thought experiments and questions to pursue.

First, let's think through the idea that rhetoric might be just for classrooms. Take a moment and think of a goal or purpose that you would like to convince an audience to accomplish. It can be anything, from getting a friend to stop smoking to persuading a Congressman to vote a certain way on a bill. Now, take out a sheet of paper or open a new document on your computer and do some freewriting. Working quickly, and without editing yourself, try to convince your audience to accomplish or do what you want them to do without using any speech that could be considered "rhetoric." Think creatively here. Now, review what you have written and think about your audience. Do you think you were able to write in a way that was not rhetorical? Why or why not? Would your writing convince your audience?

Second, let's do what we might call "field-research" based upon our normal day-to-day discourse. In your journal, or on a piece of paper or new document on your computer, keep track of the different forms of communication that you used for one full day. Include conversations, requests, emails, social network posts, the things you yell to your friends, etc. Then, at the end of the day or the next day think back through these examples. How did your rhetoric change based upon your rhetorical situation, your audience, context, and purpose? You might be surprised to find that you speak and write in many more ways than you imagined.

Finally, try to get your feet wet in rhetorical analysis by applying the aspects of the rhetorical situation we discussed here to a text. You might pick a song, a newspaper editorial, a flyer, or any other text you find interesting. Pick a text you are willing to share with your classmates and then try to reason through the audience it is designed for, the different contexts that it reflects, and the purposes it seeks to fulfill. Write up a quick analysis paragraph of the text and then exchange it, and a copy of the text, with a classmate to see if they interpreted it similarly.

Analyzing Rhetorical Texts

Chapter 1

Narrative Analysis: Argument through Story

By Margaret Jay Jessee

Narrative

A **narrative** is a story that is constructed to describe a sequence of events. These events can be either fictional or non-fictional. Fictional narratives include short stories, novels, movies, and narrative poetry. As you probably discussed in other English or writing courses, fictional narratives do indeed create arguments and lend themselves to analyses. In this chapter, however, we will explore how narrative is used in non-fiction to present something that actually happened in real life, and how we can analyze this type of narrative by paying attention to how the argument of the non-fiction piece is created through a story.

We use narrative in our everyday lives when we talk and write to each other. As an example, take a moment to recall a car accident you have been involved in or witnessed. Now, try to tell someone else about that experience without creating a story with a beginning, a middle, and an end. Try to merely describe the incident without making a story out of your descriptions. It's difficult, yes? And, if you are able to come up with a series of descriptions without a narrative, is that how you would actually talk to a friend about the incident? Typically, we use narrative in order to convey a message, in order to explain what has happened, why it has happened, and how it has happened. Those narratives create arguments in themselves. For example, would your story about the car accident convey who was at fault in the crash? Your story might begin with your claim that you were sitting at a red light doing nothing wrong when a car ran into your car. Or, you might say that you slid on a patch of ice and lost control of your car. Either way, that presents an argument through the story, even if you don't literally say the other driver or the weather was to blame for the accident. Your listener can gather, from the way you portray your narrative about the event, where you place the blame and thus what your argument is.

Of course, the way you choose to tell your story is rhetorical; that is, all of the choices you make in how you convey the narrative to your audience are rhetorical choices. If you were to tell your parents about the accident, you would likely make different choices than you would if telling your story to a close friend. The version you tell your parents likely emphasizes the other driver or the weather making your ability to avoid the accident impossible while the version you present to your friend might emphasize how scared you were when you thought of having to tell your story to your parents. This is what makes all narrative, even non-fiction narrative, rhetorical. While you may be presenting "facts" in a story of something that actually happened, non-fiction narratives require the author to make a series of choices, decisions based on what they would like to convey to their audiences.

Narratives function by creating a sense of identification with the writer or speaker (or narrator). We understand someone else's story by listening to or reading his or her narrative, but we also come to learn something about ourselves, too. Politicians often use narrative in order to create a sense of identification and thus persuade an audience to feel that their life story is similar to the life story the politician provides. Bill Clinton is famous for describing his birth "in a little place called Hope." In this speech, former President Clinton goes on to create an argument about how important hope is to the American people, all the while referring back to his birthplace, Hope, Arkansas. This move, a rhetorical series of choices, conveys the idea that Clinton was not born into an elite family. His opponent, George H. W. Bush, was born into a prominent, successful family in New England while Clinton came from a poor, broken family in a tiny town in the south. Rather than emphasizing the advantages his opponent had in terms of opportunity and access to education, culture, and political knowledge, Clinton used his personal story to convey the sense that he, like the average voter, was born poor and believed in the American Dream. By telling his story of going from being poor in Hope, Arkansas to governor to presidential candidate in the way he did, he attempted to persuade voters that his birth was actually an advantage, not a disadvantage.

Even Abraham Lincoln's famous Gettysburg Address begins as a story would, "Four score and seven years ago, our forefathers brought forth upon this continent a new nation…" (Lincoln 732). This emphasizes the fact that all Americans have a shared history. Remember that this speech was delivered after the country had, essentially, broken in two: the North and the South. During the Civil War, Lincoln's address told a story, a narrative that all Americans share, emphasizing unity after this divide. Other powerful speakers use narrative in order to connect readers to the speaker's vision, to tell a story that others want to participate in and make their own narratives. Martin Luther King Jr. references Abraham Lincoln's story in his "I Have a Dream" speech when he claims that "Five score years ago, a great American, in whose symbolic shadow we stand today, signed the emancipation proclamation" (King 556). In a different speech, King describes his trip "to the mountaintop" where he has "seen the promised land,"("Speech at Mason Temple" 692) something he says all Americans, regardless of race, will get to see eventually. These are stories meant to persuade the audience to identify and see the story of the African American as their own story, regardless of the audience member's race. What these examples have in common is their attempt to tell stories in order to persuade, to create an argument in order to convey a message to an audience. These speakers all chose the way they told their stories in order to best persuade their audiences. Even though the stories are true stories, they were structured carefully in order to best emphasize certain elements, deemphasize other elements, and create a cohesive story best suited for a particular rhetorical situation.

Ways to Analyze Narrative

By taking apart the narrative, inspecting each part in order to see how it relates to the whole, we are able to analyze how an author makes rhetorical choices in order to craft an argument. So, we are conducting a rhetorical analysis much like the others in this book, but we are focusing on the particular choices of narration in our analysis. Thus, we are conducting a **narrative analysis**. In order to help us to analyze how and why certain authors construct their narrative arguments, there are a few key rhetorical choices we should look for:

- **The point of view of the narrator.** The point of view is the perspective of the person telling the story. In literature, the narrator is not assumed to be the same as the author, but in non-fiction, we can more readily assume the narrator and the writer or speaker are the same person. For conducting a narrative analysis of a nonfiction piece, it is important to see how the author (the narrator) sets up the perspective of the story. The important questions to consider are: Is the author of the story an observer, relaying facts and events at a distance? Is the author telling the story as a participant relaying facts and events from a very closely involved position? Did the action happen to or is the author an observer? Does the narrator assume that his or her story is also our story? Does the narrator have knowledge of the story that the audience does not? What is the purpose or effect of that narrative position or point of view? And the most important questions are: How does the narrative reveal the narrative point of view, or how does the author use their point of view to persuade their audiences?

- **Time.** When telling a story, a certain amount of time takes place within the narrative. This time might cover a matter of minutes, to hours, to years, to centuries. A famous example of a fictive narrative dealing with time is Kate Chopin's "The Story of an Hour." The story itself takes place over the course of one hour in the life of the main character. The reader follows the main character through that one hour but sees nothing else, no other time in her life. Everything about the character that happens outside of that hour must be inferred by what the character thinks and does within that hour. On the other hand, Abraham Lincoln's Gettysburg Address, mentioned earlier in the chapter, summarizes the entire history of the United States from its birth of independence to post-Civil War America in order to establish a shared history. A large number of narratives have multiple time frames functioning in the same story. These narratives might refer back several years, they may follow the writer's life from childhood forward while actually focusing on one issue in the present, or they might deal with the past, move to the present, and then reference the future. The important questions to consider are: how much ground (in terms of time) is covered in the narrative? Does the narrative take place over a specific time period or does the time move back and forth between present, past and future? Do we see a whole history as well as a personal experience in the story? Is the story focusing on a very brief moment, and if so, why is that particular point in time important? And the most important question is: How does the author focus the time in the story in order to persuade their audience?

- **Order or Sequencing.** Writers and speakers of any text have to decide what comes first, second, third, and so on in their text. When you write an essay for a class, you must decide what your essay will begin with and why you should begin with that. Often, what comes next depends on what you decided to begin with, and what you choose to end your essay with is equally as important as all of the other sequence choices you had to make. This is true, too, of narratives. Narratives begin in one place and end in another, and that is not always congruent with **time**. That is, narrative ordering does not always follow chronological order. A narrative might begin in the middle of the chronological time sequence of the story and work backwards and forwards or it might begin at the end of the chronological time and fill in the middle and beginning. Choosing what to begin with, what to place second, third and so on is as equally important in a narrative as it is in your essays for class. The important questions to consider are: How is the narrative arranged? What comes first? What comes next? What comes third, etc.? Why does it end with whatever it ends with? Why does it begin with whatever it begins with? Why are the pieces arranged in the order they are in the middle? And the most important question is: How does the narrative reveal its ordering and how does the author order the text in a way that persuades the audience?

- **Description.** How an author describes the people, places, and things that make up the story is crucial to understanding the purpose of the story. A great deal can be gleaned from how an author chooses to describe something in the narrative. One author may describe a storm as dark, foreboding, and frightening while another might describe that same storm as exciting, refreshing, and beautiful. The author's purpose of persuasion is often conducted through description in narratives. When you analyze a narrative, it is important to notice *how* an author describes certain things as well as *what* the author describes. The important questions to consider are: What is described in detail in the narrative? What descriptions seem important? How does the author describe those things? What is the purpose of that type of description? And the most important question is: How does the narrative reveal those descriptions and how are these descriptions used to emphasize the author's meaning or persuade their audience?

The following article uses elements of narrative in order to create an argument about race and identity. As you're reading the article, take the time to ask yourself about the point of view, time, order, and description. Annotate (or make notes of summary) what you notice about Liu's rhetorical choices in his narrative.

Eric Liu—Notes of a Native Speaker

"The Chinatown Idea," from The Accidental Asian: Notes of a Native Speaker, *by Eric Liu. Copyright © 1998 by Eric Liu. Used by permission of Random House, Inc.*

Here are some of the ways you could say I am "white":

I listen to National Public Radio.

I wear khaki Dockers.

I own brown suede bucks.

I eat gourmet greens.

I have few close friends "of color."

I married a white woman.

I am a child of the suburbs.

I furnish my condo a la Crate & Barrel.

I vacation in charming bed-and-breakfasts.

I have never once been the victim of blatant discrimination.

I am a member of several exclusive institutions.

I have been in the inner sanctums of political power.

I have been there as something other than an attendant.

I have the ambition to return.

I am a producer of the culture.

I expect my voice to be heard.

I speak flawless, unaccented English.

I subscribe to Foreign Affairs.

I do not mind when editorialists write in the first person plural.

I do not mind how white television casts are.

I am not too ethnic.

I am wary of minority militants.

I consider myself neither in exile nor in opposition.

I am considered "a credit to my race."

I never asked to be white. I am not literally white. That is, I do not have white skin or white ancestors. I have yellow skin and yellow ancestors, hundreds of generations of them. But like so many other Asian Americans of the second generation, I find myself now the bearer of a strange new status: white, by acclamation. Thus it is that I have been described as an "honorary white," by other whites, and as a "banana," by other Asians. Both the honorific and the epithet take as a given this idea: To the extent that I have moved away from the periphery and toward the center of American life, I have become white inside. Some are born white, others achieve whiteness, still others have whiteness thrust upon them. This, supposedly, is what it means to assimilate.

There was a time when assimilation did quite strictly mean whitening. In fact, well into the first half of this century, mimicry of the stylized standards of the WASP gentry was the proper, dominant, perhaps even sole method of ensuring that your origins would not be held against you. You "made it" in society not only by putting on airs of anglitude, but also by assiduously bleaching out the marks of a darker, dirtier past. And this bargain, stifling as it was, was open to European immigrants almost exclusively; to blacks, only on the passing occasion; to Asians, hardly at all.

Times have changed, and I suppose you could call it progress that a Chinaman, too, may now aspire to whiteness. But precisely because the times have changed, that aspiration—and the imputation of the aspiration—now seems astonishingly outmoded. The meaning of "American" has undergone a revolution in the 29 years I have been alive, a revolution of color, class and culture. Yet the vocabulary of "assimilation" has remained fixed all this time: fixed in whiteness, which is still our metonym for power; and fixed in shame, which is what the colored are expected to feel for embracing the power.

I have assimilated. I am of the mainstream. In many ways I fit the psychological profile of the so-called banana: imitative, impressionable, rootless, eager to please. As I will admit in this essay, I have at times gone to great lengths to downplay my difference, the better to penetrate the "establishment" of the moment. Yet I'm not sure that what I did was so cut and dried as "becoming white." I plead guilty to certain charges: achieving, learning the ways of the upper middle class, distancing my-self from radicals of any hue. But having confessed, I still do not know my crime.

To be an accused banana is to stand at the ill-fated intersection of class and race. And because class is the only thing Americans have more trouble talking about than race, a minority's climb up the social ladder is often willfully misnamed and wrongly portrayed. There is usually, in the portrayal, a strong whiff of betrayal: The assimilist is a traitor to his kind, to his class, to his own family. He cannot gain the world without losing his soul. To be sure, something is lost in any migration, whether from place to place or from class to class. But something is gained as well. And the result is always more complicated than the monochrome language of "whiteness" and "authenticity" would suggest.

My own assimilation began long before I was born. It began with my parents, who came here with an appetite for Western ways already whetted by films and books and music and, in my mother's case, by a father who'd been to the West. My parents, who traded Chinese formal-ity for the more relaxed stance of this country. Who made their way by hard work and quiet adaptation. Who fashioned a comfortable life in a quiet development in a second-tier suburb. Who, unlike your "typical" Chinese parents, were not pushy, status-obsessed, rigid, disciplined or prepared. Who were haphazard about passing down ancestral traditions and "lessons" to their children. Who did pass down, however, the sense that their children were entitled to mix or match, as they saw fit, what-ever aspects of whatever cultures they encountered.

I was raised, in short, to assimilate, to claim this place as mine. I don't mean that my parents told me to act like an American. That's partly the point: They didn't tell me to do anything except to be a good boy. They trusted I would find my way, and I did, following their ex-ample and navigating by the lights of the culture that encircled me like a dome. As a function of my parents' own half-conscious, half-finished acculturation, I grew up feeling that my life was Book II of an ongoing saga. Or that I was running the second leg of a relay race. Slap! I was out of the womb and sprinting, baton in hand. Gradually more sure of my stride, my breathing, the feel of the track beneath me. Eyes forward, never backward.

Today, nearly seven years after my father's death and two years after my marriage into a large white family, it is as if I have come round a bend and realized that I am no longer sure where I am running or why. My sprint slows to a trot. I scan the unfamiliar vista that is opening up. I am somewhere else now, somewhere far from the China that yielded my mother and father; far, as well, from the modest horizons I knew as a boy. I look at my limbs and realize I am no longer that boy; my gait and grasp exceed his by an order of magnitude. Now I want desperately to see my face, to see what time has marked and what it has erased. But I can find no mirror except the people who surround me. And they are mainly pale, powerful.

How did I end up here, in what seems the very seat of whiteness, gazing from the promontory of social privilege? How did I cover so much ground so quickly? What was it, in my blind journey, that I felt I should leave behind? And what did I leave behind? This, the jettisoning of one mode of life to send another aloft, is not only the immigrant's tale; it is the son's tale, too. By coming to America, my parents made themselves into citizens of a new country. By traveling the trajectory of an assimilist, so did I.

As a child, I lived in a state of "amoebic bliss," to borrow the felicitous phrase of the author of *Nisei Daughter*, Monica Sone. The world was a gossamer web of wonder that began with life at home, extended to my friendships, and made the imaginary realm of daydream seem as immediate as the real. If something or someone was in my personal web of meaning, then color or station was irrelevant. I made no distinctions in fourth grade between my best friend, a black boy named Kimathi, and my next-best friend, a white boy named Charlie—other than the fact that one was number one, the other number two. I did not feel, or feel for, a seam that separated the textures of my Chinese life from those of my American life. I was not "bicultural" but omnicultural, and omnivorous, too. To my mind, I differed from others in only two ways that counted: I was a faster runner than most, and a better student. Thus did work blend happily with play, school with home, Western culture with Eastern: It was all the same to a self-confident boy who believed he'd always be at the center of his own universe.

As I approached adolescence, though, things shifted. Suddenly, I could no longer subsume the public world under my private concept of self. Suddenly, the public world was more complicated than just a parade of smiling teachers and a few affirming friends. Now I had to contend with the unstated, inchoate, but inescapable standards of cool. The essence of cool was the ability to conform. The essence of conformity was the ability to anticipate what was cool. And I wasn't so good at that. For the first time, I had found something that did not come effortlessly to me. No one had warned me about this transition from happy amoeboid to social animal; no one had prepared me for the great labors of fitting in.

And so in three adjoining arenas—my looks, my loves, my manners—I suffered a bruising adolescent education. I don't mean to overdramatize: There was, in these teenage banalities, usually something humorous and nothing particularly tragic. But in each of these realms, I came to feel I was not normal. And obtusely, I ascribed the difficulties of that age not to my age but to my color. I came to suspect that there was an order to things, an order that I, as someone Chinese, could perceive but not quite crack. I responded not by exploding in rebellion but by dedicating myself, quietly and sometimes angrily, to learning the order as best I could. I was never ashamed of being Chinese; I was, in fact, rather proud to be linked to a great civilization. But I was angry that my difference should matter now. And if it had to matter, I did not want it to defeat me.

Consider, if you will, my hair. For the first 11 years of my life, I sported what was essentially the same hairstyle: a tapered bowl cut, the handiwork of my mother. For those 11 joyful years, this low-maintenance do was entirely satisfactory. But in my 12th year, as sixth grade got under way, I became aware—gradually at first, then urgently—that bangs were no longer the look for boys. This was the year when certain early bloomers first made the height-weight-physique distribution in our class seem startlingly wide—and when I first realized that I was lingering near the bottom. It was essential that I compensate for my childlike mien by cultivating at least a patina of teenage style.

This is where my hair betrayed me. For some readers the words "Chinese hair" should suffice as explanation. For the rest, particularly those who have spent all your lives with the ability to comb back, style and part your hair at will, what follows should make you count your blessings. As you may recall, 1980 was a vintage year for hair that was parted straight down the middle, then feathered on each side, feathered so immaculately that the ends would meet in the back like the closed wings of angels. I dreamed of such hair. I imagined tossing my head back casually, to ease into place the one or two strands that had drifted from their positions. I dreamed of wearing the fluffy, tailored locks of the blessed.

Instead, I was cursed. My hair was straight, rigid and wiry. Not only did it fail to feather back; it would not even bend. Worse still, it grew the wrong way. That is, it all emanated from a single swirl near the rear edge of my scalp. Combing my hair in any direction except back to front, the way certain balding men stage their final retreat, was a physical impossibility. It should go without saying that this was a disaster. For the next three years, I experimented with a variety of hairstyles that ranged from the ridiculous to the sublimely bad. There was the stringy pothead look. The mushroom do. Helmet head. Bangs folded back like curtains. I enlisted a blow-dryer, a Conair set on high heat, to force my hair into stiff postures of submission. The results, though sometimes innovative, fell always far short of cool.

I feigned nonchalance, and no one ever said anything about it. But make no mistake: This was one of the most consuming crises of my inner life as a young teen. Though neither of my parents had ever had such troubles, I blamed this predicament squarely on my Chinese genes. And I could not abide my fate. At a time when homogeneity was the highest virtue, I felt I stood out like a pigtailed Manchu.

My salvation didn't come until the end of junior high, when one of my buddies, in an epiphany as we walked past the Palace of Hair Design, dared me to get my head shaved. Without hesitation, I did it—to the tearful laughter of my friends and, soon afterward, the tearful horror of my mother. Of course, I had moments of doubt the next few days as I rubbed my peach-fuzzed skull. But what I liked was this: I had managed, without losing face, to rid myself of my greatest social burden. What's more, in the eyes of some classmates, I was now a bold (if bald) iconoclast. I've worn a crew cut ever since.

Well-styled hair was only one part of a much larger preoccupation during the ensuing years: wooing girls. In this realm I experienced a most frustrating kind of success. I was the boy that girls always found "sweet" and "funny" and "smart" and "nice." Which, to my highly sensitive ear, sounded like "leprous." Time and again, I would charm a girl into deep friendship. Time and again, as the possibility of romance came within reach, I would smash into what I took to be a glass ceiling.

The girls were white, you see; such were the demographics of my school. I was Chinese. And I was convinced that this was the sole obstacle to my advancement. It made sense, did it not? I was, after all, sweet and funny and smart and nice. Hair notwithstanding, I was not unattractive, at least compared with some of the beasts who had started "going out" with girls. There was simply no other explanation. Yet I could never say this out loud: It would have been the whining of a loser. My response, then, was to secretly scorn the girls I coveted. It was they who were sub-par, whose small-mindedness and veiled prejudice made them unworthy.

My response, too, was to take refuge in my talents. I made myself into a Renaissance boy, playing in the orchestra but also joining the wrestling team, winning science prizes but also editing the school paper. I thought I was defying the stereotype of the Asian American male as a one-dimensional nerd. But in the eyes of some, I suppose, I was simply another "Asian overachiever."

In hindsight, it's hard to know exactly how great a romantic penalty I paid for being Chinese. There may have been girls who would have had nothing to do with me on account of my race, but I never knew them. There were probably girls who, race aside, simply didn't like me. And then there were girls who liked me well enough but who also shied from the prospect of being part of an interracial couple. With so many boys out there, they may have reasoned, why take the path of greater resistance? Why risk so many status points? Why not be "just friends" with this Chinese boy?

Maybe this stigma was more imagined than real. But being an ABC ("American-born Chinese," as our parents called us) certainly affected me another way. It made me feel like something of a greenhorn, a social immigrant. I wanted so greatly to be liked. And my earnestness, though endearing, was not the sort of demeanor that won girls' hearts. Though I was observant enough to notice how people talked when flirting, astute enough to mimic the forms, I was oblivious to the subterranean levels of courtship, blind to the more subtle rituals of "getting chicks" by spurning them. I held the view that if you were manifestly a good person, eventually someone of the opposite sex would do the rational thing and be smitten with you. I was clueless. Many years would pass before I'd wise up.

It wasn't just dating rituals that befuddled me as a youth. It was ritual of all kinds. Ceremony, protocol, etiquette—all these made me feel like an awkward stranger. Things that came as second nature to many white kids were utterly exotic to me. American-style manners, for instance. Chinese families often have their own elaborate etiquette, but "please" and "may I" weren't the sort of words ever heard around my house. That kind of ritual seemed so beside the point. I was never taught by my parents to write thank-you notes. I didn't even have the breeding to say "Thank you" after sleeping over at a friend's house. I can recall the awful, sour feeling in my stomach when this friend told me his mother had been offended by my impoliteness. (At that point, I expressed my thanks.)

Eating dinner at the home of a yangren could be especially trying. The oaken furniture seemed scaled-up, chairs like thrones. The meal would begin with someone, usually the father, mumbling grace. Furtively, I'd steal a glance at the heads bowed in prayer. What if they asked me to say something? I looked back down and kept my mouth shut. Next was the question of silverware: which pieces to use, in which order, and so forth. I'd be reminded that at home I ate by using chopsticks to shove rice and meat straight from bowl to slurping mouth. Then the whole thing about passing platters of food around the table, instead of just reaching over and getting what you wanted. I would hear myself ask, in too-high tones, "Would you please pass the carrots, please?" It was usually at that point that I would notice that my napkin was the only one still folded neatly on the table.

All this, of course, was in the context of being with my friends and having a nice time. But something made me feel vaguely sad while I sat there, swallowing huge servings of gravy-drenched food with this other family. These were the moments when I realized I was becoming something other than my parents. I wanted so badly then just to be home, in my own kitchen, taking in the aroma of stir-fry on the wok and the chattery sounds of Chinglish. And yet, like an amphibian that has just breached the shore, I could not stop inhaling this wondrous new atmosphere. My moist, blinking eyes opened wide, observing and recording the customs and predilections of these "regular" Americans. The more time I spent in their midst, the more I learned to be like them. To make their everyday idioms and idiosyncrasies familiar. To possess them.

This, the mundane, would be the locus of my conversion. It was through the small things that I made myself over. I wish, if only for storytelling purposes, that I could offer a more dramatic tale, a searing incident of racism that sent me into deep, self-abnegating alienation.

The truth is, I can't. I was sometimes uncomfortable, but never really alienated. There were one or two occasions in seventh grade when the toughs in the back of the bus taunted me, called me chink, shot spitballs at me. I didn't like it. But each time, one of my friends—one of my white friends, in whose house I'd later eat dinner—would stand with me and fire back both spitballs and insults. Our insults were mean, too: scornful references to the trailer parks where these kids lived or the grubby clothes they wore or the crummy jobs their parents had. These skirmishes weren't just about race; they were also about mobility.

The same could be said, ultimately, about my own assimilation. To say simply that I became a banana, that I became white-identified, is somewhat simplistic. As an impressionable teen, I came to identify not with white people in general but with that subset of people, most of them white, who were educated, affluent: going places. It was their cues that I picked up, their judgments that I cared about. It was in their presence that old patterns of thought began to fall away like so much scaffolding around my psyche. It was in their presence that I began to imagine myself beyond race.

I recently dug up a photograph of myself from freshman year of college that made me smile. I have on the wrong shoes, the wrong socks, the wrong checkered shirt tucked the wrong way into the wrong slacks. I look like what I was: a boy sprung from a middlebrow burg who affected a secondhand preppiness. I look nervous. Compare that image with one from my senior class dinner: Now I am attired in a gray tweed jacket with a green plaid bow tie and a sensible button-down shirt, all purchased at the Yale Co-op. I look confident, and more than a bit contrived.

What happened in between those two photographs is that I experienced, then overcame, what the poet Meena Alexander has called "the shock of arrival." When I was deposited at the wrought-iron gates of my residential college as a freshman, I felt more like an outsider than I'd thought possible. It wasn't just that I was a small Chinese boy standing at a grand WASP temple; nor simply that I was a hayseed neophyte puzzled by the refinements of college style. It was both: Color and class were all twisted together in a double helix of felt inadequacy.

For a while I coped with the shock by retreating to a group of my own kind—not fellow Asians, but fellow marginal public school grads who resented the rah-rah Yalies to whom everything came so effortlessly. Aligning myself this way was bearable—I was hiding, but at least I could place myself in a long tradition of underdog exiles at Yale. Aligning my-self by race, on the other hand, would have seemed too inhibiting.

I know this doesn't make much sense. I know also that college, in the multicultural era, is supposed to be where the deracinated minority youth discovers the "person of color" inside. To a point, I did. I stud-ied Chinese, took an Asian American history course, a seminar on race politics. But ultimately, college was where the unconscious habits of my adolescent assimilation hardened into self-conscious strategy.

I still remember the moment, in the first week of school, when I came upon a table in Yale Station set up by the Asian American Student Association. The upperclassman staffing the table was pleasant enough. He certainly did not strike me as a fanatic. Yet, for some reason, I flashed immediately to a scene I'd witnessed days earlier, on the corner outside. Several Lubavitch Jews, dressed in black, their faces bracketed by dan-gling side curls, were looking for fellow travelers at this busy crossroads. Their method was crude but memorable. As any vaguely Jewish-looking male walked past, the zealots would quickly approach, extend a pam-phlet, and ask, "Excuse me, sir, are you Jewish?" Since most were not, and since those who were weren't about to stop, the result was a frantic, nervous, almost comical buzz all about the corner: Excuse me, are you Jewish? Are you Jewish? Excuse me. Are you Jewish?

I looked now at the clean-cut Korean boy at the AASA table (I think I can distinguish among Asian ethnicities as readily as those Hasidim thought they could tell Gentile from Jew), and though he had merely offered an introductory hello and was now smiling mutely at me, in the back of my mind I heard only this: Excuse me, are you Asian? Are you Asian? Excuse me. Are you Asian? I took one of the flyers on the table, even put my name on a mailing list, so as not to appear impolite. But I had already resolved not to be active in any Asians-only group. I thought then: I would never choose to be so pigeonholed.

This allergic sensitivity to "pigeonholing" is one of the unhappy hallmarks of the banana mentality. What does the banana fear? That is, what did I fear? The possibility of being mistaken for someone more Chinese. The possibility of being known only, or even primarily, for being Asian. The possibility of being written off by whites as a self-seg-regating ethnic clumper. These were the threats—unseen and, frankly, unsubstantiated—that I felt I should keep at bay.

I didn't avoid making Asian friends in college or working with Asian classmates; I simply never went out of my way to do so. This distinction seemed important—it marked, to my mind, the difference between self-hate and self-respect. That the two should have been so proximate in the first place never struck me as odd, or telling. Nor did it ever occur to me that the reasons I gave myself for dissociating from Asians as a group—that I didn't want to be part of a clique, that I didn't want to get absorbed and lose my individuality—were the very developments that marked my own assimilation. I simply hewed to my ideology of race neutrality and self-reliance. I didn't need that crutch, I told myself nervously, that crutch of racial affinity. What's more, I was vaguely insulted by the presumption that I might.

But again: Who was making the presumption? Who more than I was taking the mere existence of Korean volleyball leagues or Taiwanese social sets or pan-Asian student clubs to mean that all people of Asian descent, myself included, needed such quasi-kinship groups? And who more than I interpreted this need as infirmity, as a failure to fit in? I resented the faintly sneering way that some whites regarded Asians as an undifferentiated mass. But whose sneer, really, did I resent more than my own?

I was keenly aware of the unflattering mythologies that attach to Asian Americans: that we are indelibly foreign, exotic, math and science geeks, numbers people rather than people people, followers and not leaders, physically frail but devious and sneaky, unknowable and potentially treacherous. These stereotypes of Asian otherness and inferiority were like immense blocks of ice sitting before me, challenging me to chip away at them. And I did, tirelessly. All the while, though, I was oblivious to rumors of my own otherness and inferiority, rumors that rose off those blocks like a fog, wafting into my consciousness and chilling my sense of self.

As I had done in high school, I combated the stereotypes in part by trying to disprove them. If Asians were reputed to be math and science geeks, I would be a student of history and politics. If Asians were supposed to be feeble subalterns, I'd lift weights and go to Marine officer candidate school. If Asians were alien, I'd be ardently patriotic. If Asians were shy and retiring, I'd try to be exuberant and jocular. If they were narrow-minded specialists, I'd be a well-rounded generalist. If they were perpetual outsiders, I'd join every establishment outfit I could and show that I, too, could run with the swift.

I overstate, of course. It wasn't that I chose to do all these things with no other purpose than to cut against a supposed convention. I was neither so Pavlovian nor so calculating that I would simply remake myself into the opposite of what people expected. I actually liked history, and wasn't especially good at math. As the grandson of a military officer, I wanted to see what officer candidate school would be like, and I enjoyed it, at least once I'd finished. I am by nature enthusiastic and allegiant, a joiner, and a bit of a jingo.

At the same time, I was often aware, sometimes even hopeful, that others might think me "exceptional" for my race. I derived satisfaction from being the "atypical" Asian, the only Chinese face at OCS or in this club or that.

The irony is that in working so duteously to defy stereotype, I became a slave to it. For to act self-consciously against Asian "tendencies" is not to break loose from the cage of myth and legend; it is to turn the very key that locks you inside. What spontaneity is there when the value of every act is measured, at least in part, by its power to refute a presumption about why you act? The typical Asian I imagined, and the atypical Asian I imagined myself to be, were identical in this sense: Neither was as much a creature of free will as a human being ought to be.

Let me say it plainly, then: I am not proud to have had this mentality. I believe I have outgrown it. And I expose it now not to justify it but to detoxify it, to prevent its further spread.

Yet it would be misleading, I think, to suggest that my education centered solely on the discomfort caused by race. The fact is, when I first got to college I felt deficient compared with people of every color. Part of why I believed it so necessary to achieve was that I lacked the connections, the wealth, the experience, the sophistication that so many of my classmates seemed to have. I didn't get the jokes or the intellectual references. I didn't have the canny attitude. So, in addition to all my course work, I began to puzzle over this, the culture of the influential class.

Over time, I suppose, I learned the culture. My interests and vocabulary became ever more wordly. I made my way onto what Calvin Trillin once described as the "magic escalator" of a Yale education. Extracurriculars opened the door to an alumni internship, which brought me to Capitol Hill, which led to a job and a life in Washington after commencement. Gradually, very gradually, I found that I was not so much of an outsider anymore. I found that by almost any standard, but particularly by the standards of my younger self, I was actually beginning to "make it."

It has taken me until now, however, to appraise the thoughts and acts of that younger self. I can see now that the straitening path I took was not the only or even the best path. For while it may be possible to transcend race, it is not always necessary to try. And while racial identity is sometimes a shackle, it is not only a shackle. I could have spared myself a great deal of heartache had I understood this earlier, that the choice of race is not simply "embrace or efface."

I wonder sometimes how I would have turned out had I been, from the start, more comfortable in my own skin. What did I miss by distancing myself from race? What friendships did I forgo, what self-knowledge did I defer? Had certain accidents of privilege been accidents of privation or exclusion, I might well have developed a different view of the world. But I do not profess to know just how my view would have differed.

What I know is that through all those years of shadow-dancing with my identity, something happened, something that had only partially to do with color. By the time I left Yale I was no longer the scared boy of that freshman photo. I had become more sure of myself and of my place—sure enough, indeed, to perceive the folly of my fears. And in the years since, I have assumed a sense of expectation, of access and belonging, that my younger self could scarcely have imagined. All this happened incrementally. There was no clear tipping point, no obvious moment of mutation. The shock of arrival, it would seem, is simply that I arrived.

"The world is white no longer, and it will never be white again." So wrote James Baldwin after having lived in a tiny Swiss village where, to his knowledge, no black man had ever set foot. It was there, in the icy heart of whiteness, that the young expatriate began to comprehend the desire of so many of his countrymen to return to some state of nature where only white people existed. It was there too that he recognized just how impossible that was, just how intertwined were the fates and identities of the races in America. "No road whatever will lead Americans back to the simplicity of this European village where white men still have the luxury of looking on me as a stranger," he wrote. "I am not, really, a stranger any longer for any American alive."

That is precisely how I feel when I consider my own journey, my own family's travels. For here I am now, standing in a new country. Not as an expatriate or a resident alien, but as a citizen. And as I survey this realm—this Republic of Privilege—I realize certain things, things that my mother and father might also have realized about their new country a generation ago. I realize that my entry has yielded me great opportunities. I realize, as well, that my route of entry has taken a certain toll. I have neglected my ancestral heritage. I have lost something. Yes, I can speak some Mandarin and stir-fry a few easy dishes. I have been to China and know something of its history. Still, I could never claim to be Chinese at the core.

Yet neither would I claim, as if by default, to be merely "white inside." I do not want to be white. I only want to be integrated. When I identify with white people who wield economic and political power, it is not for their whiteness but for their power. When I imagine myself among white people who influence the currents of our culture, it is not for their whiteness but for their influence. When I emulate white people who are at ease with the world, it is not for their whiteness but for their ease. I don't like it that the people I should learn from tend so often to be white, for it says something damning about how opportunity is still distributed. But it helps not at all to call me white for learning from them. It is cruel enough that the least privileged Americans today have colored skin, the most privileged fair. It is crueler still that by our very language we should help convert this fact into rule. The time has come to describe assimilation as something other than the White Way of Being.

The time has also come, I think, to conceive of assimilation as more than a series of losses—and to recognize that what is lost is not necessarily sacred. I have, as I say, allowed my Chinese ethnicity to become diluted. And I often resolve to do more to preserve, to conserve, my inheritance. But have my acts of neglect thus far, my many omissions, been inherently wrong? G.K. Chesterton once wrote that "conservatism is based upon the idea that if you leave things alone, you leave them as they are. But you do not. If you leave a thing alone, you leave it to a torrent of change." I may have been born a Chinese baby, but it would have taken unremitting reinforcement, by my parents and by myself, for me to have remained Chinese. Instead, we left things alone. And a torrent of change washed over me.

This, we must remember, has been an act of creation as much as destruction. Something new is emerging from the torrent, in my case and the many millions like it. Something undeveloped, speaking the unformed tongue of an unformed nation. Something not white, and probably more Chinese than I know. Whatever it is that I am becoming, is it any less authentic for being an amalgam? Is it intrinsically less meaningful than what I might otherwise have been? In every assimilation, there is a mutiny against history—but there is also a destiny, which is to redefine history. What it means to be American—in spirit, in blood —is something far more borrowed and commingled than anything previous generations ever knew. Alongside the pain of migration, then, and the possibility, there is this truth: America is white no longer, and it will never be white again.

Analyzing Eric Liu's Narrative

As you probably noticed, Eric Liu's **point of view** in his narrative is not as a mere observer, uninvolved in the action of the narrative and watching from afar. He is not telling a story of some other, foreign person or land (though issues of foreignness and homeland are important in the narrative). Liu's point of view is quite personal and active. The question, of course, is how this affects our reading and understanding of the essay. In other parts of this book, you have been introduced to the author's ethos, or how the author of a text establishes his or her own credibility. Do you think Liu's narrative position affects his ethos in a negative or in a positive way? Why? How do you, as the reader, identify with the perspective of Liu's story? Do you think your response is the one Liu intended when he chose this point of view?

Liu, like all authors, had choices when he decided on his particular point of view. He could have taken a more distant approach or he might have told a less personal story. How might the narrative have been different with another or opposing point of view? Is the point of view Liu chose significant to the purpose of his narrative? Does his point of view give you any indication of what his argument is?

We establish what Liu's point of view is by looking closely at the choices he made when crafting his narrative. How does Liu establish his perspective, exactly? That is, if someone were to ask you how you knew that the point of view was not as a distant observer, how would you explain how you knew that?

Time is complicated in Liu's narrative. He covers a large number of years, yet he stops and pauses over particular instances, exact moments. Why did Liu choose the moments he did?

One of the effects of time in a narrative is ***pacing***. Some parts of Liu's narrative seem to move more quickly over time than others. In some parts, Liu slows the time down and at other times, he speeds up the pacing. How does the pacing of the narrative shift between larger history and specific moments? What causes the sense of pacing? How does Liu create a sense of speed in some parts and not in others?

Liu's narrative covers a great deal of past, present, and even future. He discusses a time that hasn't even actually been conceived of as yet. What is the effect of the amount of time covered in the narrative? Do you get the sense that even the time covered in the narrative doesn't encompass all of the time implied by the narrative?

Liu begins his narrative in a rather jarring and intriguing way. He arranges the narrative to begin with a list. Why do you think Liu might have made that choice? What did you first think when you encountered the opening lines? What effect does Liu's choice have now that you've finished the narrative and realize how that first choice relates to the **order** of the rest of the narrative?

The narrative order does not exactly follow the chronological time covered in the narrative. Instead, Liu shifts back and forth between what happened in his childhood to the present and back again, sometimes following chronological order in between shifts. What do you make of the order of the narrative? Is it effective? What would change about the narrative if Liu had chosen to follow strict chronological time?

Liu's narrative relies heavily on **description** in order to present his argument. Liu claims that his hair "betrayed" him and then goes on to call it "straight, rigid, and wiry." How does this description affect how we read what Liu means about his hair? What does the description have to do with betrayal? What is Liu's argument here? Is he merely discussing hair in this section?

Note how Liu describes eating at a friend's house, the sights, smells, and feelings Liu experienced while in this setting. What do we learn about his experience through this description? How might someone else describe the same moment, maybe the friend or parent? What makes Liu's description persuasive?

We know that all authors choose each part of their narratives very carefully, so why do you think Liu chose to focus his descriptions on the things he does? Why doesn't he focus on other descriptions? Would it matter which thing he described as long as his description reflected his argument or is it important that he chose the elements he did?

What conclusions do you draw from Liu's description? How does he construct his narrative in such a way as to give you the impressions you do about his hair, his clothes, his napkin at the dinner table and other descriptions? Ultimately, what is the overall purpose of how Liu creates that impression?

Conducting a Narrative Analysis

Analyzing narrative means thinking about how the author of the narrative went about creating the narrative and why. A narrative analysis is your own piece of rhetoric in which you write about—in a structured, organized way—the discoveries you made when you analyzed the narrative. When you analyze a narrative, you will come to conclusions about why the author made certain choices, and you will be able to support your conclusions with examples from the text because you paid attention to how the narrative revealed the choices the author made. In order to conduct a narrative analysis, you will write down your conclusions supported with evidence. This, too, is an argument. You will draw conclusions that might be slightly different than the conclusions another reader drew. Your analysis of the narrative will never be exactly like some other reader's analysis. Thus, when you formulate your analysis, providing supporting reasons for your interpretation, you are conducting your own argument about the narrative. In your narrative analysis, you, as the author, will have a series of rhetorical choices to make based on your own rhetorical situation. You will need to choose how to establish an ethos, how to arrange your essay, what elements you wish to emphasize in your essay, which elements you wish to deemphasize, what examples would best illustrate your claims, and so on. Thus, you will use your own rhetorical choices in order to analyze the rhetorical choices of another.

As you think about how you might take your analysis of a narrative and craft a narrative analysis from it, consider the way we analyzed Liu's narrative as a framework for how to begin to make your rhetorical choices. If you were to answer all of the questions posed in the analysis of Liu's narrative, you would have more than enough to get started with forming some interesting and strong conclusions about the text as a whole. By taking apart a narrative and studying various elements separately, you can then say something about how investigating those parts led you to a larger conclusion about the whole. A narrative analysis would then present that conclusion about the whole early on as a thesis statement. Then, you would show your readers exactly what led you to that whole by showing them the pieces you discovered yourself. You might then conclude your essay by telling your audience about the significance of the analysis you conducted.

Works Cited

King, Martin Luther, Jr. "Address at the March on Washington." *American Speeches: Political Oratory from the Revolution to the Civil War.* Volume 2. Ed. Ted Widmer. New York: Library of America, 2006. Print.

---. "Speech at Mason Temple." *American Speeches: Political Oratory from the Revolution to the Civil War.* Volume 2. Ed. Ted Widmer. New York: Library of America, 2006. Print.

Lincoln, Abraham. "Address at Gettysburg Pennsylvania." *American Speeches: Political Oratory from the Revolution to the Civil War.* Volume 1. Ed. Ted Widmer. New York: Library of America, 2006. Print.

Chapter 2

Classical Rhetorical Analysis: Turning Daydreams into Rhetorical Analysis

By Rebecca Richards

It's happened to us all. We get into an argument with a friend or family member that escalates to a point where neither person is listening or being heard. After that conversation, we walk away, drive home, call a friend to complain about the other person, make dinner, and go to bed—all the while thinking about what we *should* have said. We replay the conversation in our minds, re-evaluating the reactions of our audience, wishing we had used a different tone, phrase, or strategy. Perhaps the worst daydream is when we leave the argument wishing we had *not* used certain argumentative tactics. When we re-imagine the conversation, our audience responds differently, perhaps they now agree with what we said or they are moved to take action. Perhaps after replaying that conversation, we realize that we need to have another conversation with that person in order to apologize or clarify what we meant. In these daydreams, we pull apart what we said, what the other person said, the facial and hand gestures used, the timing, and the context of the argument.

These daydreams are really just a *rhetorical analysis* of the confrontation or conversation. A *rhetorical analysis* determines the available means of persuasion for a given speaker/writer (sometimes called the *rhetor*), audience, and the situation. For example, in your daydreams you consider the different strategies, or "available means" for persuading your friend in an argument. If the person you were speaking to was angry and aggressive, you could:

1. use a calm, smooth tone and try to convince him or her that you find his or her thoughts to be valid

2. meet his or her aggression with aggression by speaking over the person who is angered and hostile, using a list of logical facts.

But these are only two of the possible "available means" from your daydreams. I am certain you could think of more—the possibilities are endless. Often, this analysis happens quickly and instinctively. Unfortunately, when we are confronted, we are not given the time to deliberate on or think through *every* available means of persuasion. In fact, we probably do not have the time to be aware of the decisions we are making in our pursuit to be persuasive.

Therefore, in a situation such as a conflict with a friend, we must quickly decide upon what we believe is the most effective means of persuasion for this rhetorical situation. In making that decision, we rely on our practical wisdom, or *phronesis*. Phronesis is a tricky idea. When the ancient Greeks discussed "practical wisdom," they used this term to address a situation for which there was not a certain "correct" answer. However, this does not mean that science and fact could not be a part of that practical wisdom. In fact, quite the opposite. For example, when looking at storm clouds accumulating in the sky, you and I could debate about the time and the severity of the storm. You could argue that given the type of storm clouds and the barometric pressure that the storm will occur at 7 pm. But even with that scientific data, there is no way in that given moment to prove this to be correct. In fact, I could counter that argument to say that it will not rain at all because my grandmother who suffers from arthritis can predict rainfall, and she told me that she does not feel impending rain.

Likewise, as we run over the confrontational scene between ourselves and a friend again and again in our heads, wondering if we argued the best we can, we cannot know *for certain* if we chose different strategies for the rhetorical situation if the outcome would have been different, better, or worse. In fact, rhetorical situations exist when we are using our practical wisdom, or *phronesis*, to argue for an uncertain knowledge or an answer. Therefore, we can imagine (and hope) that a different strategy would have a different outcome or effect, but there is no way to prove beyond a doubt that this different strategy would have a given outcome. Yet we can make an argument for why we could or should have done or said something differently and the effect of that choice.

Rhetorically analyzing a conversation for your own personal purpose is something that you are not only familiar with but also very good at doing in interpersonal situations such as a disagreement with a loved one. But perhaps you are less familiar with using those same strategies to rhetorically analyze a document or text for an academic purpose. Being able to rhetorically analyze a text will help you better understand how to use texts, documents, and artifacts in your academic research, academic writing, and public writing. As you should remember from the introduction, analyzing texts rhetorically is directly related to the process of rhetorical practice. It will help you evaluate sources to determine which ones will be persuasive for your given audience and make stronger arguments. Also, by understanding your audience, you will be able to choose which rhetorical strategies will be the most effective. Perhaps more importantly, developing your rhetorical analysis skills will help you become a more active citizen because you will learn how to engage in democratic discussions.

In order to understand just how you can turn your daydreaming into a rhetorical argument that you can use in your writing, you should skim the following two texts. The longer of the two is

Canons of Rhetoric

Rhetoric is usually broken into five elements, also called "canons":

(1) **invention**: the creation of an argument by selecting various proofs, appeals, and strategies

(2) **arrangement**: the organization and sequencing various strategies of an argument

(3) **style**: the written/spoken expression of an argument; the actual words and signs used to communicate an argument

(4) **memory**: memorization of argument. Techniques given for texts that are recited.

(5) **delivery**: the performance of an argument

In this analysis, we are going to focus on invention, arrangement, and style in order to help you learn how to do this type of analysis for other texts.

Analyzing invention means looking at the available means of persuasion and deciding which strategies would be most effective for the given purpose. In this type of analysis, we look at how credibility, logic, and emotion are used to persuade the audience.

In looking at arrangement, we consider the order of the strategy used in invention. What is the effect of appealing to an expert authority before giving a personal anecdote?

Finally, style is one of the most complex elements to analyze. We can look at how repetition and metaphor are used and for what purpose. What do these elements do for the argument?

Dr. Martin Luther King Jr.'s "Letter from a Birmingham Jail." The shorter is an editorial, "A Call for Unity." Do not spend your time learning all of the various details. Instead, look over the two texts to get an idea of their purpose and audience. Then, we will develop a rhetorical analysis of this very famous rhetorical situation.

A Call for Unity

Reprinted by arrangement with the Heirs to the Estate of Martin Luther King, Jr., c/o Writers House as agent for the proprietor, New York, NY. Copyright © 1963 Martin Luther King, Jr.; Copyright renewed 1991 by Coretta Scott King.

12 April 1963

1   We the undersigned clergymen are among those who, in January, issued "An Appeal for Law and Order and Common Sense," in dealing with racial problems in Alabama. We expressed understanding that honest convictions in racial matters could properly be pursued in the courts, but urged that decisions of those courts should in the meantime be peacefully obeyed.

2   Since that time there had been some evidence of increased forbearance and a willingness to face facts. Responsible citizens have undertaken to work on various problems which cause racial friction and unrest. In Birmingham, recent public events have given indication that we will have opportunity for a new constructive and realistic approach to racial problems.

3   However, we are now confronted by a series of demonstrations by some of our Negro citizens, directed and led in part by outsiders. We recognize the natural impatience of people who feel that their hopes are slow in being realized. But we are convinced that these demonstrations are unwise and untimely.

4   We agree rather with certain local Negro leadership which has called for honest and open negotiation of racial issues in our area. And we believe this kind of facing of issues can best be accomplished by citizens of our own metropolitan area, white and Negro, meeting with their knowledge and experience of the local situation. All of us need to face that responsibility and find proper channels for its accomplishment.

5   Just as we formerly pointed out that "hatred and violence have no sanction in our religious and political traditions," we also point out that such actions as incite to hatred and violence, however technically peaceful those actions may be, have not contributed to the resolution of our local problems. We do not believe that these days of new hope are days when extreme measures are justified in Birmingham.

6   We commend the community as a whole, and the local news media and law enforcement officials in particular, on the calm manner in which these demonstrations have been handled. We urge the public to continue to show restraint should the demonstrations continue, and the law enforcement officials to remain calm and continue to protect our city from violence.

7   We further strongly urge our own Negro community to withdraw support from these demonstrations, and to unite locally in working peacefully for a better Birmingham. When rights are consistently denied, a cause should be pressed in the courts and in negotiations among local leaders, and not in the streets. We appeal to both our white and Negro citizenry to observe the principles of law and order and common sense.

Signed by:
C.C.J. Carpenter, D.D., LL.D., Bishop of Alabama; Joseph A. Durick, D.D., Auxiliary Bishop, Diocese of Mobile-Birmingham; Rabbi Milton L. Grafman, Temple Emanu-El, Birmingham, Alabama; Bishop Paul Hardin, Bishop of the Alabama-West Florida Conference of the Methodist Church; Bishop Nolan B. Harmon, Bishop of the North Alabama Conference of the Methodist Church; George M. Murray, D.D., LL.D., Bishop Coadjutor, Episcopal Diocese of Alabama; Edward V. Ramage, Moderator, Synod of the Alabama Presbyterian Church in the United States; Earl Stallings, Pastor, First Baptist Church, Birmingham, Alabama

[handwritten margin note: Ethos/Pathos]

Martin Luther King Jr. — "Letter from a Birmingham Jail"

16 April 1963

[handwritten: Primary audience / secondary (blacks) us]

My Dear Fellow Clergymen:

While confined here in the Birmingham city jail, I came across your recent statement calling my present activities "unwise and untimely." Seldom do I pause to answer criticism of my work and ideas. If I sought to answer all the criticisms that cross my desk, my secretaries would have little time for anything other than such correspondence in the course of the day, and I would have no time for constructive work. But since I feel that you are men of genuine good will and that your criticisms are sincerely set forth, I want to try to answer your statement in what I hope will be patient and reasonable terms.

[handwritten margin note: States purpose explicitly]

I think I should indicate why I am here in Birmingham, since you have been influenced by the view which argues against "outsiders coming in." I have the honor of serving as president of the Southern Christian Leadership Conference, an organization operating in every southern state, with headquarters in Atlanta, Georgia. We have some eighty five affiliated organizations across the South, and one of them is the Alabama Christian Movement for Human Rights. Frequently we share staff, educational and financial resources with our affiliates. Several months ago the affiliate here in Birmingham asked us to be on call to engage in a nonviolent direct action program if such were deemed necessary. We readily consented, and when the hour came we lived up to our promise. So I, along with several members of my staff, am here because I was invited here. I am here because I have organizational ties here.

But more basically, I am in Birmingham because injustice is here. Just as the prophets of the eighth century B.C. left their villages and carried their "thus saith the Lord" far beyond the boundaries of their home towns, and just as the Apostle Paul left his village of Tarsus and carried the gospel of Jesus Christ to the far corners of the Greco Roman world, so am I compelled to carry the gospel of freedom beyond my own home town. Like Paul, I must constantly respond to the Macedonian call for aid.

Moreover, I am cognizant of the interrelatedness of all communities and states. I cannot sit idly by in Atlanta and not be concerned about what happens in Birmingham. Injustice anywhere is a threat to justice everywhere. We are caught in an inescapable network of mutuality, tied in a single garment of destiny. Whatever affects one directly, affects all indirectly. Never again can we afford to live with the narrow, provincial "outside agitator" idea. Anyone who lives inside the United States can never be considered an outsider anywhere within its bounds.

You deplore the demonstrations taking place in Birmingham. But your statement, I am sorry to say, fails to express a similar concern for the conditions that brought about the demonstrations. I am sure that none of you would want to rest content with the superficial kind of social analysis that deals merely with effects and does not grapple with underlying causes. It is unfortunate that demonstrations are taking place in Birmingham, but it is even more unfortunate that the city's white power structure left the Negro community with no alternative.

In any nonviolent campaign there are four basic steps: collection of the facts to determine whether injustices exist; negotiation; self purification; and direct action. We have gone through all these steps in Birmingham. There can be no gainsaying the fact that racial injustice engulfs this community. Birmingham is probably the most thoroughly segregated city in the United States. Its ugly record of brutality is widely known. Negroes have experienced grossly unjust treatment in the courts. There have been more unsolved bombings of Negro homes and churches in Birmingham than in any other city in the nation. These are the hard, brutal facts of the case. On the basis of these conditions, Negro leaders sought to negotiate with the city fathers. But the latter consistently refused to engage in good faith negotiation.

Then, last September, came the opportunity to talk with leaders of Birmingham's economic community. In the course of the negotiations, certain promises were made by the merchants—for example, to remove the stores' humiliating racial signs. On the basis of these promises, the Reverend Fred Shuttlesworth and the leaders of the Alabama Christian Movement for Human Rights agreed to a moratorium on all demonstrations. As the weeks and months went by, we realized that we were the victims of a broken promise. A few signs, briefly removed, returned; the others remained. As in so many past experiences, our hopes had been blasted, and the shadow of deep disappointment settled upon us. We had no alternative except to prepare for direct action, whereby we would present our very bodies as a means of laying our case before the conscience of the local and the national community. Mindful of the difficulties involved, we decided to undertake a process of self purification. We began a series of workshops on nonviolence, and we repeatedly asked ourselves: "Are you able to accept blows without retaliating?" "Are you able to endure the ordeal of jail?" We decided to schedule our direct action program for the Easter season, realizing that except for Christmas, this is the main shopping period of the year. Knowing that a strong economic-withdrawal program would be the by product of direct action, we felt that this would be the best time to bring pressure to bear on the merchants for the needed change.

Then it occurred to us that Birmingham's mayoral election was coming up in March, and we speedily decided to postpone action until after election day. When we discovered that the Commissioner of Public Safety, Eugene "Bull" Connor, had piled up enough votes to be in the run off, we decided again to postpone action until the day after the run off so that the demonstrations could not be used to cloud the issues. Like many others, we waited to see Mr. Connor defeated, and to this end we endured postponement after postponement. Having aided in this community need, we felt that our direct action program could be delayed no longer.

You may well ask: "Why direct action? Why sit ins, marches and so forth? Isn't negotiation a better path?" You are quite right in calling for negotiation. Indeed, this is the very purpose of direct action. Nonviolent direct action seeks to create such a crisis and foster such a tension that a community which has constantly refused to negotiate is forced to confront the issue. It seeks so to dramatize the issue that it can no longer be ignored. My citing the creation of tension as part of the work of the nonviolent resister may sound rather shocking. But I must confess that I am not afraid of the word "tension." I have earnestly opposed violent tension, but there is a type of constructive, nonviolent tension which is necessary for growth. Just as Socrates felt that it was necessary to create a tension in the mind so that individuals could rise from the bondage of myths and half truths to the unfettered realm of creative analysis and objective appraisal, so must we see the need for nonviolent gadflies to create the kind of tension in society that will help men rise from the dark depths of prejudice and racism to the majestic heights of understanding and brotherhood. The purpose of our direct action program is to create a situation so crisis packed that it will inevitably open the door to negotiation. I therefore concur with you in your call for negotiation. Too long has our beloved Southland been bogged down in a tragic effort to live in monologue rather than dialogue.

One of the basic points in your statement is that the action that I and my associates have taken in Birmingham is untimely. Some have asked: "Why didn't you give the new city administration time to act?" The only answer that I can give to this query is that the new Birmingham administration must be prodded about as much as the outgoing one, before it will act. We are sadly mistaken if we feel that the election of Albert Boutwell as mayor will bring the millennium to Birmingham. While Mr. Boutwell is a much more gentle person than Mr. Connor, they are both segregationists, dedicated to maintenance of the status quo. I have hope that Mr. Boutwell will be reasonable enough to see the futility of massive resistance to desegregation. But he will not see this without pressure from devotees of civil rights. My friends, I must say to you that we have not made a single gain in civil rights without determined legal and nonviolent pressure. Lamentably, it is an historical fact that privileged groups seldom give up their privileges voluntarily. Individuals may see the moral light and voluntarily give up their unjust posture; but, as Reinhold Niebuhr has reminded us, groups tend to be more immoral than individuals.

We know through painful experience that freedom is never voluntarily given by the oppressor; it must be demanded by the oppressed. Frankly, I have yet to engage in a direct action campaign that was "well timed" in the view of those who have not suffered unduly from the disease of segregation. For years now I have heard the word "Wait!" It rings in the ear of every Negro with piercing familiarity. This "Wait" has almost always meant "Never." We must come to see, with one of our distinguished jurists, that "justice too long delayed is justice denied."

We have waited for more than 340 years for our constitutional and God given rights. The nations of Asia and Africa are moving with jet-like speed toward gaining political independence, but we still creep at horse and buggy pace toward gaining a cup of coffee at a lunch counter. Perhaps it is easy for those who have never felt the stinging darts of segregation to say, "Wait." But when you have seen vicious mobs lynch your mothers and fathers at will and drown your sisters and brothers at whim; when you have seen hate filled policemen curse, kick and even kill your black brothers and sisters; when you see the vast majority of your twenty million Negro brothers smothering in an airtight cage of

credibility w/ negros

Credibility/pathos

poverty in the midst of an affluent society; when you suddenly find your tongue twisted and your speech stammering as you seek to explain to your six year old daughter why she can't go to the public amusement park that has just been advertised on television, and see tears welling up in her eyes when she is told that Funtown is closed to colored children, and see ominous clouds of inferiority beginning to form in her little mental sky, and see her beginning to distort her personality by developing an unconscious bitterness toward white people; when you have to concoct an answer for a five year old son who is asking: "Daddy, why do white people treat colored people so mean?"; when you take a cross county drive and find it necessary to sleep night after night in the uncomfortable corners of your automobile because no motel will accept you; when you are humiliated day in and day out by nagging signs reading "white" and "colored"; when your first name becomes "nigger," your middle name becomes "boy" (however old you are) and your last name becomes "John," and your wife and mother are never given the respected title "Mrs."; when you are harried by day and haunted by night by the fact that you are a Negro, living constantly at tiptoe stance, never quite knowing what to expect next, and are plagued with inner fears and outer resentments; when you are forever fighting a degenerating sense of "nobodiness"—then you will understand why we find it difficult to wait. There comes a time when the cup of endurance runs over, and men are no longer willing to be plunged into the abyss of despair. I hope, sirs, you can understand our legitimate and unavoidable impatience. You express a great deal of anxiety over our willingness to break laws. This is certainly a legitimate concern. Since we so diligently urge people to obey the Supreme Court's decision of 1954 outlawing segregation in the public schools, at first glance it may seem rather paradoxical for us consciously to break laws. One may well ask: "How can you advocate breaking some laws and obeying others?" The answer lies in the fact that there are two types of laws: just and unjust. I would be the first to advocate obeying just laws. One has not only a legal but a moral responsibility to obey just laws. Conversely, one has a moral responsibility to disobey unjust laws. I would agree with St. Augustine that "an unjust law is no law at all."

maintains integrity. Patience/poise

Now, what is the difference between the two? How does one determine whether a law is just or unjust? A just law is a man made code that squares with the moral law or the law of God. An unjust law is a code that is out of harmony with the moral law. To put it in the terms of

St. Thomas Aquinas: An unjust law is a human law that is not rooted in eternal law and natural law. Any law that uplifts human personality is just. Any law that degrades human personality is unjust. All segregation statutes are unjust because segregation distorts the soul and damages the personality. It gives the segregator a false sense of superiority and the segregated a false sense of inferiority. Segregation, to use the terminology of the Jewish philosopher Martin Buber, substitutes an "I it" relationship for an "I thou" relationship and ends up relegating persons to the status of things. Hence segregation is not only politically, economically and sociologically unsound, it is morally wrong and sinful. Paul Tillich has said that sin is separation. Is not segregation an existential expression of man's tragic separation, his awful estrangement, his terrible sinfulness? Thus it is that I can urge men to obey the 1954 decision of the Supreme Court, for it is morally right; and I can urge them to disobey segregation ordinances, for they are morally wrong.

Let us consider a more concrete example of just and unjust laws. An unjust law is a code that a numerical or power majority group compels a minority group to obey but does not make binding on itself. This is difference made legal. By the same token, a just law is a code that a majority compels a minority to follow and that it is willing to follow itself. This is sameness made legal. Let me give another explanation. A law is unjust if it is inflicted on a minority that, as a result of being denied the right to vote, had no part in enacting or devising the law. Who can say that the legislature of Alabama which set up that state's segregation laws was democratically elected? Throughout Alabama all sorts of devious methods are used to prevent Negroes from becoming registered voters, and there are some counties in which, even though Negroes constitute a majority of the population, not a single Negro is registered. Can any law enacted under such circumstances be considered democratically structured?

Sometimes a law is just on its face and unjust in its application. For instance, I have been arrested on a charge of parading without a permit. Now, there is nothing wrong in having an ordinance which requires a permit for a parade. But such an ordinance becomes unjust when it is used to maintain segregation and to deny citizens the First-Amendment privilege of peaceful assembly and protest.

I hope you are able to see the distinction I am trying to point out. In no sense do I advocate evading or defying the law, as would the rabid segregationist. That would lead to anarchy. One who breaks an unjust law must do so openly, lovingly, and with a willingness to accept the penalty. I submit that an individual who breaks a law that conscience tells him is unjust, and who willingly accepts the penalty of imprisonment in order to arouse the conscience of the community over its injustice, is in reality expressing the highest respect for law.

logic

Of course, there is nothing new about this kind of civil disobedience. It was evidenced sublimely in the refusal of Shadrach, Meshach and Abednego to obey the laws of Nebuchadnezzar, on the ground that a higher moral law was at stake. It was practiced superbly by the early Christians, who were willing to face hungry lions and the excruciating pain of chopping blocks rather than submit to certain unjust laws of the Roman Empire. To a degree, academic freedom is a reality today because Socrates practiced civil disobedience. In our own nation, the Boston Tea Party represented a massive act of civil disobedience.

We should never forget that everything Adolf Hitler did in Germany was "legal" and everything the Hungarian freedom fighters did in Hungary was "illegal." It was "illegal" to aid and comfort a Jew in Hitler's Germany. Even so, I am sure that, had I lived in Germany at the time, I would have aided and comforted my Jewish brothers. If today I lived in a Communist country where certain principles dear to the Christian faith are suppressed, I would openly advocate disobeying that country's antireligious laws.

I must make two honest confessions to you, my Christian and Jewish brothers. First, I must confess that over the past few years I have been gravely disappointed with the white moderate. I have almost reached the regrettable conclusion that the Negro's great stumbling block in his stride toward freedom is not the White Citizen's Counciler or the Ku Klux Klanner, but the white moderate, who is more devoted to "order" than to justice; who prefers a negative peace which is the absence of tension to a positive peace which is the presence of justice; who constantly says: "I agree with you in the goal you seek, but I cannot agree with your methods of direct action"; who paternalistically believes he can set the timetable for another man's freedom; who lives by a mythical concept of time and who constantly advises the Negro to wait for a "more convenient season." Shallow understanding from people of good will is more frustrating than absolute misunderstanding from people of ill will. Lukewarm acceptance is much more bewildering than outright rejection.

I had hoped that the white moderate would understand that law and order exist for the purpose of establishing justice and that when they fail in this purpose they become the dangerously structured dams that block the flow of social progress. I had hoped that the white moderate would understand that the present tension in the South is a necessary phase of the transition from an obnoxious negative peace, in which the Negro passively accepted his unjust plight, to a substantive and positive peace, in which all men will respect the dignity and worth of human personality. Actually, we who engage in nonviolent direct action are not the creators of tension. We merely bring to the surface the hidden tension that is already alive. We bring it out in the open, where it can be seen and dealt with. Like a boil that can never be cured so long as it is covered up but must be opened with all its ugliness to the natural medicines of air and light, injustice must be exposed, with all the tension its exposure creates, to the light of human conscience and the air of national opinion before it can be cured.

In your statement you assert that our actions, even though peaceful, must be condemned because they precipitate violence. But is this a logical assertion? Isn't this like condemning a robbed man because his possession of money precipitated the evil act of robbery? Isn't this like condemning Socrates because his unswerving commitment to truth and his philosophical inquiries precipitated the act by the misguided populace in which they made him drink hemlock? Isn't this like condemning Jesus because his unique God consciousness and never ceasing devotion to God's will precipitated the evil act of crucifixion? We must come to see that, as the federal courts have consistently affirmed, it is wrong to urge an individual to cease his efforts to gain his basic constitutional rights because the quest may precipitate violence. Society must protect the robbed and punish the robber. I had also hoped that the white moderate would reject the myth concerning time in relation to the struggle for freedom. I have just received a letter from a white brother in Texas. He writes: "All Christians know that the colored people will receive equal rights eventually, but it is possible that you are in too great a religious hurry. It has taken Christianity almost two thousand years to accomplish what it has. The teachings of Christ take time to come to earth." Such an attitude stems from a tragic misconception of time, from the strangely irrational notion that there is something in the very flow of time that will inevitably cure all ills. Actually, time itself is neutral; it can be used either destructively or constructively. More and more I feel that the people of ill will have used time much more effectively than have the people of good will. We will have to repent in this generation not merely for the hateful words and actions of the bad people but for the appalling silence of the good people. Human progress never rolls in on wheels of inevitability; it comes through the tireless efforts of men willing to be coworkers with God, and without this hard work, time itself becomes an ally of the forces of social stagnation. We must use time creatively, in the knowledge that the time is always ripe to do right. Now is the time to make real the promise of democracy and transform our pending national elegy into a creative psalm of brotherhood. Now is the time to lift our national policy from the quicksand of racial injustice to the solid rock of human dignity.

You speak of our activity in Birmingham as extreme. At first I was rather disappointed that fellow clergymen would see my nonviolent efforts as those of an extremist. I began thinking about the fact that I stand in the middle of two opposing forces in the Negro community. One is a force of complacency, made up in part of Negroes who, as a result of long years of oppression, are so drained of self respect and a sense of "somebodiness" that they have adjusted to segregation; and in part of a few middle-class Negroes who, because of a degree of academic and economic security and because in some ways they profit by segregation, have become insensitive to the problems of the masses. The other force is one of bitterness and hatred, and it comes perilously close to advocating violence. It is expressed in the various black nationalist groups that are springing up across the nation, the largest and best known being Elijah Muhammad's Muslim movement. Nourished by the Negro's frustration over the continued existence of racial discrimination, this movement is made up of people who have lost faith in America, who have absolutely repudiated Christianity, and who have concluded that the white man is an incorrigible "devil."

I have tried to stand between these two forces, saying that we need emulate neither the "do nothingism" of the complacent nor the hatred and despair of the black nationalist. For there is the more excellent way of love and nonviolent protest. I am grateful to God that, through the influence of the Negro church, the way of nonviolence became an integral part of our struggle. If this philosophy had not emerged, by now many streets of the South would, I am convinced, be flowing with blood. And I am further convinced that if our white brothers dismiss as "rabble rousers" and "outside agitators" those of us who employ nonviolent

Pathos

50

direct action, and if they refuse to support our nonviolent efforts, millions of Negroes will, out of frustration and despair, seek solace and security in black nationalist ideologies—a development that would inevitably lead to a frightening racial nightmare.

Oppressed people cannot remain oppressed forever. The yearning for freedom eventually manifests itself, and that is what has happened to the American Negro. Something within has reminded him of his birthright of freedom, and something without has reminded him that it can be gained. Consciously or unconsciously, he has been caught up by the Zeitgeist, and with his black brothers of Africa and his brown and yellow brothers of Asia, South America and the Caribbean, the United States Negro is moving with a sense of great urgency toward the promised land of racial justice. If one recognizes this vital urge that has engulfed the Negro community, one should readily understand why public demonstrations are taking place. The Negro has many pent up resentments and latent frustrations, and he must release them. So let him march; let him make prayer pilgrimages to the city hall; let him go on freedom rides—and try to understand why he must do so. If his repressed emotions are not released in nonviolent ways, they will seek expression through violence; this is not a threat but a fact of history. So I have not said to my people: "Get rid of your discontent." Rather, I have tried to say that this normal and healthy discontent can be channeled into the creative outlet of nonviolent direct action. And now this approach is being termed extremist. But though I was initially disappointed at being categorized as an extremist, as I continued to think about the matter I gradually gained a measure of satisfaction from the label. Was not Jesus an extremist for love: "Love your enemies, bless them that curse you, do good to them that hate you, and pray for them which despitefully use you, and persecute you." Was not Amos an extremist for justice: "Let justice roll down like waters and righteousness like an ever flowing stream." Was not Paul an extremist for the Christian gospel: "I bear in my body the marks of the Lord Jesus." Was not Martin Luther an extremist: "Here I stand; I cannot do otherwise, so help me God." And John Bunyan: "I will stay in jail to the end of my days before I make a butchery of my conscience." And Abraham Lincoln: "This nation cannot survive half slave and half free." And Thomas Jefferson: "We hold these truths to be self evident, that all men are created equal ..." So the question is not whether we will be extremists, but what kind of extremists we will be. Will we be extremists for hate or for love? Will we be extremists for the preservation of injustice or for the extension of justice? In that dramatic scene on Calvary's hill three men were crucified. We must never forget that all three were crucified for the same crime—the crime of extremism. Two were extremists for immorality, and thus fell below their environment. The other, Jesus Christ, was an extremist for love, truth and goodness, and thereby rose above his environment. Perhaps the South, the nation and the world are in dire need of creative extremists.

I had hoped that the white moderate would see this need. Perhaps I was too optimistic; perhaps I expected too much. I suppose I should have realized that few members of the oppressor race can understand the deep groans and passionate yearnings of the oppressed race, and still fewer have the vision to see that injustice must be rooted out by strong, persistent and determined action. I am thankful, however, that some of our white brothers in the South have grasped the meaning of this social revolution and committed themselves to it. They are still all too few in quantity, but they are big in quality. Some—such as Ralph McGill, Lillian Smith, Harry Golden, James McBride Dabbs, Ann Braden and Sarah Patton Boyle—have written about our struggle in eloquent and prophetic terms. Others have marched with us down nameless streets of the South. They have languished in filthy, roach infested jails, suffering the abuse and brutality of policemen who view them as "dirty nigger-lovers." Unlike so many of their moderate brothers and sisters, they have recognized the urgency of the moment and sensed the need for powerful "action" antidotes to combat the disease of segregation. Let me take note of my other major disappointment. I have been so greatly disappointed with the white church and its leadership. Of course, there are some notable exceptions. I am not unmindful of the fact that each of you has taken some significant stands on this issue. I commend you, Reverend Stallings, for your Christian stand on this past Sunday, in welcoming Negroes to your worship service on a nonsegregated basis. I commend the Catholic leaders of this state for integrating Spring Hill College several years ago.

But despite these notable exceptions, I must honestly reiterate that I have been disappointed with the church. I do not say this as one of those negative critics who can always find something wrong with the church. I say this as a minister of the gospel, who loves the church; who was nurtured in its bosom; who has been sustained by its spiritual blessings and who will remain true to it as long as the cord of life shall lengthen.

When I was suddenly catapulted into the leadership of the bus protest in Montgomery, Alabama, a few years ago, I felt we would be supported by the white church. I felt that the white ministers, priests and rabbis of the South would be among our strongest allies. Instead, some have been outright opponents, refusing to understand the freedom movement and misrepresenting its leaders; all too many others have been more cautious than courageous and have remained silent behind the anesthetizing security of stained glass windows.

In spite of my shattered dreams, I came to Birmingham with the hope that the white religious leadership of this community would see the justice of our cause and, with deep moral concern, would serve as the channel through which our just grievances could reach the power structure. I had hoped that each of you would understand. But again I have been disappointed.

I have heard numerous southern religious leaders admonish their worshipers to comply with a desegregation decision because it is the law, but I have longed to hear white ministers declare: "Follow this decree because integration is morally right and because the Negro is your brother." In the midst of blatant injustices inflicted upon the Negro, I have watched white churchmen stand on the sideline and mouth pious irrelevancies and sanctimonious trivialities. In the midst of a mighty struggle to rid our nation of racial and economic injustice, I have heard many ministers say: "Those are social issues, with which the gospel has no real concern." And I have watched many churches commit themselves to a completely other worldly religion which makes a strange, un-Biblical distinction between body and soul, between the sacred and the secular.

I have traveled the length and breadth of Alabama, Mississippi and all the other southern states. On sweltering summer days and crisp autumn mornings I have looked at the South's beautiful churches with their lofty spires pointing heavenward. I have beheld the impressive outlines of her massive religious education buildings. Over and over I have found myself asking: "What kind of people worship here? Who is their God? Where were their voices when the lips of Governor Barnett dripped with words of interposition and nullification? Where were they when Governor Wallace gave a clarion call for defiance and hatred? Where were their voices of support when bruised and weary Negro men and women decided to rise from the dark dungeons of complacency to the bright hills of creative protest?"

Yes, these questions are still in my mind. In deep disappointment I have wept over the laxity of the church. But be assured that my tears have been tears of love. There can be no deep disappointment where there is not deep love. Yes, I love the church. How could I do otherwise? I am in the rather unique position of being the son, the grandson and the great grandson of preachers. Yes, I see the church as the body of Christ. But, oh! How we have blemished and scarred that body through social neglect and through fear of being nonconformists.

There was a time when the church was very powerful—in the time when the early Christians rejoiced at being deemed worthy to suffer for what they believed. In those days the church was not merely a thermometer that recorded the ideas and principles of popular opinion; it was a thermostat that transformed the mores of society. Whenever the early Christians entered a town, the people in power became disturbed and immediately sought to convict the Christians for being "disturbers of the peace" and "outside agitators.'" But the Christians pressed on, in the conviction that they were "a colony of heaven," called to obey God rather than man. Small in number, they were big in commitment. They were too God-intoxicated to be "astronomically intimidated." By their effort and example they brought an end to such ancient evils as infanticide and gladiatorial contests. Things are different now. So often the contemporary church is a weak, ineffectual voice with an uncertain sound. So often it is an archdefender of the status quo. Far from being disturbed by the presence of the church, the power structure of the average community is consoled by the church's silent—and often even vocal—sanction of things as they are.

But the judgment of God is upon the church as never before. If today's church does not recapture the sacrificial spirit of the early church, it will lose its authenticity, forfeit the loyalty of millions, and be dismissed as an irrelevant social club with no meaning for the twentieth century. Every day I meet young people whose disappointment with the church has turned into outright disgust.

Perhaps I have once again been too optimistic. Is organized religion too inextricably bound to the status quo to save our nation and the world? Perhaps I must turn my faith to the inner spiritual church, the church within the church, as the true ekklesia and the hope of the world. But again I am thankful to God that some noble souls from the ranks of organized religion have broken loose from the paralyzing chains of conformity and joined us as active partners in the struggle for freedom.

They have left their secure congregations and walked the streets of Albany, Georgia, with us. They have gone down the highways of the South on tortuous rides for freedom. Yes, they have gone to jail with us. Some have been dismissed from their churches, have lost the support of their bishops and fellow ministers. But they have acted in the faith that right defeated is stronger than evil triumphant. Their witness has been the spiritual salt that has preserved the true meaning of the gospel in these troubled times. They have carved a tunnel of hope through the dark mountain of disappointment. I hope the church as a whole will meet the challenge of this decisive hour. But even if the church does not come to the aid of justice, I have no despair about the future. I have no fear about the outcome of our struggle in Birmingham, even if our motives are at present misunderstood. We will reach the goal of freedom in Birmingham and all over the nation, because the goal of America is freedom. Abused and scorned though we may be, our destiny is tied up with America's destiny. Before the pilgrims landed at Plymouth, we were here. Before the pen of Jefferson etched the majestic words of the Declaration of Independence across the pages of history, we were here. For more than two centuries our forebears labored in this country without wages; they made cotton king; they built the homes of their masters while suffering gross injustice and shameful humiliation—and yet out of a bottomless vitality they continued to thrive and develop. If the inexpressible cruelties of slavery could not stop us, the opposition we now face will surely fail. We will win our freedom because the sacred heritage of our nation and the eternal will of God are embodied in our echoing demands. Before closing I feel impelled to mention one other point in your statement that has troubled me profoundly. You warmly commended the Birmingham police force for keeping "order" and "preventing violence." I doubt that you would have so warmly commended the police force if you had seen its dogs sinking their teeth into unarmed, nonviolent Negroes. I doubt that you would so quickly commend the policemen if you were to observe their ugly and inhumane treatment of Negroes here in the city jail; if you were to watch them push and curse old Negro women and young Negro girls; if you were to see them slap and kick old Negro men and young boys; if you were to observe them, as they did on two occasions, refuse to give us food because we wanted to sing our grace together. I cannot join you in your praise of the Birmingham police department.

It is true that the police have exercised a degree of discipline in handling the demonstrators. In this sense they have conducted themselves rather "nonviolently" in public. But for what purpose? To preserve the evil system of segregation. Over the past few years I have consistently preached that nonviolence demands that the means we use must be as pure as the ends we seek. I have tried to make clear that it is wrong to use immoral means to attain moral ends. But now I must affirm that it is just as wrong, or perhaps even more so, to use moral means to preserve immoral ends. Perhaps Mr. Connor and his policemen have been rather nonviolent in public, as was Chief Pritchett in Albany, Georgia, but they have used the moral means of nonviolence to maintain the immoral end of racial injustice. As T. S. Eliot has said: "The last temptation is the greatest treason: To do the right deed for the wrong reason."

I wish you had commended the Negro sit inners and demonstrators of Birmingham for their sublime courage, their willingness to suffer and their amazing discipline in the midst of great provocation. One day the South will recognize its real heroes. They will be the James Merediths, with the noble sense of purpose that enables them to face jeering and hostile mobs, and with the agonizing loneliness that characterizes the life of the pioneer. They will be old, oppressed, battered Negro women, symbolized in a seventy two year old woman in Montgomery, Alabama, who rose up with a sense of dignity and with her people decided not to ride segregated buses, and who responded with ungrammatical profundity to one who inquired about her weariness: "My feets is tired, but my soul is at rest." They will be the young high school and college students, the young ministers of the gospel and a host of their elders, courageously and nonviolently sitting in at lunch counters and willingly going to jail for conscience' sake. One day the South will know that when these disinherited children of God sat down at lunch counters, they were in reality standing up for what is best in the American dream and for the most sacred values in our Judaeo Christian heritage, thereby bringing our nation back to those great wells of democracy which were dug deep by the founding fathers in their formulation of the Constitution and the Declaration of Independence.

Never before have I written so long a letter. I'm afraid it is much too long to take your precious time. I can assure you that it would have been much shorter if I had been writing from a comfortable desk, but what else can one do when he is alone in a narrow jail cell, other than write long letters, think long thoughts and pray long prayers?

If I have said anything in this letter that overstates the truth and indicates an unreasonable impatience, I beg you to forgive me. If I have said anything that understates the truth and indicates my having a patience that allows me to settle for anything less than brotherhood, I beg God to forgive me.

I hope this letter finds you strong in the faith. I also hope that circumstances will soon make it possible for me to meet each of you, not as an integrationist or a civil rights leader but as a fellow clergyman and a Christian brother. Let us all hope that the dark clouds of racial prejudice will soon pass away and the deep fog of misunderstanding will be lifted from our fear drenched communities, and in some not too distant tomorrow the radiant stars of love and brotherhood will shine over our great nation with all their scintillating beauty.

Yours for the cause of Peace and Brotherhood, Martin Luther King, Jr.

After skimming these texts, you have a rough idea of the rhetorical situation that Dr. King encountered in 1963. If asked, I am sure you could give a brief summary of the situation. However, in order to push past summary and into an analysis of the situation, we need to examine the three elements of a rhetorical situation: the writer, the audience, and the context. In order to do so, we will do a **close reading** of the text together and uncover questions that you must consider when engaging in a rhetorical analysis. Some of these questions you probably answered subconsciously as you skimmed the texts. But in order to guide you through a rhetorical analysis, I am going to write out some questions and brief answers. My answers are not meant to provide totalizing answers. Instead, they should give you a jumping off point for your own analysis of the rhetorical situation to which Dr. King responded. You should read the questions I have provided and then flip back to the text to do a closer evaluation.

Close Reading: A close reading is a term from literary analysis, and is exactly what it sounds like—a deliberate, slow and sustained consideration of the text. Close reading is a method of analysis and will be helpful for your studies when you are asked to evaluate and interpret a source.

The first set of questions lists questions you should consider first as the building blocks of more complicated analysis. These are questions you should be asking as you read any text. Consider them to be pre-reading questions. In each question set, you will be asked to "Take Action" with the text. When doing a rhetorical analysis, you cannot just passively read. Therefore, use the Take Action suggestions to mark up the text to help you in your analysis.

TAKE ACTION: While Dr. King directly states this one purpose, his other purposes are more nuanced. As you continue reading the letter and working through these questions, write some of the other purposes for this letter in the margin of the book. Highlight the moments when the purpose of the letter shifts and returns to various purposes.

When evaluating future texts for *kairos*, ask yourself if there is a sense of urgency to the text. If so, where do you get that sense? How does the writer/speaker create that sense of urgency? Is the sense of urgency the same for all readers? Think about how the urgency of Dr. King's letter differs between a reader today and a reader back in 1963.

TAKE ACTION: Make a list of the shared values of the audiences for both texts. How does Dr. King appeal to those values? How do the clergymen? Choose one shared value of both audiences and place a star in each text where the writer(s) appeal to that.

What is the occasion that gives rise to this letter? What is Dr. King's letter's broadest purpose?

In April 1963, Dr. King was arrested following a non-violent protest organized by the Southern Christian Leadership Conference (SCLC) in Birmingham, Alabama. The participants protested the continued segregation and oppression of blacks and whites in Alabama. Meanwhile, eight white clergymen publicly accused Dr. King of being an outside agitator since he was from Georgia.

After skimming the first paragraph, we can already see that one purpose of this letter is to "answer criticism of [Dr. King's] work and ideas." However, there are many specific purposes for this letter.

The clergymen's letter and Dr. King's imprisonment gave him a very unique opportunity to write such a long letter. The Greeks called this type of opportunity *kairos*. They believed that action should take place at the most advantageous time, especially since time and opportunity are fleeting concepts. Note how Dr. King used *kairos* to justify the length of his letter, "I can assure you that it [the letter] would have been much shorter if I had been writing from a comfortable desk, but what else can one do when he is alone in a narrow jail cell other than write long letters, think long thoughts, and pray long prayers?" In this moment of the text, Dr. King gives an emotional and logical justification of his long letter, thus reminding his readers that he has been jailed for his non-violent actions. He is highlighting how this moment uniquely positions him to write this letter. Giving the unique details of the historical situation appeals to the urgency of this issue.

Who is the audience?

Dr. King's letter directly addresses the eight clergymen who criticized him, making this the easy answer to this question. Dr. King often speaks directly to these eight people at the beginning of paragraphs in order to highlight that he is responding to their criticism (e.g., "you deplore the demonstrations taking place in Birmingham" and "you express a great deal of anxiety over our willingness to break laws"). But in these moments, the "you" is actually a larger group of people. We cannot forget that this is an open letter, meaning that it was published for a general audience. Therefore, to whom else could he be speaking? The congregants that these eight men lead? Perhaps. Most likely, Dr. King wanted to speak to those who sympathize with their point of view.

Furthermore, some could argue (and have) that Dr. King had been working on this piece of writing for a while and took advantage of this moment (*kairos*) of responding to the clergymen to publish the work.

What are the values of the audience?

This might be a bit complex to answer, seeing as there are many audiences for Dr. King's letter and these audiences might have a wide variety of values. But Dr. King is transparent in appealing to values in the moments where he dissects very loaded terminology. One prominent example of this occurs midway through the text where he takes on the label of "extremist." He uses the language of the clergymen's letter and their religious values to reclaim this word as a positive label for his work. He cites Jesus Christ as an extremist, "Was not Jesus an extremist for love: 'Love your enemies, bless them that curse you, do good to them that hate you, and pray for them which despitefully use you, and persecute you'." What is the effect of Dr. King using the clergymen's values of Christianity in reclaiming the label of "extremist"?

Basically, he removes the negative connotation from this label that they have given him, which would force this group of men to re-consider using this term against him in the future. Both texts make appeals to the same values but in very different ways. Looking back to the "A Call for Unity," we find that the clergymen argued for peaceful resolutions, negotiation, obeying laws, and trusting in the courts and police force, and local citizens leading community activism. We also know that these men were Christian leaders of various churches in Alabama so their values will be based in their religious traditions as well as their local Alabama culture. What are the similarities and differences between the values of both audiences of "A Call for Unity" and Dr. King's letter?

However, a more public audience of Dr. King's letter will probably share some of these values with the clergymen, but many will also disagree. Those who disagree with the clergymen will have a completely different understanding of the letter than those who agree with the clergy. Remember, there is no totalizing "right way" to interpret a text. Each person or audience will bring a unique set of values, experiences, and beliefs that shape the way in which they read the text.

TAKE ACTION: Dr. King makes sure that his readers understand the timeliness of his argument. Find other moments in the text where he appeals to the *kairos*, or the advantageous opportunity, in which he found himself in writing this letter. Use a highlighter to mark the paragraphs, and write *kairos* in the margins.

TAKE ACTION: Find paragraphs that clearly address other readers beyond the eight clergymen. Draw a line down the side of that paragraph and write the name/identifying characteristic of those people in the margin. Also, consider whether or not you are targeted in this letter. If so, find a place in the text where Dr. King is speaking to you. How does he do this?

TAKE ACTION: Dr. King often reexamined abstract vocabulary words in his letter in order to increase or decrease the value of them. Make a list of all the terminology that he dissects and investigates. Then, look at this list and consider what these values tell us about the audience. Why did Dr. King select these words in particular? Why did he not choose other words like "racism"?

59

TAKE ACTION: In Dr. King's letter, underline passages where he addresses the values that are different from the clergymen. These moments are complex rhetorical strategies to make Dr. King's public letter appeal to a broader audience. Take note on how these moments are different than those you starred before. Do they use more emotional appeals? Do they employ empirical data or facts? Do they use the authority of Dr. King's position or that of another well-respected expert? Or do they use stylish writing strategies like catch phrases, commonplaces, or repetition?

Who is the speaker/writer?

Dr. Martin Luther King, Jr. is a very recognizable figure, which means that many of you will assume you *know* who he is. Did you know that, like his father, he was a minister of the Baptist church? Perhaps you did not know how young he was when he began his activist work. Did you know that he first became a minister when he was 25 years old, and by the time he was 28 he was elected the president of the SCLC? Did you know about his education and that he received his Bachelor's degree from Morehouse College in Atlanta and his PhD in Systematic Theology from Boston University? Finally, did you know that Dr. King's views were influenced by Ghandi's philosophies of non-violence? In fact, he visited India and Ghandi's family in 1959. Perhaps you know little about his personal life, such as his marriage to Coretta Scott and his four children, all of whom continued his activist work.

Ok, now that we've established the rhetorical situation of "Letter from a Birmingham Jail," we can really start to critique what means of persuasion, arrangement, and style that Dr. King used to address this situation.

TAKE ACTION: If you do not know specific details about who Dr. King was, this would be a good moment to do a quick Internet search about his background and his work. Jot down notes in this book about Dr. King that will help you understand who Dr. King was and why he wrote this letter.

How does the speaker/writer establish credibility?

With this question, we need to look for moments in the text where Dr. King establishes his credibility on the subject or *ethos*[1]. A writer or speaker can employ ethos by proving to be of good character, demonstrating good will, or proving his or her intelligence/expertise on the subject. Therefore, we can evaluate a writer or speaker's ethos based on their interpersonal relationship and situation to the audience as well as their attitude towards them.

Dr. King decided to assert his ethos on all three accounts very early on in the letter. First, he establishes good will by saying that he is responding to the clergymen, not out of spite, but because he felt that they were "men of genuine good will and that [their] criticisms [were] genuinely set forth." In this gesture, he disarms his audience from receiving his message with a hostile tone. He has just validated the men for their own credibility—a generous gesture of his own character.

---

1 In classical rhetoric, *ethos* carries overtones as to the moral character of the speaker. Aristotle believed that ethos was the most persuasive out of the three invention strategies: ethos, pathos, and logos. However, Aristotle was not concerned with the moral character of the speaker. Instead he believed that speakers should concern themselves with the *appearance* of ethical characteristics in their speaking.

Another way Dr. King proves his credibility as a writer is through his expert knowledge of race relations, religion, and regional issues. He does so by citing various reliable sources and giving concrete examples of the civil rights work he has done in Atlanta, quoting Bible passages, and recounting conflicts of the Alabama community. He even goes as far to give very concrete descriptions of the south to prove that he knows the region: "On sweltering summer days and crisp autumn mornings, I have looked at the South's beautiful churches with their lofty spires pointing heavenward." Anyone who has ever been to the South will immediately identify with the humidity of the South in the summer, thus giving him credibility on his knowledge of the region. This is just one example of how Dr. King establishes his credibility, or enables his audience to identify with him.

How does the speaker/writer appeal to the audience's values?

Besides using his own credibility, Dr. King also uses the emotions and values of his audience to be persuasive. For example, Dr. King knew that his critics called for peaceful resolutions to racial tensions. Therefore, he cites the logic of nonviolence when he details how the protestors prepared for the demonstration in workshops. He writes, "In your statement you assert that our actions, even though peaceful, must be condemned because they precipitate violence. But is this a logical assertion? Isn't this like condemning a robbed man because his possession of money precipitated the evil act of robbery?" In this quotation, Dr. King highlights the flaw of the *enthymeme*, or deductive reasoning that might read like this, "Anyone who provokes a crime should be punished. Dr. King and the peaceful protesters provoked violence. Peaceful protesters must be punished." He refutes this enthymeme, or logical proof, in a very stylistic way, by showing how if you replace "peaceful protesters" with "money" and "violence" with "robbery," the logic falls apart.

He also addresses the clergymen's desire for "negotiations" by detailing how negotiation is "the very purpose of direct action." These two moments are logical appeals, or *logos*, where Dr. King uses the values and logic of his audience to be persuasive.

After establishing *ethos* and using logical appeals, Dr. King uses the third appeal to speak to his audience—*pathos*. *Pathos* is an appeal to the emotions of the audience. Dr. King uses many emotional

---

Does this moment come across as genuine or forced? Consider that perhaps the Dr. King who physically wrote the letter does not find these men to be of "good will" since they are not fighting the injustices of racism with direct action. However, for this letter (and other pieces of writing), Dr. King has created a version of himself that is patient and willing to give the benefit of the doubt to his critics. This is called "invented ethos." Can you find other moments that might be invented ethos strategies?

TAKE ACTION: Find other moments where he writes to appeal to his credibility and underline those moments twice. Then write in the margins whether those moments establish good will, good character, or intelligence/expertise. Don't forget to think about how these moments change the dynamic of the relationship between reader and writer!

TAKE ACTION: Besides this paragraph, when does Dr. King use pathetic appeals? Put an exclamation point next to these appeals and write *pathos* in the margins.

appeals throughout his letter. But the paragraph beginning "We have waited for more than 340 years for our constitutional and God given rights" is a particularly strong example of how Dr. King uses the emotions of his audience to be persuasive. As he recounts the experience of black Americans, he invokes pity, anger, hostility, and impatience. When he tells his readers about the 6-year-old daughter who cannot go to the amusement park, he uses descriptive words to paint the picture of every child who has been disappointed. The image of a young child crying seeks to create sympathy and identification of the audience member with the parent who has to explain to the child why she cannot go inside.

TAKE ACTION: What are some other logical appeals that Dr. King uses? Highlight these moments in the text and then write *logos* in the margins.

Does the form of the message match the purpose/audience?

Finally, we can consider King's choice to respond to this public criticism through a public letter. Why did he choose to make his letter public when he could have responded to the men privately, collectively or individually? We could make an argument that the clergymen's criticism came in the form of a public announcement. Therefore, Dr. King wanted to clear the air with not only those who wrote the criticism but also those who read it. You will learn about how to evaluate the genre of a given text in future chapters.

Just from the brief answers to the above questions, we can see that there was no one "right way" for Dr. King to answer criticism of his work. There was not just one purpose or outcome of this letter. But this is where you, the writer, come in. You need to use your rhetorical analysis skills to argue for a different interpretation of this piece. While a rhetorical analysis of Dr. King's work will require you to pay closer attention, it will employ many of the same skills that you use when you daydream about your own rhetorical situations. Perhaps, it is hard to imagine the different means of persuasion for Dr. King's rhetorical situation—especially because he is a civil rights hero and skilled writer and orator. However, there are always other options that he could have employed. Therefore, on your own, ask yourself these questions:

1. Was Dr. King effective in achieving his purpose for his given audience? What would you have done differently to improve his chances of efficacy? What would have been a worse response in your mind? Find moments in the text to support your claims.

2. What are some other purposes of this letter, besides responding to the clergymen in Alabama? What in the text or your research of the context leads you to believe this?

3. How could Dr. King have established his *ethos* differently? Can you imagine how he might have demonstrated intelligence, proven his good character, or shown his good will differently? What might be the effect of this on his audience?

4. What if he had given this message as a speech for SCLC upon his release from prison? How would he have to change his appeals to logic, emotion, and his credibility? How would the purpose change?

Chapter 3

Visual-Spatial Analysis

By Adrienne Crump and Elise Verzosa

How Are You Persuaded by What You See?

What we see is directly related to how we experience the world and correspondingly informs what we know and how we come to know it. We live in a culture in which our daily experiences—including our assumptions, beliefs, and actions—are mediated or shaped by a wide range of visual and spatial texts. From the moment we wake-up in the morning and throughout the course of the day, we shape, interpret, and participate in multiple forms of meaning-making based on the things we see and the spaces we inhabit. Think about the various things you see and the spaces you inhabit in a given day; even a simple walk through your college campus, for example, will reveal multiple sites for visual and spatial analysis. One such place is the student union—a hub of campus life. Numerous people have daily experiences in this space: students may

Seeing comes before words. The child looks and recognizes before it can speak. But there is also another sense in which seeing comes before words. It is seeing that establishes our place in the surrounding world; we explain that world with words, but words can never undo the fact that we are surrounded by it. The relation between what we see and what we know is never settled.

—John Berger, *Ways of Seeing*

65

linger to eat here and hang out with their friends or they may simply walk in to buy a soda on their way to class. Regardless of the ways in which the space is used, a place such as the student union is ripe with visual and spatial clues that help us navigate the space. From the posters and ads we see on the walls, to the brightly colored neon signs and menus of eateries, to the way the physical space is manipulated by the placement of tables and chairs or the barriers telling us where to stand in line, we are constantly interpreting what we see within the space. How we interpret these elements necessarily shapes our different life experiences.

Consider the University of Arizona bookstore, for example. Located in the heart of the Memorial Student Union, the bookstore is a space where students buy academic textbooks for college courses. In essence, the purpose of all university bookstores is to provide a space and a service that supports students in their learning by selling textbooks. However, through visual and spatial analyses, we can see that the UA bookstore is doing quite a bit more than providing textbooks—it is also a purveyor of certain messages and values of our culture. A closer examination allows us to see what messages and values are being promoted and whether or not the space fulfills its primary purpose—to sell academic textbooks for university courses.

The first step in learning how to apply visual and spatial analyses is simply to take note of what you see and how a particular place is laid out. What do you see when you walk into the UA bookstore, for example? Upon entering the space, we notice that it looks very much like a commercial bookstore—perhaps something along the lines of a Borders or a Barnes and Noble—complete with its own Starbucks coffee shop. The books are organized neatly into sections that divide genres into shelves with signs that read "Fiction," "Non-Fiction," "New in Paperback," etc. On the other side of the UA bookstore, we see racks of clothing—shirts, jackets, and hats, among other things—branded with either the University of Arizona logo or Wilbur the Wildcat. After grabbing a cup of coffee, perusing the books, looking through the racks of UA clothing, and perhaps even stopping by the Clinique counter, you might begin to wonder, "Where are the textbooks?" After all, this is a university bookstore, right?

Because the textbooks don't seem to be available on the first floor, you might walk down the stairs to the floor below. Once you get there, you'll likely notice a space that looks very much like an electronics store complete with computers, laptops, software, and iPods. As you turn the corner, however, you notice that you have finally stumbled across the textbooks for various courses offered in the university—remember that the primary purpose of a university bookstore is to offer a space and service that supports student education. Now, let's think critically about what you saw:

- What kinds of places or spaces in our culture does the UA bookstore remind you of? Why?

- Why might the textbooks be "hidden" away from the main floor of the bookstore?

- Is it significant that the UA bookstore offers more than just textbooks? Why or why not?

- What kinds of values are being communicated in the UA bookstore?

One way of reading the UA bookstore might include some kind of commentary about how our culture—and thus our students—value commercialism and capitalism over simple access to education. Another reading might concern the benefits of having multiple kinds of items available in one space. Regardless of your reading of the UA bookstore, looking to visuals and spaces as texts can help us to see how visual and spatial elements communicate messages that inform our worldviews.

Rhetorical Analysis of Visual and Spatial Texts

As demonstrated by our "tour" of the University of Arizona Bookstore, it is evident that a key to analyzing the persuasive effects of a particular space is paying close attention to the visual imagery of that space. Likewise, the visual imagery found in a particular space (be it a physical, virtual, or printed space) can be read as persuasive in and of itself. Hopefully, it is becoming clearer that any space, place, visual, or written text can be "read" and analyzed from a rhetorical perspective.

Rhetorical analysis of visual and spatial texts aims to uncover the ways in which we are persuaded by these texts. One way of getting at the persuasive effects of such a text is to identify the purpose of the text in addition to the argument that text is trying to make. In order to fully analyze the persuasive effect of a visual or spatial argument, identifying the purpose is equally as important as identifying the argument. We can call this combination of purpose and argument the "function" of the text. Identifying a text's function by sorting out and identifying the difference between its purpose and its argument can seem confusing at first, perhaps even silly. But the distinction is important when considering a text's effects on different audiences and its success or failure to persuade.

EXERCISE: Develop this thesis statement further by examining the implications of the assumptions made by the creator about what students "know" about being bone marrow donors, the effectiveness and persuasiveness of the poster board. What negative implications could arise from this assumption? What other assumptions could the creators have made? How would these different assumptions change the contents of the poster board?

Take, for instance, a booth on the University Mall aimed at recruiting bone marrow donors. Different visual cues, such as poster boards, informational pamphlets on the tables, and t-shirts and buttons worn by the representatives, easily identify that the purpose of this booth is to persuade passersby to become bone marrow donors. But *are* passersby persuaded to become donors, and if so, how? A closer look at the visual imagery reveals some assumptions made about the audience for this booth. A large poster board is displayed next to the booth listing, then dispelling, several "myths" about becoming a bone marrow donor. The contents of this poster board indicate that its creator(s) assumes that college students are misinformed about the details of being a bone marrow donor, and it is only these misconceptions that are preventing them from becoming donors.

An initial or "working" thesis statement for a rhetorical analysis of this bone marrow donor display on the UA Mall might read: *The function of the blood donor display booth is to recruit donors by persuading passersby that what they believe about becoming a blood donor is incorrect.*

As with any rhetorical artifact, a writer's argument for a particular function of a text is likely only one valid interpretation among many. In addition, the writer may identify more than one function for the text. Rhetorician Sonja Foss provides examples of function: "A critic may see the function of a painting of Elvis on velvet, for example, as a loving memorial to Elvis; the function of a kitchen painted a sunny yellow as the expression of warmth; and the function of a non-representational painting of maroon, blue, and gold forms as an invitation to viewers to break old patterns and to transcend the limitations they represent" (Foss, 215).

A Step-by-Step Approach to Analysis

The following steps provide a framework for approaching and analyzing visual and spatial texts that centers on identifying its possible function (purpose and argument). This analytical approach can be used for the myriad of visual and spatial texts we encounter daily, from Web sites, to advertising images, to the layout of commercial spaces, such as grocery or department stores, as well as to art forms, such as graffiti and sculptures.

Step One: The student writer "reads" the text, noting her or his initial reactions in a journal entry. In the same entry, the student should write a very detailed description of the argument, noting all of its dimensions (i.e., size, shape, color, material composition), including where the argument is placed (i.e., displayed or published), and any spatial aspects (physical location, design layout) that contribute to the effect of the visual or space. Lastly, the student writer should reflect upon the reaction she or he had to the text forming a thesis as to why a certain reaction was evoked and what about the visual might have contributed to that reaction.

Step Two: Formulate a working thesis as to the function of the text that includes a claim about both the text's argument and purpose. Drawing upon their initial reader response to the visual, some questions the student writer might consider in identifying a visual's function are: What does the text do to viewers (i.e., does it draw or direct their attention to something specific; or elicit particular reactions?)?

Visual Imagery and Words

When analyzing texts that include both images and text, it is important to also consider how the function is propelled by the relationship between the two. Some questions the writer might address include: How do the words function by themselves? Do they? How do the images function by themselves? Do they? Are the words dependent on the image (is the text **anchored** by the image) to convey meaning? Is the image dependent on the words (is the image **anchored** by the text) to convey meaning? Or are the text language and image interdependent (**relay**) in controlling the **function** or conveying meaning?

Analyses of visual and spatial texts often raise the following kinds of questions:

- What are your eyes first drawn to when you see a visual or encounter a certain space? Why did you notice these things first? How might the visuals or the space have been created to influence what you see?
- What roles do visuals (for example, advertisement, art, comic, sign, poster, film, map, etc.) or spaces (for example, classroom, shopping mall, playground, etc.) play in shaping our experiences? What are the purposes of a visual or a space? How does it fulfill these purposes? For whom does it fulfill such purposes? Why?
- What kinds of cultural values are communicated by a visual or a space? How do we know?
- What does a particular visual, or a particular space, communicate about what is not valued?
- How might different people with different personal backgrounds interpret such values?
- Who has the power to influence us through the creation of a particular visual or a particular space?

What might the text persuade viewers to think/feel/identify with/ do? How do the identified purpose and argument interact? How do we know?

Step Three: In this step, the writer assesses the function of the visual, identified in the previous step—detailing dimensions of the text that contribute to or detract from the visual's success is fulfilling its supposed function. Questions she or he might address include: How well is the function communicated? What aspects of the text support the writer's argument of function? These aspects might include subject matter, medium, materials, forms, colors, organization, craftsmanship, and context, as well as genre specific attributes such as those found in film, comics, or web pages. Writers might also draw comparisons between the visual and others visuals with arguably the same or similar function as a means of supporting their argument.

Step Four: Here the writer critiques the function itself. In other words, this step attempts to answer the question, "So What?" Some questions she or he might address are: What are the implications of the function? What are the immediate consequences of the function? Under what circumstances and for whom? These questions are based on the writer's reason for analyzing the image in the first place.

For instance, consider the image of the visual depicted below. A writer might argue that the function of this visual is to convey complicity on both sides of the U.S./Mexico border in maintaining the "imagined" barrier between the two countries. Does the sculpture actually function to communicate this complicity? In what ways is this complicity conveyed? In what ways does the image actually impede its function?

Some Key Terms for Analysis:

Visual Rhetoric: a focus on visual elements and materials in communication

Visual Function: a visual's argument and purpose

Visual Composition: texts that individuals or groups design/compose, primarily of visual elements and materials, for the purposes of communicating

Visual Impact: The overall effect and appeal that a visual composition has on an audience

Visual Coherence: The extent to which visual elements of a composition are tied together with color, shape image, lines of sight, theme, etc.

Visual Salience: Importance or prominence of a visual element in relation to the composition as a whole

Visual Organization: Pattern of arrangement that relates the elements of the visual essay to one another in a way that makes them easier for readers/viewers to comprehend.

A Sample Visual/Spatial Analysis:

This visual-spatial analysis below was designed as an article for a student newspaper.

Arizona Student Times

Wednesday, May 6, 2009

Border Dynamics. Artists: Alberto Morackis and Guadalupe Serrano. Photograph by Melissa Koblenz

A Constant Reminder

By Melissa Koblenz

The other day I asked a few of my friends what they thought of the monstrously large and politically significant statue in front of the Harvell building on campus. The response I received was not too shocking. My friends seemed to have no idea which statue I was even talking about. These friends of mine are smart girls, girls that walk by that piece of art every single day, and yet they have never even noticed it, and the meaning behind it for that matter. This statue on the University of Arizona's campus is not just a statue; it's not even just a piece of art. This metal sculpture represents a serious social issue that affects America and its citizens every single day—the issue of illegal immigration across the southern border between the U.S. and Mexico.

This extraordinarily powerful statue not only conveys the significance of illegal immigration, but it also manifests how citizens on both sides of the fence, so to speak, feel about the issue. The entire piece features a large, thin metal wall with four men, two on either side, pushing against it. On one side, which represents the Mexican people, the men are ferociously pushing all of their might onto the wall. Their faces show great pain through their struggle to break down the metal barrier. Yet, on the other side, representing the American people, the men seem as though they are not exerting as much force against the wall as those on the other side. Their faces look somewhat bored; one man even has his head tilted downward to symbolize his apathy towards the entire situation. This same man is leaning his back against the wall, indicating that he, like many other Americans, does not forwardly confront the issue, but rather just goes along with the ideas of others within his community.

How does the wall stay perfectly straight if on one side the men are putting all their weight and force against the wall, where as the other men seem as though they aren't even trying? Well that's simple. The side representing the U.S. is shown as a powerhouse, with Mexico shown as the weaker country. Obviously, the United States' citizens clearly do not actually care about the situation. They are merely more powerful, giving them the strength to keep the Mexican people from knocking down the so-called "fence." Although the Mexican men are seen as weak and struggling, they put their whole bodies, hands, arms, and shoulders into their efforts against the other side. Their astounding willpower is the symbol of their fortitude. In contrast to the artwork's display of diversity, in the way of ideals and strength between the two cultures, it is also able to capture their similarities. The long pieces of metal that comprise the sculpture have painted sections of human muscle on the four men. What the artist expresses with the muscles is that even though the men might look different in reality and they might be from different backgrounds, they are all still human beings and should be treated equally and with respect.

In my own opinion, this particular artist, along with many other United States citizens, believes that illegal immigration across the U.S./Mexican border creates a positive impact on the country and allows the impoverished Mexican people to have a chance at freedom and greatness. This is shown through the American men seeming so unconcerned with holding up the fence. In opposition to this thought, and although it is not displayed in the statue due to the artist's views, a large amount of Americans believe that illegal aliens provide a negative outcome towards the United States' economy, dealing with issues of work and crime. Yet, the most important aspect of this sculpture is that it was specifically made to raise awareness of illegal immigration.

I have used this sculpture to provide an example of how important issues, such as illegal immigration, are being completely overlooked by people, even when it is so blatantly obvious that they demand attention. People miss the enormous statue on campus in a manner similar to the ignorance of the issue that it stands for. Like I had said earlier, it is imperative that more and more United States citizens become aware and more involved with the social and political issues and events that are becoming increasingly prevalent in the country. In addition, people should take a stand for what they believe in, or better yet, research the issue of illegal immigration, or any other controversial social issue and event, to better understand what is going on in today's world, rather than being oblivious to something that severely affects our lives.

Works Cited

Berger, John. *Ways of Seeing.* New York: Penguin, 1972. Print.

Foss, S.K. "A Rhetorical Schema for the Evaluation of Visual Imagery." *Communication Studies* 45 (2003): 213–224. Print.

Analyzing the Contexts of
Rhetorical Texts

Chapter 4

Contexts: Reading Culture in Rhetorical Texts

By Christopher Minnix

Each piece of writing that we read displays different facets of our society and culture. A play by Shakespeare exposes us to a viewpoint of the culture and society of Elizabethan England. A speech by a former President presents us with a view of a former time or moment in American history. Or, a bit more close to home, an old letter or email might bring us back to a specific moment when we were living in a particular local culture. In this sense, each time we pick up a piece of writing and read it we observe its relationship to the society or culture where it was written. We also read the text's relationship to ourselves and our own cultural and societal background. As we read, we may find points where the society or culture of the writing connects to or disconnects to our own viewpoints, and we may even find that others who are reading the same piece of writing feel a deep connection to it when we do not, or feel apathy towards it when we are moved by it. This is because the contexts that shape our reading are like the contexts that shaped the writing of the text: they form a dialogue or conversation between the many different viewpoints, beliefs, values, and opinions that make up our culture.

Now that you have a firm grasp of the basics of analyzing the forms, language, and strategies of different types of texts, we will focus in this chapter on analyzing the connection between the texts we read and their social and cultural contexts. Keep in mind that the texts we read are often designed to move us to identify with a particular view of the world that we live in. When you analyze the context of a piece of writing, you develop a picture of the society and culture that the writing portrays and then draw upon your own important ideas to interpret, understand, and respond. Just as societies and cultures are made up of many different groups of people, values, beliefs, and perspectives, the many pieces of writing that are written at any one time reflect these differences. The multiple viewpoints we encounter force us to challenge our assumptions about the different cultures and times that we read about. Our reading opens us to a deeper understanding of the people, societies, and cultures that we encounter and can even challenge us to think more deeply about how we define ourselves.

How Social Contexts Shape Our Reading

We find ourselves in many different social and cultural contexts throughout our lives. Contexts can be thought of as **social or cultural settings**, and these settings *reflect the cultural values, beliefs, attitudes, laws, and norms of behavior of a particular society.* Social settings are constantly adapting and changing, and there are many values, beliefs, laws, and norms from earlier points in the history of our society that no longer reflect our society. However, many historical elements of our cultural or social setting remain highly important. For example, our belief in liberty or freedom is still vitally important to our social or cultural setting and shapes our politics to this day. If the text is from another country or culture, we will encounter a different social or cultural setting from our own and often read the text as being in dialogue with our own values, attitudes, beliefs, and norms. Even science fiction, which often creates worlds that seem distant from our own, often portrays its futuristic or alien worlds in a way that comments upon the society or culture it was written in. In this sense, we often find ourselves comparing and contrasting the view of the culture or society presented in a piece of writing with our own knowledge and experience of that culture. We can think of reading for context in three different ways:

(1) **Analyzing How the Text or Writing Interacts with Its Culture or Society:** Every piece of writing reveals something about the context that it was written in, and often, in the case of rhetorical texts and literary texts, it provides a particular way of viewing or understanding that culture. Part of our job as readers and writers is to look critically at this perspective and interpret it. Writing

not only portrays different aspects of culture or society, but it also plays a role in moving us to react in a certain way to that society. When we read for cultural and social contexts, we are looking at the reaction that the text is attempting to create and the strategies that the text is using to move us to react in this way.

Questions We Might Ask When Analyzing the Text's Relationship to Its Social or Cultural Setting

1. What values, ideas, norms, beliefs, even laws of the culture play an important role in the text?
2. Does the text address these cultural values, beliefs, etc., directly (by directly mentioning and responding to them) or indirectly (by presenting a scenario or narrative that addresses them)?
3. What is the relationship of the text to the values, beliefs, etc.? Is it critical of these aspects of the culture? Is it supportive? Does it seek to modify these aspects of the culture in a certain way?

---

(2) **Analyzing the Text in the Context of Other Viewpoints:** It is unlikely that the writing you are reading was the only thing written on the issue. Think, for example, of the differences in values that you witnessed when you read "The Call to Unity" by eight Alabama clergymen and Martin Luther King Jr's "Letter from a Birmingham Jail." These documents were written at the same time and in the same culture, but reflect different perspectives on the struggle for civil rights. While you could analyze the different cultural or societal ideas presented in one piece of writing, it is often illuminating to compare and contrast that piece of writing with another perspective from the same period. By doing so, you are able to understand the full context of the text. Look for texts written in response to the text you are analyzing, or for texts written about the same issue or problem around the same time and compare their perspectives.

> ### Analyzing the Text's Relationship to Other Viewpoints
> 1. In what ways are the arguments of the texts similar or different?
> 2. Do the two texts point to similar or different cultural or social values, beliefs, etc., to support their argument?
> 3. If the texts or one of the texts is written in response to the other, does it criticize the other text's values, beliefs, etc.?
> 4. Do the texts define or use certain values or beliefs differently— their definition of the word "justice" or "democracy" for example?

(3) **Analyzing How the Text Connects to Our Own Cultural Assumptions as Readers:** Even ancient texts, such as Homer's *Odyssey*, tell us something intriguing about our own culture. As we analyze the contexts of texts, part of our job is to compare and contrast the view of culture and society that they present with our own cultural and intellectual viewpoints. This requires quite a bit of reflection, as we have to be careful not to pronounce other cultures or cultural periods inferior to our own just because they differ from our values or come from a time before our own.

> ### Analyzing the Text's Relationship to Our Own Cultural Assumptions
> 1. What cultural or social values, beliefs, etc., do we share with the society or culture in which the text was written? Why have they endured?
> 2. What cultural or social values, beliefs, etc., do we not share? Why not?
> 3. If the text is written in a culture distant or different from our own, what social values, beliefs, etc., connect to or reflect our own culture? What social values, beliefs, etc., can we not see in our own culture?
> 4. If the text is written in our culture but in a different historical time, how have the social values, beliefs, etc., developed or changed over time?

How Cultural Contexts Connect to Narrative, Rhetorical, and Visual-Spatial Analysis

The skills of narrative, rhetorical, and visual-spatial analysis that you have read about and developed so far are vital to your ability to analyze social contexts. Narrative, rhetorical, and visual-spatial strategies are what writers use to move us to identify with their particular perspective on their culture or society. You are still looking for these strategies when you conduct a contextual analysis. Now, however, you are looking at how these strategies inform your understanding of the relationship between the writing, the culture it was written in, and even our own culture.

Analyzing Social Contexts: Some Important Steps

Like any analysis, contextual analysis begins with a deep reading of the writing being analyzed. When you choose a text for contextual analysis, use the active reading strategies that we discussed in the introduction to textual analysis. The key is to remember that you are adding to your skills of narrative, rhetorical, and visual-spatial analysis instead of engaging in a different activity. As you actively read and annotate the text you have chosen to analyze, make sure to note both the rhetorical strategies and cultural and social codes that you observe. Here are several processes to make this sophisticated process of analysis more manageable. One important thing to note is that the following steps are steps for **rereading** the text you are analyzing. You will want to give the text you are writing a good first reading before using the processes on the following page.

Previewing:
Look at the materials that introduce the text, or do some quick research on the time and culture of the text. Why is the issue it addresses so important at that time? What are some of the different perspectives or ideas about the issue at that time? If the text is well-known, try to find some quick information about how people have reacted to and used the text.

Skim for cultural references:
Skim the text for references to its context or culture. Look for points when the author refers to important cultural events, ideas, institutions, etc.

Skim for cultural values:
Skim the text for references to the value system that the author uses to make their argument. Highlight the important references to these contexts, such as religious beliefs, political ideals or beliefs, cultural norms of behavior, national identity, etc.

Reread and narrow your focus:
Now that you have annotated the text, give it one more thorough rereading. While you do, get out a notebook or open a blank word document, and copy down the examples that you think are most important. These references will be those that are most helpful to your written analysis.

After scanning the text, rereading it, and then narrowing your focus to the cultural references that you think are most important, it's time to take inventory of what you have found and examine your findings. Use the steps below to help you think through the process of your cultural analysis.

1. First, look at your list and choose two to three cultural keywords that you feel are most important to the overall argument of the text. Look for cultural keywords that are repeated and that play a major role in setting up the argument.

2. Second, as you read back through the text, circle each time these keywords or cultural values are used.

3. Third, try to write out the basic thesis or the main argument of the text in the center of a blank page. You may not find a thesis statement, so you may have to write out the main idea of the text based upon your reading of the whole text.

4. Fourth, draw lines out from the thesis and write out the passages where the cultural keyword or value is used.

5. Finally, looking back at these passages, freewrite for a moment about the connection between the cultural keywords, the passages that you have listed, and the thesis. How do these keyword help support the argument that the author is making? Why might an audience be more likely to support this argument if it is connected to these values?

Cultural Messages in a Political Speech

Cultural values are reflected in all texts, though we are sometimes so used to seeing them that they become invisible to us. In the following section, we are going to put our knowledge of rhetorical analysis and cultural analysis to work by analyzing a political speech. Political speeches are rich sources of cultural values, and can provide us with a deep understanding of our culture and what audiences in our culture find persuasive. Now that we have a clear understanding of what cultural values and cultural keywords are, let's try to put our knowledge to work by analyzing one of the most well-known American political speeches, Ronald Reagan's "First Inaugural Address." Look for both the different cultural values Reagan utilizes and how he uses them to give his ideas authority and persuade his audience to identify with them. There are several important cultural values or ideological terms throughout the speech. We will focus our analysis on one of these important terms: "Americans." As you read, circle each time this important term or synonyms for this term are used. This will help you keep track of how the cultural value is used in each point of Reagan's speech.

Ronald Reagan—"First Inaugural Address"

January 20, 1981

Thank you. Thank you.

Senator Hatfield, Mr. Chief Justice, Mr. President, Vice President Bush, Vice President Mondale, Senator Baker, Speaker O'Neill, Reverend Moomaw, and my fellow citizens:

To a few of us here today this is a solemn and most momentous occasion. And, yet, in the history of our nation it is a commonplace occurrence. The orderly transfer of authority as called for in the Constitution routinely takes place as it has for almost two centuries and few of us stop to think how unique we really are. In the eyes of many in the world, this every-four-year ceremony we accept as normal is nothing less than a miracle.

Mr. President, I want our fellow citizens to know how much you did to carry on this tradition. By your gracious cooperation in the transition process you have shown a watching world that we are a united people pledged to maintaining a political system which guarantees individual liberty to a greater degree than any other. And I thank you and your people for all your help in maintaining the continuity which is the bulwark of our republic.

The business of our nation goes forward.

These United States are confronted with an economic affliction of great proportions. We suffer from the longest and one of the worst sustained inflations in our national history. It distorts our economic decisions, penalizes thrift, and crushes the struggling young and the fixed-income elderly alike. It threatens to shatter the lives of millions of our people. Idle industries have cast workers into unemployment, human misery and personal indignity.

Those who do work are denied a fair return for their labor by a tax system which penalizes successful achievement and keeps us from maintaining full productivity. But great as our tax burden is, it has not kept pace with public spending. For decades we have piled deficit upon deficit, mortgaging our future and our children's future for the temporary convenience of the present. To continue this long trend is to guarantee tremendous social, cultural, political, and economic upheavals.

You and I, as individuals, can, by borrowing, live beyond our means, but for only a limited period of time. Why then should we think that collectively, as a nation, we are not bound by that same limitation?

We must act today in order to preserve tomorrow. And let there be no misunderstanding—we're going to begin to act beginning today. The economic ills we suffer have come upon us over several decades. They will not go away in days, weeks, or months, but they will go away. They will go away because we as Americans have the capacity now, as we have had in the past, to do whatever needs to be done to preserve this last and greatest bastion of freedom.

In this present crisis, government is not the solution to our problem; government is the problem. From time to time we've been tempted to believe that society has become too complex to be managed by self-rule, that government by an elite group is superior to government for, by, and of the people. But if no one among us is capable of governing himself, then who among us has the capacity to govern someone else?

All of us together—in and out of government—must bear the burden. The solutions we seek must be equitable with no one group singled out to pay a higher price. We hear much of special interest groups. Well our concern must be for a special interest group that has been too long neglected. It knows no sectional boundaries, or ethnic and racial divisions, and it crosses political party lines. It is made up of men and women who raise our food, patrol our streets, man our mines and factories, teach our children, keep our homes, and heal us when we're sick—professionals, industrialists, shopkeepers, clerks, cabbies, and truck drivers. They are, in short, "We the People." This breed called Americans.

Well, this Administration's objective will be a healthy, vigorous, growing economy that provides equal opportunities for all Americans with no barriers born of bigotry or discrimination. Putting America back to work means putting all Americans back to work. Ending inflation means freeing all Americans from the terror of runaway living costs.

All must share in the productive work of this "new beginning," and all must share in the bounty of a revived economy.

With the idealism and fair play which are the core of our system and our strength, we can have a strong and prosperous America at peace with itself and the world. So as we begin, let us take inventory.

We are a nation that has a government—not the other way around. And this makes us special among the nations of the earth. Our Government has no power except that granted it by the people. It is time to check and reverse the growth of government which shows signs of having grown beyond the consent of the governed.

It is my intention to curb the size and influence of the Federal establishment and to demand recognition of the distinction between the powers granted to the Federal Government and those reserved to the states or to the people.

All of us—all of us need to be reminded that the Federal Government did not create the states; the states created the Federal Government.

Now, so there will be no misunderstanding, it's not my intention to do away with government. It is rather to make it work—work with us, not over us; to stand by our side, not ride on our back. Government can and must provide opportunity, not smother it; foster productivity, not stifle it. If we look to the answer as to why for so many years we achieved so much, prospered as no other people on earth, it was because here in this land we unleashed the energy and individual genius of man to a greater extent than has ever been done before.

Freedom and the dignity of the individual have been more available and assured here than in any other place on earth. The price for this freedom at times has been high, but we have never been unwilling to pay that price.

It is no coincidence that our present troubles parallel and are proportionate to the intervention and intrusion in our lives that result from unnecessary and excessive growth of Government.

It is time for us to realize that we are too great a nation to limit ourselves to small dreams. We're not, as some would have us believe, doomed to an inevitable decline. I do not believe in a fate that will fall on us no matter what we do. I do believe in a fate that will fall on us if we do nothing.

So with all the creative energy at our command, let us begin an era of national renewal. Let us renew our determination, our courage, and our strength. And let us renew our faith and our hope. We have every right to dream heroic dreams.

Those who say that we're in a time when there are no heroes—they just don't know where to look. You can see heroes every day going in and out of factory gates. Others, a handful in number, produce enough food to feed all of us and then the world beyond. You meet heroes across a counter—and they're on both sides of that counter. There are entrepreneurs with faith in themselves and faith in an idea who create new jobs, new wealth and opportunity.

There are individuals and families whose taxes support the Government and whose voluntary gifts support church, charity, culture, art, and education. Their patriotism is quiet but deep. Their values sustain our national life.

Now I have used the words "they" and "their" in speaking of these heroes. I could say "you" and "your" because I'm addressing the heroes of whom I speak—you, the citizens of this blessed land. Your dreams, your hopes, your goals are going to be the dreams, the hopes, and the goals of this Administration, so help me God.

We shall reflect the compassion that is so much a part of your make-up. How can we love our country and not love our countrymen—and loving them reach out a hand when they fall, heal them when they're sick, and provide opportunity to make them self-sufficient so they will be equal in fact and not just in theory? Can we solve the problems confronting us? Well the answer is an unequivocal and emphatic "Yes." To paraphrase Winston Churchill, I did not take the oath I've just taken with the intention of presiding over the dissolution of the world's strongest economy. In the days ahead, I will propose removing the roadblocks that have slowed our economy and reduced productivity. Steps will be taken aimed at restoring the balance between the various levels of government. Progress may be slow—measured in inches and feet, not miles—but we will progress. It is time to reawaken this industrial giant, to get government back within its means, and to lighten our punitive tax burden. And these will be our first priorities, and on these principles there will be no compromise.

On the eve of our struggle for independence a man who might've been one of the greatest among the Founding Fathers, Dr. Joseph Warren, president of the Massachusetts Congress, said to his fellow Americans,

"Our country is in danger, but not to be despaired of. On you depend the fortunes of America. You are to decide the important question upon which rest the happiness and the liberty of millions yet unborn. Act worthy of yourselves."

Well I believe we, the Americans of today, are ready to act worthy of ourselves, ready to do what must be done to insure happiness and liberty for ourselves, our children, and our children's children. And as we renew ourselves here in our own land, we will be seen as having greater strength throughout the world. We will again be the exemplar of freedom and a beacon of hope for those who do not now have freedom.

To those neighbors and allies who share our freedom, we will strengthen our historic ties and assure them of our support and firm commitment. We will match loyalty with loyalty. We will strive for mutually beneficial relations. We will not use our friendship to impose on their sovereignty, for our own sovereignty is not for sale.

As for the enemies of freedom, those who are potential adversaries, they will be reminded that peace is the highest aspiration of the American people. We will negotiate for it, sacrifice for it; we will not surrender for it—now or ever. Our forbearance should never be misunderstood. Our reluctance for conflict should not be misjudged as a failure of will. When action is required to preserve our national security, we will act. We will maintain sufficient strength to prevail if need be, knowing that if we do so, we have the best chance of never having to use that strength.

Above all we must realize that no arsenal or no weapon in the arsenals of the world is so formidable as the will and moral courage of free men and women. It is a weapon our adversaries in today's world do not have. It is a weapon that we as Americans do have. Let that be understood by those who practice terrorism and prey upon their neighbors.

I am—I'm told that tens of thousands of prayer meetings are being held on this day; and for that I am deeply grateful. We are a nation under God, and I believe God intended for us to be free. It would be fitting and good, I think, if on each inaugural day in future years it should be declared a day of prayer.

This is the first time in our history that this ceremony has been held, as you've been told, on this West Front of the Capitol.

Standing here, one faces a magnificent vista, opening up on this city's special beauty and history. At the end of this open mall are those shrines to the giants on whose shoulders we stand. Directly in front of me, the monument to a monumental man. George Washington, father of our country. A man of humility who came to greatness reluctantly. He led America out of revolutionary victory into infant nationhood. Off to one side, the stately memorial to Thomas Jefferson. The Declaration of Independence flames with his eloquence. And then beyond the Reflecting Pool, the dignified columns of the Lincoln Memorial. Whoever would understand in his heart the meaning of America will find it in the life of Abraham Lincoln.

Beyond those moments—those monuments to heroism is the Potomac River, and on the far shore the sloping hills of Arlington National Cemetery, with its row upon row of simple white markers bearing crosses or Stars of David. They add up to only a tiny fraction of the price that has been paid for our freedom.

Each one of those markers is a monument to the kind of hero I spoke of earlier. Their lives ended in places called Belleau Wood, the Argonne, Omaha Beach, Salerno, and halfway around the world on Guadalcanal, Tarawa, Pork Chop Hill, the Chosin Reservoir, and in a hundred rice paddies and jungles of a place called Vietnam.

Under one such a marker lies a young man, Martin Treptow, who left his job in a small town barber shop in 1917 to go to France with the famed Rainbow Division. There, on the Western front, he was killed trying to carry a message between battalions under heavy fire. We're told that on his body was found a diary. On the flyleaf under the heading, "My Pledge," he had written these words:

"America must win this war. Therefore, I will work; I will save; I will sacrifice; I will endure; I will fight cheerfully and do my utmost, as if the issue of the whole struggle depended on me alone."

The crisis we are facing today does not require of us the kind of sacrifice that Martin Treptow and so many thousands of others were called upon to make. It does require, however, our best effort, and our willingness to believe in ourselves and to believe in our capacity to perform great deeds; to believe that together with God's help we can and will resolve the problems which now confront us.

And after all, why shouldn't we believe that? We are Americans. God bless you and thank you. Thank you very much.

You may notice that the speech taps into the cultural keyword "Americans" in conjunction with the word "heroes." While we noted several others down, we chose this term because it is used consistently throughout the speech. Reagan uses these cultural keywords to produce a strong sense of identification in his audience, as he is asking them to see themselves as having the power to change the direction of the country. Observe how Reagan links his audience to his vision of government:

All of us together—in and out of government—must bear the burden. The solutions we seek must be equitable with no one group singled out to pay a higher price. We hear much of special interest groups. Well our concern must be for a special interest group that has been too long neglected. It knows no sectional boundaries, or ethnic and racial divisions, and it crosses political party lines. It is made up of men and women who raise our food, patrol our streets, man our mines and factories, teach our children, keep our homes, and heal us when we're sick—professionals, industrialists, shopkeepers, clerks, cabbies, and truck drivers. They are, in short, "We the People." This breed called Americans.

In this example, we see that the heroes that Reagan had stated had the power to reform the government in an earlier paragraph are none other than everyday Americans.

You might have noticed another important point here. Reagan uses this term to move his audience to identify with his vision of American government. Look closely at how Reagan describes the role of government:

Well I believe we, the Americans of today, are ready to act worthy of ourselves, ready to do what must be done to insure happiness and liberty for ourselves, our children, and our children's children. And as we renew ourselves here in our own land, we will be seen as having greater strength throughout the world. We will again be the exemplar of freedom and a beacon of hope for those who do not now have freedom.

Notice how "Americans" lends authority to Reagan's argument here. The key phrase is "ready to act worthy of ourselves." These words raise the stakes of Reagan's audience, as to not act in the way he describes might mean that we are not acting "worthy of ourselves" and that we are not taking the steps to protect the "happiness and liberty" of future generations.

While there are more cultural values at play here than "Americans," focusing on this one cultural keyword can tell us a lot about the speech's connection to its audience.

Looking at each of our questions, it would seem that we can definitely make the argument that "Americans" is an important cultural value in Reagan's speech, one that reflects a deep-seated American ideology that is based on both the power of American citizens to reform government and address national crises through their ingenuity and common values. We also witness the way that this cultural keyword is used to endorse one particular view of government. Now that we have located this cultural keyword, we have to think through how we might interpret it in our own analysis.

As we mentioned above, there is a close connection between "Americans" and Reagan's description of government. Reagan's understanding of the role of government in America is shaped by his ideology of the American people. In the example below, Reagan uses the cultural value "Americans" to directly support his vision of a more limited government. Looking back through Reagan's speech, we see that he endorses his view of government by pointing to the ability of Americans to rule themselves and take control of their own destinies.

Reagan explains that

> *We are a nation that has a government—not the other way around. And this makes us special among the nations of the earth. Our Government has no power except that granted it by the people. It is time to check and reverse the growth of government which shows signs of having grown beyond the consent of the governed.*

In this passage we see that "the people" and "the governed" serve as synonyms for "Americans." We see here that Reagan develops a set of values for "Americans" and then contrasts these values to a government that is no longer reflecting their interests.

Speaking of the responsibility of each American in reforming the country, Reagan states,

> *It does require, however, our best effort, and our willingness to believe in ourselves and to believe in our capacity to perform great deeds; to believe that together with God's help we can and will resolve the problems which now confront us.*

> *And after all, why shouldn't we believe that? We are Americans.*

As we read back through the speech and trace this cultural value even more closely, we see that Reagan uses "Americans" to support his vision of a more limited government, or a government that places more of an emphasis on the opportunity and responsibility of its citizens to fulfill their own needs.

It is his vision of the strength, heroism, and capacity of "Americans" that helps support his argument that government should be more limited.

Reagan's vision of "Americans" portrays common Americans as the heroes of democracy, but this cultural keyword is also used to exclude the idea that Reagan might refer to as "big government." He contrasts the power of the American people to the philosophy that the government should be made up of an "elite" set of representatives. Reagan states that

> From time to time we've been tempted to believe that society has become too complex to be managed by self-rule, that government by an elite group is superior to government for, by, and of the people. But if no one among us is capable of governing himself, then who among us has the capacity to govern someone else?

The rhetorical question at the end of this passage is designed to move us to consider if our democracy is possible at all without the realization that citizens have the power to govern. This is what Reagan means by the reference to "self-rule."

Reagan's use of rhetorical strategies is extensive throughout his speech, and we will only focus on a few examples. Take time to read back through the speech and look for even more examples of his rhetorical appeals. Reagan's rhetorical ethos is aligned with the cultural value "Americans." He portrays his own role as a leader as being inseparable from the ideals and goals of the American people. His ethos is that of a leader who will restore the role of the American people in government and limit the government from being too intrusive. He states,

> Now I have used the words "they" and "their" in speaking of these heroes. I could say "you" and "your" because I'm addressing the heroes of whom I speak—you, the citizens of this blessed land. Your dreams, your hopes, your goals are going to be the dreams, the hopes, and the goals of this Administration, so help me God.

By addressing his audience as heroes and linking the goals of administration to the goals of his Presidency, Reagan portrays his character as not only trustworthy but as reflective of the character of the American people.

Reagan builds upon the connection he established between himself and average Americans by drawing upon several moving examples. In this rhetorical vision of the American worker, each person plays a role in the success of the country as a whole. Reagan states,

You can see heroes every day going in and out of factory gates. Others, a handful in number, produce enough food to feed all of us and then the world beyond. You meet heroes across a counter—and they're on both sides of that counter. There are entrepreneurs with faith in themselves and faith in an idea who create new jobs, new wealth and opportunity. There are individuals and families whose taxes support the Government and whose voluntary gifts support church, charity, culture, art, and education. Their patriotism is quiet but deep. Their values sustain our national life.

Notice how he mentions the values of these people but does not explicitly define them. Instead, they are to be read through the actions Reagan describes. Their values can be seen in their ingenuity, work ethic, and generosity. By defining "Americans" in this way, with these values, Reagan is able to align his audience with the values of his administration.

Reagan's logos or logical argument is more complex than we can discuss in full here. One example can help us understand the link between the logic of his argument and the cultural value "Americans." Reagan argues that

Now, so there will be no misunderstanding, it's not my intention to do away with government. It is rather to make it work—work with us, not over us; to stand by our side, not ride on our back. Government can and must provide opportunity, not smother it; foster productivity, not stifle it. If we look to the answer as to why for so many years we achieved so much, prospered as no other people on earth, it was because here in this land we unleashed the energy and individual genius of man to a greater extent than has ever been done before.

Reagan's logic here is that government needs to be reformed because it is over-involved in the lives of American citizens. His logical argument can be broken down in the same way that we might break down a basic thesis statement:

Claim: Government works and prospers when it works alongside citizens to provide opportunities and foster productivity.

Reason: Because, historically, when government worked alongside rather than over citizens, great prosperity followed.

In this example, we see that "Americans" are defined by their "individual genius" and that a large government must not interfere with this genius. A historical understanding of the power of Americans to create prosperity for the nation supports Reagan's argument. His logic, or his logical description of why government must be limited, is supported by an appeal to the history of American prosperity and its causes.

Our discussion of this speech has only touched the surface of Reagan's speech, and we encourage you to read back through the speech and look for even more examples of cultural values and how they are used in the speech.

Conclusion

Culture is a very complex concept, and by taking on a cultural analysis, you will push your skills of rhetorical analysis and close reading to new levels. Cultural analysis asks us to reflect deeply upon how cultural values and ideas shape texts and how texts speak to these values and ideas. As you develop a cultural analysis, remember that culture is too complex to sum up in one analysis. Instead, you will want to be selective, choosing one cultural keyword to focus upon and analyzing how this keyword helps support the argument of the text. Remember that cultural analysis utilizes the skills of rhetorical analysis that you have developed through narrative, classical, and visual-spatial analysis. These forms of close textual analysis inform your cultural analysis. Cultural analysis uses these skills and adds an understanding of cultural values that can be used to support appeals to logic, character, and emotion.

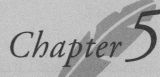

Chapter 5

Cultural Analysis in Context: Reading and Writing in a World of Assumptions— Gender, Audience, and *Vogue*

By Marlowe Daly-Galeano

You have a good imagination. It's one of your special skills. If someone says to you, "I'm pretty much your average first-grade teacher," you will probably be able to come up with a vivid image of that person. Let's try it right now. What does your image look like? How old is the person you imagine? What is this person's body type? What type of clothing does your imagined first-grade teacher wear? What race is this first-grade teacher? How tall is she? What does her voice sound like? Does she wear glasses? Carry a purse? Ah, have you caught me? I've made an **assumption** here: "Your average first-grade teacher" is a woman. When I make an assumption, I draw a conclusion based on the information and ideas that have shaped the way I view the world. My first-grade teacher was a woman, and all the first-grade teachers at my elementary school were women. When I think of the average first-grade teacher, it is not necessarily surprising that I assume this person will be a woman. Statistically, of course, the numbers will support my assumption: nearly three quarters of elementary school teachers are women (Nelson). There is nothing inherently wrong with this assumption. In seventy-five percent of cases, my assumption, and perhaps yours too, will match the gender of the actual individual. But what if the speaker of this statement is not a woman? How does this change the statement? How does a male utter, "I'm pretty much your average first-grade teacher"? To whom does he make this statement? What are his intentions when he says it? And how is this different from the way a female would say, "I'm pretty much your average first-grade teacher." I am drawing your attention to the fact that any time we read or write we are working with, within, or against a world of assumptions.

This was a fairly easy example. I'm going to give you a few more. Think about the assumptions that will likely follow the statements below. Think about who might make each statement and who might receive or respond to the statement. Then, think about an *unlikely* way to imagine the subject or subjects of the statement. Try these:

- "The cutest couple was sitting in front of me at the movies last night."

- "Wow! Now that is what I call a *great* parent!"

- "My doctor is the best. If you want I can try to get you an appointment."

- "That looks so sleazy."

What kind of assumptions do you form? The point of this exercise is not to show you that something is wrong with you if you make assumptions. The point is to illustrate the fact that we all can and do make assumptions. Having this awareness helps us to think critically about the conversations, or **discourses** (the ways thoughts are expressed more formally in written or spoken language), that surround us every day. In the previous essay in this section, you learned the basic techniques of ideological analysis. In this piece, by looking more closely at particular texts, you will see these techniques in practice. Starting with an awareness of assumptions and the way they relate to the **audience** helps you to begin analyzing texts and situations and to make your own choices as a writer. For example, if you understand that several people will assume that "the cutest couple" in front of you at the theater means a relatively young man and a relatively young woman (probably attractive, probably clean, probably thin, probably middle-class, probably of the same race), then when you write about this couple, you know that you are writing to people who are likely to have these assumptions. Reflecting on these assumptions can also lead you to another step in critical thinking: determining what most people will probably *not* assume about "the cutest couple." We can think of these as **anti-assumptions**. When you think up anti-assumptions about "the cutest couple," you might think about a same-sex couple, a mixed-race couple, a couple in which the woman appears to be twenty years older than the man, and so on. While there is no reason that any of these couples would not be "cute," there is a sense that the "average" cute couple will fall into the first set of descriptors. The assumptions and the anti-assumptions that you might make can help us to understand the way culture influences how we think about difference and identity.

This in turn allows us to think about gender and our assumptions about gender when we read and write. As the examples above should illustrate, we all have assumptions about gender. We don't all have the same assumptions, but there are several assumptions that are common and widely held. In order to be able to communicate more effectively about gender assumptions, it will be helpful to have a **shared vocabulary** of terms related to gender-based assumptions. In the previous section, I spent some time explaining the way I understand assumptions and anti-assumptions. You spent some time reading about my understanding of assumptions and anti-assumptions. In these practices of reading and writing, we added the terms **assumption** and **anti-assumption** to our shared vocabulary. As you may have noticed when performing a **rhetorical analysis**, creating and using a shared vocabulary is one way that writers establish credibility with their readers. For the sake of our discussion of gender assumptions, I propose that we accept and use the following terms and definitions. It is important to know that the vocabulary used in discussions of gender is often contested. Different writers may ask you to use terms like "sex" or "gender" in different ways. That is why it is so critical to understand the shared vocabulary within a particular discourse community. The definitions below have been adapted from *The Bedford Glossary of Critical and Literary Terms*, but as you continue to read, think, and write about gender, you may find definitions that are better suited to your purpose and the needs of your audience. Our shared vocabulary will include:

> **gender:** a term referring to the socially constructed identities *man,
> woman, masculine, feminine*. Gender is distinguished from *sex*, the
> biological designation of male or female. Unlike *sex*, which is ana-
> tomical, gender is widely held to be a product of the prevailing mores,

expectations, and stereotypes of a particular culture. Thus, what it means to be "masculine" or "feminine" (rather than "male" or "female") is determined by culture and may vary from one culture to the next.

sex: the *biological* designation of male or female.

masculine: a description of someone who complies with the *social* expectations for males.

feminine: a description of someone who complies with the *social* expectations for females.

queer: a term based on the assumption that sexual identities are fluid, not fixed; a sexual practice or behavior without reproductive aims and without regard for social or economic considerations; a term used for texts or ideas that question generally accepted associations and identities involving sex, gender, and sexuality.

heteronormative: a term describing the view that heterosexuality is the *normal* sexual orientation; a system that marginalizes non-heterosexual lifestyles and people.

When you perform cultural and rhetorical analysis of a text, you can use this shared vocabulary to analyze and critique the text's ideas about gender. When you approach a text with the intention of identifying its ideas and assumptions about gender, you might start by turning this list of terms into a list of questions.

- To start, does the text *directly* address the issue of gender difference? Does it use the words "gender" or "sex"? What do those words mean in the text? (Remember that the definitions I have provided might be different from the definitions of "sex" or "gender" used by another writer.) Or, does the text instead include more subtle messages or ideas about gender even if it does not directly engage this topic?

- Think about the text's audience. Does the text seem to be directed toward a specifically male or female audience? If so, what assumptions does the text seem to make about its intended audience? Does the text appeal to certain values or tastes that are associated with gender?

- What words are used to describe men or women? What connotations do these words have?

- What pronouns does the text contain? If a text seems to be written about women, a writer's choice to use the pronoun "we" rather than "they" will have a very specific effect.

- Does the text include references to masculinity or femininity? If so, how does the text define or depict "masculine" or "feminine"? How do these meanings help to construct an idea of gender? In other words, does the text provide some sort of answer to the questions "What is masculine?" or "What is feminine?" Do the answers to these questions (as the text answers them) directly or indirectly answer the questions "What is male?" or "What is female?"

- Does the text contain visual messages? If the text contains images of men or women, what are these images like? How do the images relate to the language used? What ideas about gender do the images create?

- Does the text contain ideas about sexuality? Does it assume heteronormativity? Does the text challenge any traditional ideas about gender or gender roles? Or rather, does the text queer any of these traditional ideas?

The ways that you answer these questions will help you to think and eventually write a gender analysis as I have done with the magazine *Vogue*.

I am flipping through an issue of *Vogue* magazine. I am not a regular reader of *Vogue*, and I admit to finding several surprises when reading the magazine. As I begin analyzing a text, I like to try to assess its **rhetorical situation,** or to consider its audience, purpose, and context. *Vogue* is generally considered a women's magazine; I imagine that by reading this magazine, I will be able to define and understand the assumptions that CondeNast, the publisher of *Vogue*, makes about women. One of the first surprises is that the 380-page magazine seems to be almost completely composed of advertisements. The editor's letter doesn't occur until more than one hundred pages into the magazine, while the first feature story turns up at page 150. And before that? Advertisements—many, many advertisements. Although I am not generally a fan of advertisements, the advertisements that make up the bulk of *Vogue* are truly fascinating. First, they, like much of the magazine, give off the air of *money*. The quality of the photographs is above average; and, in some cases, similar to what you could see at a photography exhibit in a gallery. The models look professional and confident. The products being sold—shoes, clothing, handbags, cosmetics, jewelry, and fragrances—are classy (and expensive).

The articles in *Vogue* surprise me too. They are all several pages long, drawing on the research and opinions of experts. They are well written. The topics include a full-length interview with actress Rachel Weisz, a tribute to Valerie Jarrett (a chief advisor to Barack Obama), a discussion of fashion trends that draw attention to social and political issues, the development of new alternatives to Botox, and an article that I will explore at more length, which describes the unusual and long-enduring marriage of Christina Thompson (the editor of the *Harvard Review*) and her tool-manufacturer husband. So what are the assumptions about women in this magazine? When I perform a rhetorical analysis of the entire magazine, I conclude that the purpose of the magazine is to sell several products and also to promote a particular idea and image of women. This image of women is constructed through the written and visual texts that comprise the magazine.

Vogue appears to believe its female readers are educated and value education, as we can see in the length and complexity of its articles and in the story about Christina Thompson, a well-known academic. The writers assume that women readers are interested in the stories of successful women like political advisor Valerie Jarrett and actress Rachel Weisz. However, these stories are not merely success stories. They also reveal complex situations and conflicts. The assumption, then, is that the readers of *Vogue* are complicated individuals themselves who are interested in the complex lives of other women. The following excerpt from Christina Thompson's article illustrates this complexity. While reading the article, I annotated it, as I do with anything I read closely. My notes address some of the gender analysis questions from the previous section:

I had always been curious about other people and interested in anything different from what I knew. It was one of the things that had attracted me to my husband in the first place, what had drawn me to his far-flung corner of the world. I flattered myself that I was immune to these socially constructed prejudices, regardless of whether they arose from differences of ethnicity, race, religion, or social class. And then, one day, quite by accident I came face-to-face with a set of feelings that, if you had asked me, I would certainly have denied having had.

We had been married for about five years when my husband and I moved to a city where, for the first time, he had difficulty finding employment. I had been awarded a fellowship at the local university and was supporting a family of four—me, my husband, our first child, and my husband's youngest sister, who had come to live with us—on a postdoctoral stipend. It was, therefore, imperative that my husband get some kind of work. He'd had a number of different jobs in the past: dispatching cars, casting boat parts, riding as a bicycle messenger—but none of these was an option in the place where we now lived. He talked about becoming a taxi driver and worked for a while as a janitor in a factory where they made salads for supermarket chains. He did a brief stint as a builder's laborer, and then one day he came home and told me that he had taken a job selling vacuum cleaners door-to-door.

I still have difficulty explaining the effect this announcement had on me, but it was a bit like being dropped into a cold, dark well. At the time, I didn't even understand my reaction: I just knew I couldn't tolerate the idea, and I begged him to go back and tell them he'd decided against taking the job. My husband thought I was being unreasonable. There was nothing about the job, he argued, that made it any worse or better than any of the other things he'd ever done. In fact, it was a lot easier than cycling and cleaner than foundry work. But nothing he could say made any difference, because my reasons for feeling the way I did were, in fact, entirely irrational, arising as they did from something I'd experienced as a child.

When I was growing up, a traveling salesman paid a visit to my parents' house once or twice a year. He had a large old car and a shabby coat, and he came in the late fall or early spring so that it was

Thompson seems to treat her husband as an exotic object rather than a partner of twenty years. I'm not quite sure why she does this. Is it because she is writing for a popular magazine instead of the *Harvard Review*?

She does not mention gender or sex in this list of markers of difference. It suggests her treatment of gender difference will be much more subtle than her treatment of class.

Throughout the article, she almost never gives his name. It's always "my husband." This really emphasizes the importance of the institution of marriage for this writer in this text.

She's not afraid to draw attention to a queered family image, though. She is the breadwinner of the family that not only includes her child (no stay-at-home mom figure here!) but also an extra family member, the sister.

Her class position makes her unable to conceive that anyone might enjoy this kind of work. "Nice home" privileges the hetero-normative (and capitalistic) idea of family and home, just like her repeated use of "my husband" does.

Aha! "Masculine integrity—so in some ways what is lost in the vacuum-salesman job is not so much class status (even though earlier she writes, "The trickier thing is marrying across class"), *it's masculinity*.

For Thompson, masculinity is associated with physical labor—it contrasts starkly with her white-collar "parody" job, so she's also constructing an idea of white-collar, academic work as feminine. This is unusual since academia is still male-dominated.

Thompson goes on to analyze her own reaction in much more depth. The full article is included in the October 2008 issue of *Vogue*.

always damp and cold whenever I saw him. I still have a vivid image of the way he looked, with his rounded shoulders and his heavy case and the way he shuffled across the gravel to our front door. I felt quite sad about this man and also a bit scared of him, but mostly what I felt was guilt. It was clear to me that no one would want to do what he was doing out there in the drizzle while we were snug and warm in our nice home. And so, when my husband told me that he had taken a job as a door-to-door salesman, the shadow of this man washed over me, and for the first time, in our marriage, I wondered what I had done.

Until that point, I had viewed my husband's various occupations with humor and something like pride. There was a certain masculine integrity in being a bicycle messenger, for example, or a machinist. I never cared that he wasn't white-collar. My own work was like a parody of professional employment (I still haven't had a job outside a university), and it reminds me that it was sensible to have someone in the family who was good with his hands. But selling, particularly this dodgy variety, did not fit into any of these acceptable categories, and it was only the greatest of mercies that my husband proved inept at selling, and after a couple weeks of pointless demonstrations, voluntarily gave it up.

I can see from Thompson's article and others that *Vogue* assumes that women are not limited by **gender** in their professional careers. The stories focus on women who have reached high levels of achievement and status in fields that are still often dominated by men: academia, politics, and the arts. These women, while working against the norms, have not necessarily been limited by them. *Vogue* also assumes that the female audience is financially successful and able to buy both the four-dollar magazine, and the four-hundred dollar handbags advertised throughout its pages. At the same time, articles like Thompson's also reflect a traditional romanticized (idealized) view of more traditional institutions (like marriage) and the potential conflicts of trying to maintain some aspects of a traditional gender role (wife) while functioning in a less traditional gender role (*Harvard Review* editor). The article and the entire magazine seem to be dealing with several potential conflicts faced by successful women. The text assumes that these conflicts are interesting and relevant to its readers. The assumptions in *Vogue* do not stop there, though. The magazine also assumes that successful women *want* (or should want) to buy the products featured on nearly every page. They want to acquire nice things, and they want to be attractive.

The repeated image of the attractive woman is where *Vogue*'s concept of woman gets even more complicated. I can see that the financially and professionally successful woman is a departure from the more traditional **feminine** image of women found in some women's magazines. The women pictured in *Vogue* are definitely not housewives or stay-at-home moms. In fact, it seems unlikely that they are moms at all. We might even say that by showing images of women who are not having babies, *Vogue* **queers** one traditional image of women. But *Vogue* also presents an idea of the feminine woman that is dependent on her **sex** and her sexuality. The images of women in the ads, the fashion shots, and the feature photos all show beautiful, sexy, and sexual women. The women are usually pictured alone, seemingly aware that they are being watched (or that they are objects of the viewer's *gaze*) but when they are pictured with others, they are usually shown as part of a heterosexual pair. In this way, the texts present a **heteronormative** image of women. *Vogue* assumes women want to be wealthy, successful, beautiful, and in a sexual relationship with a man. By using text and images about this type of woman, they appeal to what they think their readers want to be.

The magazine also offers a **message**, a suggestion for how readers can become like the women on the pages of *Vogue*, and this is done with advertising. Because of the aesthetic quality of the advertisements, they appeal to women who appreciate artistic photography that has been achieved with quality cameras, highly trained models, and good editing. And because there are so *many* advertisements, the reader cannot just forget about them. Remember, I had to flip through more than one hundred pages of ads before I even reached the editor's letter. Before I reached the editor's description of the issue's featured photographer, Patrick Demarchelier, I flipped through pages of seductive advertisements by vendors like Saks Fifth Avenue, Dolce & Gabana, Giorgio Armani, Valentino, Oscar de la Renta, Ralph Lauren, Gucci, and Prada. While the editor's letter begins with a statement about a museum exhibit of Demarchelier's photography, the first pages of *Vogue* are like a museum exhibit themselves. Not only is the advertising a "Who's Who?" of the designing world, these advertisements use a surprising variety of styles and camera techniques. Some are in color, some are in black and white. Some feature the product alone, others focus on a woman. Several ads form part of a series, in which more than one page image contributes to the overall desirable image of the product. The ads, in their variety, add to the complex and aesthetic design of the entire magazine. A reader's first experiences in the opening pages of *Vogue* create consumer desire. The articles and letters reflect human accomplishment; the combined impression is that possessing certain items (those featured in the ads, in particular) is related to being successful.

I take a closer look at one of *Vogue*'s ads. The ad is one in a series of ads for Gucci jewelry that appear in this issue. It is a particularly beautiful shot of an attractive woman. The color scheme of the ad uses shades of gold. The woman's jewelry is gold, her hair is gold, her skin is gold, and she is lying on something gold. In one sense, this ad and all those in the series confuse me. This woman is lying down, with her finger and perhaps a piece of jewelry from Gucci's "Horsebit Collection" in her mouth. The idea of woman presented in the ad does not seem much like the idea of woman contained in the inspiring story about Valerie Jarrett's political success.

By lying down, the woman in the Gucci ad seems powerless. By putting her fingers in her mouth, she is made to seem like a child. Worse yet, if the jewelry is supposed to be a "horsebit," this woman is being compared to a dominated, domesticated animal! But the most striking aspect of this ad is that the woman is highly sexualized. The look on her face seems to be one of both sexual pleasure and sexual desirability. And the use of the gold and the jewelry suggests she is "rich." The message of this ad is that women will be sexual and happy if they own Gucci. There's even a queer element to this message, because it suggests the possibility that a woman does not need a man to be sexually or personally satisfied. All she needs is gold, or rather, Gucci. Oddly, though, this image feels very much like an image that would be appealing to a male viewer. The passivity and the feminine sexuality here seem to appeal to the **male gaze**, a concept that the scholar Laura Mulvey described in detail. According to Mulvey, "In a world ordered by sexual imbalance, pleasure in looking has been split between active/male and passive/female" (Mulvey 11). The woman is

Several scholars have researched and written about the male gaze. If you would like to know more about this concept, you might start by looking at the work of Laura Mulvey. For more on the male gaze within popular advertising, see GenderAds.com.

presented as a figure who is always being watched; by being the object
of the male gaze, the woman gratifies the gazing male (or the viewer
who is aligned with a male) and begins to see herself as a figure "to-be-
looked-at." Thus if I had to make an assumption about who is watching this woman, I would assume that she is being watched (or gazed
at) by a man. This is an interesting and potentially problematic point,
since I know that *Vogue* is generally considered a magazine for and
about women. It shows that even as the magazine and the ad try to
connect ideas of female power and success, there remains an underlying idea that women act (often passively) for the benefit of men. As the
objects of the male gaze, they provide gratification for the male viewer,
and this is weirdly connected, in the pages of *Vogue*, to female success.

Advertisers know the importance of "developing a concept that
is effective and powerful" (Adbusters 541). The concept that Gucci
uses is the visual link between beauty, sexuality, and wealth. Because
Vogue seems to assume that successful women want to (and will)
purchase attractive things, this ad works very well into the larger
concept and message of the magazine. *Vogue* assumes that its readers want to be successful, but even more than that, they want to be
like the woman in the Gucci ad. In her interview with *Vogue's* writer
Eve MacSweeney, Rachel Weisz describes the entire complicated
relationship between *Vogue* and its audience. Weisz says, "I remember someone once telling me that the definition of good styling is
when you look at the picture and you want to be the woman in the
photos. Well, I want to be that girl!" (MacSweeney 330).

Vogue has turned out to be a great case study, because it shows
just how complicated assumptions about gender can get. In some
ways, *Vogue* works against certain stereotypical ideas about women
in society, for example, the idea that women are all or should all be
mothers. It shows women achieving success equal or superior to men
in business, art, and academics. But it also relies on other assumptions about gender that are not necessarily in agreement with this
image of women, like the idea that a woman's success is inextricable
from her sexuality, or the idea that women are somehow powerless
to consumer culture. I've discussed several of the assumptions that
seem to influence the way *Vogue* is created. But the next step would

be to address the assumptions that affected the way I read the magazine. Why was I surprised at the artistic quality of the advertisements? Why was I surprised at the complex and often nontraditional ideas contained in the articles? Why did I assume the writing would be simpler and less well-written? You probably know the reason for this by now. I was surprised because I picked up my copy of *Vogue* with my own set of assumptions guiding me. And as I began to read and then to write this essay, I realized that many of my assumptions were limiting me.

Assumptions *can* cause us to misread a text or misjudge a writer. They can cause us to completely miss an important idea. So what should we do with assumptions? When we perform rhetorical analysis we are constantly on the lookout for assumptions. What are the author's assumptions about her topic? What is assumed about the audience? If we can answer these questions, we can learn a lot about a text, a writer, and the society in which the text is written and read. What should we do with assumptions? We should look for them, we should find them, we should analyze them. We should be aware that we are *always* reading and writing in a world of assumptions.

Works Cited

Adbusters. "Create Your Own Print Ad." *Adbusters*. 28 May, 2008. Web. 1 June, 2008.

MacSweeney, Eve. "The Beauty Down the Block." *Vogue* Oct. 2008: 330+. Print.

Mulvey, Laura. "Visual Pleasure and Narrative Cinema." *Screen* 16.3 (1975):6–18. Print.

Murfin, Ross, and Supriya M. Ray, eds. *The Bedford Glossary of Critical and Literary Terms*. 2nd ed. Boston: Bedford St. Martin's, 2003. Print.

Nelson, Bryan G. "They're Few But They're Proud." *Men Teach*, 11 Apr. 2009. Web. 15 May, 2009.

Thompson, Christina. "Up Front: Beyond Borders, Opposites Attract." *Vogue* Oct. 2008: 150–56. Print.

Warner, Judith. "Dangerous Resentment." *The New York Times.com*. New York Times, 9 July, 2009. Web. 10 July 2009.

Chapter 6

Genre Analysis

By Rachel Lewis

As you have learned, rhetorical analysis evaluates the available means of persuasion for a given speaker/audience/situation. Genre analysis is a type of rhetorical analysis that looks at the patterns that emerge from reoccurring rhetorical situations. Reoccurring rhetorical situations are those writing, reading, and speaking tasks that we encounter over and over again. For instance, you've probably encountered hundreds of birthday invitations in your lifetime. Each may be different—in color, theme, and even medium (think Facebook or Evite vs. a paper card)—but they probably all share certain traits: a positive tone, clearly placed date, time, and location information, and a way to respond to the host. When you sit down to write a birthday invitation, you already know to include some of these traits. Why? Because you've written and read birthday invitations before. The rhetorical situation of the birthday invitation is reoccurring.

What exactly is a genre? You may have heard the term used in English classes to classify forms of literature like fiction, poetry, or non-fiction. Perhaps you've even heard the term genre used to describe the types of writing you do in school, like personal narrative, persuasive argument, or literary analysis. When it's used for rhetorical analysis, the word genre means any reoccurring form of communication with conventions that we use to communicate effectively within that form. Every text that you read and write falls within a genre because no rhetorical situation is ever entirely new, from the diary entries you write to the emails you read and the text messages you send. There may be no rulebook for the diary entry,

107

but have you ever noticed that many open like letters (e.g., "Dear Diary")? And why do most diary entries use "I" more than "You"? Is there a reason so few diary entries are written in academic jargon? The answer is genre. When you write a diary entry, you are responding to a reoccurring rhetorical situation. Each reoccurring rhetorical situation produces patterns of rhetorical response.

Imagine you are applying to college and you are asked to submit a college application essay. Even though this might be the first college application essay you've ever written, you would likely already know (or conduct research to learn) some of the common traits of college application essays in general. No matter the prompt, you would probably infer that this occasion calls for you to include a personal story from your life that illustrates some of your most positive characteristics (invention). You would also be likely to conclude by discussing the ways these positive characteristics prepare you to be a successful, serious, and academically focused college student (arrangement). Similarly, you would also be able to predict what sorts of rhetorical choices *not* to make. You would know not to mention that this college is just your "backup," for instance, or that what you're most excited about are college parties. You would hesitate to open your essay too casually, with a "Waz up?" or to conclude with three explanation marks and a smile icon ☺ (style). Of course, you would not be the only one to make these rhetorical choices; other college applicants make very similar choices because they face a nearly identical rhetorical situation when they sit down to write their college application essays. So, yours is not an entirely new rhetorical situation; rather, the means of persuasion available to you are similar to those that were available to the millions of other students who have ever written college application essays. Because rhetorical situations like this one reoccur, the texts they produce usually reflect certain patterns. You can use genre analysis to consider what these patterns tell us about the social contexts from which they emerge.

Social contexts are key components of genre analysis. You can think of them as the communities, locations, or institutions where people communicate with one another. All genres occur within a social context. English papers occur within the social context of English classes. Lawyers' closing remarks occur within the social context of courtrooms. Eulogies occur within the social context of funerals. Before you begin a genre analysis, you should think of a social context that you are interested in learning more about. This could be a particular major you plan to declare (like Sociology or Biology), a profession you aspire to enter (like the medical field, or the film industry), or any other social context you are curious about (like social networking sites, presidential elections, weddings, or the Peace Corps). If this is an assignment for class, your teacher may give you a more focused assignment that defines that context for you. Either way, before you begin a genre analysis, you will need to choose a genre to analyze. Let's say you choose weddings as a social context that you're interested in learning more about. You might consider choosing wedding announcements, wedding invitations, or a new genre like wedding Web sites as a genre for analysis. (What if you chose social networking sites as a social context? Can you think of some genres that would help you analyze Facebook or MySpace? Try listing as many genres related to social networking sites as you can and then choose the one you think would lead to the most interesting analysis.)

Once you've chosen a genre to study, you're ready to get started. A genre analysis involves four basic steps:

1. collecting samples of a genre,

2. describing the social context of the genre,

3. describing the rhetorical patterns that emerge within the genre, and

4. analyzing what those patterns reveal about the social context of the genre.[2]

Step One: Collect Samples of a Genre

When you collect samples of a genre, you will want to collect as many as you can from as many different sources as possible. For example, if you're choosing to study the genre of the Biology lab report, you'll want to ask several different teachers and students on your campus for samples, as well as look for samples publicly available in the library and online. You may even consider contacting

2 The four steps of genre analysis are adapted from Anis Bawarshi's "Guidelines for Analyzing Genres" in *Genre and the Invention of the Writer* (159–160).

teachers and students at other schools to gather a range of different samples. The more samples you collect, and the more diverse their sources, the more patterns will emerge for your analysis.

Step Two: Describe the Social Context of the Genre

Consider the following questions:

- *Where is the genre typically set?*

- *What is the subject of the genre?*

- *Who uses the genre?*

- *When and why is the genre used? What purposes does the genre serve for the people who use it?*

Step Three: Describe the Rhetorical Patterns that Emerge Within the Genre

Consider the following questions:

- *What type of content is usually included and excluded?*

- *What rhetorical appeals are used most often? Do you notice any patterns in the appeals to logos, pathos, or ethos?*

- *How are the texts organized? Do they generally open in similar ways? Conclude in similar ways? What common parts do the samples share?*

- *Do sentences in the genre share a certain style? Are they mostly active, passive, simple, or complex? Is there an abundance or lack of questions, exclamation points, or semicolons?*

- *What type of word choice is used? Do many of the words fit in a particular category of jargon or slang? Is the overall effect of the word choice formal, informal, humorous, or academic?*

Step Four: Analyze What Those Patterns Reveal about the Social Context of the Genre

- *Who does the genre include and who does it exclude?*

- *What roles for writers and readers does the genre encourage?*

- *What values and beliefs are assumed about or encouraged from users of the genre?*

- *What content does the genre treat as most valuable? Least valuable?*

Analyzing the Genre of the College Application Essay

Now let's walk through the four steps of genre analysis together. Let's say I'm interested in learning more about the social context of college admissions. I could be interested in this topic for a number of reasons. Maybe I was rejected from the college of my choice and I'm still trying to figure out why. Maybe I was accepted to my current college but am just waiting for someone to knock on my dorm-room door to tell me they made a mistake. Maybe I found the process of applying to college overly stressful. Maybe I have a political interest in affirmative action. Whatever the reason, now that I have my social context, the thing I need to decide is what genre to analyze. I'll begin by coming up with a list of genres related to college admissions:

✔ the application itself
✔ admissions Web sites
✔ the application essay
✔ college guidebooks
✔ college rankings
✔ acceptance letters
✔ rejection letters

Each of these genres would have something to tell me about the context of college admissions. I choose to analyze the genre of the **college application essay** because I think it will lead to the most interesting analysis.

Step One: Now that I've chosen the genre of the college application essay, I need to collect my samples. Lucky for me, there are thousands of sample essays available online. To gather a good range, I will collect some from the model essays listed on essay help Web sites, some from those published in guidebooks like *The College Application for Dummies*, and some from my friends. I could try asking an admissions officer on my campus to share some samples, but it's likely he/ she will not be allowed to share private application information. Of course, I can't read every sample that I find, but I will try to gather enough essays to show me a range of different rhetorical responses to the reoccurring situation. Some about family background, others about academic interests. Some about trips abroad, others about part-time jobs. I'll look for all the different versions of the college application essay that I can find.

Step Two: Once I have my samples, it's time to think more carefully about the social situation of the college application essay.

Where is the college application typically set?
The college application essay is usually set as a blank box on the back page of a paper application. Students sometimes write their essays by hand in that box, but most type it on a separate page. Nowadays, most college application essays are submitted online.

What is the subject of the college application essay?
The subject of the college application essay is an applicant's readiness or qualification for higher education. It usually includes a personal narrative, or story, that illustrates why an applicant should be admitted to a particular school.

Who uses the genre?
College applicants write the genre, and college admissions officers read it.

When and why is the genre used? What purposes does the genre serve for the people who use it?
The college application essay is used at competitive universities that receive a high number of applications. Often, it is used to help admissions officers make decisions about students whose GPA and test scores are borderline. The essay can help give a student that extra push to be admitted or rejected. Students often use the application essay as a way to demonstrate areas of their character that are not apparent from their transcripts, test scores, or lists of extracurricular activities, scholarships, and awards.

Step Three: After taking notes on these observations, it's time to think about what rhetorical patterns I notice emerging in the college application essay.

Below is a sample essay I analyzed.

"I am sure you will find something to do." When my eighth grade geometry teacher asked everyone in class what they wanted to study in college, they all named their dream schools, spoke of their majors, and described how they would achieve success or even change the world. I was not given the chance. Instead, my teacher simply said, "I am sure you will find something to do." It was clear that this something had nothing to do with going to college. I wasn't all that bad of a student, even given the fact that I had always wanted to study literature and not mathematics. It wasn't as much aptitude as place.

My entire life since leaving the local elementary school across from my house has been leading to one place in the educational system. I am a "back parking lot kid." This space must have been assigned to me at birth, as all my childhood friends all seem to have ended up here. We are the working class kids who park in the back parking lot in the high school. Our trucks and cars are old, often two-toned, and are enveloped in a haze of cigarette smoke. Like the smoke that clings to our skin, we carry this place on our flannel shirts, jeans, and cheap shoes. We are easy to recognize and easy to forget.

I often flash forward from the experience in my geometry class to my high school orientation. My guidance counselor reviewed my file as if I were a patient in a hospital and looked at me as though I was a specimen in a Petri dish. I was present, but there to be observed not talked to. He spoke to my father. He pointed at me. "Have you considered sending your son part time to the local vocational college?" I knew this place. I had toured it with the other back parking lot kids last year, and my cousin studied auto-repair there. One could escape from the back parking lot, but this place was a well-designed mousetrap. You entered, made friends, learned your trade, and never escaped. Your life became an extension of these classrooms. Curiously, it was a school almost completely free of paper. There were few books and anyone caught with one was immediately considered an outsider, someone "too good." In that moment, with the vision of this place as a possible life, I watched my world narrowing, closing like a lower-class fist.

My father waived his hand in front of the file and said, "No. He's going to college." In my mind, the fist that held me was still tightened, and my father's words had not changed anything. I knew that he just didn't understand the system that was working against me. I was a "North-brook Kid," someone who came from a neighborhood that served as the back parking lot of my community. I had learned this in Middle School, but my father was proud of his home, his community, and his work in the textile mill. The guidance counselor understood the system well enough, though. "Given your son's academic background, I believe he might thrive at the vocational college," he said. My father didn't balk: "He's going to a real college." Conversation over. I was enrolled in college prep courses that afternoon.

As we walked back to the car that late summer afternoon, I looked at the back parking lot. I knew that I would end up there, I had heard about it from my cousin. However, walking next to my father, it seemed as though I could claim any space that I wanted. He didn't say a lot to me at first. He was still angry. Finally, in a thick drawl muffled by a cigarette in the left corner of his mouth, he said, "Sometimes you have fight to get where you want." While these words are not as poetic as the Whitman that I would read in College Prep English in my junior year, they taught me what I feel good books teach: how to survive. Since that time I haven't simply worked as a student, I have fought to succeed in classes where front parking-lot kids surround me. My academic success comes from these experiences. Attending college, for me, is not about money. It is about the chance to become a teacher, a teacher who will perhaps recognize in many other back-parking lot kids what my father recognized in me.

What type of content is usually included and excluded?

The content tends to show applicants in their moments of strength, determination and hard work on the way to a college education. Noticeably excluded are stories that show applicants' uncertainty, fears, or doubts about attending college.

What rhetorical appeals are used most often? Do you notice any patterns in the appeals to logos, pathos, or ethos?

I notice a pattern of pathetic (emotional) appeals being used to establish ethos (the character of the writer). Usually these begin with an applicant describing a personal hardship that he/she has overcome. However, the pattern that really sticks out is the way each of these stories is told in a way that shows the student's strength, hard work, and determination as a result of overcoming the personal hardship.

That is, the college application essay seems to encourage students to discuss personal hardships, but it discourages them from wallowing in self-pity. What results are appeals to pathos that establish the student's credibility (or ethos) as a college student.

How are the texts organized? Do they generally open in similar ways? Conclude in similar ways? What common parts do the samples share?
The college application essay usually opens with a personal story and concludes with the positive character traits that the applicant has developed as a result of that personal story. The conclusion usually speaks directly to the applicant's goals as a college student. The structure of the stories often opens with hardship and ends with redemption, or the positive results of the personal hardship. Personal redemption is important to the college application essay because it is important that applicants show the ways they have overcome the hardships of their background. A college education is very often alluded to in the conclusion as either a necessary step to or the logical progression of the applicant's personal redemption.

Do sentences in the genre share a certain style? Are they mostly active, passive, simple, or complex? Is there an abundance or lack of questions, exclamation points, or semi-colons?
The sentences are mostly active, and in the first-person. There is a lack of questions.

What type of word choice is used? Do many of the words fit in a particular category of jargon or slang? Is the overall effect of the word choice formal, informal, humorous, or academic?
The overall effect of word choice, or diction, in the college application essay, is informal. Applicants take on an intimate, storytelling voice in the genre in order to share the personal details of their lives. At the same time, it is clear that applicants are writing to an audience with authority over them, because they often use overly academic words to sound "college-ready."

Step Four: In the final stage of analysis, I need to think through what these rhetorical patterns reveal about the social context of college admissions. As you can see, many, many patterns emerged from the previous stage of my analysis, but one of them interested me more than the others—my observation that a good number of college application essays focus on an applicant overcoming some kind of personal obstacle. Because this pattern interests me, I will use it to focus my answers to the next set of questions, and perhaps arrive at a paper topic or thesis. I will need to consider: What can I learn about the context of college admissions by the reoccurrence of stories about overcoming personal obstacles in college application essays? What about these stories appeals to college admission officers and why? These same stories would not be fit for a job application letter; why do they reoccur in college application essays?

Who does the genre include and who does it exclude?
The genre seems to include students who have a compelling story of personal hardship; in turn, it excludes students who do not have a compelling story of personal hardship. In the context of college admissions, a story of personal hardship is "compelling" if it ends with redemption—that is, if it leads to a positive outcome for the applicant that prepares him/her for a college education. It is not compelling if the applicant appears weak, angry, or discouraged as a result of the personal hardship.

What roles for writers and readers does the genre encourage?
The genre encourages writers to play the role of a disadvantaged person who has pulled him/herself up by the bootstraps. It encourages readers (admissions officers) to play the role of hero by admitting applicants who have overcome personal hardships. Likewise, the genre discourages writers from playing the role of an angry, discouraged, or "down-and-out" victim of difficult life circumstances.

What values and beliefs are assumed about or encouraged from users of the genre?
Users of the genre are assumed to value individualism and self-reliance. The bootstraps story requires that applicants have overcome the personal obstacle on their own, without help or support, through personal characteristics like determination and a strong work ethic.

What content does the genre treat as most valuable? Least valuable?
The disadvantages that applicants have overcome are treated as most valuable. The advantages that would have given an applicant a leg up are treated as least valuable.

These responses reveal only the beginning stages of my analysis, but they have prepared me to write a very strong first draft of a genre analysis essay. Can you see how the four steps of genre analysis have led me toward a focused argument about the college application essay? I now have a clear focus—appeals to pathos in the college application essay—and a clear argument—that appeals to pathos in the college application essay both reflect and respond to the "bootstraps" narrative in college admissions. This is the kind of claim that could be used to structure a focused genre analysis essay in your first-year composition class. Not only does it make a claim about a rhetorical pattern of a genre, but it also reveals something interesting about the rhetorical context of college admissions. A strong genre analysis will do more than list observations about a genre; it will make a focused, insightful claim about the relationship between a genre and its social context.

A Question to Consider

- Even though genres produce rhetorical patterns, no two responses to a genre are exactly the same. What accounts for the differences within genres?

Work Cited

Bawarshi, Anis. *Genre and the Invention of the Writer.* Logan: Utah State P, 2003. Print.

Chapter 7

Writing Your Rhetorical Analysis

By Christopher Minnix

As we develop as writers, we often learn that writing about what we read involves different processes than discussing what we read. By this point, you have probably had many discussions in class about different types of rhetorical texts. As you sit down to write, you will find that translating the ideas that you have developed in discussion into a written analysis requires learning how to say what you want to say in a certain context. No matter how abstract our ideas, we express them in specific contexts. These contexts are made up of specific audiences, bodies of knowledge, and the types or forms of writing that people in these contexts use to communicate. As we learned in the last chapter, we call these forms of writing **genres**. Genres are *forms of writing that are typically used to fulfill the purposes of specific groups in specific contexts*. We are surrounded by genres all of the time. Some are written, some are conversational, and some are visual or auditory.

We likely know genre from literary analysis, and there are many different types of genres that fit into categories that we might have studied in the past, such as Novel, Drama, Poetry. All of this is true for the types of writing that we do across college campuses. We have big container words, such as Analytical Writing, but when we speak about actual assignments we are speaking about specific genres, such as the rhetorical analysis. This means that rhetorical analysis is one genre or form of analytical writing and there are other forms of analysis, such as literary analysis and historical analysis. Learning to say what you want to say in this context means learning to use the genre of rhetorical analysis.

So, why do we use rhetorical analysis in the humanities? What goals does rhetorical analysis help us achieve? Rhetoric moves audiences to identify with specific values and worldviews and motivates audiences to take action on specific issues. When we think about rhetoric in this way, there is a lot at stake when we talk about persuasion. As we respond to rhetorical texts, we have the responsibility of judging whether or not we should allow the text to persuade us to act in a certain way. Writing a rhetorical analysis is not simply fulfilling an assignment for a course, but an opportunity to reflect upon whether or not you and those around you should take up the ideas of a specific text. In the classroom, rhetorical analysis enables us to develop and hone our skills of critical reading, interpretation, and argument. Outside of the classroom, rhetorical analysis enables us to think through the consequences of ideas that shape the way we act in the world.

The Form of Rhetorical Analysis

Genres or forms of writing have what we call *conventions* or typical patterns of organization, argument, and style that they use to communicate effectively. You are more than likely writing in an academic context, within an English course, as you write your rhetorical analysis. Rhetorical analyses in this context do not all look the same, but they so share some patterns of organization, argument, and style. Knowing what these are can help you write a more successful rhetorical analysis. Before reading any further, however, I want to encourage you to do one important thing: **read your assignment sheet for the rhetorical analysis**. Assignment sheets not only let you know the requirements, but give you a good overview of the genre conventions that you are being asked to use. Look specifically at what the assignment says about the following conventions:

- Purpose: the reason you are being asked to write, or the main task that the assignment asks you to accomplish.

- Thesis: the main statement of interpretation or argument.

- Paragraph Organization: how the introduction, body paragraphs, and conclusion are supposed to be organized.

- Textual Evidence: how you are supposed to support your argument with examples, quotations, and paraphrases from the text.

Now that you have covered those important elements of your assignment sheet, you are ready to look at a few of the typical conventions of a rhetorical analysis in an academic context. We will break these up by Argument, Organization, and Style.

Argument

Is a rhetorical analysis an argument? Not in the sense that you are writing an argument about the issue of the text. For example, you would not discuss your own viewpoints and the viewpoints of your family on racial justice if you were analyzing Martin Luther King's "Letter from a Birmingham Jail." This does not mean that your views are not important. They are highly important, and they will shape the way that you interpret a text like King's. The key point is that the goal is different. In a rhetorical analysis, *your goal is to analyze and evaluate the persuasiveness of a text's argument.* This means that you will want to stay focused on your analysis and evaluation of the text. Before we move on, let's define those words a bit more precisely:

Analysis: analyzing the major rhetorical strategies of the text and how they are used to persuade the audience and to potentially take further action.

Evaluation: this term is part of analysis rather than a separate activity. As you analyze the rhetorical strategies, you will want to develop your own arguments about whether or not the text is persuasive. You will draw upon your own ideas and views, as well as your analysis of the text, to support your analysis.

In the sense that you are *evaluating* the text, you are making an argument, an argument about why the text is potentially persuasive or not persuasive for an audience. The rhetorical strategies that you have learned to read for—such as ethos, pathos, logos, visual elements, cultural keywords—give you a vocabulary for talking about why the text is persuasive or not. What we need to understand now is how your argument might be developed in the different sections of your paper.

The Sections of the Paper

We can start by looking at three basic sections: Introduction, Body, and Conclusion.

Introduction: How do you introduce a rhetorical analysis? Do you begin with a general idea, a history, of the text, or do you dive right into your analysis? Like all genres, rhetorical analysis allows for variety in the way that it is structured. Not all rhetorical analyses begin the same way. Instead of looking for one single way of introducing your analysis, it is more important to shape your introduction in a way that helps you achieve the goal or purpose of your analysis.

Your goal is to analyze the persuasive strategies of a specific text, so that means that you will want to focus the bulk of your writing on the text itself rather than on general ideas about the issue that it addresses. This means that your introduction is there to set up your particular perspective or reading of the text. There are many different ways to meet this goal. You might draw on necessary background information on the text and the issue it addresses, but the amount of background you use is limited by your focus on the text. Use just enough background to frame your specific focus on the text. Stay focused on the main idea or point of your analysis in your introduction.

Thesis: Your evaluation of the text becomes a key part of your argument: the main claim for your thesis. The thesis of a rhetorical analysis is an important convention of the genre because it is the main focus and purpose of your writing.

You can think of yourself as answering an important question: *What do we observe or understand about the ways it tries to persuade its audience?* This is a general question and not how your thesis should read. It does, however, help our readers understand the results of our analysis, or what you feel they should think about the text. We might respond analytically, pointing to the way a strategy like pathos is designed to move the audience emotionally. We might also respond to this question by evaluating, noting that the text is not persuasive.

1. *Develop an Analytical Claim:* a claim is the major argument or point of your thesis statement. An analytical claim is your major argument or point about the text that you are analyzing. For a rhetorical analysis, your main claim should explain what your major argument or point about the text you are analyzing will be. Your claim will need to go beyond a statement of fact about the text or a statement of an obvious point about it. In this sense it will need to be two things:

   • Debatable: this means that your analysis is not self-explanatory, but must be supported and defended with supporting arguments. For example, "Martin Luther King Jr.'s 'Letter from a Birmingham Jail' is a strong argument for racial equality" is not a debatable claim. In contrast, "Martin Luther King Jr.'s 'Letter from a Birmingham Jail' effectively refutes the arguments of the Alabama Clergymen who wrote against him by subtly illustrating the contradictions in their theological arguments" is debatable. This last thesis claim would require further discussion and support, where the first thesis claim really did not leave much to be said about the text.

   • Supportable: this means that your thesis claim has to be grounded in what the text actually argues. As you write an analysis, you are making claims about the persuasive strategies and arguments of a text. In order to show that these claims are valid, you have to show readers that what you are claiming about the text can be observed in the words of the text. If you cannot find evidence—quotations, ideas, scenes—from the text that support your claims, then the interpretation cannot be supported.

2. *Support the Analytical Claim with Good Reasons:* it is not often that people will accept our statements without reasons to support them. If you had developed the claim that King's "Letter from a Birmingham Jail" refutes the arguments of the Alabama Clergymen, you would have to explain how his text does this. This means that you would need a reason that supports your claim. For example, you might argue that he refutes their reason by illustrating how the logic of their arguments for inaction contrasts with their Christian values. In this sense, your reason explains how the text does what you are saying it does.

Body: You have introduced and framed the argument of your rhetorical analysis. Now, what are the conventions of the body paragraphs? Body paragraphs in a rhetorical analysis are focused upon a specific aspect of the text that you are analyzing and they serve as evidence to support your reading or analysis of the text.

It is all too easy to say, OK, I'll just write one paragraph for ethos, one for pathos, and one for logos, or one for plot, one for dialogue, and one for character. The problem with this organizational sequence is that it leads to analyses that try to cover too many aspects of the text. Instead, you will want to focus on analyzing one or two of the strategies that you feel are most essential to the persuasiveness of the text. Here are some important tips.

Developing Body Paragraphs in a Rhetorical Analysis

1. Develop a focus for your body paragraphs that goes beyond simply stating the strategy that they address. You might be tempted to say, for example, "Martin Luther King's Jr's logos is very effective." This does not really say all that much. Instead, you might develop the focus of the paragraph by explaining why King's logos or logic in "Letter from a Birmingham Jail" effectively disproves the argument that nonviolent protest will cause violent reactions in Alabama.

2. Use strong textual evidence to back up your focus or supporting arguments. To support your analysis, you will want to show that what you are saying about the text can be observed in the text itself. Short quotations and examples from the text are there to prove the point of your analysis.

3. Think through the different aspects of each rhetorical strategy you discuss. Instead of trying to sum up each rhetorical strategy in one paragraph, consider tracing out different aspects of the rhetorical strategies. For example, after reading "Letter from a Birmingham Jail," I know that King's logical arguments or logos are far to ocomplex to sum up in one paragraph. Instead, I might devote my entire focus to this strategy. If I did so, I might develop paragraphs that looked at his logical arguments against waiting for change, the connection between his logic and his Christian belief, and the way in which he links his Christian values to the logical aims of the civil rights movement.

4. Draw strong conclusions in your paragraphs. The final sentences of your paragraph will need to explain why the information that you have presented them with is important to the persuasiveness of the text.

Conclusion: There is a myth out there about conclusions—that all they do is restate the main points of an essay. In fact, they should do much more. Think back to the purpose of your analysis: to analyze how the text attempts to persuade its readers and whether or not it is persuasive. The body of your analysis focuses upon the most significant rhetorical strategies that the text uses to persuade its readers. Now, in your conclusion, you have an opportunity to think about the implications of your analysis, or why you feel these strategies make the text persuasive or not. Consider the text as part of an ongoing conversation. In what ways has it been or not been persuasive in the past and in what ways does it continue to be persuasive? These are just a few questions that you might explore, and you should feel free to develop your own implications for your conclusions.

A Sample Rhetorical Analysis

Shelly Jackson
Dr. Minnix
English 102
18 February 2010

"The Gospel of Black Nationalism": a Rhetorical Analysis of Malcolm X's "The Ballot or the Bullet"

During the political and social upheaval of the civil rights movement there were two types of leaders, those who urged peaceful protests and those who urged success by any means possible. Malcolm X, being the latter, urges his audience of African Americans to stand up for their rights and be violent if necessary, in his speech "The Ballot or the Bullet". Malcolm X speaks and acts in ways that are completely opposite of the famous Martin Luther King Jr. He sets himself apart by being provocative and presenting a different type of plan of action, one that can better achieve his ultimate goal of Black Nationalism. Malcolm X urges his audience to be violent by drawing upon the emotional suffering that they have endured, but in addition he points out their mistakes that they have made; mistakes that have not fixed any of their problems, but only have prolonged them. After having pointed out their mistakes, he then presents his plan and his ideology that will change the black community. X first taps into his audience on an emotional level because he wants them to be angered by the injustices they are facing and if he can get them to see that he understands their plight then they are more

125

likely to agree to his plan. By connecting with his audience emotionally, explaining to them that their actions thus far have not been effective and presenting them with his plan, Malcolm X delivers a powerful and provocative speech that captivates his audience and promotes his view.

By understanding his primary audience of African Americans, Malcolm X can utilize his common ground to connect with them. One way in which he does this is by saying that no matter where they are from or what their religion is, that it is, "time for us to submerge our differences and realize that it is best for us to first see that we have the same problem, a common problem" (X). By drawing upon the one thing they have in common, Malcolm X uses this to get his audience to feel a sense of camaraderie. He further unifies them for his cause and emotionally connects with his primary audience when he says, "We're all in the same boat and we all are going to catch the same hell from the same man. He just happens to be white" (Malcolm X). This puts his audience of African Americans and himself on the same side and under the same 'thumb', further helping his audience to see that he is understanding and capable of leading them because he knows what they are going through. He goes on to say that, "Now in speaking like this, it doesn't mean that we're anti-white, but it does mean we're anti-degradation, we're anti-oppression" (X). He creates a common enemy of the white people and anyone who has treated them in a way that is unjust and unkind. When there is a common enemy people are more likely to group together, like the weak against the strong. By using "we" and creating a common enemy, X uses the "us against them" mentality that is commonly used by leaders to unite their group, because it is a lot easier to be united under one goal when there is a common enemy.

Malcolm X also issues an underlying threat to his second audience, his enemies who are the aforementioned white people who degrade and oppress the African-Americans. They are his second audience because X wants his enemies to fear what they will do to them if they do not treat the African Americans equally. He borders on giving a direct threat when he says, "It is constitutionally legal to own a shotgun or a rifle. This doesn't mean you're going to get a rifle and form battalions and go out looking for white folks, although you'd be within your rights – I mean, you'd be justified; but that would be illegal and we don't do anything illegal" (X). When he says this he endorses the use of a gun but at the same time says 'I didn't tell anyone to do that'. It is like when someone says I don't condone nor support an action. By saying this,

X's enemies can perceive the threat because it is implied, but he doesn't completely urge his comrades to use violence. By twisting his words he in essence covers his back from anyone saying that he specifically said to use violence. Malcolm X further threatens his enemies that if they, "don't want that non-nonviolent army going down there, tell them to bring the filibuster to a halt" (X). By primarily addressing the African Americans and threatening his enemies Malcolm X casts his primary audience into the role of provocation against those who oppress and deprive them of their natural rights.

To unite his primary audience and to get them to listen to him, Malcolm X reaches them on an emotional level, by talking about the injustices around them and the sacrifices they have made. He discusses the perils they have faced in hopes that his audience will understand that he knows what they are going through and that he can help lead them to the equality that they deserve. One of the things he mentions throughout his speech is African Americans who have sacrificed their life overseas for their country. He says, "If they draft you, they send you to Korea and make you face 800 million Chinese. If you can be brave over there, you can be brave right here"(X). If his audience can fight for a government that does not recognize their individual rights, then according to X, they can fight for their rights against the government and anyone who opposes them. X also says, "Not only did we give our free labor, we gave our blood. Every time he had call to arms, we were the first one in uniform. We died on every battlefield the white man had. We have made a greater contribution and have collected less" (X). Malcolm X effectively gets his audience angry, for all that they have sacrificed they have never received even the most basic of rights that all Americans, no matter the color of the skin, should be guaranteed.

Once he has gotten his audience to see that he is on their side and he understands their plight he then insists that they "wake up" and see the reality of the situation. Malcolm X uses logic to undermine his audience for the mistakes they have made. He rebukes them for their actions and shows them that they need to realize that, "It's time for you and me to wake up and start looking at it like it is, and trying to understand it like it is; and then we can deal with it" (X). When he states this Malcolm X also uses kairos to let his audience realize that today is the day to stand up for injustices and to do so with whatever means possible, either the ballot or the bullet. He also criticizes his audience for thinking that their vote has made a difference. X talks about the Democratic majority in the House and Senate which should be an advantage to the Civil Rights movement but is not. He states, "Why, the Democrats have got the government sewed up, and you're the one who sewed it up for them. And what have they given you for it?" (X). He urges them to realize that the people they are putting into office are not keeping their promises and that it is time for someone from their own community to rise up and change the political ways.

Malcolm X further blames his audience for the government not making any progress on a civil rights act, because their vote was unwise. He said, "It was the black man's vote that put the present administration in Washington, D.C. Your vote, your dumb vote, your ignorant vote, your wasted vote put in an administration in Washington, D.C., that has seen fit to pass every kind of legislation imaginable, saving you until last, then filibustering on top of that" (X). He blames them and calls them names, so as to say to his audience that what they think they are doing by elected officials is not helping and that it is high time for them to help themselves. This blunt charge that Malcolm X states helps the people to realize they need to act instead of react and after telling them basically that they have been stupid, he tells his audience to, "become more politically mature and realize what the ballot is for; what we're supposed to get when we cast a ballot; and that if we don't cast a ballot, it going to end up in a situation where we're going to have to cast a bullet" (X). This is completely opposite from when he connects with his audience by talking about all the injustices he faces. One might suppose that this would hinder his efforts, but in fact him saying this is so shocking that his brutal honesty completely works to tell his audience that what they are doing is not working and instead they need to follow his plan.

After using pathos, logos and kairos to urge his audience, Malcolm X then goes on to unite his audience under the ideology of "Black Nationalism", where X tells his audience that in order achieve his ultimate goal that, "We have to get together and remove the evils, the vices, alcoholism, drug addiction, and other evils that are destroying the moral fiber of our community. We ourselves have to lift the level of our community, the standard of our community to a higher level, make our own society beautiful so that we will be satisfied in our own social circles and won't be running around here trying to knock our way into a social circle where we're not wanted" (X). Malcolm X wants his people to know that they have not only fight for their rights at a political level, but that they also need to clean up their communities and improve them so as to better the black society as a whole. His ultimate goal is that the black people will, like the whites, control their own school, bank, community, economy and politics. (X) By setting up this "Black Nationalism" ideology and issuing a way in which they can achieve it, Malcolm X effectively shows his audience what can be achieved through his ways and means and not by the ways of other activist leaders.

Malcolm X presents a very effective speech by knowing his audience and utilizing that knowledge to connect with them emotionally, rebuke them for their actions and then unite them under his plan for Black Nationalism. He successfully gets his audience angered at the injustices they have come across at the hand of the white man. After convincing his audience that they need to change their methods, and then getting them angry at their plight, he then pulls them under the idea of Black Nationalism, an ideal of a community that is run by African Americans who have more power in their communities, areas and even in the United States. By presenting this notion Malcolm X unites his audience under his activist front which calls for a fight for their rights by either the ballot or the bullet. Malcolm X correctly utilizes rhetorical appeals within his speech to address his primary audience and to gain support for his fight against those who have oppressed them and to use whatever means possible, whether it be "the ballot or the bullet".

Works Cited

X, Malcolm. "The Ballot or the Bullet." *Social Justice Speeches.* EdChange Multicultural Pavilion. 2005. Web. 16 Feburary, 2010.

Rhetorical Analysis: Some Questions for Revision

These questions do not cover every aspect of rhetorical analysis. Instead, they present you with a list of areas that you might focus upon and review during the revision of your work. In this sense, this list is most helpful after you have written a full draft of your rhetorical analysis and can help you determine where to spend the most time in revision.

- Is your analysis focused on interpreting the rhetoric of the specific text rather than general observations about the topic of the text?

- Does your analysis focus on what the text is trying to persuade its readers to think, do, experience, etc.?

- Is your analysis focused on the rhetorical strategies that you think are most important to the text's persuasiveness or are you trying to cover too many strategies?

- Does your introduction set up or frame the focus of your essay, explaining the aspect(s) of the text you will focus upon, giving sufficient background, and setting up the idea or problem that your analysis will analyze clearly?

- Does your analysis develop an analytical thesis that makes a claim about the text's rhetoric and supports that claim with reasons?

- Do the body paragraphs explain, expand, and support the main thesis?

- Are the body paragraphs supported by textual evidence or quotations from the text?

- Are the Illustrations introduced fully and discussed fully? Do they illustrate what the author is saying about the text?

- Do the body paragraphs develop strong conclusions so they end with sentences that explain the relevance or importance of the ideas in the paragraphs?

- Does the conclusion go beyond the typical restatement of the thesis and towards explaining the implications of the ideas in the analysis?

Readings for Rhetorical Analysis

Defining and Envisioning Ourselves

Introduction

We live in a world where identity has become more and more complicated. We inhabit various networks—social, political, virtual (online), media, etc.—and these networks often shape our outlook on the world. The rise of online social networks illustrates just how complex our identities are becoming. As we post on these networks, we are often inventing and reinventing our image or ethos, shaping ourselves in front of a virtual audience. Understanding how we "see" ourselves and how we represent ourselves has perhaps become more complicated in our time than in any other. The readings in this section question, challenge, and redefine the way that we see ourselves or understand our identity. The essays, interview, and images in this section point us to an important point that we have learned throughout this first chapter: *much of what we take for granted as "reality" or "culture" is constructed through our rhetoric.*

As you read these essays, we encourage you to analyze how each author challenges a particular rhetorical argument about or vision of our identity. Utilize the skills of rhetorical analysis that you have learned in this chapter to analyze how each author or artist challenges some of our most important assumptions about our physical, cultural, and national identities.

SECTION ONE
Readings

David Brooks—People Like Us

The Atlantic Monthly. *September 2003. Reprinted with permission from the author.*

 Maybe it's time to admit the obvious. We don't really care about diversity all that much in America, even though we talk about it a great deal. Maybe somewhere in this country there is a truly diverse neighborhood in which a black Pentecostal minister lives next to a white antiglobalization activist, who lives next to an Asian short-order cook, who lives next to a professional golfer, who lives next to a postmodern-literature professor and a cardiovascular surgeon. But I have never been to or heard of that neighborhood. Instead, what I have seen all around the country is people making strenuous efforts to group themselves with people who are basically like themselves.

Human beings are capable of drawing amazingly subtle social distinctions and then shaping their lives around them. In the Washington, D.C., area Democratic lawyers tend to live in suburban Maryland, and Republican lawyers tend to live in suburban Virginia. If you asked a Democratic lawyer to move from her $750,000 house in Bethesda, Maryland, to a $750,000 house in Great Falls, Virginia, she'd look at you as if you had just asked her to buy a pickup truck with a gun rack and to shove chewing tobacco in her kid's mouth. In Manhattan the owner of a $3 million SoHo loft would feel out of place moving into a $3 million Fifth Avenue apartment. A West Hollywood interior decorator would feel dislocated if you asked him to move to Orange County. In Georgia a barista from Athens would probably not fit in serving coffee in Americus.

It is a common complaint that every place is starting to look the same. But in the information age, the late writer James Chapin once told me, every place becomes more like itself. People are less often tied down to factories and mills, and they can search for places to live on the basis of cultural affinity. Once they find a town in which people share their values, they flock there, and reinforce whatever was distinctive about the town in the first place. Once Boulder, Colorado, became known as congenial to politically progressive mountain bikers, half the politically progressive mountain bikers in the country (it seems) moved there; they made the place so culturally pure that it has become practically a parody of itself.

But people love it. Make no mistake—we are increasing our happiness by segmenting off so rigorously. We are finding places where we are comfortable and where we feel we can flourish. But the choices we make toward that end lead to the very opposite of diversity. The United States might be a diverse nation when considered as a whole, but block by block and institution by institution it is a relatively homogeneous nation.

When we use the word "diversity" today we usually mean racial integration. But even here our good intentions seem to have run into the brick wall of human nature. Over the past generation reformers have tried heroically, and in many cases successfully, to end housing discrimination. But recent patterns aren't encouraging: according to an analysis of the 2000 census data, the 1990s saw only a slight increase in the racial integration of neighborhoods in the United States. The number of middle-class and upper-middle-class African-American families is rising, but for whatever reasons—racism, psychological comfort—these families tend to congregate in predominantly black neighborhoods.

In fact, evidence suggests that some neighborhoods become more segregated over time. New suburbs in Arizona and Nevada, for example, start out reasonably well integrated. These neighborhoods don't yet have reputations, so people choose their houses for other, mostly economic reasons. But as neighborhoods age, they develop personalities (that's where the Asians live, and that's where the Hispanics live), and segmentation occurs. It could be that in a few years the new suburbs in the Southwest will be nearly as segregated as the established ones in the Northeast and the Midwest.

Even though race and ethnicity run deep in American society, we should in theory be able to find areas that are at least culturally diverse. But here, too, people show few signs of being truly interested in building diverse communities. If you run a retail company and you're thinking of opening new stores, you can choose among dozens of consulting firms that are quite effective at locating your potential customers. They can do this because people with similar tastes and preferences tend to congregate by ZIP code.

The most famous of these precision marketing firms is Claritas, which breaks down the U.S. population into sixty-two psycho-demographic clusters, based on such factors as how much money people make, what they like to read and watch, and what products

SECTION ONE
Readings

they have bought in the past. For example, the "suburban sprawl" cluster is composed of young families making about $41,000 a year and living in fast-growing places such as Burnsville, Minnesota, and Bensalem, Pennsylvania. These people are almost twice as likely as other Americans to have three-way calling. They are two and a half times as likely to buy Light n' Lively Kid Yogurt. Members of the "towns & gowns" cluster are recent college graduates in places such as Berkeley, California, and Gainesville, Florida. They are big consumers of DoveBars and Saturday Night Live. They tend to drive small foreign cars and to read *Rolling Stone* and *Scientific American*.

Looking through the market research, one can sometimes be amazed by how efficiently people cluster—and by how predictable we all are. If you wanted to sell imported wine, obviously you would have to find places where rich people live. But did you know that the sixteen counties with the greatest proportion of imported-wine drinkers are all in the same three metropolitan areas (New York, San Francisco, and Washington, D.C.)? If you tried to open a motor-home dealership in Montgomery County, Pennsylvania, you'd probably go broke, because people in this ring of the Philadelphia suburbs think RVs are kind of uncool. But if you traveled just a short way north, to Monroe County, Pennsylvania, you would find yourself in the fifth motor-home-friendliest county in America.

Geography is not the only way we find ourselves divided from people unlike us. Some of us watch Fox News, while others listen to NPR. Some like David Letterman, and others— typically in less urban neighborhoods—like Jay Leno. Some go to charismatic churches; some go to mainstream churches. Americans tend more and more often to marry people with education levels similar to their own, and to befriend people with backgrounds similar to their own.

My favorite illustration of this latter pattern comes from the first, noncontroversial chapter of *The Bell Curve*. Think of your twelve closest friends, Richard J. Herrnstein and Charles Murray write. If you had chosen them randomly from the American population, the odds that half of your twelve closest friends would be college graduates would be six in a thousand. The odds that half of the twelve would have advanced degrees would be less than one in a million. Have any of your twelve closest friends graduated from Harvard, Stanford, Yale, Princeton, Caltech, MIT, Duke, Dartmouth, Cornell, Columbia, Chicago, or Brown? If you chose your friends randomly from the American population, the odds against your having four or more friends from those schools would be more than a billion to one.

Many of us live in absurdly unlikely groupings, because we have organized our lives that way.

It's striking that the institutions that talk the most about diversity often practice it the least. For example, no group of people sings the diversity anthem more frequently and fervently than administrators at just such elite universities. But elite universities are amazingly undiverse in their values, politics, and mores. Professors in particular are drawn from a rather narrow segment of the population. If faculties reflected the general population, 32 percent of professors would be registered Democrats and 31 percent would be registered Republicans. Forty percent would be evangelical Christians. But a recent study of several universities by the conservative Center for the Study of Popular Culture and the American Enterprise Institute found that roughly 90 percent of those professors in the arts and sciences who had registered with a political party had registered Democratic. Fifty-seven professors at Brown were found on the voter-registration rolls. Of those, fifty-four were Democrats. Of the forty-two professors in the English, history, sociology, and political-science departments, all were Democrats. The results at Harvard, Penn State, Maryland, and the University of California at Santa Barbara were similar to the results at Brown.

What we are looking at here is human nature. People want to be around others who are roughly like themselves. That's called community. It probably would be psychologically difficult for most Brown professors to share an office with someone who was pro-life, a member of the National Rifle Association, or an evangelical Christian. It's likely that hiring committees would subtly—even unconsciously—screen out any such people they encountered. Republicans and evangelical Christians have sensed that they are not welcome at places like Brown, so they don't even consider working there. In fact, any registered Republican who contemplates a career in academia these days is both a hero and a fool. So, in a semi-self-selective pattern, brainy people with generally liberal social mores flow to academia, and brainy people with generally conservative mores flow elsewhere.

The dream of diversity is like the dream of equality. Both are based on ideals we celebrate even as we undermine them daily. (How many times have you seen someone renounce a high-paying job or pull his child from an elite college on the grounds that these things

SECTION ONE
Readings

are bad for equality?) On the one hand, the situation is appalling. It is appalling that Americans know so little about one another. It is appalling that many of us are so narrowminded that we can't tolerate a few people with ideas significantly different from our own. It's appalling that evangelical Christians are practically absent from entire professions, such as academia, the media, and filmmaking. It's appalling that people should be content to cut themselves off from everyone unlike themselves.

The segmentation of society means that often we don't even have arguments across the political divide. Within their little validating communities, liberals and conservatives circulate half-truths about the supposed awfulness of the other side. These distortions are believed because it feels good to believe them.

On the other hand, there are limits to how diverse any community can or should be. I've come to think that it is not useful to try to hammer diversity into every neighborhood and institution in the United States. Sure, Augusta National should probably admit women, and university sociology departments should probably hire a conservative or two. It would be nice if all neighborhoods had a good mixture of ethnicities. But human nature being what it is, most places and institutions are going to remain culturally homogeneous.

It's probably better to think about diverse lives, not diverse institutions. Human beings, if they are to live well, will have to move through a series of institutions and environments, which may be individually homogeneous but, taken together, will offer diverse experiences. It might also be a good idea to make national service a rite of passage for young people in this country: it would take them out of their narrow neighborhood segment and thrust them in with people unlike themselves. Finally, it's probably important for adults to get out of their own familiar circles. If you live in a coastal, socially liberal neighborhood, maybe you should take out a subscription to *The Door*, the evangelical humor magazine; or maybe you should visit Branson, Missouri. Maybe you should stop in at a megachurch. Sure, it would be superficial familiarity, but it beats the iron curtains that now separate the nation's various cultural zones.

Look around at your daily life. Are you really in touch with the broad diversity of American life? Do you care?

Nancy Mairs—On Being a Cripple

From Plaintext. *Copyright © 1986 The Arizona Board of Regents.*
Reprinted by permission of the University of Arizona Press.

> *To escape is nothing. Not to escape is nothing.*
> —*Louise Bogan*

The other day I was thinking of writing an essay on being a cripple. I was thinking hard in one of the stalls of the women's room in my office building, as I was shoving my shirt into my jeans and tugging up my zipper. Preoccupied, I flushed, picked up my book bag, took my cane down from the hook, and unlatched the door. So many movements unbalanced me, and as I pulled the door open I fell over backward, landing fully clothed on the toilet seat with my legs splayed in front of me: the old beetle-on-its-back routine. Saturday afternoon, the building deserted, I was free to laugh aloud as I wriggled back to my feet, my voice bouncing off the yellowish tiles from all directions. Had anyone been there with me, I'd have been still and faint and hot with chagrin. I decided that it was high time to write the essay

First, the matter of semantics. I am a cripple. I choose this word to name me. I choose from among several possibilities, the most common of which are "handicapped" and "disabled." I made the choice a number of years ago, without thinking, unaware of my motives for doing so. Even now, I'm not sure what those motives are, but I recognize that they are complex and not entirely flattering. People—crippled or not—wince at the word "cripple," as they do not at "handicapped" or "disabled." Perhaps I want them to wince. I want them to see me as a tough customer, one to whom the fates/gods/viruses have not been kind, but who can face the brutal truth of her existence squarely. As a cripple, I swagger.

But, to be fair to myself, a certain amount of honesty underlies my choice. "Cripple" seems to me a clean word, straightforward and precise. It has an honorable history, having made its first appearance in the Lindisfarne Gospel in the tenth century. As a lover of words, I like the accuracy with which it describes my condition: I have lost the full use of my limbs. "Disabled," by contrast, suggests any incapacity, physical or mental. And I certainly don't like "handicapped," which implies that I have deliberately been put at a disadvantage, by whom I can't imagine (my God is not a Handicapper General), in order to equalize chances in the great race of life. These words seem to me to be moving away from my condition, to be widening the gap between word and reality. Most remote is the recently coined euphemism "differently abled," which partakes of the same semantic hopefulness that transformed countries from "undeveloped" to "underdeveloped," then to "less developed," and finally to "developing" nations. People have continued to starve in those countries during the shift. Some realities do not obey the dictates of language.

Mine is one of them. Whatever you call me, I remain crippled. But I don't care what you call me, so long as it isn't "differently abled," which strikes me as pure verbal garbage designed, by its ability to describe anyone, to describe no one. I subscribe to George Orwell's thesis that "the slovenliness of our language makes it easier for us to have foolish thoughts." And I refuse to participate in the degeneration of the language to the extent that I deny that I have lost anything in the course of this calamitous disease; I refuse to pretend that the only differences between you and me are the various ordinary ones that distinguish any one person from another. But call me "disabled" or "handicapped" if you like. I have long since grown accustomed to them; and if they are vague, at least they hint at the truth. Moreover, I use them myself. Society is no readier to accept crippledness than to accept death, war, sex, sweat, or wrinkles. I would never refer to another person as a cripple. It is the word I use to name only myself.

I haven't always been crippled, a fact for which I am soundly grateful. To be whole of limb is, I know from experience, infinitely more pleasant and useful than to be crippled; and if that knowledge leaves me open to bitterness at my loss, the physical soundness I once enjoyed (though I did not enjoy it half enough) is well worth the occasional stab of regret. Though never any good at sports, I was a normally active child and young adult. I climbed trees, played hopscotch, jumped rope, skated, swam, rode my bicycle, sailed. I despised team sports, spending some of the wretchedest afternoons of my life, sweaty and humiliated, behind a field-hockey stick and under a basketball hoop. I tramped alone for miles along the bridle paths that webbed the woods behind the house I grew up in. I swayed through countless dim hours in the arms of one man or another under the scattered shot of light from mirrored balls, and gyrated through countless more as Tab Hunter and Johnny Mathis gave way to the Rolling Stones, Credence Clearwater Revival, Cream. I walked down the aisle. I pushed baby carriages, changed tires in the rain, marched for peace.

When I was twenty-eight I started to trip and drop things. What at first seemed my natural clumsiness soon became too pronounced to shrug off. I consulted a neurologist, who told me that I had a brain tumor. A battery of tests, increasingly disagreeable, revealed no tumor. About a year and a half later I developed a blurred spot in one eye. I had, at last, the episodes "disseminated in space and time" requisite for a diagnosis: multiple sclerosis. I have never been sorry for the doctor's initial misdiagnosis, however. For almost a week, until the negative results of the tests were in, I thought that I was going to die right away. Every day for the past nearly ten years, then, has been a kind of gift. I accept all gifts.

Multiple sclerosis is a chronic degenerative disease of the central nervous system, in which the myelin that sheathes the nerves is somehow eaten away and scar tissue forms in its place, interrupting the nerves' signals. During its course, which is unpredictable and uncontrollable, one may lose vision, hearing, speech, the ability to walk, control of bladder and/or bowels, strength in any or all extremities, sensitivity to touch, vibration, and/or pain, potency, coordination of movements—the list of possibilities is lengthy and, yes, horrifying. One may also lose one's sense of humor. That's the easiest to lose and the hardest to survive without.

In the past ten years, I have sustained some of these losses. Characteristic of MS are sudden attacks, called exacerbations, followed by remissions, and these I have not had. Instead, my disease has been slowly progressive. My left leg is now so weak that I walk with the aid of a brace and a cane; and for distances I use an Amigo, a variation on the electric wheelchair that looks rather like an electrified kiddie car. I no longer have much use of my left hand. Now my right side is weakening as well. I still have the blurred spot in my right eye. Overall, though, I've been lucky so far. My world has, of necessity, been circumscribed by my losses, but the terrain left me has been ample enough for me to continue many of the activities that absorb me: writing, teaching, raising children and cats and plants and snakes, reading, speaking publicly about MS and depression, even playing bridge with people patient and honorable enough to let me scatter cards every which way without sneaking a peek.

SECTION ONE
Readings

Lest I begin to sound like Pollyanna, however, let me say that I don't like having MS. I hate it. My life holds realities—harsh ones, some of them—that no right-minded human being ought to accept without grumbling. One of them is fatigue. I know of no one with MS who does not complain of bone-weariness; in a disease that presents an astonishing variety of symptoms, fatigue seems to be a common factor. I wake up in the morning feeling the way most people do at the end of a bad day, and I take it from there. As a result, I spend a lot of time *in extremis* and, impatient with limitation, I tend to ignore my fatigue until my body breaks down in some way and forces rest. Then I miss picnics, dinner parties, poetry readings, the brief visits of old friends from out of town. The offspring of a puritanical tradition of exceptional venerability, I cannot view these lapses without shame. My life often seems a series of small failures to do as I ought.

I lead, on the whole, an ordinary life, probably rather like the one I would have led had I not had MS. I am lucky that my predilections were already solitary, sedentary, and bookish—unlike the world-famous French cellist I have read about, or the young woman I talked with one long afternoon who wanted only to be a jockey. I had just begun graduate school when I found out something was wrong with me, and I have remained, interminably, a graduate student. Perhaps I would not have if I'd thought I had the stamina to return to a full-time job as a technical editor; but I've enjoyed my studies.

In addition to studying, I teach writing courses. I also teach medical students how to give neurological examinations. I pick up freelance editing jobs here and there. I have raised a foster son and sent him into the world, where he has made me two grandbabies, and I am still escorting my daughter and son through adolescence. I go to Mass every Saturday. I am a superb, if messy, cook. I am also an enthusiastic laundress, capable of sorting a hamper full of clothes into five subtly differentiated piles, but a terrible housekeeper. I can do italic writing and, in an emergency, bathe an oil-soaked cat. I play a fiendish game of Scrabble. When I have the time and the money, I like to sit on my front steps with my husband, drinking Amaretto and smoking a cigar, as we imagine our counterparts in Leningrad and make sure that the sun gets down once more behind the sharp childish scrawl of the Tucson Mountains.

This lively plenty has its bleak complement, of course, in all the things I can no longer do. I will never run again, except in dreams, and one day I may have to write that I will never walk again. I like to go camping, but I can't follow George and the children along the trails that wander out of a campsite through the desert or into the mountains. In fact, even on the level I've learned never to check the weather or try to hold a coherent conversation: I need all my attention for my wayward feet. Of late, I have begun to catch myself wondering how people can propel themselves without canes. With only one usable hand, I have to select my clothing with care not so much for style as for ease of ingress and egress, and even so, dressing can be laborious. I can no longer do fine stitchery, pick up babies, play the piano, braid my hair. I am immobilized by acute attacks of depression, which may or may not be physiologically related to MS but are certainly its logical concomitant.

These two elements, the plenty and the privation, are never pure, nor are the delight and wretchedness that accompany them. Almost every pickle that I get into as a result of my weakness and clumsiness—and I get into plenty—is funny as well as maddening and sometimes painful. I recall one May afternoon when a friend and I were going out for a drink after finishing up at school. As we were climbing into opposite sides of my car, chatting, I tripped and fell, flat and hard, onto the asphalt parking lot, my abrupt departure interrupting him in mid-sentence. "Where'd you go?" he called as he came around the back of the car to find me hauling myself up by the door frame. "Are you all right?" Yes, I told him, I was fine, just a bit rattly, and we drove off to find a shady patio and some beer. When I got home an hour or so later, my daughter greeted me with "What have you done to yourself?" I looked down. One elbow of my white turtleneck with the green froggies, one knee of my white trousers, one white kneesock were blood-soaked. We peeled off the clothes and inspected the damage, which was nasty enough but not alarming. That part wasn't funny: The abrasions took a long time to heal, and one got a little infected. Even so, when I think of my friend talking earnestly, suddenly, to the hot thin air while I dropped from his view as though through a trap door, I find the image as silly as something from a Marx Brothers movie.

SECTION ONE
Readings

I may find it easier than other cripples to amuse myself because I live propped by the acceptance and the assistance and, sometimes, the amusement of those around me. Grocery clerks tear my checks out of my checkbook for me, and sales clerks find chairs to put into dressing rooms when I want to try on clothes. The people I work with make sure I teach at times when I am least likely to be fatigued, in places I can get to, with the materials I need. My students, with one anonymous exception (in an end-of-the-semester evaluation), have been unperturbed by my disability. Some even like it. One was immensely cheered by the information that I paint my own finger-nails; she decided, she told me, that if I could go to such trouble over fine details, she could keep on writing essays. I suppose I became some sort of bright-fingered muse. She wrote good essays, too.

The most important struts in the framework of my existence, of course, are my husband and children. Dismayingly few marriages survive the MS test, and why should they? Most twenty-two- and nineteen-year-olds, like George and me, can vow in clear conscience, after a childhood of chicken pox and summer colds, to keep one another in sickness and in health so long as they both shall live. Not many are equipped for catastrophe: the dismay, the depression, the extra work, the boredom that a degenerative disease can insinuate into a relationship. And our society, with its emphasis on fun and its association of fun with physical performance, offers little encourage-ment for a whole spouse to stay with a crippled partner. Children experience similar stresses when faced with a crippled parent, and they are more helpless, since parents and children can't usually get divorced. They hate, of course, to be different from their peers, and the child whose mother is tacking down the aisle of a school audi-torium packed with proud parents like a Cape Cod dinghy in a stiff breeze jolly well stands out in a crowd. Deprived of legal divorce, the child can at least deny the mother's disability, even her existence, forgetting to tell her about recitals and PTA meetings, refusing to accompany her to stores or church or the movies, never inviting friends to the house. Many do.

But I've been limping along for ten years now, and so far George and the children are still at my left elbow, holding tight. Anne and Matthew vacuum floors and dust furniture and haul trash and rake up dog droppings and button my cuffs and bake lasagna and Toll House cookies with just enough grumbling so I know that they don't have brain fever. And far from hiding me, they're forever dragging me by racks of fancy clothes or through teeming school corridors, or welcoming gaggles of friends while I'm wandering through the house in Anne's filmy pink babydoll pajamas. George generally calls before he brings someone home, but he does just as many dumb thankless chores as the children. And they all yell at me, laugh at some of my jokes, write me funny letters when we're apart—in short, treat me as an ordinary human being for whom they have some use. I think they like me. Unless they're faking....

Faking. There's the rub. Tugging at the fringes of my consciousness always is the terror that people are kind to me only because I'm a cripple. My mother almost shattered me once, with that instinct mothers have—blind, I think, in this case, but unerring nonetheless—for striking blows along the fault-lines of their children's hearts, by telling me, in an attack on my selfishness, "We all have to make allowances for you, of course, because of the way you are." From the distance of a couple of years, I have to admit that I haven't any idea just what she meant, and I'm not sure that she knew either. She was awfully angry. But at the time, as the words thudded home, I felt my worst fear, suddenly realized. I could bear being called selfish: I am. But I couldn't bear the corroboration that those around me were doing in fact what I'd always suspected them of doing, professing fondness while silently putting up with me because of the way I am. A cripple. I've been a little cracked ever since.

Along with this fear that people are secretly accepting shoddy goods comes a relentless pressure to please—to prove myself worth the burdens I impose, I guess, or to build a substantial account of goodwill against which I may write drafts in times of need. Part of the pressure arises from social expectations. In our society, anyone who deviates from the norm had better find some way to compensate. Like fat people, who are expected to be jolly, cripples must bear their lot meekly and cheerfully. A grumpy cripple isn't playing by the rules. And much of the pressure is self-generated. Early on I vowed that, if I had to have MS, by God I was going to do it well. This is a class act, ladies and gentlemen. No tears, no recriminations, no faint-heartedness.

One way and another, then, I wind up feeling like Tiny Tim, peering over the edge of the table at the Christmas goose, waving my crutch, piping down God's blessing on us all. Only sometimes I

SECTION ONE

Readings

don't want to play Tiny Tim. I'd rather be Caliban, a most scurvy monster. Fortunately, at home no one much cares whether I'm a good cripple or a bad cripple as long as I make vichyssoise with fair regularity. One evening several years ago, Anne was reading at the dining-room table while I cooked dinner. As I opened a can of tomatoes, the can slipped in my left hand and juice spattered me and the counter with bloody spots. Fatigued and infuriated, I bellowed, "I'm so sick of being crippled!" Anne glanced at me over the top of her book. "There now," she said, "do you feel better?" "Yes," I said, "yes, I do." She went back to her reading. I felt better. That's about all the attention my scurviness ever gets.

Because I hate being crippled, I sometimes hate myself for being a cripple. Over the years I have come to expect—even accept—attacks of violent self-loathing. Luckily, in general our society no longer connects deformity and disease directly with evil (though a charismatic once told me that I have MS because a devil is in me) and so I'm allowed to move largely at will, even among small children. But I'm not sure that this revision of attitude has been particularly helpful. Physical imperfection, even freed of moral disapprobation, still defies and violates the ideal, especially for women, whose confinement in their bodies as objects of desire is far from over. Each age, of course, has its ideal, and I doubt that ours is any better or worse than any other. Today's ideal woman, who lives on the glossy pages of dozens of magazines, seems to be between the ages of eighteen and twenty-five; her hair has body, her teeth flash white, her breath smells minty, her underarms are dry; she has a career but is still a fabulous cook, especially of meals that take less than twenty minutes to prepare; she does not ordinarily appear to have a husband or children; she is trim and deeply tanned; she jogs, swims, plays tennis, rides a bicycle, sails, but does not bowl; she travels widely, even to out-of-the-way places like Finland and Samoa, always in the company of the ideal man, who possesses a nearly identical set of characteristics. There are a few exceptions. Though usually white and often blonde, she may be black, Hispanic, Asian, or Native American, so long as she is unusually sleek. She may be old, provided she is selling a laxative or is Lauren Bacall. If she is selling a detergent, she may be married and have a flock of strikingly messy children. But she is never a cripple.

Like many women I know, I have always had an uneasy relationship with my body. I was not a popular child, largely, I think now, because I was peculiar: intelligent, intense, moody, shy, given to unexpected actions and inexplicable notions and emotions. But as I entered adolescence, I believed myself unpopular because I was homely: my breasts too flat, my mouth too wide, my hips too narrow, my clothing never quite right in fit or style. I was not, in fact, particularly ugly, old photographs inform me, though I was well off the ideal; but I carried this sense of self-alienation with me into adulthood, where it regenerated in response to the depredations of MS. Even with my brace I walk with a limp so pronounced that, seeing myself on the videotape of a television program on the disabled, I couldn't believe that anything but an inchworm could make progress humping along like that. My shoulders droop and my pelvis thrusts forward as I try to balance myself upright, throwing my frame into a bony S. As a result of contractures, one shoulder is higher than the other and I carry one arm bent in front of me, the fingers curled into a claw. My left arm and leg have wasted into pipe-stems, and I try always to keep them covered. When I think about how my body must look to others, especially to men, to whom I have been trained to display myself, I feel ludicrous, even loathsome.

At my age, however, I don't spend much time thinking about my appearance. The burning egocentricity of adolescence, which assures one that all the world is looking all the time, has passed, thank God, and I'm generally too caught up in what I'm doing to step back, as I used to, and watch myself as though upon a stage. I'm also too old to believe in the accuracy of self-image. I know that I'm not a hideous crone, that in fact, when I'm rested, well dressed, and well made up, I look fine. The self-loathing I feel is neither physically nor intellectually substantial. What I hate is not me but a disease.

I am not a disease.

And a disease is not—at least not single-handedly—going to determine who I am, though at first it seemed to be going to. Adjusting to a chronic incurable illness, I have moved through a process similar to that outlined by Elizabeth Kubler-Ross in *On Death and Dying*. The major difference—and it is far more significant than most people recognize—is that I can't be sure of the outcome, as the terminally ill cancer patient can. Research studies indicate that, with proper medical care, I may achieve a "normal" life span. And in our society, with its vision of death as the ultimate evil, worse even than decrepitude, the response to such news is, "Oh well, at least you're not going to die." Are there worse things than dying? I think that there may be.

I think of two women I know, both with MS, both enough older than I to have served me as models. One took to her bed several years ago and has been there ever since. Although she can sit in a high-backed wheelchair, because she is incontinent she refuses to go out at all, even though incontinence pants, which are readily available at any pharmacy, could protect her from embarrassment. Instead, she stays at home and insists that her husband, a small quiet man, a re-tired civil servant, stay there with her except for a quick weekly foray to the supermarket. The other woman, whose illness was diagnosed when she was eighteen, a nursing student engaged to a young doc-tor, finished her training, married her doctor, accompanied him to Germany when he was in the service, bore three sons and a daughter, now grown and gone. When she can, she travels with her husband; she plays bridge, embroiders, swims regularly; she works, like me, as a symptomatic-patient instructor of medical students in neurology. Guess which woman I hope to be.

At the beginning, I thought about having MS almost inces-santly. And because of the unpredictable course of the disease, my thoughts were always terrified. Each night I'd get into bed wonder-ing whether I'd get out again the next morning, whether I'd be able to see, to speak, to hold a pen between my fingers. Knowing that the day might come when I'd be physically incapable of killing my-self, I thought perhaps I ought to do so right away, while I still had the strength. Gradually I came to understand that the Nancy who might one day lie inert under a bedsheet, arms and legs paralyzed, unable to feed or bathe herself, unable to reach out for a gun, a bottle of pills, was not the Nancy I was at present, and that I could not presume to make decisions for that future Nancy, who might well not want in the least to die. Now the only provision I've made for the future Nancy is that when the time comes—and it is likely to come in the form of pneumonia, friend to the weak and the old—I am not to be treated with machines and medications. If she is unable to communicate by then, I hope she will be satisfied with these terms.

Thinking all the time about having MS grew tiresome and intrusive, especially in the large and tragic mode in which I was accustomed to considering my plight. Months and even years went by without catastrophe (at least without one related to MS), and really I was awfully busy, what with George and children and snakes and students and poems, and I hadn't the time, let alone the inclination, to devote myself to being a disease. Too, the richer my life became, the funnier it seemed, as though there were some connection between largesse and laughter, and so my tragic stance began to waver until, even with the aid of a brace and a cane, I couldn't hold it for very long at a time.

After several years I was satisfied with my adjustment. I had suffered my grief and fury and terror, I thought, but now I was at ease with my lot. Then one summer day I set out with George and the children across the desert for a vacation in California. Part way to Yuma I became aware that my right leg felt funny. "I think I've had an exacerbation," I told George. "What shall we do?" he asked. "I think we'd better get the hell to California," I said, "because I don't know whether I'll ever make it again." So we went on to San Diego and then to Orange, up the Pacific Coast Highway to Santa Cruz, across to Yosemite, down to Sequoia and Joshua Tree, and so back over the desert to home. It was a fine two-week trip, filled with friends and fair weather, and I wouldn't have missed it for the world, though I did in fact make it back to California two years later. Nor would there have been any point in missing it, since in MS, once the symptoms have appeared, the neurological damage has been done, and there's no way to predict or prevent that damage.

The incident spoiled my self-satisfaction, however. It renewed my grief and fury and terror, and I learned that one never finishes adjusting to MS. I don't know now why I thought one would. One does not, after all, finish adjusting to life, and MS is simply a fact of my life—not my favorite fact, of course—but as ordinary as my nose and my tropical fish and my yellow Mazda station wagon. It may at any time get worse, but no amount of worry or anticipation can prepare me for a new loss. My life is a lesson in losses. I learn one at a time.

SECTION ONE
Readings

And I had best be patient in the learning, since I'll have to do it like it or not. As any rock fan knows, you can't always get what you want. Particularly when you have MS. You can't, for example, get cured. In recent years researchers and the organizations that fund research have started to pay MS some attention even though it isn't fatal; perhaps they have begun to see that life is something other than a quantitative phenomenon, that one may be very much alive for a very long time in a life that isn't worth living. The researchers have made some progress toward understanding the mechanism of the disease: It may well be an autoimmune reaction triggered by a slow-acting virus. But they are nowhere near its prevention, control, or cure. And most of us want to be cured. Some, unable to accept incurability, grasp at one treatment after another; no matter how bizarre: megavitamin therapy, gluten-free diet, injections of cobra venom, hypothermal suits, lymphocytopharesis, hyperbaric chambers. Many treatments are probably harmless enough, but none are curative.

The absence of a cure often makes MS patients bitter toward their doctors. Doctors are, after all, the priests of modern society, the new shamans, whose business is to heal, and many an MS patient roves from one to another, searching for the "good" doctor who will make him well. Doctors too think of themselves as healers, and for this reason many have trouble dealing with MS patients, whose disease in its intransigence defeats their aims and mocks their skills. Too few doctors, it is true, treat their patients as whole human beings, but the reverse is also true. I have always tried to be gentle with my doctors, who often have more at stake in terms of ego than I do. I may be frustrated, maddened, depressed by the incurability of my disease, but I am not diminished by it, and they are. When I push myself up from my seat in the waiting room and stumble toward them, I incarnate the limitation of their powers. The least I can do is refuse to press on their tenderest spots.

This gentleness is part of the reason that I'm not sorry to be a cripple. I didn't have it before. Perhaps I'd have developed it anyway—how could I know such a thing?—and I wish I had more of it, but I'm glad of what I have. It has opened and enriched my life enormously. This sense that my frailty and need must be mirrored in others, that in searching for and shaping a stable core in a life wrenched by change and loss, change and loss, I must recognize the same process, under individual conditions, in the lives around me. I do not deprecate such knowledge, however I've come by it.

All the same, if a cure were found, would I take it? In a minute. I may be a cripple, but I'm only occasionally a loony and never a saint. Anyway, in my brand of theology God doesn't give bonus points for a limp. I'd take a cure; I just don't need one. A friend who also has MS startled me once by asking, "Do you ever say to yourself, 'Why me, Lord?'" "No, Michael, I don't," I told him, "because whenever I try, the only response I can think of is 'Why not?'" If I could make a cosmic deal, whom would I put in my place? What in my life would I give up in exchange for sound limbs and a thrilling rush of energy? No one. Nothing. I might as well do the job myself. Now that I'm getting the hang of it.

SECTION ONE
Readings

Gloria Anzaldúa—How to Tame a Wild Tongue

From Borderlands: The New Mestiza/La Frontera, *2nd ed. Aunt Lute Books, 1999, pp. 75–86. Reprinted with permission.*

 "We're going to have to control your tongue," the dentist says, pulling out all the metal from my mouth. Silver bits plop and tinkle into the basin. My mouth is a motherlode.

The dentist is cleaning out my roots. I get a whiff of the stench when I gasp. "I can't cap that tooth yet, you're still draining," he says.

"We're going to have to do something about your tongue," I hear the anger rising in his voice. My tongue keeps pushing out the wads of cotton, pushing back the drills, the long thin needles. "I've never seen anything as strong or as stubborn," he says. And I think, how do you tame a wild tongue, train it to be quiet, how do you bridle and saddle it? How do you make it lie down?

> "Who is to say that robbing a people of its language is less violent than war?"
>
> —Ray Gwyn Smith[1]

I remember being caught speaking Spanish at recess—that was good for three licks on the knuckles with a sharp ruler. I remember being sent to the corner of the classroom for "talking back" to the Anglo teacher when all I was trying to do was tell her how to pronounce my name. "If you want to be American, speak 'American.' If you don't like it, go back to Mexico where you belong."

"I want you to speak English. *Pa' hallar buen trabajo tienes que saber hablar el inglés bien. Qué vale toda tu educación si todavía hablas inglés con un* 'accent'," my mother would say, mortified that I spoke English like a Mexican. At Pan American University, I and all Chicano students were required to take two speech classes. Their purpose: to get rid of our accents.

Attacks on one's form of expression with the intent to censor are a violation of the First Amendment. *El Anglo con cara de inocente nos arrancó la lengua.* Wild tongues can't be tamed, they can only be cut out.

Overcoming the Tradition of Silence

Ahogadas, escupimos el oscuro.
Peleando con nuestra propia sombra
el silencio nos sepulta.

En boca cerrada no entran moscas. "Flies don't enter a closed mouth" is a saying I kept hearing when I was a child. *Ser habladora* was to be a gossip and a liar, to talk too much. *Muchachitas bien criadas*, well-bred girls don't answer back. *Es una falta de respeto* to talk back to one's mother or father. I remember one of the sins I'd recite to the priest in the confession box the few times I went to confession: talking back to my mother, *hablar pa' 'trás, repelar. Hocicona, repelona, chismosa*, having a big mouth, questioning, carrying tales are all signs of being *mal criada*. In my culture they are all words that are derogatory if applied to women—I've never heard them applied to men.

The first time I heard two women, a Puerto Rican and a Cuban, say the word "*nosotras*," I was shocked. I had not known the word existed. Chicanas use *nosotros* whether we're male or female. We are robbed of our female being by the masculine plural. Language is a male discourse.

> And our tongues have become
> dry the wilderness has
> dried out our tongues and
> we have forgotten speech.
>
> —Irena Klepfisz[2]

Even our own people, other Spanish speakers *nos quieren poner candados en la boca.* They would hold us back with their bag of *reglas de academia.*

Oyé como ladra: el lenguaje de la frontera

Quien tiene boca se equivoca.

—Mexican saying

"*Pocho*,[3] cultural traitor, you're speaking the oppressor's language by speaking English, you're ruining the Spanish language," I have been accused by various Latinos and Latinas. Chicano Spanish is considered by the purist and by most Latinos deficient, a mutilation of Spanish.

But Chicano Spanish is a border tongue which developed naturally. Change, *evolución, enriquecimiento de palabras nuevas por invención o adopción* have created variants of Chicano Spanish, *un Nuevo, lenguaje. Un lenguaje que corresponde a un modo de vivir.* Chicano Spanish is not incorrect, it is a living language.

For a people who are neither Spanish nor live in a country in which Spanish is the first language; for a people who live in a country in which English is the reigning tongue but who are not

Anglo; for a people who cannot entirely identify with either standard (formal, Castillian) Spanish nor standard English, what recourse is left to them but to create their own language? A language which they can connect their identity to, one capable of communicating the realities and values true to themselves—a language with terms that are neither *español ni inglés*, but both. We speak a patois, a forked tongue, a variation of two languages.

Chicano Spanish sprang out of the Chicanos' need to identify ourselves as a distinct people. We needed a language with which we could communicate with ourselves, a secret language. For some of us, language is a homeland closer than the Southwest—for many Chicanos today live in the Midwest and the East. And because we are a complex, heterogeneous people, we speak many languages. Some of the languages we speak are:

1. Standard English
2. Working class and slang English
3. Standard Spanish
4. Standard Mexican Spanish
5. North Mexican Spanish dialect
6. Chicano Spanish (Texas, New Mexico, Arizona, and California have regional variations)
7. Tex-Mex
8. *Pachuco* (called *caló*)

My "home" tongues are the languages I speak with my sister and brothers, with my friends. They are the last five listed, with 6 and 7 being closest to my heart. From school, the media, and job situations, I've picked up standard and working class English. From Mamagrande Locha and from reading Spanish and Mexican literature, I've picked up Standard Spanish and Standard Mexican Spanish. From *los recién llefgados*, Mexican immigrants, and *braceros*, I learned the North Mexican dialect. With Mexicans I'll try to speak either Standard Mexican Spanish or the North Mexican dialect. From my parents and Chicanos living in the Valley,[4] I picked up Chicano Texas Spanish, and I speak it with my mom, younger brother (who married a Mexican and who rarely mixes Spanish with English), aunts, and older relatives.

With Chicanas from *Nuevo México* or *Arizona* I will speak Chicano Spanish a little, but often they don't understand what I'm saying. With most California Chicanas I speak entirely in English (unless I forget). When I first moved to San Francisco, I'd rattle off something in Spanish, unintentionally embarrassing them. Often it is only with another Chicana *tejana* that I can talk freely.

Words distorted by English are known as anglicisms or *pochismas*. The *pocho* is an anglicized Mexican or American of Mexican origin who speaks Spanish with an accent characteristic of North Americans and who distorts and reconstructs the language according to the influence of English.[5] Tex-Mex, or Spanglish, comes most naturally to me. I may switch back and forth from English to Spanish in the same sentence or in the same word. With my sister and my brother Nune and with Chicano *tejano* contemporaries I speak in Tex-Mex.

From kids and people my own age I picked up *Pachuco*. *Pachuco* (the language of the zoot suiters) is a language of rebellion, both against Standard Spanish and Standard English. It is a secret language. Adults of the culture and outsiders cannot understand it. It is made up of slang words from both English and Spanish. *Ruca* means girl or woman, *valo* means guy or dude, *chale* means no, *simón* means yes, *churro* is sure, talk is *periquiar*, *pigionear* means petting, *que gacho* means how nerdy, *ponte águila* means watch out, death is called *la pelona*. Through lack of practice and not having others who can speak it, I've lost most of the *Pachuco* tongue.

SECTION ONE
Readings

Chicano Spanish

Chicanos, after 250 years of Spanish/Anglo colonization, have developed significant differences in the Spanish we speak. We collapse two adjacent vowels into a single syllable and sometimes shift the stress in certain words such as *maíz/maiz, cohete/cuete*. We leave out certain consonants when they appear between vowels: *lado/lao, mojado/mojao*. Chicanos from South Texas pronounce *f* as *j* as in *jue* (*fue*). Chicanos use "archaisms," words that are no longer in the Spanish language, words that have been evolved out. We say *semos, truje, haiga, ansina*, and *naiden*. We retain the "archaic" *j*, as in *jalar*, that derives from an earlier *h* (the French *halar* or the Germanic *halon* which was lost to standard Spanish in the 16th century), but which is still found in several regional dialects such as the one spoken in South Texas. (Due to geography, Chicanos from the Valley of South Texas were cut off linguistically from other Spanish speakers. We tend to use words that the Spaniards brought over from Medieval Spain. The majority of the Spanish colonizers in Mexico and the Southwest came from Extremadura—Hernán Cortés was one of them—and Andalucía.[6] Andalucians pronounce *ll* like a *y*, and their *d*'s tend to be absorbed by adjacent vowels: *tirado* becomes *tirao*. They brought *el lenguaje popular, dialectos y regionalismos*.)[7]

Chicanos and other Spanish speakers also shift *ll* to *y* and *z* to *s*.[8] We leave out initial syllables, saying *tar* for *estar*, *toy* for *estoy*, *hora* for *ahora* (*cubanos* and *puertorriqueños* also leave out initial letters of some words). We also leave out the final syllable such as *pa* for *para*. The intervocalic *y*, the *ll* as in *tortilla, ella, botella*, gets replaced by *tortia* or *tortiya, ea, bolea*. We add an additional syllable at the beginning of certain words: *atocar* for *tocar*, *agastar* for *gastar*. Sometimes we'll say *lavaste las vacijas*, other times *lavates* (substituting the ates verb endings for the *aste*).

We use anglicisms, words borrowed from English: *bola* from ball, *carpeta* from carpet, *máchina de lavar* (instead of lavadora) from washing machine. Tex-Mex argot, created by adding a Spanish sound at the beginning or end of an English word such as *cookiar* for cook, *watchar* for watch, *parkiar* for park, and *rapiar* for rape, is the result of the pressures on Spanish speakers to adapt to English.

We don't use the word *vosotros/as* or its accompanying verb form. We don't say *claro* (to mean yes), *imagínate*, or *me emociona*, unless we picked up Spanish from Latinas, out of a book, or in a classroom. Other Spanish-speaking groups are going through the same, or similar, development in their Spanish.

Linguistic Terrorism

Deslenguadas. Somas los del español deficienle. We are your linguistic nightmare, your linguistic aberration, your linguistic *mestizaje*, the subject of your *burla*. Because we speak with tongues of fire we are culturally crucified. Racially, culturally, and linguistically *somos huérfanos*—we speak an orphan tongue.

Chicanas who grew up speaking Chicano Spanish have internalized the belief that we speak poor Spanish. It is illegitimate, a bastard language. And because we internalize how our language has been used against us by the dominant culture, we use our language differences against each other.

Chicana feminists often skirt around each other with suspicion and hesitation. For the longest time I couldn't figure it out. Then it dawned on me. To be close to another Chicana is like looking into the mirror. We are afraid of what we'll see there. *Pena.* Shame. Low estimation of self. In childhood we are told that our language is wrong. Repeated attacks on our native tongue diminish our sense of self. The attacks continue throughout our lives.

Chicanas feel uncomfortable talking in Spanish to Latinas, afraid of their censure. Their language was not outlawed in their countries. They had a whole lifetime of being immersed in their native tongue; generations, centuries in which Spanish was a first language, taught in school, heard on radio and TV, and read in the newspaper.

If a person, Chicana or Latina, has a low estimation of my native tongue, she also has a low estimation of me. Often with *mexicanas y latinas* we'll speak English as a neutral language.

Even among Chicanas we tend to speak English at parties or conferences. Yet, at the same time, we're afraid the other will think we're *agringadas* because we don't speak Chicano Spanish. We oppress each other trying to out-Chicano each other, vying to be the "real" Chicanas, to speak like Chicanos. There is no one Chicano language just as there is no one Chicano experience. A monolingual Chicana whose first language is English or Spanish is just as much a Chicana as one who speaks several variants of Spanish. A Chicana from Michigan or Chicago or Detroit is just as much a Chicana as one from the Southwest. Chicano Spanish is as diverse linguistically as it is regionally.

SECTION ONE
Readings

By the end of this century, Spanish speakers will comprise the biggest minority group in the U.S., a country where students in high schools and colleges are encouraged to take French classes because French is considered more "cultured." But for a language to remain alive it must be used.[9] By the end of this century English, and not Spanish, will be the mother tongue of most Chicanos and Latinos.

So, if you want to really hurt me, talk badly about my language. Ethnic identity is twin skin to linguistic identity—I am my language. Until I can take pride in my language, I cannot take pride in myself. Until I can accept as legitimate Chicano Texas Spanish, Tex-Mex, and all the other languages I speak, I cannot accept the legitimacy of myself. Until I am free to write bilingually and to switch codes without having always to translate, while I still have to speak English or Spanish when I would rather speak Spanglish, and as long as I have to accommodate the English speakers rather than having them accommodate me, my tongue will be illegitimate.

I will no longer be made to feel ashamed of existing. I will have my voice: Indian, Spanish, white. I will have my serpent's tongue—my woman's voice, my sexual voice, my poet's voice. I will overcome the tradition of silence.

> My fingers
> move sly against your palm
> Like women everywhere, we speak in code...
> —Melanie Kaye/Kantrowitz[10]

"Vistas," corridos, y comida: My Native Tongue

In the 1960s, I read my first Chicano novel. It was *City of Night* by John Rechy,[11] a gay Texan, son of a Scottish father and a Mexican mother. For days I walked around in stunned amazement that a Chicano could write and could get published. When I read *I Am Joaquin*[12] I was surprised to see a bilingual book by a Chicano in print. When I saw poetry written in Tex-Mex for the first time, a feeling of pure joy flashed through me. I felt like we really existed as a people. In 1971, when I started teaching High School English to Chicano students, I tried to supplement the required texts with works by Chicanos, only to be reprimanded and forbidden to do so by the principal. He claimed that I was supposed to teach "American" and English literature. At the risk of being fired, I swore my students to secrecy and slipped in Chicano short stories, poems, a play. In graduate school, while working toward a Ph.D., I had to "argue" with one advisor after the other, semester after semester, before I was allowed to make Chicano literature an area of focus.

Even before I read books by Chicanos or Mexicans, it was the Mexican movies I saw at the drive-in—the Thursday night special of $1.00 a carload—that gave me a sense of belonging. "*Vámonos a las vistas*," my mother would call out and we'd all—grandmother, brothers, sister, and cousins—squeeze into the car. We'd wolf down cheese and bologna white bread sandwiches while watching Pedro Infante in melodramatic tearjerkers like *Nosotros los pobres*,[13] the first "real" Mexican movie (that was not an imitation of European movies). I remember seeing *Cuando los hijos se van*[14] and surmising that all Mexican movies played up the love a mother has for her children and what ungrateful sons and daughters suffer when they are not devoted to their mothers. I remember the singing-type "westerns" of Jorge Negrete and Miquel Aceves Mejía.[15] When watching Mexican movies, I felt a sense of homecoming as well as alienation. People who were to amount to something didn't go to Mexican movies, or *bailes*, or tune their radios to *bolero*, *rancherita*, and *corrido* music.

The whole time I was growing up, there was *norteño* music sometimes called North Mexican border music, or Tex-Mex music, or Chicano music, or *cantina* (bar) music. I grew up listening to conjuntas, three- or four-piece bands made up of folk musicians playing guitar, *bajo sexto*,[16] drums, and button accordion, which Chicanos had borrowed from the German immigrants who had come to Central Texas and Mexico to farm and build breweries. In the Rio Grande Valley, Steve Jordan and Little Joe Hernández were popular, and Flaco Jimenez[17] was the accordion king. The rhythms of Tex-Mex music are those of the polka, also adapted from the Germans, who in turn had borrowed the polka from the Czechs and Bohemians.

I remember the hot, sultry evenings when *corridos*—songs of love and death on the Texas-Mexican borderlands—reverberated out of cheap amplifiers from the local *cantinas* and wafted in through my bedroom window.

Corridos first became widely used along the South Texas/ Mexican border during the early conflict between Chicanos and Anglos. The corridos are usually about Mexican heroes who do valiant deeds against the Anglo oppressors. Pancho Villa's song, "*La*

SECTION ONE
Readings

cucaracha," is the most famous one. *Corridos* of John F. Kennedy[18] and his death are still very popular in the Valley. Older Chicanos remember Lydia Mendoza,[19] one of the great border *corrido* singers who was called *la Gloria de Tejas.* Her "*El tango negro,*" sung during the Great Depression, made her a singer of the people. The everpresent *corridos* narrated one hundred years of border history, bringing news of events as well as entertaining. These folk musicians and folk songs are our chief cultural mythmakers, and they made our hard lives seem bearable.

I grew up feeling ambivalent about our music. Country-western and rock-and-roll had more status. In the 50s and 60s, for the slightly educated and *agringado* Chicanos, there existed a sense of shame at being caught listening to our music. Yet I couldn't stop my feet from thumping to the music, could not stop humming the words, nor hide from myself the exhilaration I felt when I heard it.

There are more subtle ways that we internalize identification, especially in the forms of images and emotions. For me food and certain smells are tied to my identity, to my homeland. Woodsmoke curling up to an immense blue sky; woodsmoke perfuming my grandmother's clothes, her skin. The stench of cow manure and the yellow patches on the ground; the crack of a .22 rifle and the reek of cordite. Homemade white cheese sizzling in a pan, melting inside a folded *tortilla.* My sister Hilda's hot, spicy *menudo,*[20] *chile colorado* making it deep red, pieces of *panza* and hominy floating on top. My brother Carito barbequing *fajitas* in the backyard. Even now and 3,000 miles away, I can see my mother spicing the ground beef, pork, and venison with *chile.* My mouth salivates at the thought of the hot steaming *tamales* I would be eating if I were home.

Si le preguntas a mi mama, "¿Qué eres?"

"Identity is the essential core of who
we are as individuals, the conscious
experience of the self inside."

—Gershen Kaufman[21]

Nosotros los Chicanos straddle the borderlands. On one side of us, we are constantly exposed to the Spanish of the Mexicans, on the other side we hear the Anglos' incessant clamoring so that we forget our language. Among ourselves we don't say *nosotros los americanos, o nosotros los españoles, o nosotros los hispanos*. We say *nosotros los mexicanos* (by mexicanos we do not mean citizens of Mexico; we do not mean a national identity, but a racial one). We distinguish between *mexicanos del otro lado* and *mexicanos de este lado*. Deep in our hearts we believe that being Mexican has nothing to do with which country one lives in. Being Mexican is a state of soul—not one of mind, not one of citizenship. Neither eagle nor serpent,[22] but both. And like the ocean, neither animal respects borders.

> *Dime con quien andas y te diré quien eres.*
> (Tell me who your friends are and I'll tell you who you are.)
>   —Mexican saying

Si le preguntas a mi mamá, "¿Qué eres?" te dirá, "Soy mexicana." My brothers and sister say the same. I sometimes will answer *"soy mexicana"* and at others will say *"soy Chicana" o "soy tejana."* But I identified as *"Raza"* before I ever identified as *"mexicana"* or "Chicana."

As a culture, we call ourselves Spanish when referring to ourselves as a linguistic group and when copping out. It is then that we forget our predominant Indian genes. We are 70–80 percent Indian.[23] We call ourselves Hispanic[24] or Spanish-American or Latin American or Latin when linking ourselves to other Spanish-speaking peoples of the Western hemisphere and when copping out. We call ourselves Mexican-American[25] to signify we are neither Mexican nor American, but more the noun "American" than the adjective "Mexican" (and when copping out). Chicanos and other people of color suffer economically for not acculturating. This voluntary (yet forced) alienation makes for psychological conflict, a kind of dual identity—we don't identify with the Anglo-American cultural values and we don't totally identify with the Mexican cultural values. We are a synergy of two cultures with various degrees of Mexicanness or Angloness. I have so internalized the borderland conflict that sometimes I feel like one cancels out the other and we are zero, nothing, no one. *A veces no soy nada ni nadie. Pero hasta cuando no lo soy, lo soy.*

SECTION ONE
Readings

When not copping out, when we know we are more than nothing, we call ourselves Mexican, referring to race and ancestry; *mestizo* when affirming both our Indian and Spanish (but we hardly ever own our Black ancestry); Chicano when referring to a politically aware people born and/or raised in the U.S.; *Raza* when referring to Chicanos; (*tejanos* when we are Chicanos from Texas.

Chicanos did not know we were a people until 1965, when Cesar Chavez[26] and the farmworkers united and *I Am Joaquin* was published and *la Raza Unida*[27] party was formed in Texas. With that recognition, we became a distinct people. Something momentous happened to the Chicano soul—we became aware of our reality and acquired a name and a language (Chicano Spanish) that reflected that reality. Now that we had a name, some of the fragmented pieces began to fall together—who we were, what we were, how we had evolved. We began to get glimpses of what we might eventually become.

Yet the struggle of identities continues, the struggle of borders is our reality still. One day the inner struggle will cease and a true integration take place. In the meantime *tenemos que hacerla lucha. ¿Quién está protegiendo los ranchos de mi gente? ¿Quién está tratando de cerrar la fisura entre la india y el blanco en nuestra sangre? El Chicano, sí, el Chicano que anda como un ladrón en su propia casa.*[28]

Los Chicanos, how patient we seem, how very patient. There is the quiet of the Indian about us. We know how to survive. When other races have given up their tongue, we've kept ours. We know what it is to live under the hammer blow of the dominant *norteamericano* culture. But more than we count the blows, we count the days the weeks the years the centuries the eons until the white laws and commerce and customs will rot in the deserts they've created, lie bleached. *Humildes* yet proud, *quietos* yet wild, *nosotros los mexicanos* Chicanos will walk by the crumbling ashes as we go about our business. Stubborn, persevering, impenetrable as stone, yet possessing a malleability that renders us unbreakable, we, the *mestizas* and *mestizos*, will remain.

Notes

1. Ray Gwyn Smith [(b. 1944), Welsh painter and art educator active in the United States], *Moorland Is Cold Country*, unpublished book [Anzaldúa's note].

2. Irena Klepfisz [(b. 1941) North American Critic], "Di rayze aheym/The Journey Home," in *The Tribe of Dina: A Jewish Women's Anthology*, Melanie Kaye/Kantrowitz and Irena Klepfisz, eds. (Montpelier, VT: Sinister Wisdom Books, 1986), 49 [Anzaldúa's note].

3. An anglicized Mexican or American of Mexican origin who speaks Spanish with an accent characteristic of North Americans and who distorts and reconstructs the language according to the influence of English. Anzaldúa offers a definition later in this selection.

4. i.e., of the Rio Grande River in southern Texas, bordering Mexico.

5. R. C. Ortega, *Dialectologia Del Barrio*, trans. Hortencia S. Alwan (Los Angeles. CA: R. C. Ortega Publisher & Bookseller, 1977), 132 [Anzaldúa's note].

6. Region in southern Spain. Extremadura is a city in central Spain. Cortés (1485–1547), Spanish soldier and explorer active in Mexico.

7. Eduardo Hernandéz-Chavéz, Andrew D. Cohen, and Anthony F. Beltramo, *El Lenguaje de los Chicanos: Regional and Social Characteristics of Language Used by Mexican Americans* (Arlington, VA: Center for Applied Linguistics, 1975), 39 [Anzaldúa's note].

8. Hernandez-Chavez, xvii. [Anzaldúa's note]

9. Irena Klepfisz, "Secular Jewish Identity: Yidishkayt in America," in *The Tribe of Dina*, Kaye/Kantrowitz and Klepfisz, eds., 43. [Anzaldúa's note]

10. Melanie Kaye/Kantrowitz, "Sign," in *We Speak in Code: Poems and Other Writings* (Pittsburgh, PA: Motheroot Publications, Inc., 1980), 85. [Anzaldúa's note]

11. American novelist (b. 1934). The book was published in 1963.

SECTION ONE
Readings

12. Rodolfo Gonzales [(b. 1928). Chicano novelist], *I Am Joaquin/Yo Soy Joaquin* (New York, NY: Bantam Books, 1972). It was first published in 1967. [Anzaldúa's note]

13. A 1947 film. Infante (1917–1957), Mexican film actor and singer.

14. A 1941 film.

15. Mexican singer and film actor (b. 1916). Negrete (1911–1953), Mexican singing actor.

16. Twelve-string guitar tuned one octave lower than normal.

17. Mexican American musicians. Esteban Jordán (b. 1939). José María De Leon Hérnandez (b. 1940), Leonardo Jiménez (b. 1939).

18. Thirty-fifth U.S. president (1917–1963), assassinated in Dallas, Texas. Villa (ca. 1877–1923), born Doroteo Arango, Mexican Revolutionary leader.

19. Mexican American singer, songwriter, and musician (b. 1916).

20. Mexican soup made of simmered tripe, onion, garlic, chili, and hominy.

21. Gershen Kaufman [(b. 1943), American psychologist], *Shame: The Power of Caring* (Cambridge, MA: Schenkman Books, Inc., 1980), 68. This book was instrumental in my understanding of shame [from Anzaldúa's note].

22. Respectively, male and female cultural figurations.

SECTION ONE

Readings

23. John R. Chavez [(b. 1949), American scholar and educator], *The Lost Land: The Chicano Images of the Southwest* (Albuquerque, NM: University of New Mexico Press, 1984), 88–90 [from Anzaldúa's note].

24. "Hispanic" is derived from Hispanis (*España*, a name given to the Iberian Peninsula in ancient times when it was a part of the Roman Empire) and is a term designated by the U.S. government to make it easier to handle us on paper. [from Anzaldúa's note]

25. The Treaty of Guadalupe Hidalgo created the Mexican-American in 1848. [from Anzaldúa's note]

26. Chicago union organizer (1927–1993).

27. Known in America as the United Farm Workers; founded in 1962.

28. Anglos, in order to alleviate their guilt for dispossessing the Chicano, stressed the Spanish part of us and perpetrated the myth of the Spanish Southwest. We have accepted the fiction that we are Hispanic, that is Spanish, in order to accommodate ourselves to the dominant culture and its abhorrence of Indians. Chavez, 88–91 [from Anzaldúa's note].

SECTION ONE
Readings

Patrick Baliani—Four-Fingered Smile, Five-Fingered Grin: Face to Face with Bailey Doogan

This essay was written especially for Writing Public Lives *by Patrick Baliani. Patrick is an accomplished writer, playwright, and translator. This essay features the dynamic and penetrating art of Bailey Doogan. As you view these images, and read Patrick's essay, we encourage you to think back to the chapter on visual-spatial analysis. We encourage you to also try your hand at rhetorically analyzing this innovative and creative text.*

Bailey Doogan, "Four-Fingered Smile,"
reprinted by permission of Bailey Doogan.

1.

I met Bailey Doogan on consecutive Saturdays last semester at the Etherton Gallery in Tucson. My assignment, for this anthology, was to write an essay about her recent artwork on exhibit there. And there she stood, at the top of the stairs to the viewing rooms—five feet four inches tall—her luminescence pulling me toward her. Strangely, her right arm was twisted over her head as she clutched and contorted the left side of her face. She looked intense—eyes closed, lips curled—rueful, sensual, contemplative, at once dispirited and heartened. I was compelled to do as others did stepping into the Gallery after me—lean in for a closer look. I spent the rest of the morning gazing at this one image of her.

Four-Fingered Smile is a large (64" × 52") charcoal drawing, part of *TRANSLATIONS*, an Etherton Gallery exhibit with recent paintings and drawings by Tucson artists Bailey Doogan, Alice Leora Briggs, and Chris Rush. Doogan, whose body of work includes painting and drawing, three dimensional construction, and film, was on the faculty of art at the University of Arizona for thirty-two years and continues to mentor and inspire other artists. Her work has been shown in major galleries and museums across the country, including The Brooklyn Museum, The New Museum of Contemporary Art in New York, The San Jose Institute of Contemporary Art, The Speed Museum of Art, Louisville, The Phoenix Art Museum, and The University of Arizona Museum of Art. A retrospective, Bailey Doogan: Selected Works 1971–2005, was published by Etherton Gallery for exhibitions at the Etherton and the Tucson Museum of Art. Significantly, Doogan was the first painter Terry Etherton showed in his Gallery, in 1985, after years of exhibiting photographers exclusively (Etherton).

Four-Fingered Smile is remarkably translucent, with two emissions of light—one behind the head, the other emanating from the flesh itself. And Doogan's process—etching the charcoal to expose primed paper—reveals a theme: the clawing away of facades to unveil inner truth.

SECTION ONE
Readings

"Between the fall of 2006 and the spring of 2008 I was not myself. A series of ailments, and major and minor surgeries, left me depressed … One day I was in my bathroom posing in front of the mirror to mimic socially acceptable facial expressions: smiles, grins, thoughtful concern, etc. I was going to an opening and wanted to look normal. My face was a blank slate that my hands could compress, push, or stretch to create an image … I wanted to make art again." (Doogan, 8)

Student essays often explore similar content—social disgraces, personal inadequacies, cultural shocks, mental recoveries. College life and art openings, it appears, have much in common. As undergraduates or mature artists, we can become trapped by the public constructions we stiffly and often unwillingly inhabit. Still, we put on the front.

Doogan's "clear eyed realism about the aging human body will remind one of Rembrandt ..." writes Mary Garrard, in a foreword to an earlier Doogan catalogue (Garrard 7). Especially in Rembrandt's more dramatic paintings, concealed light and facial incandescence enhance the paintings' more theatrical qualities. But as Garrard is quick to point out, "the differential of gender is critical" (7). Influenced by preceding generations of women artists who reshaped portraiture, Doogan renders her female subjects not as women often make themselves seem, or as men perennially imagine them to be, but more precisely as they are. Women's aging is provocatively rendered, hard to take *and* alluring—seductive in its aggressive honesty, assertive sincerity, unfolding beauty. What we see is not what society expects us to perceive and we are unaccustomed to appreciating such mature physicality, the contours and folds of older women incitefully portrayed.

"Women artists of the post-1968 generation have also dealt with the implications of producing self-portrait images which do not fix the 'self' to simple definitions, but reveal the multiplicity of 'selves' available to one individual" (Meskimmon 87). Though most of us recognize our public selves residing in ever shifting contexts, fine lines differentiate dissembling from multiplicity. Realizing an integrated identity—if such a one exists—is daunting. This makes realistic self-portraiture elusive, especially for women artists, given that male paradigms have historically dominated the genre and limited its possibilities. A woman as the "object" of a drawing or painting has traditionally meant something other than a man as one.

Of course, whether women were altogether more objectified in Rembrandt's day than in ours is debatable. That women today have greater artistic license is not. "Doogan's people are bodies first," writes Lucy Lippard. "Yet being bodies first does not mean that they are objectified as bodies are in the mass media. On the contrary, they are subjectified, or intensified to an extreme" (Lippard 9). This subjectification gains intensity, in part, because the viewpoint is distilled repeatedly, from individual artistic perception to artistic expression to public perception to public reflection and reconsideration. Collaborating with photographer Jack Kulawik, Doogan interpreted herself as seen—and posed for—in his photos. As viewers, we further subjectify the etchings that have emerged and, as we are impacted by them and change, we change our perceptions. This transference of awareness speaks to the title of the exhibit, *TRANSLATIONS*. As the transformations occur across media, so too people before and after Doogan refigure her images. In this way, the more traditional roles of spectactor and performer are blurred—they "translate" from one to the other. Furthermore, the role of the artist, as "sitter," in relation to herself and to the viewer, has occurred in spaces without literal mirrors. "What we can begin to infer about the self-portraiture of [contemporary] women artists, is that these works constantly renegotiate the boundaries which defined them as both 'woman' and 'artist', and that they cannot rely on fixed and simple sets of identifications" (Meskimmon 87).

There is also something jarring and enveloping about the size of Doogan's work. Rembrandt never painted faces this *big*. Typically, the more out of proportion something is to its human scale the less likely we relate to it on realistic terms (Mohr). Here, though, the effect is a kind of *magna*-realism—the drawing is strikingly realistic almost despite its size. Doogan's hands pull at more than her flesh; they tug at the viewer too, as they seem to extend beyond the picture plane. Her knuckles—the size of fists—are particularly arresting. The tiny swirly faces they seem to contain invite further reflection. Clearly these fingers have long toiled and are not letting go. "I also love the way hands weather; how they show the effects of the kind of work we do" (Doogan 39). The hand shaping the face has also molded the art. "And of course we connect the hand with writing and gesturing. So there was something about the manipulation of one expressive part of my body with another communicating part of my body that was important to me" (37).

Faces and hands. Are there more telling—or more beautiful—aspects of the human body? No wonder artists at every level struggle so in depicting them.

SECTION ONE
Readings

Bailey Doogan, "Five-Fingered Grin,"
reprinted by permission of Bailey Doogan.

2.

Tell me, Bailey—what is the difference between a smile and a grin? Seeing you again one week later, I am as taken by your *Five-Fingered Grin* as I was by *Four-Fingered Smile*. But I find it harder to embrace you today. My impulse is to step away, not toward you, for the better look. I tell my students to establish a relationship with the art they experience; the relation today is a difficult one. I am aware of the dynamics of the gallery affecting me—how any gallery contributes to the experience of the work it displays—and I can look at you today from angles not afforded me a week ago. Does "Grin" gaze in the direction of "Smile?" Beyond it? What is it I imagine you see? What is so disturbing about your "Grin?"

Smiles are broader, more inviting, more infectious. Grins are deliberate, sometimes forced. They can be snarls. Your "Grin" is equally pellucid, your contortions as palpable as a week ago. Gone, though, is the delightful curl of your lip, the endearing water smear on your neck. "Smile" conjured visions within; "Grin" sees all too clearly an outside world. "Smile" may have acquiesced, supplicated. Your eyes were closed and male vanities are readily piqued. "Grin," I realize, transcends gender. Something beyond you threatens us here.

My friend Tilly Warnock suggests I let the essay unfold as it will, allow its two halves to commune more with each other. Any essay is an attempt—from the French, *assai*, to try—to see things anew, not jump to conclusions. A week ago, I hadn't noticed—your shoulder isn't raised to accommodate the reach of your arm. The hand in each image extends from the psyche, not the anatomy. I have to rethink both works.

As I am revising, images of "Neda," the twenty-six year old Iranian dying in the streets of Tehran has me divided—needing to know more about this terrible event and turning away. In class we are reading *Richard III*—how could Lady Anne willfully submit to Richard's sadistic advances? My own doubts and insecurities seem trivial in these contexts.

Bailey, I am as trapped as most by our culture's craze for surface beauty. And there is something starkly beautiful—seductive—about the texture of your work. You have said you "can never get it physical enough" (Doogan 29). I have tried and tried to work this notion into my essay, assuming I knew what this meant—something like the writer never getting the words right, or realism being the truest way for you to know the world, or sublimity as inherent in physical beauty. I have considered and reconsidered *Five-Fingered Grin*—the look in your eye—seeing you reflected, then me, then something else. Etchings are like words and your charcoal has become my looking glass. The more I contemplate "Grin," the more I want to look and yet look away.

I recall my college days decades ago—heading to my room after work, desperate for release, wedging past drunken partiers in the dorm hall as dense and suffocating as claustrophobia. Was it a forced smile or reluctant grin I wore amid the smell of keg beer and cheap colognes? How have I grown?

And what now do I expect from you? Resistance? Deliverance? As the hobbled King Richard says, waking from nightmares, "What do I fear? Myself? There's none else by" (Shakespeare 751). "Having mastered the significant gesture," writes Lippard, "Doogan paints

SECTION ONE
Readings

and draws with radical compassion" (Lippard 12). For me, what's radical—*from the root*—is your daring to be known intimately, without pretense. Your folds are open to me and I see myself better knowing you.

"There is some artwork that burrows under your skin and crackles in the nerve endings. It is work you cannot stop looking at for fear the excitement within might go away, that the images will disappear before the hunger for them fades" (Etherton 5). I will continue to look. How will I make my face? What masks will I wear? When will I turn away?

You have said we live in a society where popularly projected images of people being other than themselves is a norm; that what we knew as reality has become rather unreal; that being true to one's self is suspect (Doogan 32). Tomorrow, your self-portraits will move across the country to another gallery. The reproductions here, greatly reduced, will remain. As will the catalogue. And the relationships you've engendered. Your resilience is encouraging. Each of your images is unflinching in its own way. When we shed debilitating personas worn for public consumption, luminescence emerges. The rewards don't come easy. "Coming out of a period where I didn't feel well for so long, my future plans have been very simple: keep breathing, moving, and making art. I finally realize the enormity of those acts" (39). Will students, at whatever age, see their own resilience, their courage, as beautiful?

Tell us, Bailey—what hard earned smiles and grins are in the making? How will our perceptions of them shift in time? Is it clear the discussion is critical and must be continued collectively? John Updike has said: "The efforts of an art critic must be, in an era beset by visual stimulants, mainly one of appreciation, of letting the works sink in as a painting hung on the wall of one's home sinks in, never quite done with unfolding all that is in it to see" (Updike xv). Here's to the unfolding to come and to the enormity of your next acts.

Until we meet again.

Works Cited

Doogan, Bailey. Personal interview. Tucson. May 12, 2009.

Doogan, Bailey and Etherton, Terry. *TRANSLATIONS*. Published by Etherton Gallery on the occasion of the exhibition TRANS-LATIONS: Bailey Doogan, Alice Leora Briggs, Chris Rush. Tucson, January 20–April 11, 2009. Print.

Etherton, Terry. Personal interview. April 10, 2009.

Garrard, Mary D. *Bailey Doogan and the Beauty of Truth*; and Lippard, Lucy R. *Body and Soul. Bailey Doogan, Selected Works, 1971–2005*, published by Etherton Gallery, Tucson, 2005. Print.

Meskimmon, Marsha. *The Art of Reflection: Women Artists' Self-Portraiture in the Twentieth Century*. New York: Columbia University Press, 1996. Print.

Mohr, Paul. *Fundamentals of Drawing I. The Drawing Studio*. Class notes. Tucson, April 7, 2009.

Updike, John. *Still Looking: Essays on American Art*. New York: Alfred A. Knopf, 2005. Print.

SECTION ONE
Readings

William Deresiewicz—The Dispossessed

The American Scholar, Winter 2006. Reprinted with permission of the author.

 Sometimes you don't realize that something's been missing—it doesn't matter how big it is—until, for a moment or two, it isn't. About 10 years ago, I was listening to an interview with the choreographer Bill T. Jones, who had just published his memoirs. Jones is gay and black, and when the interviewer asked him what his father had thought about his becoming a dancer, Jones, somewhat testily, said something like, "You don't understand. This wasn't a middle-class family. The goal wasn't to become a professional: the goal was to better yourself." The first thing that hit me about this was that it had nothing to do with race or sexuality. The second thing that hit me was that it had everything to do with class, specifically the working class—which, I suddenly realized, I never heard anyone talk about. A little while later, I read a profile of Roseanne Barr in *The New Yorker*. Only middle-class women care about feminism, Barr claimed. Working-class women already have power, because they're the ones in charge at home.

Working-class career expectations, working-class family structures: two things I knew nothing about. Each revelation gratified me with the feeling of learning something interesting and important and new, but together they enraged me with the recognition that the reason they felt new, the reason I was so abysmally ignorant about this world that lay all around me—the American working class—was that such knowledge had been withheld from me by my culture. It's not just that I'm middle class myself. I'm white, too, but mainstream culture (popular entertainment, the news media) has exposed me to a steady stream of images and information about blacks. I suspect that American gentiles also know quite a lot about Jews. But the working class is American culture's great lost continent.

There are exceptions: Roseanne's show was one, Michael Moore's *Roger & Me* (as well as the whole persona he's constructed) is another, as was the recent HBO series *Family Bonds*. But much of what was seen as important and "edgy" in those productions was their working-class subject matter, which shows how rare any serious, extended, or sympathetic popular treatment of the working class now is. (Analogous things could be said about Bruce Springsteen, or novelists like Richard Russo and Russell Banks, or *The New York*

SECTION ONE

Readings

Times's recent multipart series on class in America. Imagine how superfluous it would have been for the *Times* to do a series about race or sexuality, topics that permeate half the stories it publishes.) Among mainstream films of the last decade, *Mystic River* and *Good Will Hunting* come to mind, but far more typical is the kind of thing we got in *Million Dollar Baby*, where the heroine's family was presented as loutis, contemptible trailer trash, or on the *Simpsons*, where Homer's working-class characteristics (and he seems to be the working-class breadwinner of a middle-class family) are played strictly for laughs. There are working-class characters all over the place: cops on detective shows, nurses and orderlies on doctor shows, and so forth. But it's the nature of such dramas to present people only in terms of their jobs, asking few or no questions about the rest of their lives. Look at a show or a movie that takes you into its characters' homes, and you'll find that the homes you're being taken into are almost always middle or upper class, even when the characters belong to that vast, imaginary social group we might call the pseudo-working class, people with working-class jobs but middle-class lifestyles, like the *Simpsons* or the *Gilmore Girls* or those lucky kids on *Friends*.

What we don't have in this country, in other words, is anyone like Mike Leigh, who makes art out of working-class lives by refusing to prettify them. We no longer have anyone, among our major novelists, like Steinbeck or Dos Passos. We don't even have any TV shows like *The Honeymooners* or *All in the Family*, whose frank depictions of the material conditions of working-class life (think of the Kramdens' kitchen, with its bridge table and two chairs) didn't prevent them from achieving a monumental universality. When we do get the rare serious mainstream treatment of working-class life, it comes from a middle-class observer like Barbara Ehrenreich. So why is it that the only working-class person anyone will pay attention to these days is a middle-class journalist masquerading as one? More fundamentally, why is it that the working class is treated as an exotic species, while the middle class, which it heavily outnumbers, is regarded as normal and normative?

It's not hard to begin to answer these questions. First, the people who get paid to create mainstream culture—journalists, editors, writers, producers—are, ipso facto, members of the middle class. As social mobility slows, more and more of them originate in that class. The middle class is not only what they know and identify with,

SECTION ONE
Readings

it often seems to be the only thing they're aware of. Today's army of cultural commentators, who speak so confidently about the way "we" live now—the crazy hours, the overscheduled kids, the elite colleges and nursery schools—mistake their tiny world of urban and university-town professionals for the whole of society. Second, as TV's creation of a pseudo-working class suggests, looking at the real one is kind of a bummer. Just as everyone on TV has to be beautiful, so does everyone have to have money, or at least live like they do. Nobody wants to watch a show about some fat guy struggling to make the rent. Finally and most important, we simply don't talk about class at all anymore. Why should we, when we're all supposedly part of a single one, the great middle? What we talk about is race and sexuality. (Or in the academy, race, gender, and sexuality, the great triumvirate. The humanities, despite their claim to transformative significance, have all but forgotten about class.) Instead of Steinbeck and Dos Passos, we have Toni Morrison, Maxine Hong Kingston, Oscar Hijuelos, Jhumpa Lahiri, and Michael Cunningham.

It was Morrison, in fact, who provided one of the most telling indications of our loss of the working class as an imaginative category, her famous anointment of Bill Clinton as our "first black president": "Clinton displays almost every trope of blackness: single-parent household, born poor, working-class, saxophone-playing, McDonald's-and-junk-food-loving boy from Arkansas." At least Morrison still employs the term working class, but it's still merely a secondary category for her. If it weren't, she would have seen that what those attributes really added up to wasn't that Clinton was black (or "black"), but that he was our first working-class president, if not ever, then in a while, and our most flamboyantly so in a long while. But of course working-class attributes are going to look like tropes of blackness. Just about the only images we have of the working class are images of black people, understood as black people. In fact, many of the things we think of as characteristically black are really true of the working class as a whole (and aren't true of middle-class blacks). Consider the realm of family structure: having children at an early age, having them outside of marriage, raising them as a single parent, raising them with the help of an older relative—and not being stigmatized by your community for doing any of these things. It's an old American story: race becomes a surrogate for class, which is to say, a way of not thinking about it at all.

On the rare occasions when we do think about class, our fixation on race makes us confuse the working class with the poor, as the response to the Katrina disaster demonstrated. For an interval that proved predictably brief, Americans started talking about class again, but we still missed the true picture. For one thing, our discussion of poverty was all too quickly subsumed, again, into a discussion about race. (It's funny how few images we saw of poor, dispossessed whites, though many such people must have existed.) More important is that most of the blacks we saw wandering the highways or abandoned at the Convention Center were surely not the truly indigent (the homeless, the unemployed); they were laborers and waitresses and hospital workers and maids, members of New Orleans's socially cohesive and culturally vibrant working-class black communities. These are the same communities that are now struggling for the right to rebuild themselves, struggling to get the rest of us to acknowledge that their neighborhoods were more than just slums. The people who lived in these communities may have looked dirty and disheveled on TV, and some of them may have acted desperately at times, but how would you have looked, and how would you have acted after four or five days in those circumstances? Yet so deeply has the notion of a working class been pushed to the recesses of our consciousness, and so powerful is the link in our minds between poverty and race, that when we're shown a working-class black, we see a poor person—and when we're shown a working-class white, we don't see anything at all.

What is the working class? As a first approximation, I'd suggest that a member of the working class is someone who receives an hourly wage. (There are exceptions both ways: airline pilots on the one hand, secretaries on the other.) The virtue of this definition is that it not only excludes the true middle class—professionals, managers, and small-business owners—it also reminds us that working-class people have a very different relationship to their work and their workplace than do those who earn a salary. By this criterion, the working class comprises about 80 percent of the American workforce. Even if one claims that the cop or fireman or unionized factory worker, who might well live in the suburbs and drive a big car, actually belongs to the middle class, the working class still comprises a large majority of the country. (Besides, as Paul Krugman recently argued in a *New York Times* column on the wage-and-benefit

SECTION ONE
Readings

squeeze in the auto industry, a lot of those factory workers—the "working middle class"—will find themselves squarely back in the working class soon anyway.) The poor may literally be "invisible in America," as the subtitle of David K. Shipler's recent book puts it, out of sight in the human garbage heaps of ghettos and trailer parks, but the great bulk of the working class—which is to say, most of America—is invisible only because "we" aren't seeing what's right in front of our faces: the people who serve our food, ring up our purchases, fix our cars, change our bedpans.

It's as if the vast space between the poor and the middle class didn't exist. The term working class has been erased from our political discourse, replaced by working poor and the insidious working families. Working poor is a valuable term, because it reminds us how meagerly many jobs pay these days and belies the notion of what used to be called the idle poor. But working poor is not at all the same as working class, though the trailer-trash stereotype would have us think so. Some working-class people are poor, but the great majority are not, they just aren't well-off enough to be middle class. Working families isn't the same as working class, either. Whether in the mouth of a Clinton or a Bush, the term is designed to treat the working and middle classes as a monolith. By conflating the two (the doctor struggling to pay for his kids to go to Harvard, the cashier struggling to pay for medicine), the term eliminates the working class as a political as well as a cultural category.

But class hasn't completely dropped out of our political discourse. In fact, it's made a comeback of late, only in a particularly devious new guise, our new ruling paradigm of red state vs. blue state—where ideology is rewritten as region (Republicans are from red states, Democrats from blue), region as culture (red-staters drink beer, blue-staters drink wine), and culture as class, though only implicitly (what do you think beer and wine really mean?). Fifty-seven million people voted for John Kerry in the last election; to speak as if all of them were Chardonnay-sipping professors, or even professionals, is ridiculous. Simple arithmetic tells us that millions of them were members of the working class. But according to the dominant syllogism, if Kerry voters are effete elitists while Bush voters are "ordinary Americans" (the closest anyone comes to actually saying working class anymore) then the working class looks like the stereotypical Bush voter: rural, Southern, conservative, nationalist, and fundamentalist—in other words, redneck. This is as gross an oversimplification as imagining that the middle class is composed exclusively of leftist academics. But absent any other or better images of the working class, the redneck myth not only means that Republicans get to present themselves as champions of the working class while ostensibly denying its existence (as Thomas Frank has argued in *What's the Matter with Kansas*), it also means that the true character of the working class, in all its enormous breadth and diversity, remains hidden.

It remains hidden, in particular, from the working class itself, among whom the redneck myth does in fact seem to be taking hold. I lived in Portland, Oregon, last year, a heavily working-class town, and I was struck by the affinity the working class there seems to feel with Southern culture. (Country Music Television, for example, is part of the basic cable package.) The South is the one place where the white working class doesn't hide itself, as the essayist Richard Rodriguez recently noted, and its leading cultural expressions—country music and NASCAR—are becoming those of the white working class as a whole. This southernization of the working class surely owes a lot to the red-state/blue-state nonsense, to the ascendancy of southern Republicans, and to the scarcity of other kinds of working-class images.

But it also owes a lot to the decline of organized labor. I've suggested that working-class images haven't always been so hard to find in the mainstream, and it's no accident that their virtual disappearance over the past few decades has coincided with that decline. Fifty years ago, more than one in three American workers were unionized; today, one in eight is. Along with a huge loss in political power has come the loss of a confident, self-conscious, working-class culture. Not only were workers visible to the classes above them, they had their own voices, their own cultural institutions, their own sense of who they were and what they did; in short, they weren't dependent on the middle class to define them. People used to speak of the "dignity of labor," and the phrase meant that being a worker was something to be proud of, that the working class saw itself as something more than a collection of people who couldn't make it, that it had its own traditions and values, constituted its own community.

I've spent a lot of time thinking about the working class in the 10 years since those inciting recognitions. I've kept my eyes open to whatever I could glean from the media and from my immediate

SECTION ONE
Readings

surroundings. I've had long talks on the subject with my wife, who spent many years in a working-class environment, and with a former student, who grew up in one. I've come to believe not only that the working class constitutes a coherent culture very different from the middle-class one that's presented to us as natural and universal, but that that culture possesses a genuine set of virtues. *New York Times* columnist David Brooks has been singing the praises lately of bourgeois values like industry, temperance, prudence, and thrift. I have nothing against these things, especially since, as a member of the middle class, I practice them myself. But industry, temperance, prudence, and thrift are not the be-all and end-all of the good life. In fact, they are apt to be accompanied by a countervailing array of bourgeois vices, like narrowness, prudery, timidity, and meanness, not to mention hypocrisy and self-conceit.

As for the working class, I'll grant, for the sake of argument, that its vices tend to be the negative of bourgeois values, that working-class people are, compared to the middle class, less temperate, prudent, thrifty, and industrious (though that last seems a rather unfair description of people who do manual labor, work two jobs, or put up with forced overtime). But by the same token, working-class life breeds its own virtues: loyalty, community, stoicism, humility, and even tolerance. Not that every working-class person is a paragon of these virtues; like Brooks, I'm trying to articulate the general contours of a class culture as it arises from the facts of everyday existence. If only because of their limited possibilities in life, working-class people care more about their families and their friends and the places they're from than they do about their careers. Because they haven't been taught to believe that they're entitled to the best of everything, they take what life brings them without whining or self-pity. Because they don't preen themselves on where they went to school or what kind of job they have, they don't act like they're better than everyone else. And when it comes right down to it, they aren't any more prejudiced than the middle class, and may even be less so. Middle-class prejudices are just more respectable—in fact, they tend to be directed against the working class itself—as well as more carefully concealed. What's more, while the middle class espouses tolerance, working-class people, because they can't simply insulate themselves from those they don't like with wads of money, are much more likely, in practice, to live and let live. Maybe what this country needs are fewer bourgeois values and more proletarian ones.

William Deresiewicz, who teaches English at Yale, is the author of Jane Austen and the Romantic Poets.

Source Citation

Deresiewicz, William. "The Dispossessed: First We Stopped Noticing Members of the Working Class, and Now We're Convinced They Don't Exist." *American Scholar* 75.1 (2006): 17+. Academic OneFile. Web. 26 Oct. 2010.

SECTION ONE
Readings

Kehinde Wiley—Interview

Originally published in INTERVIEW *magazine, November 2008, Interview, Inc. Reprinted with permission from Brant Publications.*

You may want to look at the images on pages 191–192 before reading this interview. Each of Wiley's paintings are paired with the original painting he is adapting.

 The public perception of black male youth has arguably changed since artist Kehinde Wiley began painting his formal portraits while in residency at New York's Studio Museum in Harlem in 2000. Part of Wiley's process was lifting his subjects straight from the street and rendering them—complete with sneakers, track pants, tank tops, and team caps—in the visual language of classic European portraiture; the result wasn't so much brashly iconoclastic as brilliantly inclusive, a mash-up of museum treasure and the urban life outside of its gates. What remains so surprising about these works today is that the 31-year-old Los Angeles native's black males remain a rarity in the fine-art world, despite their prevalence, even dominance in pop culture. Wiley may have redefined portrait painting for a new century, but he's still cutting his own path in a field that purports to be progressive.

Wiley's practices have changed in the last decade and the results are increasingly visible. His recent show at the Studio Museum in Harlem called "The World Stage" took him all over the globe, from Lagos to New Delhi, to cast his models from the street and capture them in poses representing a larger world. His solo exhibition "Down" opens at Deitch Projects in New York City this month; "Down" features eight large-scale paintings of black youths based on iconic images of fallen warriors in art—from bullfighters to Christ. Here he talks about his work with his friend, fellow sampler, and pop star M.I.A. She managed to get stung by a bee during the interview, but the two still got around to tackling the demise of hip-hop and the death of the New York art scene.

M.I.A.: I wanted to ask you about the progression of your work these days. How are you finding it? Because New York is a really different place to make art compared to what it used to be.

KEHINDE WILEY: I came here almost 10 years ago now. It was my first experience of making a life for myself outside of school, and my career kind of snowballed at once. So there's really not much in the way of an alternative experience for me to contrast it with. These days I'm spending quite a bit of time on the road, which finally has allowed me to get some perspective. I'm starting a new project where I open up studios in different nations and do street casting. I just got back from Brazil and Nigeria and Senegal. Actually, tomorrow I'm leaving for New Delhi.

M: Does leaving New York change your art?

KW: That type of process becomes the work in many ways—physically removing yourself from what your work was based on before. By and large what I'd been doing was mining the streets of African America, using a sort of urban vernacular. That changes radically when you remove yourself physically, especially around the world.

M: Manhattan seems pretty developed, you know what I mean? Like it has peaked in culture. The Village Voice called it McHattan. It's just become impossible for young, creative artists to live in New York.

KW: Where do you find it most fruitful to work?

M: I think traveling really helps. I know some musicians who have studios in Trinidad. There's a collective of artists and painters there now who went to Central Saint Martins College [in London] with me. They live there and make art. It's neat to see that—[people] not led by money or pretentiousness. It's a small community, but you really have the space to observe and digest the culture. You go to a place where social commentary is rare and important and you can serve people. That's what's inspiring to me—finding someplace where people haven't already seen themselves in a certain light.

KW: Yeah, I know.

M: You create that light, you create that visual or image. In America, everything has been done. We've had everything. And now we're rerunning what's already been done.

SECTION ONE
Readings

181

KW: Right, recycling. The recycled object.

M: Exactly! I performed at a show at the MoMA. There was this big dinner there, and I was seated in this hall with the mayor of New York and all these extremely wealthy art-supporting and art-buying people. There was a piece of work hanging in the hall—it was a fan. This fan was supposed to swing by the momentum of its own propeller. So, while we were having dinner, the fan was stopped, and the guy next to me, a curator at P.S.1, said, "Look, this is what art symbolizes today." Like, that piece of art is supposed to be moving, but just to have dinner we've stopped the art. That's what New York is like today. You can't have real art happen in an institution because rich people can make the world stop. The stuff on the street is a lot more interesting.

KW: I think so, too. There's a freshness. I remember being in West Africa and thinking about my father's country—he's from Nigeria—and I was there, opening up a studio, doing a lot of street casting, stopping people, and there was this film crew with me because we were doing a documentary on my process, and I was contrasting the experience I had there with the experience I had doing the exact same street casting in places like the Fulton Street Mall, in Brooklyn. And it's amazing how, in New York, there is almost a feeling of entitlement by the public—this very palpable lack of surprise at being stopped in the street and being asked to be the subject of a 12-foot monumental painting. I think part of that is mediated by a very televisual sense of instant celebrity, something that's sort of "just add water"—an age where reality television mediates the way that we see new faces entering our lives. Whereas when I was in Nigeria, in places like Lagos and Calabar, there was a very ineffable exchange where these guys were really curious but also so far removed from this artificial environment that I was creating. It gave something new to the work. In some ways, there is a look in the paintings that seems a bit more fragile.

M: It's like cinema, when you put someone onscreen who's never been on before. You show it to them and say, "This is you. This is what you look like on a 60-by-60-foot screen." It's a different understanding of art. Take India: Even though it's got a major movie industry, when it comes to contemporary art, artists on the streets don't see themselves as artists—it's like a skilled job. When they're painting a car and they decorate it with all this crazy stuff, I think, "Wow, this is amazing! It's something I would hang on my wall." But they're always really shocked when I go up to them and ask them to do something for me. Do you think that's what you're going for, looking for ideas outside of the disposable "just add water" kind of thing?

KW: My desire is to restart the conversation. It's akin to this idea that most 18-year-olds who are going to be voting for the first time this year in the American elections were 10 and 11 years old during the 9/11 attacks—this idea that we're all kind of collectively correcting and rebooting, this desire to throw away the old rules. This is something that, as artists, we constantly deal with—throwing away the past, slaying the father, and creating the new.

M: Yeah, change. You know, what really drives me mad about art is that, in America, the only thing you can do is to take it apart. As artists, that's the best commentary you can do because there's just so much vacuous content. For example, yesterday I stayed in bed for 24 hours and watched TV. I do that, like, every six months, where I just don't answer phone calls and the only thing I do is watch television. And it's insane! I couldn't tell the difference between the news and an advert. It's all Fox News, 30-second sound bites, and there was nothing I got from it at all. Where the fuck are all the Michael Moores in our culture? Where are the cool Democrats? Where are cool people on television? Where has cleverness gone?

KW: The trouble is that the traditional targets have been so co-opted. It's hard to know where to cast your aim. So much of what changed American society in the '60s had to do with a very strong set of targets—what we can physically do with ourselves and our bodies. Now it's much more subtle. It's almost debilitating in a way because we can't organize either, artistically or politically or socially, against any specific thing, because it's more like an essence, an ether that floats in the air, poisoning our ability to really have an authentic moment.

SECTION ONE
Readings

M: That's what I miss, being a real human. Like, I'm just so grateful for the 10 years that I had in Sri Lanka when it was in the middle of a war and I was getting shot at, because now and again I remember glimpses of those times and I just go, "Wow, I'll never, ever see that again in my life. And I'm never gonna feel that, and I'm never gonna feel for a human being like that."

KW: When was the last time you were back in Sri Lanka?

M: Just before September 11th happened. After that it was insane to even try to go back, with all the new restrictions. When I was there I was already having a machine gun held to my head every five seconds, and every 50 yards I'd have to show my ID. I wasn't a singer at the time—I was just a random girl, an artist. I was making films, and I had just graduated from Saint Martins in London. I thought I was invincible. Like, I'm getting harassed and I have a British passport. I have a letter from the Ministry of Defence! What if I were just a random Tamil girl from the village. I could be dead! It was the weirdest experience. I couldn't even make a movie because you can't make one without having it okayed by the Sri Lankan embassy. So you can only have a one-sided story. Do you think art in America is like all other industries? That there are certain parameters you can't go past?

KW: Certainly. I think I've come through the art-industrial complex— I've been educated in some of the best institutions and been privy to some of the insider conversations around theory and the evolution of art. But that doesn't necessarily get spoken about outside of a very small group. When you operate outside those rules, you are changing the vernacular. I think that's partly the success of my work—the ability to straddle both of those worlds, the ability to have a young black girl walk into the Brooklyn Museum and see paintings she recognizes not because of their art or historical influence but because of their inflection, in terms of colors, their specificity and presence.

M: Yeah, that's how I felt about your work the first time I saw it. It felt establishment, but it was also breaking it a little bit and twisting it. Do you feel a responsibility to teach something in your work?

KW: That's a question I have always grappled with. Is that even my job? Is that gonna slow you down?

M: In the beginning I definitely felt a responsibility because I was representing a bunch of people who never got represented before. I felt this responsibility to correct that situation, to be like, "Look, you can't discriminate against refugees and Muslim people and blah, blah, blah …" Now I don't feel that so much … It's complicated. Hold on a second. Are you there? I just got stung by a bee.

KW: Are you serious?

M: Yeah. It's the first time I've ever been stung.

KW: You have to be careful with that. Some people have major allergic reactions!

M: I know. I'm wearing flower-print pants. I think he thought I was a bunch of flowers.

KW: Drawn in by the flowers. That's great.

M: Anyway, getting back, do you feel a responsibility?

KW: That's a very complicated question. When I was growing up and going to art school and learning about African-American art, much of it was a type of political art that was very didactic and based on the '60s, and a social collective. I feel sometimes constrained by the expectation that the work should be solely political. I try to create a type of work that is at the service of my own set of criteria, which have to do with beauty and a type of utopia that in some ways speaks to the culture I'm located in. But Americans are so overly fixated on racial identity—and on identity in general.

SECTION ONE
Readings

M: I know. As an artist I could either sit there with a chip on my shoulder and just chip away every day, or I could transcend all of it, which really makes it about what you're actually saying—not being based on the burdens of the past but trying to make the world

185

make more sense to you. If I actually had a chip on my shoulder and started, like, race bashing, they would have been more used to that. In school I was like, "I want to be a filmmaker." And they were like, "Well, you can't be a serious filmmaker if you're not wearing a plaid shirt." You can't turn up at college in stilettos and say you're gonna be a filmmaker. They were teaching me avant-garde filmmaking, where I had to make films that were, like, an hour long about nothing. [Wiley laughs] I just refused to do it, you know?

KW: It seems incredibly self-indulgent.

M: I just couldn't be like that, because this week this is what's happening in my life: So-and-so is going to jail, so-and-so got evicted, I'm getting busted for this, and blah, blah, blah. There was just, like, real-life shit going down in my house all the time. There was no need for me to go to college and learn how to film a blue screen for half an hour. I did my thesis on CB4 [1993]. Everyone freaked out. They tried to have me kicked out of school. They thought I was disgusting.

KW: I think there's something important in going against the grain, and perhaps finding value in things that aren't necessarily institutionally recognized.

M: Exactly! I want to find a taxi driver in India and ask him where he got the sticker that goes across his windshield. That decorative choice comes from the idea that maybe it's good to tell your vehicle apart from everyone else's when you get off of break.

KW: Right, very real.

M: They also do it because they want to show off. If they buy a shop, they're gonna name the shop after their kid. If they drive a taxi, they name the taxi after their mom.

KW: This sort of reminds me of growing up in South Central Los Angeles back in the '80s, you know, where so many people were flossing down Crenshaw Boulevard with their lowriders and hydraulics and stuff, and it was this major scene. For me it was always important to internalize that type of flossing. When I was at Yale, most of the students there were obsessed with this type of neo-minimalism that thought that any garish display or show of emotion or visceral beauty was something to be scoffed at. I think conversely it made me revert back to some of the more ornate or baroque features of black American culture.

M: That's exactly what happened with me. Because I spent time in L.A., too, growing up on gangster rap. My cousin was a gangster bitch, and she knew the Bloods and the Crips and she was Sri Lankan, so we'd go to all these clubs down on Crenshaw. Then I would come back to college at Saint Martins, and I was learning a whole other way. Like having that whole '90s hip-hop from L.A. and then going to Saint Martins, where it's all the Britpop stuff about being shy and hating yourself. I was a Sri Lankan refugee, like, the scum of society, and then I went right to Los Angeles, into African-American culture, and it was just incredible. I've never seen black people like that in England. In England black people still live within the parameters of white society. It was an eye-opener. Then I'd be in school and the students would be like, "I'm white, and I'm male, and I don't know what to do, I hate myself." I was just like, there is this contemporary culture in America that's writhing with so much good shit and bad shit that no one is really making art out of yet, you know?

KW: Sometimes there's that tipping point, where societies embrace who they are without necessarily needing a dominant culture or center to recognize the periphery. I remember being in Nigeria back in 1997 and meeting a bunch of MCs practicing their skills outside this bar and I was just like, "This is an amazing scene!" And how many people really know about what was going on in the hip-hop scene in Nigeria back in the early '90s? These guys were really complaining about how they just couldn't get any play at home and how most of what was consumed in terms of black culture was American. Of course, now you go to Nigeria and it's a completely different scene. It's just overrun with amazing acts. And I think that's kind of indicative of a type of self-confidence that people develop when they recognize their own ability to create.

SECTION ONE
Readings

187

M: Yeah. Also, it could be the sort of declining grip of the American MTV-nation culture—the fact that MTV doesn't play so much music anymore. When I would go to Africa I used to get really pissed off that people would listen to 50 Cent in, like, a mud hut and want DVD players and a GPS in their SUVs, you know?

KW: Now, why would that piss you off?

M: I felt pissed off because I realized that you have to teach people in a clichéd way how to be happy—and happiness has become too one thing in American media. Achieving happiness is not really about having a flat stomach and the best car.

KW: Personally—and this comes from my experiences of seeing people from very hard lives, working their way toward a sort of middle class, and really wanting to embrace the signifiers for success-the question has always been, who am I to tell them that that's crap? You know, it's not for me, perhaps it's not my style but . . . [sighs] I know your feelings.

M: That's fine! You can say, "Get the SUV," but you can't say, "Get the SUV before you get a house." You know what I mean? Okay, there's a kid in a mud hut. I don't want to teach him bad habits because I live in Brooklyn. Brooklyn, New York City! And I feel like I'm living in the dead weeds of hip-hop. I live in the graveyard of what went wrong with hip-hop.

KW: Well, what went wrong with gangster rap?

M: It's not even gangster rap—it's just what's wrong with hip-hop. It became so one-dimensional; it became like a businessman thing. It's run out of creativity. It went so far off about making money that now everyone can do it.

KW: I wonder, though, because I think about this quite a bit when I think of someone like Jeff Koons, whom I admire quite a bit, but aesthetically this type of emptiness is the point—this type of soullessness and devotion to the signifiers of happiness and consumption. Are you prepared to say that that type of hip-hop—soulless, empty hip-hop-is interesting on some level?

M: Well, I would have said, "yeah, it was," 10 years ago. But now I've had 10 years—

KW: [laughs] It's not funny anymore!

M: Yeah, it's not funny anymore. It's good you're taking your work everywhere and you're making it global. I think all relevant work needs to be like that.

KW: One of the really great things about working in Lagos is that it's such a crazy assault on the senses. The population has been rising since oil was discovered there in the late '60s, but public sculpture has been there since even before the colonial years. All my models are asked to choose which pose they're going to assume, and those poses are derived from portraits of former colonial masters or generals or military dictators or what have you, many of them cast in public squares. What comes out of people's minds about which person they'd prefer to be, now that they've been asked to sort of open their eyes to what's been there in their own backyard.

M: I have this artist I work with called Afrikan Boy. He was on my album, and he's from Lagos, Nigeria, and he's always like, "I want to be the African dream!" I think that's so cool. I like the way he represents more than that modern outsider.

KW: If I were going to paint you, if I could paint you as any historical figure, who would it be? Now, you have to realize it's all your look and feel, but I'm asking you about the pose.

M: A historical figure?

KW: And think about it in terms of a preexisting iconic work of art. For instance, when Ice-T came by, he wanted to be this really great painting of Napoleon by Ingres.

M: It's really hard. There are so many people who inspire me. I'll have to think about it and email you.

KW: Okay.

SECTION ONE
Readings

Now that you have read about Kehinde Wiley's aesthetics, or views on art, take a moment to compare his images to the paintings he is drawing inspiration from. Look back through Wiley's interview with M.I.A. and underline passages that you feel capture his views on his art, and then use the space beside the images to annotate them with your own interpretations. Try to develop a list that compares and contrasts the visual elements in the paintings, and use the ideas in your list to explore the following questions.

1. What statements from the Wiley's interview are illustrated in Wiley's paintings? How are Wiley's views of art and our culture illustrated in his paintings?

2. Review the questions from Chapter 3 of this book—"Visual-Spatial Analysis" by Adrienne Crump and Elise Verzosa (page 65)—and try to answer them for each set of paintings.

3. Now that you have completed a visual-spatial analysis, think about the effects of the visual elements in the paintings. What is the purpose of the visual rhetoric in the paintings? Why do you feel this visual rhetoric is effective or ineffective?

SECTION ONE
Readings

Théodore Géricault—Officer of the Imperial Guard
Scala/Art Resource, NY. Louvre, Paris, France.

Kehinde Wiley—Officer of the Hussars
Reprinted by permission of Kehinde Wiley Studio.

SECTION ONE
Readings

Andrea Mantegna—The Lamentation Over the Dead Christ
Scala/Art Resource, NY. Pinacoteca di Brera, Milan, Italy.

Kehinde Wiley—The Lamentation Over the Dead Christ
Reprinted by permission of Kehinde Wiley Studio.

Section Two

Controversy Analysis

Introduction: Getting Ready to Join the Conversation

By Carol Nowotny-Young

There's nothing like a controversy to get a conversation going. Sometimes the conversation is among people who agree about a certain point and are discussing their opinions to hear them validated by others who are of like mind. At other times, the conversation occurs among people who disagree about an issue, who perhaps have widely opposing opinions about it, who discuss their opinions to further explore them with people who challenge their views. Sometimes the conversation is completely polarized, with the people involved divided into opposing viewpoints. At other times, the conversation involves a number of different viewpoints on the issue. The conversations sometimes get very heated, even angry, and once in a while somewhat violent. But most conversations about controversies are engaging and stimulating, testing our intellectual and verbal mettle.

In academia, this intellectual and verbal testing is precisely why we engage in conversations about controversies. They expand our abilities to think and reason, prompt us to go out and gather more evidence to support our views, or even cause us to change our minds about what we think. In this way, we create new knowledge about the world and how it works.

But as a student, you may have found arguments troubling and intimidating in the past, equating controversies with angry words, hurt feelings, or putdowns. But the arguments we encounter in our private lives are nothing like the controversies that people discuss within the discipline of their fields or even in public debates and political spheres. Nevertheless, it may still be intimidating to involve yourself in academic and public controversies because you think of yourself as being somehow less knowledgeable or experienced than the people doing all the talking. Therefore, when you are asked to write an argument, you immediately find a controversy that has been extensively written about, gather up what others have said about it, and synthesize that into an argumentative essay, all without having to explore your own true opinions about the controversy. Unfortunately, this all-too-common response to an assignment of a documented argument teaches students more about pretending to argue than actually arguing. While I am not denigrating the value of imitation in learning, at this point in your education, you are ready to begin learning how to argue for real.

Because, ready or not, many students still produce essays that are pretend arguments rather than real arguments, we are going to try a different way to approach writing an argument. We are going to break up the work of joining a conversation about a controversy (which is what an argumentative essay really is) into two separate parts. The first part, which will be discussed in this section of *Writing Public Lives*, involves preparing to join the conversation—doing the research, listening to the conversation as it were, and then analyzing this conversation as a way of explaining it to your readers (as well as yourself) in your own essay; the second part, writing your own argument and thereby actually stepping into the conversation yourself, will be discussed in the next section of the book on public argument.

Getting ready to join the conversation involves more than just reading what others have said about a controversy. It also involves listening—*really* listening—closely to not only what others are saying but also how they are saying it and even why they are saying it. In the last section on rhetorical analysis, you learned about looking past the content of a text and considering the ways the text was designed and structured, which could tell you quite a lot about who the writer of the text wanted to persuade and what he/she thought about that target audience. The design and structure of a text could also tell you about what the writer wanted to accomplish by persuading that audience, even if the thesis or parts of the text claimed to intend something else entirely. The strategies the writer used to construct the argument could even tell you something about the underlying values and beliefs of the writer him/herself, values and beliefs that could reveal a hidden agenda or biases affecting how the writer was approaching the controversy.

In a controversy analysis, you are going to employ the same skills you used to analyze a single text in your rhetorical analysis assignment to analyze several texts addressing the same controversy. Analyzing these texts—these voices, as it were, arguing different points of view about an issue—is part of your preparation to join the conversation. You are giving the controversy and the conversation about it a thorough examination, deciphering motives and agendas, biases and beliefs, tactics and strategies that affect the shape and dynamics of that conversation. After doing that, you will be well prepared to offer your own argument in a sophisticated, well-structured argument of your own.

If you've ever studied fencing or martial arts, music or dance, even acting or playing chess, you know that part of your training involves learning to read and respond to the subtle signs that reveal what your opponent or partner or fellow performer is about to do. If you fight as though your opponent is just a static force to be pummeled into submission, you will miss a lot of the strategies that your opponent is using to defeat you, and the likelihood of your defeat is much greater in fact. If you play music or act or dance as though you are the only one onstage or on the dance floor, your performance will be less than it could be. You need to listen to your fellow musicians, pay attention to the other actors onstage with you, or feel the moves of your dance partner in order to anticipate the subtle nuances of their performance and respond to them in ways that create a seamless, unified performance. But you can't just expect to be able to anticipate and respond without training in what to look for and practice in recognizing signs and finding the appropriate ways to respond.

Arguing is the same way. You can present a good argument only when you have studied your opponents and fellow arguers, learned to look into their arguments for their strengths and weaknesses and the subtle cues for what is driving them, and practiced using persuasive strategies and methods yourself. By preparing well to argue, you will be much better able to construct a successful argument.

So this is your preparation, but lest you think of your controversy analysis as just the lead-up to the more important text, your public argument, remember that preparing well requires just as much art and skill as the performance itself. Your controversy analysis is an essay in its own right. Controversy analyses are important texts helping readers to better understand the issues involved and the nature of the arguments and the conversations about them. A well-written controversy analysis can be a pleasurable read as well as a source of important knowledge.

Therefore, the purpose of this section on controversy analysis is designed to help you produce a well-crafted essay as well as teach you an important skill and further develop the skills you learned in the rhetorical analysis section. To begin with, you will learn more about how to plan and construct your controversy analysis in Chapter 8, "Discovering and Focusing on a Conversation," in which I explain more about what a controversy analysis is and does and show you ways to approach it. In Chapter 9, "Finding and Conducting Research on a Local Issue," Ashley J. Holmes models the process of discovering a local issue to write on, formulating a workable focus on it, and creating a plan for researching it. In Chapter 10, Christopher Minnix explains ideology and how to analyze the ideological clues in a text. Also in Chapter 10, "Analyzing Ideology in a Controversy" by Maggie Werner, shows you how to apply an ideological lens to the arguments you are discovering in the course of your research for your controversy analysis. You might also read her essay with an eye toward how it models using the other lenses that you learned in the rhetorical analysis section for analyzing your research. Any of those lenses could work for you in your controversy analysis project. Chapter 11 presents four controversy analysis essays written by students in English 102 during the spring semester of 2010. You may use these essays as models for structuring your own controversy analysis or as prompts for thinking about how you want to write your essay. Finally, at the end of this section are two clusters of readings, the first focused on the recent breakdown of the American economy and the second concerning the new changes in health care. Preceding the readings is an introduction suggesting some ways that you could use the two clusters to think about your own controversy analysis and the sources you might find when you research your own topic. As you read through the two clusters of readings, consider how they might prompt further research or refocusing of a thesis. Analyze the different types of arguments presented, especially with an ideological lens. What values and beliefs underlie each of these readings and inform its argument?

Chapter 8

Discovering and Focusing on a Conversation

By Carol Nowotny-Young

What a Controversy Is: A Definition

If you were to look up "controversy" in a dictionary, you might find a fairly simple definition that goes something like this: 1: a discussion marked by the expression of opposing views: DISPUTE 2: QUARREL, STRIFE (Merriam-Webster's *Collegiate Dictionary*, 11th ed.). If you also checked "controversial," the adjectival form of the word, you would find that it meant "given to arousing controversy" or "disputatious." By this definition, you might think that your argument with your best friend over the merits of last night's movie or your fight with your roommate about whose turn it was to clean the bathroom counted as a controversy. In some circles, it might, but when a teacher asks you to write a controversy analysis paper, she's probably not asking you to write about either of these arguments. "Okay," you say, "I figured that out already. Tell me something I don't know."

Fair enough. How about this: I am a hopeless night owl, often not retiring until well into the wee hours. When I want to relax before going to sleep, I'd like to watch something mildly entertaining on television, but nearly all the cable and network stations I get stop regular programming around 1:00 or 2:00 AM. Then it's just "paid programming," extended commercials, if you will. I think it's outrageous that I have to pay for cable programming that caters to morning larks but not to night owls. Programming should run 24/7, or I should get a discount for premium channels that run 24/7—a sort of "night owl discount." Does this count as a controversy? Well, yes and no. If I wrote my paper about this issue mainly as it pertained to me and my problems, it wouldn't really be a controversy. Most people, including a lot of night owls, would just say I was whining and suggest I record the morning programming and watch it at 2:00 AM. But if I approached it in a different way, say, looking at the programming and pay structures of cable and satellite companies and arguing that consumers are being charged unfairly for channels that utilize big blocks of time for paid programming and/or repetitive programming, I might get more interest. Getting interest, however, doesn't mean that everyone will agree with me; in fact, if they did, I wouldn't have a controversy. By "getting interest," I mean that readers would look at my argument as valid—worthy of arguing.

This is how we are defining "controversy" in this section and how your instructor is going to define it for the papers you write. You will want to find an issue that others will care about and take seriously, an issue that is capable of arousing valid disputes. And, as I showed you above, you can often find a valid controversy by taking something that you personally find annoying or aggravating and approaching it from a larger viewpoint that includes problems many people might find contentious.

So What Is a Controversy Analysis?

Earlier in this book, you learned about rhetorical analysis and how it works. A controversy analysis really follows the same pattern and structure as rhetorical analysis, only applied to an issue rather than to a single argument within the issue. Or, to be more precise, the controversy analysis looks at various arguments in relationship with each other within an issue. To focus and define what your analysis needs to cover, you must take a particular approach to the issue and focus a question that defines a particular aspect of the issue to limit what you analyze, rather than tackling all the arguments within the larger issue itself—which would be quite a daunting task for some issues and require that you write a lengthy book rather than a relatively short essay.

> **The main features of a controversy analysis are as follows:**
> - Its thesis is stated in the form of a focusing question.
> - It presents at least two—and frequently more—different arguments in answer to the question.
> - It has researched the arguments it presents so as to present them thoroughly and fairly, using the words of those who have made the arguments.
> - It examines how the arguments speak to each other.
> - It analyzes the arguments to show how they are constructed and what their strengths and weaknesses are.

Another way to define a controversy analysis is to look at what it is not, as follows:

- *A controversy analysis is not an argument.* You are not advocating for a particular viewpoint on an issue, nor are you refuting a particular viewpoint on the issue. You are laying out for your own audience the various arguments addressing a particular question about the issue.

- *A controversy analysis is not just a summary of the arguments.* In other words, you are not merely summarizing what different arguments say in answer to your research question. You should indeed summarize each argument you will analyze, but make sure you are also analyzing the arguments—that is, examining how all the arguments are presented, just as you did for a single argument when you wrote your rhetorical analysis essay. You could use any of the rhetorical lenses that the previous section, "Rhetorical Analysis," describes for you—such as cultural, genre, classical or Aristotelian, narrative, and so forth—to focus your analysis and get below the surface of *what* is written in each argument to *how* and *why* it is written.

- *A controversy analysis is not a report.* While it may seem like you are merely reporting on the various arguments of the issue as you have defined it, you have a greater purpose than that—you want to help your readers understand the controversy as a whole. In the course of your research into the controversy, you will want to do more than just find the various relevant arguments; you will also want to show how they speak to each other, how they intertwine and interact. In other words, in your controversy analysis, you are not merely showing each argument to your readers and then moving on to the next one. You will need to find a focus and structure for your analysis that reveals how these arguments feed into each other. What is the common ground—that is, the points of agreement—that all the arguments stand on? If there is no common ground, why isn't there? How do some or all of the arguments undermine themselves? What are the strengths and weaknesses of each one? How do points of one argument stem from the points of another? In addition to showing the interactions between the arguments, at the beginning of the essay you should also give some sort of background on the controversy, and at the conclusion of the essay you should project what seems to be the future, as you see it, of the controversy.

What might help you avoid writing a paper that falls into one of the traps listed above is using one or more of the approaches listed below.

Approaches to a Controversy

The Pro-Con Question

When asked to write about a controversy, many students look at opposing positions on an issue, creating what is also referred to as "pro-con" or "polarized" arguments, such as those used in debates. The "pro-con" approach can be very valuable when looking at some of the larger questions in the issue, as suggested by the question "Do alternative fuels contain the answer to our dependence on oil?", "Is a government-controlled health plan the answer to our current crisis in health care?" or "Should the food industry be forced to disclose the complete list of contents in all prepared foods?" As you can see, there are only two possible answers to each of these questions—"yes, because..." or "no, because..." Thus, one answer is "for" or "pro" and one "against" or "con," making this approach ideal for debates, which really aren't designed to get into more complex aspects of these issues.

However, the drawback of the pro-con approach, which is considerable, is that unless both sides base their answers on some common ground, they really will not be addressing the issue in the same way. For example, a topic students often choose to write about is abortion. When you approach abortion from a pro-con perspective, the question nearly always becomes, "Should abortion remain legal?" The "yes" or pro side, the pro-choice group, would say, "Yes, because a woman has a right to her own body and shouldn't be forced to continue a pregnancy she doesn't want and hasn't planned for." The "no" or con side, the pro-life group, would say, "No, because a fetus is a human being, and therefore abortion is murder." The issue of legality is the only point at which these two sides touch. The reasons for their answers to abortion's legality do not fall on any kind of common ground: the pro-choice group bases their answer on the Constitutional rights of women as full U.S. citizens; the pro-life group bases their answer on moral and religious beliefs about the human status of a fetus. The pro-choice group may answer as they do because they find no scientific proof for the fetus as a fully-formed human being with all the rights of born humans, making the woman's rights predominant; the pro-life group may answer as they do because their belief system tells them that a fetus's potential to become a fully-formed human being guarantees its rights as a human being, making its right to live predominant. Neither side connects with the other on its basis for argument, and thus this approach always reaches an impasse.

The same is true of many of the big issues of our culture—the drinking age, the legalization of marijuana, steroid use, euthanasia, capital punishment. The two sides of each issue's pro-con approach do not stem from any common ground, and thus, they don't really speak to each other at all.

The Problem-Solving Question

Another way to approach an issue might be from the standpoint of solving a problem. This approach phrases the question in a different way: not "Should abortion [or marijuana or capital punishment or euthanasia] be legal?" but "How can we lower the number of abortions being performed in this country?" or "How should we deal with the prevalent use of marijuana?" or "How can we prevent the unjust application of the death penalty?" or "What is the best way to prevent underage drinking?" This type of question allows for a greater degree of common ground on the answers given. For example, both pro-choice and pro-life groups can agree that prevention of unwanted pregnancy is preferable to abortion, but they might disagree on how to go about preventing unwanted pregnancies. Even within each group, there might be disagreement about the best prevention method. Some pro-choicers would say that better access of minors to birth control is the best method; other pro-choicers might say that full sex education in schools is the best way. Likewise, some pro-lifers might say that abstinence is the only sure way to prevent unwanted pregnancy, whereas other pro-lifers would advocate for more sex education and certain birth control methods. Thus, an analysis of the issue of abortion focusing on the controversy of the best way to prevent unwanted pregnancy might examine four or five different arguments rather than just two. Further, in many issues, including abortion, a number of viewpoints don't fall neatly into either pro-choice or pro-life camps. The problem-solving approach can easily include these viewpoints.

The drawback of this approach is the controversial question itself—focused too broadly, the question allows too many opinions to be examined for the scope of a short paper; focused too narrowly, the question eliminates much of the controversy that the audience might want to see addressed. Careful focusing of the "problem-solving" question needs to take place so that the number of viewpoints to be addressed is strictly limited. (*See Chapter 9, "Finding and Conducting Research on a Local Issue," for more on how to focus a research question.*)

The Cause-Effect Question

Another way to focus on the issue is to address the cause of a problem: what force or forces created the controversy in the first place. This asks a researcher to dig into the history of an issue to find what might be at the root of it. Of course, as with other aspects of the controversy, there can be quite a bit of disagreement on this point as well. For example, "Why is there disagreement about the death penalty?"

- Some might say the question is as old as the Ten Commandments and the particular commandment that orders "Thou shalt not kill." The interpretation of this commandment, according to some, should be as broad as possible—there is no reason to kill another human being, period.

- Others may claim that nobody seriously disputed the death penalty until certain groups, in the course of questioning many widely accepted beliefs about human rights, suggested that the death penalty constituted societal revenge, not deterrence of crime, and involved the government in practices that should not be the province of a just government.

- Still others may argue that criminals are motivated by deep psychological disturbances and conditions beyond their control, making them less culpable for their actions, and that the proper response to their crimes is to rehabilitate them.

- Some look at the statistics of who is being executed—largely members of minority groups, with many fewer white criminals being subjected to the death penalty.

- Still others point to the worldwide community and the trend toward eliminating the death penalty among most other nations and particularly among developed nations. They look at the reasons for this trend and its effect on Americans concerned with the issue of capital punishment.

Or you could focus on the effects of the continued use of capital punishment in the United States. This approach asks a researcher to look at other aspects of American life and culture in terms of how they are affected by the death penalty.

- Some would say the main effect is deterrence of capital crimes and point to various statistics.

- Others will say that the main effect is the view of other countries, particularly in Europe, that America is a largely barbaric and vengeful country, given to excesses in both crime and punishment.

- Still others might see the main effect as continued discrimination against criminals of minority or economically disadvantaged backgrounds while privileged white criminals "get away with murder."

The main problem with this approach, as with the "problem-solving" approach, is how to achieve the right focus on the issue to account for the audience's expectations while limiting the range of opinions you have to research.

205

The Major Figures Question

In this approach, the main question involves "Who are the main people addressing the issue and what are their arguments?" In this approach, your question leads you to looking at the major arguers— those who have most publicly and vociferously weighed in on the issue and laid out the main lines of the argument for both sides, those who represent certain groups concerned with the issue. Usually this means looking at two sides, similar to the pro-con approach, but with an eye toward the arguments of specific individuals on each side rather than on the general "yes-no" questions about the issue. This approach particularly lends itself to an ideological analysis of the issue, an analysis based on apparent values and beliefs underlying particular arguments. While you can analyze the prevailing ideology underlying the various arguments as part of your analysis in any of the other approaches, the major figures approach emphasizes the underlying beliefs and values implicit in each leader's argument.

In this approach, your examination of the issue focuses not so much on what is argued as on who is arguing and how he/she is arguing. This approach to the controversy is especially useful for the big issues, for which the arguments have been sent around the block numerous times, and everyone has heard them at least two or three times. It allows you to examine these familiar arguments from a different angle and provide a less familiar way to present them to your audiences.

The pitfall of this approach is that you will be more than ever tempted to argue against or for these figures and their arguments. Uncovering one or more ideologies and their accompanying assumptions, especially if your own ideologies oppose them, provides more than one opportunity for you to respond with points for or against not only the argument but the underlying ideology as well. It's natural to feel this way as you're analyzing, but the purpose of your controversy analysis is to analyze the arguments, not leap into the fray with both feet. You will get your chance to argue in another assignment (*see Section Three, "Public Argument"*), but for now you need to provide a fair and balanced analysis of each argument you examine.

The Call-to-Action Question

Let's say in the course of researching your issue, particularly if it is a familiar and well-argued one, you come across a little-noticed aspect of the issue that only a few have addressed. You might want to focus solely on this aspect of the issue and carefully analyze the various arguments addressing it. Your approach to your own audience is to shed light on this quieter yet no less important or pressing question that has been overshadowed by the louder voices of the main questions. You might also select this approach if you have chosen a local issue with a subtler controversy embedded in it. Your purpose would be to make your audience aware of this controversy and what others are saying about it. (*See Chapter 9, "Finding and Conducting Research on a Local Issue," for more on finding local issues and discovering controversies within them.*)

All of these approaches can help you get into your topic, formulate your thesis questions, and begin researching them. Each approach requires a different way to formulate the question, as demonstrated below in a table showing how the different approaches narrow and focus a sample topic, the issue of guns on college campuses:

Approach	Sample Thesis Question
Pro-Con	Should we allow students and faculty to carry guns on college campuses?
Problem-Solving	What regulations should be imposed if guns are allowed on college campuses?
Cause or Effect	Why has gun violence increased on campuses around the country? How will armed students and teachers affect the primary purpose of schools—education?
Major Figures	Larry Pratt, executive director of Gun Owners of America, claims that making college campuses weapons-free zones has done nothing but make campuses more vulnerable to armed criminals. On the other hand, Paul Helmke, president of Brady Campaign to Prevent Gun Violence, argues that allowing guns on college campuses will only encourage more gun violence. How do Pratt and Helmke, representing the opposing sides of the gun-control debate, address each other's concerns?
Call-to-Action	If guns are allowed on college campuses, can we expect more violence at parties where alcohol is served?

Conclusion: How Do I Get Started?

Obviously, the place to begin is with your instructor's assignment. She may ask you to use a particular approach or may give you multiple approaches to choose from. She may ask you to focus on a particular subject area or may make the choice of topic completely open to you. Undoubtedly, she will ask you to use a certain number of sources and make the paper a certain number of words or pages long.

After you have digested the requirements of the assignment as indicated in your instructor's assignment sheet and tried forming your thesis question according to the different approaches, do some preliminary research and settle on a particular question as the focus of your continued research. The preliminary research will help you see the different angles of the issue and find the particular angle you want to pursue in more depth. Now you are well on your way to finding out more about your chosen "conversation" and discovering the dynamics that are shaping it.

Chapter 9

Finding and Conducting Research on a Local Issue

By Ashley J. Holmes

From the moment your instructor passes out the assignment for your research project, the pressure of finding an issue looms large. Your instructor may require you to meet certain guidelines and expectations as you select your issue, or you may have complete freedom to follow your interests. Ideally, you will want to find an issue that connects with something you want to learn more about, whether that is a hobby, a career, an issue related to your family or hometown, etc. As researchers with free reign in our choice of topics, we often jump to the more traditionally debated issues, such as pro-life versus pro-choice, the legalization of marijuana, or steroids in baseball. These topics may be your most interesting options, but I would like to encourage you to brainstorm topics that connect with your local place and community.

Considering Local Issues for Research

It's easy to overlook issues that we can explore right in our backyards, but conducting research on issues that relate to our campus communities often leads to a more meaningful and interesting research process. Selecting a local issue gives you the opportunity to learn more about your area and region, and you can often find ways of connecting more general topics of interest to the local area. For example, if you are interested in the controversies surrounding affirmative action in college admissions, you could connect this issue to your specific campus, exploring your campus' specific policies as well as student responses to affirmative action. Another example might be an interest in college student-athletes. Again, though you can conduct more general research about student-athletes, why not complement those findings with research of student-athletes on your campus? You can also consider issues related to the community beyond the walls of the university. For instance, my hometown is on the eastern coast of North Carolina, and many controversies have risen in response to redevelopment after hurricanes. I could explore this important community issue by conducting interviews with construction companies, beachfront homeowners, and local environmental agencies. Each of these groups would likely have a different response to the controversial issue of rebuilding on beaches that have been devastated by hurricanes.

Brainstorming Ideas, Locating Research Issues

One of the first steps you should take when assigned a research essay is finding your issue. To brainstorm local issues that may interest you for research, try the activity listed in the strategy box below.

Exercise 1: Creating a Community Interest List

- Take a sheet of paper and turn it horizontally. Divide the sheet into three sections separated by columns.
- Write these categories at the top of each column: *Past Communities, Present Communities, Future Communities of Interest*
- Start brainstorming lists under each of these columns. Consider communities based geographically (neighborhood, dormitory, city, state), along gender/race/religion lines, based on special interests or hobbies, etc. The following examples may help you get started:
    - o **Past Communities**: Think about the communities you came from and how they have shaped the person you are today and where you are at this point in your life. (Hometown, sport you used to play, books you found interesting, etc.)
    - o **Present Communities:** Think about all the communities of which you are currently a part. (Clubs, sports, geographic communities, academic major, hobbies, special interests, etc.)
    - o **Future Communities of Interest:** Think about the communities you hope to enter or join later in life—perhaps a specific profession, or place to live, or group of people who share certain interests. (This could be a profession, a major, a club, a fraternity or sorority, etc.)
- Once you have listed all the communities you can think of under each column, choose five that you are interested in possibly pursuing as an issue for research and circle them.
- Turn your sheet of paper over, and list these five phrases at the top of the horizontal sheet of paper.
- Under each, start a new list of everything you can think of that you already know or may want to know more about related to this topic. Ideally, these lists will emerge as issues that could be pursued through research.
- Continue working to narrow your list of interests.

In the following pages, I will trace my journey of conducting research on a local issue of interest to me, noting common steps for all researchers throughout the process. I will use a sample issue that emerged when I created a community interest list:

Future Communities of Interest

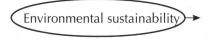 In the future, I want to learn more about how I can become involved in local environmental sustainability initiatives, such as recycling, organic food options, energy efficiency, etc.

Forming an Initial Inquiry, Narrowing Your Local Issue

After completing my community interest list and selecting "environmental sustainability" to pursue more thoroughly, I formed an initial question and then conducted preliminary research to begin narrowing my issue. See *Figure A* on the following page for a visual representation of this process.

To connect my issue with my local community, I started with a question about what environmental initiatives might currently exist on my campus, and then I brainstormed possibilities such as recycling, composting, etc. To see if any of these initiatives actually existed, I conducted a quick online search from my campus' website. This led me to an entire website devoted to campus sustainability initiatives ranging from recycling to energy efficiency, and from water conservation to food sustainability. I was curious about food initiatives, so I explored the links under that topic and found a new link of interest about the campus farmers' market. I was interested to learn more about the campus farmers' market because I enjoy shopping at markets and cooking with local produce. This helped me narrow my issue that was too broad (environmental sustainability) to an issue that was more focused (campus farmers' market). Had I kept the broad topic of environmental sustainability, I would have had to research diverse initiatives such as recycling, energy efficiency, food sustainability, etc.; certainly all of these issues are related, but trying to tackle all at once would be too much for the scope of my research project. Before I finalized my topic, though, I wanted to conduct some preliminary research to see if this would be a viable topic.

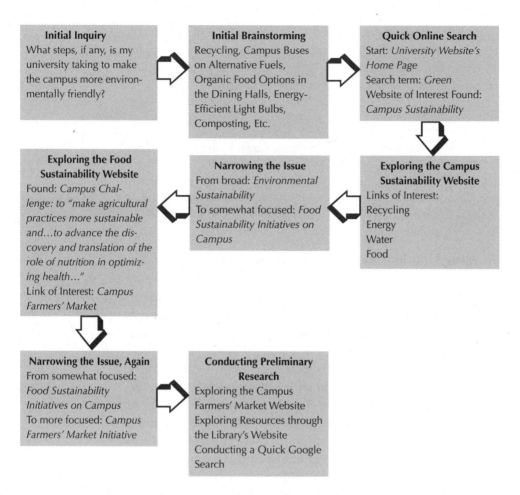

Initial Inquiry
What steps, if any, is my university taking to make the campus more environmentally friendly?

Initial Brainstorming
Recycling, Campus Buses on Alternative Fuels, Organic Food Options in the Dining Halls, Energy-Efficient Light Bulbs, Composting, Etc.

Quick Online Search
Start: *University Website's Home Page*
Search term: *Green*
Website of Interest Found: *Campus Sustainability*

Exploring the Food Sustainability Website
Found: *Campus Challenge: to "make agricultural practices more sustainable and...to advance the discovery and translation of the role of nutrition in optimizing health..."*
Link of Interest: *Campus Farmers' Market*

Narrowing the Issue
From broad: *Environmental Sustainability*
To somewhat focused: *Food Sustainability Initiatives on Campus*

Exploring the Campus Sustainability Website
Links of Interest:
Recycling
Energy
Water
Food

Narrowing the Issue, Again
From somewhat focused:
Food Sustainability Initiatives on Campus
To more focused: *Campus Farmers' Market Initiative*

Conducting Preliminary Research
Exploring the Campus Farmers' Market Website
Exploring Resources through the Library's Website
Conducting a Quick Google Search

Figure A: *Map of process from initial inquiry, to narrowing issue, to beginning preliminary research*

Conducting Preliminary Research

It is important to conduct a quick and informal search—or what most researchers call **preliminary research**—when you find an issue that you think you would like to pursue for your research project. Preliminary research is useful because it allows you to see what information is available on your issue, whether there is enough information to make the issue viable for your research assignment, and whether you are interested enough in the issue to pursue it for your assignment. Once you have an issue you are interested in pursuing, try the strategies in the box on the following page to conduct preliminary research.

Exercise 2: Strategies for Conducting Preliminary Research

- Conduct a quick online search. You may start with Google or Wikipedia, but try to go beyond those easily accessible searches to look for local, community connections. Try your school's website, websites for government agencies in the city or state, or online versions of your local city or campus newspapers.
- Talk with your instructors, classmates, friends, and family about your initial ideas for research issues. They may have some suggestions for you.
- Go to your school library's website, and search the catalog and/or databases. **[NOTE: At the preliminary research stage, you may simply want to conduct searches without gathering sources. However, it's a good idea to save your search terms and/or keep track of sources and websites that seem particularly interesting or helpful, since you may pursue this issue and will need sources in the future.]**
- Be open to the possibility of your topic shifting as a result of preliminary research. Though you'll want to finalize your topic sooner than later, at this stage in the process allow the research process to follow your interests.

For my own preliminary research on the campus farmers' market, I worked through the steps mapped in *Figure B* below. I conducted two separate searches for preliminary research: 1) exploring the campus farmers' market website and 2) exploring the library's resources. Since I found a contact for the farmers' market on campus and a series of books related to my issue, I determined that it would be a viable topic for research.

Search 1

Exploring the Campus Farmers' Market Website	**Who is Gale Welter?**	**Research Notes**
I explored links about the campus farmers' market's mission, location and hours, vendors, and contacts. The contact information gave me the phone number and email address for Gale Welter.	I wanted to find out more information about the farmers' market contact, so I went to my university's directory and typed in her name. The results indicated that Gale Welter is the Coordinator of Nutrition Services with Campus Health Service.	Because I found Gale Welter's email address and phone number, I copied this information into my research notebook. I figured it may be useful later in my research process.

Search 2

Exploring the Library's Resources	**Catalog Results**	**Research Notes**
I went to my campus library's home page and typed "farmers' market" into the search engine for the catalog.	The results included titles of books with phrases such as "the success and failure of farmers' markets" and "the new farmers' market."	Because a few of the titles in the catalog search seemed to fit well with my issue, I wrote the titles and author names in my research notebook.

Figure B: *Two paths of preliminary research*

A Note about Finding the Controversy in Local Issues

Sometimes, selecting a local issue—or any issue, for that matter—may lead you to believe that there's no controversy involved. However, many issues may require a more nuanced analysis of controversies or differences of opinion surrounding the issue. Not all issues will seem as controversial as hot-button issues like abortion or the death penalty, but give yourself time in the research process to locate the controversies.

For instance, my chosen issue of farmers' markets does not seem immediately controversial. Likely, most readers will agree that farmers' markets are a good thing, and I would be hard-pressed to find sources that say farmers' markets are bad. In this case, I've selected an issue that is not a clear-cut "pro" versus "con" issue. However, through the course of conducting library and field research, I soon learned that there are differences of opinion about how to run a farmers' market, where to locate a market, who it should serve, its primary mission, and even whether it is a better or worse option than Community Supported Agriculture (one alternative to farmers' markets). Therefore, when I began to organize my researched information for my essay, I grouped information based on these diverse opinions, and in my paper I put these positions from sources "in conversation" with one another in order to highlight the differences or controversies.

The point here is that you should not shy away from topics that are interesting to you simply because you do not initially see a clear-cut controversy. Keep researching and finding sources that help you locate differences of opinion that you can highlight as controversial in your essay. However, if after your initial round of research you are still having difficulty finding the controversy in your issue, you may need to shift the way you are framing the issue. For instance, one student I worked with selected marathons as an interest of hers, but she was having trouble finding the controversy. During the process of research, though, she found differences of opinion about how to best train for a marathon, whether it's exercise, diet, or a combination. She then shifted her issue to focus on training for marathons—where she located a controversy—rather than marathons in general.

Developing a Research Proposal/Plan

Your instructor may or may not require you to submit a research proposal. Whether or not you are required to draft a proposal, you should still create a plan for your research. Use the guidelines in the box below to help you develop your research proposal and/or plan for research.

Exercise 3: Research Proposal/Plan

- Explain which issue you selected and why.
- Describe what you already know about your issue at this point.
- Explain what you hope to learn about your issue through the process of research.
- Create a timeline (with dates) that marks milestones or indicates mini-due dates that you have set for tasks you need to complete for this assignment. (e.g., finding X number of sources, conducting interviews or surveys, reading and annotating sources, composing a first draft, revising, etc.)
- Explain your plans for conducting library research and/or conducting field research. Where and how will you look for sources? Who might you interview or survey? Why?
- Make a list of questions you have about your issue, the research process, and/or the assignment.
- Include the citations for at least two sources you found related to your issue during your preliminary research. Format your bibliography using standard MLA citation.

Conducting Library Research

You likely know by now that for college papers you should utilize resources from your campus library to add credibility to your work. Your library has many diverse resources, and you should consult your instructor and librarians about your best use of library resources. Though your library has access to archives, microfiche, and multimedia sources, the most common source types you should familiarize yourself with in your first-year writing course are books and articles. See the maps on the following pages for guides on how to find these two resources in your library: how to find books (Figure C) and how to find articles (Figure D).

| **To Find Books** Start at your library website's home page and search the library's **catalog**. The catalog lists the books and other resources that are housed in your campus library. | Type your search terms into the catalog search engine. Your results will most likely include book sources, though there may be other useful resources listed too. Click on one of the book titles that seems to fit best with your research issue. | The catalog entry for this book will give you important information that you should write in your research notebook: title, author(s) name, place and year of publication, and publisher. |

| Once you've located your book on the shelf, wait before walking away. Take a minute to flip through the book; look at the table of contents in the front and the index in the back to make sure it will be a useful resource. Also, scan the titles of books on the same shelf as the one you found. You may find other helpful sources there too. | If you decide you'd like to look at the book, find the **call number** within the catalog entry. This call number corresponds to a location on the shelves of your library. Write down the call number, and use location guides or ask a librarian to help you locate the floor and shelf that matches your book's call number. | The catalog entry may list a table of contents with the titles of chapters, which will help you determine whether this will be a useful book that you should find on the shelf. |

Figure C: *How to find books*

When researching my issue of farmers' markets, I searched the library's catalog and found a number of books that fit with my issue. I started with the search terms "farmers markets," which gave me 19 results. In a quick scan of the titles, I found three that seemed to fit best with my issue. I wrote the following information in my research notebook:

- Title: *Farmers' Markets: Success, Failure, and Management Ecology*, Author: *Garry Stephenson, Place of Publication: Amherst, NY, Publisher: Cambria Press, Year of Publication: 2008, Call Number: HF5472.U6 S74*

- Title: *Eat Here: Reclaiming Homegrown Pleasures in a Global Supermarket*, Author: *Brian Halweil, Place of Publication: New York, Publisher: W.W. Norton, Year of Publication: 2004, Call Number: TX356.H35*

- *Title: The New Farmers' Market: Farm-Fresh Ideas for Producers, Managers, & Communities,* Authors: *Vance Corum, Marcie Rosenzweig, and Eric Gibson, Place of Publication: Auburn, CA, Publisher: New World Pub., Year of Publication: 2001, Call Number: HF5472.U6 C67*

I noticed two of the titles had similar call numbers, both starting with HF5472.U6. I located these books first and found this shelf area had several other books about farmers' markets, local produce, global food issues, organic foods, etc. After finding a few books related to my issue, I searched the library's databases to find articles.

To Find Articles
Start at your library website's home page and look for a link to search **databases**. Databases search for articles in magazines, journals, and newspapers to which your library may or may not have access.

Your library likely subscribes to many databases. Each one produces different results, so it's a good idea to try a few. Some popular databases for use in firstyear writing are Academic Search Complete, Lexis-Nexis, and JSTOR.

Select one of the databases, and enter your search terms. The results on the list will be articles—some may be from academic journals, others may be from popular magazines or newspapers. Check with your instructor to see if you should use advanced search features to limit your results to academic journal articles.

See if there is a link to a PDF file or a full-text version of the article. If so, you can save, email, and/or print the article for future usage.

The database entry for this article will give you important information that you should write in your research notebook: author's name, title of the article, title of the journal or magazine, volume and issue number (if applicable), year of publication, and page numbers (if applicable).

Scan the titles of the articles, and select one that interests you and fits with your topic.

If the full text of the article is not available through the database, this does not mean that you cannot access the article. Consult with a librarian about steps you should take to locate the article in a different database, in a printed journal in the library, through inter-library loan, or other means.

Figure D: *How to find articles*

To find articles about farmers' markets, I went to my library's home page and found the link for databases. I started with Academic Search Complete and typed the search term "farmers markets." This search yielded 967 results—too many for me to search through, so I added a second search term: "farmers markets" and "campus." This resulted in 8 articles, much more manageable. I wrote the following information in my research notebook:

- *Title of Article: "Working Toward a Just, Equitable, and Local Food System: The Social Impact of Community-Based Agriculture," Author: Thomas Macias, Title of Journal: Social Science Quarterly, Volume: 89, Issue Number: 5, Year of Publication: December 2008, Page Numbers: 1086-1101.*

- *Title of Article: "Selling Fruit," Author: Jim Fruth, Title of Journal: POMONA: The Quarterly Journal of the North American Fruit Explorers, Year of Publication: Summer 2008.*

- *Title of Article: "Ohio Public Health Students Promoting Fresh Food, Nutrition." Author: Teddi Dineley Johnson, Source: The Nation's Health, Year of Publication: November 2008, Page Number: 19.*

Luckily, the database had links to full-text versions of each of these articles, so I saved the files and emailed them to myself to access later. After reading and taking notes on some of the library sources I found, I was ready to conduct field research on my issue to find out about my campus' local farmers' market.

Conducting Field Research on Your Local Issue

Two common methods of gathering field research are conducting interviews and surveys. For research in your first-year writing course, you can use these methods to enhance and complicate the information you find in sources from the library and databases. Field research requires you to get out into the local community and talk to people about your issue, and this can yield valuable information for your research project. Use the strategy boxes on the following pages to help you prepare for field research.

Exercise 4: Conducting Interviews

- Make a list of all the groups affected by your issue.
- Determine which groups you would like/need to interview for your research project, and decide how you will locate someone within that group to interview.
- Find that person's contact information email and/or phone number.
- Send an initial query through email or phone call in which you explain your research project and why you would like to interview this person for your research.
- If they agree, set up an interview plan that fits with the interviewee's schedule. You may ask to meet face-to-face, speak over the phone, or correspond over email.
- Compose your interview questions.
  - o Use the preliminary and library research you've already conducted to help you formulate the kinds of questions you'd like to ask.
  - o Phrase the questions as open-ended, rather than leading to a "yes" or "no" response.
  - o Ask a peer to review your questions before using them with your interviewee.
  - o In a face-to-face or phone interview, be ready to veer away from your written questions to respond to what the interviewee is saying.
- Conduct the interview and take detailed notes.
- Ask the interviewee if you can reference his/her interview response in your research paper for your first-year writing class. If the participant agrees, ask whether the interviewee would like you to use his/her full name or if he/she would like to remain anonymous.
- If possible, send your interviewee a thank-you card or email in the following week.

When I considered the best form of field research for my issue of the campus farmers' market, I remembered during my preliminary research coming across the contact information for Gale Welter who worked in Nutrition Services. I decided that she would likely be a great person to interview about the campus farmers' market, since she was listed as the main contact for the market. I wrote her an email explaining my research project and issue and asking if she would be willing to participate in an interview for part of my field research. She agreed and we set up a time to meet for a face-to-face interview. Ms. Welter had the great idea of meeting at the campus farmers' market the following Friday. We set our date, time, and location, and I started preparing my interview questions. I knew my major interview would be with Gale Welter, but I wanted to gather diverse perspectives. I decided to prepare interview questions for farmers at the market, as well as students at the market.

The day I met Ms. Welter for our interview at the market, I gathered a lot of research data. I interviewed Ms. Welter for approximately 30 minutes, and I took pages of handwritten notes. Ms. Welter was very knowledgeable about the campus farmers' market, since I learned that she was the first to start the market on campus. She explained how the market had evolved, including a change in location, upgrades in tents and market equipment, and more focused nutrition awareness initiatives. Her interview gave me invaluable information for my research project, and I thanked her. She gave me permission to contact her with follow-up questions if they arose when I began writing my research paper. While I was at the market that day, I also conducted other, less formal interviews. I talked with three farmers selling their goods, and I interviewed two students selling produce for a farm as part of their major requirements in nutrition. These diverse opinions on the role of the campus farmers' market made for great research. I took my pages of notes back to my work area and began to consider how to organize and put my library research in "conversation with" my field research.

Another form of field research involves distributing surveys. You may find that informal survey data would fit better with your research issue than conducting interviews. Use the strategies in the box on the following page to help you design and implement a survey as part of your field research.

Exercise 5: Surveys

- Determine what group you plan to survey before composing your questions. Do you want a random sampling of diverse groups of people? Do you want results from college students? Do you want to focus only on first-year college students? Should you include faculty members or staff? What others should you include?
- Compose the questions for your survey.
    - Decide whether you want open-ended responses or if you want participants to circle answers you provide. Providing answers for your participants to circle will make it easier for you to count the number of responses. However, open-ended responses allow you to quote from your participants' answers in their own words. There are advantages and disadvantages to each method.
    - Be sure that your survey isn't too long. Ideally you want to make it short enough that participants could complete it in a few minutes.
    - Ask a peer to review your questions before distributing them in survey form.
- Decide how many people you would like to complete your survey. In the social sciences, where surveying is an important part of field research data, it is important to have a high number of respondents to validate your data. However, for your purposes in first-year writing, you do not need hundreds of respondents. You might set a goal for 20 participants as a minimum.
- Once you've passed out and collected your surveys, read through the answers and take the time to "crunch the numbers." If participants circled responses, count how many of each response; you might even translate that information into percentages—like 75% of survey respondents said they had never made a purchase at the campus farmers' market. If you have open-ended answers, use a highlighter to indicate sentences you might want to quote from in your paper. Look for themes or recurring points made by respondents.

Chapter 10

Patterns of Belief: Analyzing Cultural Values and Ideology in Controversies

By Christopher Minnix

By now you have most likely used your research to find different stances or arguments on the controversy you are writing about. Depending upon the issue, you may be looking at sharply divided political opinions, hotly contested debates over problems and their solutions, moderate discussions of a plan or proposal, or even humorous portrayals of opposing arguments. As you continue to research, you will find that often the angry speech that you see on television news programs does not capture the full emotional and intellectual character of public controversies. Constantly interrupting hosts and forceful political pundits make for good television ratings, but they can sometimes give us a sense that all public controversy is reducible to a screaming match and that no middle ground exists between opinions in the controversy. You may be finding that your research shows that this is simply not always the case. People engaged in public controversies sometimes do find that their positions are irreconcilable, but more often than not, and especially in democratic societies like our own, they find that they have to find common ground to address the issues and problems of the controversy. This does not mean that the discussion has stopped, that the issue will not continue to be hotly debated, or that the parties involved have "sold out." What it does mean is that they had to work to create solutions based upon the situations that they found themselves in.

We can understand how people create solutions to controversies and societal problems much more deeply by understanding the rhetorical strategies they use to persuade one another to adopt a specific plan or address an issue in a specific way. Aristotle, who wrote one of the most complete early treatises on rhetoric, *On Rhetoric*, described rhetoric as "an ability in each [particular] case, to see the available means of persuasion" (2.1, 36). What did Aristotle mean? One way we can think about his statement is that understanding rhetoric helps us understand what will persuade audiences in specific contexts. Seeing the means of persuasion available means looking deeply into the social, cultural, and rhetorical contexts of our audiences and analyzing what types of rhetorical messages will speak to their values and beliefs about an issue. It means thinking deeply about their political views of an issue, their theories about an issue, their levels of knowledge about the issue, their emotional tones, and the types of arguments they are accustomed to hearing about the issue. Aristotle's statement is helpful to keep in mind as you analyze the different sources of your controversy. Thinking about how the authors you read "see the available means of persuasion," means analyzing *not only what the authors argue, but how they adapt their arguments to specific audiences.*

Controversies are often far too complex to cover in a single essay, and to cover all of the major voices in your controversy would require a much lengthier essay than you might write at this time. This means that your task is not to provide a complete history and overview of the controversy, but instead to provide an analysis of several of the major arguments that shape the controversy. This means looking for major or important points of disagreement in the controversy, and you will want to spend time sorting out the major from the minor points of disagreement. Since the controversy analysis is a rhetorical analysis, you also want to spend time analyzing how the authors seek to communicate their messages to their audiences. You might say, however, *"How do I know what the author was trying to communicate? It's not as though I can just call them up!"* You would be right to ask this question, and it makes us think deeply about what we are doing when we analyze rhetoric or analyze a controversy. While you do not have the author close by, you do have a text. We can borrow a word from archaeology to help us understand how we can analyze how others "see the available means of persuasion": artifact. Just as archaeologists analyze artifacts to help deepen and develop our understanding of a particular culture, we can think of texts as textual artifacts and analyze them to help us understand how people seek to persuade one another in our own culture.

The rhetorical texts that you have found while researching your controversy, while not thousands of years old, are nevertheless artifacts of a particular controversy, and analyzing them can help you reconstruct the controversy. Every rhetorical text has within it a vision of its audience and how they will respond to particular arguments and ideas within a given place and time. If we were to look back at Martin Luther King Jr.'s "Letter from a Birmingham Jail," we would learn an intense amount about the different arguments concerning racial progress and nonviolence, and we would also learn how King tapped into the religious beliefs of his audiences in order to persuade them that the work of the civil rights movement was God's work. When we analyze King's rhetoric, we do not just see King's argument, but how his speech reflects a deep understanding of the "available means of persuasion" of his time and place. We see, in other words, how King adapts his arguments and ideas to his audience.

In the same way that analyzing King's speech deepens our understanding of his culture, analyzing the different perspectives and sources in our controversy can help us understand our own culture and its relationship to our controversy. Perhaps one of the most important points to remember is that *audiences exist within particular cultures and that these cultures are made up of a variety of different values, beliefs, and ideologies.* It is impossible, for example, to separate King's messages about political protest in "Letter from a Birmingham Jail" from his Christian doctrine. In fact, the letter spends a large amount of time providing a Christian understanding of the civil rights movement. If we read King's letter closely, we begin to see that one of the "available means of persuasion" in his society was to tap into the religious beliefs of this time and show how supporting the civil rights movement was a Christian duty. What this example helps us understand is that analyzing the rhetoric of a controversy means looking closely at how each rhetorical text or perspective constructs a view of its audience and culture. In addition to the strategies for analyzing audience, culture, and rhetoric that you have already learned, this chapter provides you with a few more tools for your analytical toolkit. The methods and tools in this chapter can help you develop a deep analysis of the audiences and cultural contexts of your controversy.

Analyzing the Relationship between Rhetorical Texts, Audiences, and Their Cultures

Cultures are made up of various different communities of people who hold various different beliefs, values, and traditions. In his book *Keywords*, cultural historian Raymond Williams refers to culture as "one of the two or three most complicated words in the English language" (87). The difficulty of defining culture comes from the range of different activities, practices, beliefs, and values that are part of one place and time. To speak of "American Culture," for example, means to speak not only of mom, baseball, and apple pie, but also of various different cultural experiences and beliefs. What makes this concept so difficult is that we all tend to share a body of cultural knowledge or understanding while holding so many differences. Ask a group of random people on the street what the "American Dream" is and you will get remarkably similar answers, even if these people might disagree deeply over political or religious values. *This means that while our values and beliefs may differ, we nevertheless share a common understanding of the major ideas that shape our broader culture.* Likewise, as you analyze a controversy, you will begin to see certain cultural values that are brought up again and again by writers. Sometimes these values are portrayed positively, and sometimes negatively, but they are important because they reflect the cultural context of the controversy, or the beliefs and values of the authors and audiences of the controversy. As an author writes about a controversy, they are thinking through the following:

- What do my audiences know or believe about the controversy?

- What beliefs, values, or ideologies might shape their perspective on the issue?

- What intellectual and emotional responses might my message create?

- What are the key differences in opinion, belief, and values that might be found in my audiences?

- What arguments have been made before about the controversy and what are the most prevalent perspectives in the debate?

- How is the issue portrayed in the media and how could the media shape my audience's understanding of the issue?

These are just a few examples of questions that writers might think through as they determine how to best communicate their arguments to audiences. As you read through the sources that you have found, it is important to spend time thinking about how they have responded to these questions. One of the most effective ways of doing this is to spend time searching for and analyzing the value-heavy words that connect to their arguments. These words are usually broad concepts, such as "justice" or "liberty." In rhetorical studies, we call these words ideographs. The essay below will illustrate how to search for and analyze these terms in a controversy analysis, and hopefully show you why understanding the role of ideology in a controversy is an important part of understanding the "means of persuasion" available to those who would write about them.

ANALYZING IDEOLOGY IN A CONTROVERSY

By Maggie Werner

What Is Ideology?—An Introduction

Although the concept of ideology goes all the way back to the French Revolution, it is most commonly associated with the ideas of Karl Marx and Frederick Engels. Marx used the term as a way to understand the "haves" and "have nots" in society and the ways that power is held (or not held) by different economic classes. In Marxist tradition uncovering ideology shows the ways that social positions that appear to be natural and logical are really shaped by values that support the ruling class and oppress the working class. By exposing whose values and what beliefs are behind a particular ideology, as well as what values and beliefs are silenced, those people in socially subordinate positions can try to change their situations and make their voices heard (Marx and Engels).

In American society, we tend to hold an ideology of absolute equality. Many Americans and foreigners who come to this country believe that this is a land where anyone can make it, despite social or cultural position. When a person who was born without privilege achieves success, it supports this idea. For example, the election of Barack Obama, a biracial man with a modest upbringing, was widely hailed as proof of the American Dream of equality. Rhetorician Sonja K. Foss states that an ideology "includes a set or pattern of beliefs that evaluates relevant issues and topics for a group, providing interpretation of some domain of the world and encouraging particular attitudes and actions to it" (Foss 240). In the case of the American Dream and Barack Obama, we see a set of beliefs about racial equality (despite our country's past, many people believe that racism is no longer a major problem in America) and economic equality (no matter what social class you are born into, you can reach the upper echelons of society if you work hard enough).

Ideology in the Writing Class

In your writing classes, "ideology" will typically be used more generally to refer to any values and beliefs held by a defined group of people. It is important to remember that your individual values and beliefs are different from ideologies that you may hold. In order to be considered part of a recognizable ideology, values and beliefs need to reflect a specific group of people. For example, I have a belief that people who drive slowly and persistently in the left lane of the freeway are morons. This is not, however, an ideology. Many beliefs and values about driving are reflective of ideology though. It was common cultural dogma in the mid 20th century that women were inferior drivers. This changed in the latter half of the 20th century as more women were driving and studies showed that this stereotype was not true.

Becoming aware of the concept of ideology can help you as a thinker and as a writer. Ideology is useful in analysis because it is intended to make visible those aspects of culture that appear natural. Analysis requires that you go beyond the obvious and apparent to look beneath the surface and understand why arguments in texts are structured the way that they are and what groups of people benefit or suffer from those arguments. Analysis requires that you constantly ask "how" and "why" questions of texts. These are also fundamental concepts to ideology, which asks that we uncover assumptions and constructions, particularly in discourse. When you construct your own arguments, understanding your own and others' ideological positions can aid you in choosing appropriate persuasive strategies. The first step in analyzing ideology is to recognize it.

The Ideograph

Michael McGee, a rhetorical theorist who wrote about ideology, defines ideology as a "political language, preserved in rhetorical documents, with the capacity to dictate decision and control public behavior" (5). This language is "characterized by slogans" which McGee calls "ideographs." By finding the ideographs in a text, we can also identify ideology contained in the text. McGee calls them "ordinary-language term(s) found in political discourse" that are abstract and ill defined, but rarely questioned. Therefore, ideographs are difficult to define but easy to recognize, once you know what you are looking for. Some examples of ideographs that are common in American political discourse are "freedom," "terrorism," "equality," "liberty," and "family." All of these terms refer to abstract ideas, rather than specific things.

In his speech to the nation on September 20th, 2001, President George W. Bush persuasively used ideographs in order to unite the nation and prepare the way for an invasion of Iraq, by setting up a contrast between Americans and freedom and fundamentalist Muslims and terror. In the following passage, Mr. Bush employs several ideographs: "Tonight we are a country awakened to danger and called to defend freedom. Our grief has turned to anger, and anger to resolution. Whether we bring our enemies to justice, or bring justice to our enemies, justice will be done." The most obvious (and persuasive) ideographs in this passage are "country," "freedom," and "justice." Other important ideographs in the passage are "danger," "defend," and "enemies." All of these terms are abstractions—they have no specific referents—yet most Americans understand what President Bush meant when he used them. Members of Al-Qaeda would have different understandings of "freedom" and "justice"; the meanings of those words are entirely dependent on their history of their use among a group of people and their context.

The following questions can help you to find ideographs in a text.

- Is the word commonly used (not jargon)?

- Is the word an abstraction? (That is, does it represent a concept, rather than a thing?)

- Does the word have different meanings in different contexts?

- Does the meaning of the word vary according to who is using it?

Ideology and Controversy Analysis

Ideological analysis is particularly well suited for analyzing political rhetoric. Because public controversies typically have some political aspects, ideological analysis can help you in completing the controversy analysis assignment. The controversy analysis is intended to investigate the various viewpoints that different groups hold on a given issue. By exploring the major viewpoints involved, your understanding of the controversy deepens.

Ideological analysis can help you to identify the various positions in a controversy. Sometimes through such an investigation you will find that some issues do not work as well for this analysis as others because in some controversies the various participants do not listen or talk to each other. This typically happens with the grand moral issues of our time (e.g., abortion, same-sex marriage, the death penalty, etc.). Frequently the people involved don't listen to each other because they come from different ideological positions. In her book *Toward a Civil Discourse: Rhetoric and Fundamentalism*, rhetorician Sharon Crowley argues that Christian fundamentalists and liberal rationalists never get anywhere in their debates (particularly about homosexuality and abortion) because they argue from fundamentally different ideological positions. Their values and what counts as evidence in these debates is at odds. The liberal side tends to value rationality, data, and humanistic notions of free will and individuality while Christian fundamentalists value faith and religious tradition. The two sides attempt to persuade each other with evidence that the other doesn't value. Hence they argue in circles, neither listening to each other nor attempting to invent new ways of persuasion.

When you are choosing an issue, a brief assessment of the ideological positions involved can help you determine whether or not the controversy you are interested in will be one that you can work productively with throughout the semester. In order for an issue to be a controversy there have to be at least two groups of people who hold different positions, but frequently, depending on how you focus on the issue, there are more. Start your assessment of your controversy by listing the main groups that disagree with each other. Then you might want to expand your list to include any groups affected by the controversy who are not major players. Once you have identified a controversy to investigate and collected your sources, try to answer the following questions:

- Who is involved in the controversy? (Usually these will be identifiable groups.)

- Who are some of the major speakers/writers within these groups?

- What kind of social/cultural/economic/political power does each group hold?

- What resources are available to different positions?

- What does each group value?

- What counts as evidence for the different positions?

Ideological analysis can also help you to identify relations between the groups involved in a controversy. Ideological analysis is usually concerned with issues of power. What counts as power will depend on the issue, the groups involved, and their values and beliefs.

- Is there a power differential between the groups? Usually groups involved in a controversy will disagree over which side holds the power!

- Is there any acknowledged common ground between groups?

- Is there any unacknowledged common ground?

- Do the various groups listen to each other? That is, do they respond directly to the claims made by each other? Or do they only talk to people who already hold the same position?

Once you have answered the questions above, you can begin the work of looking for ideographs in various texts. A note of caution: Analyzing ideographs is most useful if you look for them in primary, rather than secondary, sources. After you have identified ideographs in primary sources from each group that you will write about, revisit the questions above and see if your answers to the questions have changed.

If we apply the list above to the controversy over the appearance of a cartoon published in *The Daily Wildcat* that included a racial slur, the issue comes into better focus.

Cartoon from The Daily Wildcat, *"The K Chronicles," 11/3/08, by Keith "Keef" Knight. Reprinted with permission.*

This particular controversy centered on several key issues: Was the cartoon racist because it contained a racial slur? Was the racism mitigated by the fact that its creator is African American? Is it ever okay to use racial slurs? If so, when? In order to understand this controversy, we can use the lists above to begin to assess the ideological positioning. In answering the first question—who is involved?—we can include individuals and groups:

- Outraged students

- Lauren LePage (Editor in Chief of *The Daily Wildcat*)

- Nickolas Seibel (Managing Editor of *The Daily Wildcat*)

- Keith "Keef" Knight (cartoon's creator)

- ASUA

At heart this was a controversy between the students who felt attacked by the printing of the word in the *Wildcat* and LePage who, whether she approved of the cartoon or not, is responsible for the content of the paper. LePage has quite a bit of power in this situation because ultimately the content in the newspaper is approved by her. The students were also a powerful group. When they began inundating the *Wildcat* with calls, letters, and e-mails, the issue was quickly center stage on campus. The students had a resource benefit in that they outnumbered the editorial board of the *Wildcat*. However, the editors had what appears to be the "ace in the hole" resource in this controversy: the cartoon's African American creator. As his race and purpose for the cartoon was established by the *Wildcat* to save face, the controversy died down. The *Wildcat* also had the power of a popular ideograph: "freedom of speech," which in this case was used as an argument ender, not a point of debate (remember that ideographs are frequently taken for granted). Both sides had the power of the ideograph "racism" and used it in different yet similarly persuasive ways.

In assessing whether or not there is common ground between the groups, a quick review of the controversy finds that all parties involved voiced disapproval of racial slurs. This is common ground that is both acknowledged and unacknowledged. The position of the *Wildcat*, enforced by the author, is that in this case, the use of the slur highlighted the continuing problem of racism in America. The position of the outraged students is that the *Wildcat*'s printing of the cartoon with "the N Word" undermined the election of the first African American president. So while both claim to be anti-racist, many outraged students did not buy that the printing was an oversight. Whether or not the groups listened to each other is, like many things, a matter of interpretation. ASUA held a meeting to discuss the issue, and LePage personally met with students who were angry. However, these meetings seemed more like a chance to vent rather than to discuss the issues of racism in America.

Behind the public face of these debates lie important issues about racism and rights to speech that did not get debated in depth. Why? What can this survey of the ideological positions of those involved reveal about the controversy? What do you want to know more about after doing this exercise? The questions above can help you get started on figuring out what needs to be covered in your controversy analysis, but it can also help you think more deeply about the issues.

Works Cited

Crowley, Sharon. *Toward a Civil Discourse: Rhetoric and Fundamentalism.* Pittsburgh: University of Pittsburgh Press, 2006. Print.

Foss, Sonja. *Rhetorical Criticism: Exploration and Practice.* 3rd ed. Long Grove, Ill.: Waveland, 2004. Print.

Marx, Karl, and Frederick Engels. *The German Ideology.* Prometheus, 1998. Print.

McGee, Michael Calvin. "The 'Ideograph': A Link Between Rhetoric and Ideology." *Quarterly Journal of Speech* 66 (February 1980): 1–16. Print.

Analyzing Ideographs: An Example

Let's take a look at an example that might be used for a controversy analysis. This example follows a student, Ashanti, as she uses ideographic analysis to understand key positions in the controversy she is analyzing. After following the discussion of the economy in recent years, Ashanti found herself interested in the controversy over corporate greed, or the controversy over the salaries of corporate CEOs. She watched the HBO film, *Too Big to Fail*, based on Andrew Ross Sorkin's *Too Big to Fail: The Inside Story of How Wall Street and Washington Fought to Save the Financial System—and Themselves* and found herself fascinated by the topic. As she researched the topic, she narrowed her focus to corporate greed and morality after she found many articles that focused on the morality of the business practices that created the banking crisis. After choosing six articles from a total of fifteen that she had marked as possible choices, she chose to first analyze an article by the writer Barbara Ehrenreich, entitled "The Power of Negative Thinking" (*also included in Controversy Cluster A elsewhere in this section*). Ashanti's notes on this article's rhetorical strategies and ideographs follow, as well as her analysis of this article's persuasiveness.

Barbara Ehrenreich—The Power of Negative Thinking

New York Times. *September 24, 2008. Reprinted with permission of PARS International Corp.*

GREED—and its crafty sibling, speculation—are the designated culprits for the financial crisis. But another, much admired, habit of mind should get its share of the blame: the delusional optimism of mainstream, all-American, positive thinking.

As promoted by Oprah Winfrey, scores of megachurch pastors and an endless flow of self-help best sellers, the idea is to firmly believe that you will get what you want, not only because it will make you feel better to do so, but because "visualizing" something—ardently and with concentration—actually makes it happen. You will be able to pay that adjustable-rate mortgage or, at the other end of the transaction, turn thousands of bad mortgages into giga-profits if only you believe that you can.

Positive thinking is endemic to American culture—from weight loss programs to cancer support groups—and in the last two decades it has put down deep roots in the corporate world as well. Everyone knows that you won't get a job paying more than $15 an hour unless you're a "positive person," and no one becomes a chief executive by issuing warnings of possible disaster.

The tomes in airport bookstores' business sections warn against "negativity" and advise the reader to be at all times upbeat, optimistic, brimming with confidence. It's a message companies relentlessly reinforced—treating their white-collar employees to manic motivational speakers and revival-like motivational events, while sending the top guys off to exotic locales to get pumped by the likes of Tony Robbins and other success gurus. Those who failed to get with the program would be subjected to personal "coaching" or shown the door.

The once-sober finance industry was not immune. On their Web sites, motivational speakers proudly list companies like Lehman Brothers and Merrill Lynch among their clients. What's more, for those at the very top of the corporate hierarchy, all this positive thinking must not have seemed delusional at all. With the rise in executive compensation, bosses could have almost anything they wanted, just by expressing the desire. No one was psychologically

---

After reading the article it seems that the author is using the ideograph "realism" against another ideograph "positive thinking."

This is an example of how the author is tapping into the cultural knowledge of her audience. By pointing to the sources of this "positive thinking," she is showing just how prevalent it is in our culture.

Her tone in the last sentence of the paragraph seems to show that she envisions her audience as seeing through the ideology of positive thinking. This ethos seems really important because if she approached her audience differently, they may feel alienated or that she is accusing them of simply buying into positive thinking stupidly.

This paragraph shows just how far the ideograph of positive thinking has invaded our consciousness. This may be one of the most powerful paragraphs in the article because it shows how the ideology of positive thinking requires us to change the way we go about our work.

This paragraph extends her argument by showing the consequences of this positive thinking. I think that the ideas in this paragraph also speak to the logic of her argument. By showing that positive thinking created a lack of preparation for hard times, she is able to defend her argument for negative thinking.

It is interesting that Ehrenreich goes back to the origins of America here, and this is an important point in her argument. She is able to show how positive thinking was a reaction to the negativity of Calvinism. This might be important here because it helps her make the case that "positive thinking" is not natural or just a natural part of being an American. It's like she's saying that positive thinking is part of our cultural language, but we don't have to accept it.

What is so interesting about her conclusion is how she defines "realism." She uses "realism" against the ideograph "positive thinking," but does not go into great detail about it. What she does say is interesting, however. She connects realism to the ability to see risks, have courage, and be prepared, all of which seem to reflect traditional American values.

prepared for hard times when they hit, because, according to the tenets of positive thinking, even to think of trouble is to bring it on.

Americans did not start out as deluded optimists. The original ethos, at least of white Protestant settlers and their descendants, was a grim Calvinism that offered wealth only through hard work and savings, and even then made no promises at all. You might work hard and still fail; you certainly wouldn't get anywhere by adjusting your attitude or dreamily "visualizing" success.

Calvinists thought "negatively," as we would say today, carrying a weight of guilt and foreboding that sometimes broke their spirits. It was in response to this harsh attitude that positive thinking arose—among mystics, lay healers and transcendentalists—in the 19th century, with its crowd-pleasing message that God, or the universe, is really on your side, that you can actually have whatever you want, if the wanting is focused enough.

When it comes to how we think, "negative" is not the only alternative to "positive." As the case histories of depressives show, consistent pessimism can be just as baseless and deluded as its opposite. The alternative to both is realism—seeing the risks, having the courage to bear bad news and being prepared for famine as well as plenty. We ought to give it a try.

After taking notes on this passage, Ashanti read back through the article and her notes and began writing a rhetorical analysis of it that would become part of her Controversy Analysis essay. Her analysis looks at how the ideograph "realism" is used against the value of "positive thinking" and analyzes how Ehrenreich uses this keyword to persuade her audience. As you read the analysis of this following article, you should note that this analysis is part of a longer controversy analysis. As Ashanti developed this paper further, she incorporated six other sources and compared and contrasted the arguments of these sources.

Ashanti's Ideographic Analysis of "The Power of Negative Thinking"

Many writers have pointed to problems with economic regulation as leading to the economic collapse, but very few have thought about the patterns of thought or attitudes might have led to the current economic crisis. In the short article "The Power of Negative Thinking," Ehrenreich points to the ideology of positive thinking that runs throughout our culture and argues that this ideology is partially to blame for how ill-prepared our society was for economic hard times. Ehrenreich shows how this ideology is everywhere in our society and challenges her audience to see beyond this ideology and to take on a more realistic view of our current situation. By pointing to cultural examples that her audience can easily relate to, she shows just how prevalent positive thinking is in our society, and how it shapes our behavior. Central to her argument is the way in which this thinking has invaded the world of work: "Everyone knows that you won't get a job paying more than $15 an hour unless you're a 'positive person,'" (6). The power of this statement lies in the fact that many in her audience would recognize this belief. In addition, she develops her argument by showing how historically we have not held to the ideology of positive thinking. By showing how this concept developed in response to the negative thinking of Calvinism, she shows her readers that this belief in positive thinking is subject to revision and change as well. Her ability to show where this ideology comes from and how prevalent it is in our society enables Ehrenreich to powerfully communicate her message without alienating her audience. If her audience has bought into positive thinking, it is because their society has required it and not because they are easily fooled. What is perhaps most interesting about her argument against "positive thinking" is her solution to this problem. She argues that we should replace the ideals of positive thinking with realism, which she defines as "seeing the risks, having the courage to bear bad news, and being prepared for famine as well as plenty" (6). Her argument for realism is fascinating because it taps into her audience's cultural ideas about individualism, or what it is to be a self-reliant American. The definition that she gives of realism reminds her readers of the rugged values that we associate with those who settled and expanded America. In this sense, she replaces the ideology of "positive thinking" with the ideology of "self-reliance."

This message would resonate with many of her readers. However, her discussion of realism is so short, and the term realism can be defined in so many different ways, that perhaps the greatest strength of her argument or rhetoric is its criticism of "positive thinking." Without a more detailed discussion of realism, her audience has little direction for addressing the problems other than bearing up to bad news well. It seems like replacing the ideograph "positive thinking" with the ideograph "realism" just does not tell readers much about how the economy might be addressed more effectively.

Ashanti's analysis focused upon two ideographs, but you may find that you focus upon just one in an analysis. While you are writing your controversy analysis, the key is not to look for ideographs in each of your sources. Instead, you are looking out for sources that draw upon ideographs to tap into the cultural values and beliefs of their audiences. In Ashanti's case, she was able to show how Ehrenreich was able to tap into her audience's beliefs in self-reliance and American individualism to argue against the idea that positive thinking should govern the way we respond to the economic crisis. Not all articles that you find will use ideographs that are this readily recognizable. They will all, however, draw upon some cultural values to develop their public messages about the controversy.

Wordle™: Using a Software Tool to Help You Spot Repeated Terms

Looking for cultural values and ideographs requires close reading of the text, and there are no quick tricks or technological tools that can substitute for this close reading. However, there is one free piece of software that can provide starting points for ideographic analysis. One interesting way to look for heavily repeated terms in a text is to use the free application Wordle, which you can access by visiting the Wordle homepage: http://www.wordle.net. Wordle is a web-based application that is designed to create "beautiful word clouds" from text. These clouds, as you see on the following page, are made up of the different words from the text you paste into Wordle. The software allows you to paste in any text, even book-length texts. Created by Jonathan Feinberg, Worldle works on principles that we have identified as being important for locating ideographs and it places heavily repeated words in larger fonts. Take a look at the example that I created by pasting in the excerpt from Reagan's "First Inaugural."

As you look at the Wordle below, notice the prominence of words like "positive" and "motivational." This Wordle reflects some of the words that frame the major arguments of Ehrenreich's article and Ashanti's analysis. Since it singles out only single words that are repeated prominently, we don't see some ideographs that might be phrases, so we might think of Wordle as a software tool that we can use to find heavily repeated words, but not as a tool that substitutes for our own critical reading. For example, one word of vital importance in the article that did not pop up in the Wordle is "realism." While some repeated words might not be ideographs, they nevertheless help us see the most repeated and important concepts in the speech. You will often find that Wordle can also present surprises, such as the prominence given to the word "believe."

Screen capture from Wordle.net, used according to the terms of the website found at: http://www.wordle.net/faq#use

Wordle can help us notice important terms like these. However, it takes our own analysis and close reading to fully determine whether this repeated word is an ideograph and to interpret why it is potentially significant to the author's argument. This is something that no piece of software can do, so as you use Wordle, you must keep in mind that it is no substitute for your own analysis.

Conclusion

Now that you have several tools for analyzing cultural contexts, think about how you might utilize this method in the texts that you encounter in public, private, and academic life. Here are some ideas to get you started.

1. This idea is adapted from Bruce McComiskey's book *Teaching Composition as a Social Process*. Visit a university's web page and click on the tab "For Prospective Students." Take a moment to read the materials about the university, its mission, student life, and the opportunities that the university affords you. As you read, look for ideographs about education, students, and the role of the university in the larger community. What do these ideographs say about the type of students that would be "ideal" for this university or who would ideally fulfill the university's mission? What do the ideographs that you find say about the way that the university views its students or its role? What do the ideographs say about the world outside of the university?

2. Reread the introduction of this textbook and look for ideographs of education and writing. What ideographs of learning, the role of study, the role of the writer, do you find? What values about education do these ideographs represent? How are the ideographs used to make the argument of the introduction? Are there contrasting ideographs or values that you believe you could use against these arguments?

3. Visit a corporate website of your choice. Click on their mission statement and any other documents that represent their public policies. What ideographs do you encounter? How are they used to enhance the ethos of the corporation? Look for contrasting ideographs or values that you believe you could use against these arguments here as well.

Works Cited

Aristotle. *On Rhetoric: A Theory of Civic Discourse*. Trans. George A. Kennedy. New York: Oxford UP, 1991. Print.

McComiskey, Bruce. *Teaching Composition as a Social Process*. Logan, UT: Utah State University Press, 2000. Print.

McGee, Michael Calvin. "The 'Ideograph': A Link Between Rhetoric and Ideology." *Contemporary Rhetorical Theory: A Reader*. Eds. John Louis Lucaites, Celeste Michelle Condit, and Sally Caudill. New York: The Guilford Press, 1999. 425–441. Print.

Williams, Raymond. "Culture." *Keywords: A Vocabulary of Culture and Society*. Revised Ed. New York: Oxford, 1983. 87–93. Print.

Chapter 11

Student Examples: Controversy Analysis Essays

By Carol Nowotny-Young

Introduction

The following essays were written by four students who took English 102 in the spring semester of 2010. Just like you, they were assigned to choose an issue they wanted to know more about, narrow their focus to a specific aspect of the issue, formulate a thesis question representing that aspect of the issue, and research the arguments answering the thesis question. Then they had to analyze the arguments, showing the strengths and weaknesses of each argument. Finally, they indicated which argument seemed the strongest based on their analysis.

As you read each of the essays, analyze how the writer puts it together. Use the following questions to help you:

• Find the thesis question. Does it give an accurate focus of what the essay discusses?

• Note how the introductory paragraphs lead into the thesis question by providing context for the issue and give an overview of the range of arguments. Does the introduction provide enough context? Do you have a good sense of how the writer will focus on the issue?

• As you read each paragraph in the essay, make a list of the arguments being presented. What has the writer focused on in the analysis of the argument? Has the writer given a thorough and fair analysis of it?

- What argument does the writer choose as the most effective? Is this choice justified by the analysis given to it? Does it bring the essay to a logical and satisfying conclusion?

- What do you think works really well in the essay? What would you advise the writer to revise?

If your instructor gave you somewhat different directions for your essay, how could each of the essays be revised to meet the requirements of your assignment? Analyzing the student essays will help you to figure out what you want to do in your essay and how to structure it.

Angelica Almader
English 102, 107
Essay 2: Controversy Analysis

Ecotourism: Benefit or Detriment?

Many of us enjoy traveling throughout various parts of the world, visiting other places, and learning about new cultures. As we vacation to distant areas, one thing that we may not be aware of is the impact that we, as tourists, have on the other countries' environments and economies. It is for this reason that various organizations have begun implementing ecotourism vacations as an alternative to the standard form of vacationing. According to the website of the International Ecotourism Society, ecotourism is defined specifically as "responsible travel to natural areas that conserves the environment and improves the well-being of local people." In this sense, ecotourism is often related to sustainable development: the core concept of sustainable development is to reduce human impacts so that global ecosystems can continue to sustain human life and societies indefinitely. Most ecotourism programs claim to offer travel accommodations that promote environmental and cultural awareness. The main difference between an ordinary tourist and an ecotourist is that an ecotourist is theoretically conserving the environment while visiting foreign areas and is more cautious of the natural surroundings. Many conventional tourists pay large sums of money to stay in luxurious resorts, which in some countries is threatening the environment and not helping the local people economically. The concern then becomes to investigate whether or not many of these programs are actually benefitting the developing countries as much as they claim to be. For this reason, I have decided to implement further research regarding ecotourism to find out what the certain financial and ecological effects are. Does it really come as an environmental and economic advantage to poor countries to have ecotourists visit, or is ecotourism providing the same outcome as ordinary tourists?

To begin with, one of the predominant supporters of ecotourism is the International Ecotourism Society (IES). The IES website portrays a strong belief that ecotourism significantly helps a country's development. They heavily focus on their ability to promote ecotourism and its effectiveness. The website claims that "for the world's 40 poorest countries, tourism is the second most important source of foreign exchange, after oil." The IES also emphasizes their interest in educating individuals through workshops. We are given a description of a workshop in El Salvador, which "featured international experts representing the Convention on Biological Diversity and the U.S. Agency for International Development…" The website instructs us that there are more than 50 national and international certification programs for sustainable tourism, and more are being created every year. In order to demonstrate their commitment to sustainability, these programs must meet "social and environmental standards created by leading third-party certification programs." Even though the website includes supporting facts for how much ecotourism contributes to poor countries, there are no credible sources related to these statistics. The website also fails to directly inform us of the specific countries that ecotourism has been favorable for; therefore, we don't know if it has truly been beneficial to anyone. The claims that are made by the website are broad and lack specific examples, so we cannot be convinced that they are completely true. On the other hand, the website did include dependable organizations that are involved in the process of promoting ecotourism. This leads us to believe that the IES is indeed a legitimate association with the right intentions for promoting their concepts. In spite of this, it seems as though the IES has failed to provide concrete evidence of ecotourism's success.

In addition to this idea of ecotourism benefitting countries environmentally, Doctor Genoveva Millan Vasquez de la Torre and Eva Agudo Gutierrez have written about the economic benefits for a rural area in Spain. Doctor Genoveva Millan Vasquez de la Torre and Eva Agudo Gutierrez are professors in the Business and Economic Sciences Faculty of the University of Cordoba and have performed different econometric studies on the tourist area in the province of Cordoba. Their article concentrates on the regions that are provided with additional income and stable employment as a result of ecotourism. De la Torre and Gutierrez recognize that ecotourism contributes to the reduction of poverty and to income redistribution and also create the notion that if a tourist wishes to stay in contact with the natural environment, ecotourism is the right choice (113). The two authors focus their research on a natural park in southern Spain and demonstrate the dependency that the local people have on ecotourists. We are given visual references in their article, such as a graph of the staff employed in rural tourism in Andalusia. This graph indicates that there has been a steady increase in the amount of employees through the year 2006 (115). The two researchers also include statistics from a survey that was conducted in Andalusia in 2004; their results exhibited that over 50% of the local population revealed an economic reliance on ecotourists (116). This certainly gives the article dependability because all the data is credibly cited. The authors' background experience also serves as a strong point for their line of reasoning.

Nevertheless, the authors display weakness in proving their argument by the limitations present in their research. There was only one small rural area that was examined, so we aren't given a complete perspective of the economic effects of ecotourism. It is entirely possible that a largely populated area would have different consequences following the implementation of ecotourism, compared to a small-populated area.

In contrast to the suggestion that ecotourism is beneficial, Martha Honey's article concerning Costa Rica takes the position that ecotourism does not help the environment whatsoever. Martha Honey is the Executive Director of the Center on Ecotourism and Sustainable Development. In her article, Honey clearly informs us that "what is currently being served up as ecotourism includes a mixture of three rather distinct phenomena: 'greenwashing' scams, ecotourism 'lite' and real ecotourism" (43). Her article contains different examples of hotels claiming to be eco-friendly, but in reality are full of the lavish resort-style accommodations of regular tourism hotels. A specific example that she mentions was from a magazine entitled *Green Luxury*, which bragged that ecotourism will meet the high life in a luxury beach resort (43). The project's main developer boasted that "environmental considerations [were] an integral part of the design," which included a system of yellow lights designed not to disturb the leatherback turtles as they lay their eggs (43). Honey later came to understand that this was all completely untrue; some scientists in Costa Rica educated her that any lights at all on a beach will scare away turtles looking for a nesting area. Honey also brings up the fact that virtually everything in Costa Rica seems to carry "eco" in its name, such as, "eco-playa (a typical beach indistinguishable from other gray-black sand beaches) and 'Ecological Rent-A-Car' (which rents the same vehicles as Hertz, Budget, or Avis)" (43). Her article targets the ecotourism programs that have little to no effect in actually protecting the environment. Consequently, the purpose of her research is to find the instances where ecotourism has failed to abide by its original intentions. For this reason, Honey's article loses credibility in the sense that it establishes a bias. She begins her article informing us that the concept of ecotourism has been completely washed out. She does not attempt to illustrate any of the occasions in which ecotourism has been proven to be advantageous. Honey also fails to investigate other countries; instead, she dedicates her studies strictly to Costa Rica. Again, this prevents us from being able to compare the ecotourism effects among different locations. Conversely, Honey's article was effective in bringing about the realization that some organizations are clearly not following the initial principles of ecotourism. She has discovered that companies will attempt to attract more commerce by including the prefix "eco" in their business name. This is important to recognize because it provides awareness for future ecotourists looking into different organizations.

Following this suspicion of ecotourism having negative effects, Eric Jaffe, a science writer, also offers his own explanations for how ecotourism harms the environment. Jaffe explains that although it is designed to be an ecologically responsible mode of travel, studies show that ecotourism may actually harm the wildlife and natural environments it seeks to protect (80). He describes the ways in which the presence of tourists in remote, uninhabited areas causes harm due to the litter and pollution caused by tourists, and how human disturbance affects animal behavior and breeding patterns (80). Jaffe also informs us that "the increased crowds lead to populations changes in some animals, such as the Humboldt penguin" (81). He explains that the penguins would sooner abandon their nests than risk personal harm, such as from an approaching human. As a result, the large numbers of ecotourists coming in cause many of the nests to be abandoned, and the chicks usually die. We are also informed of a mounting garbage problem caused by over-visitation by turtle viewers that threatens the beaches of Tortuguero in Costa Rica (81). Jaffe's studies provide reliable evidence largely due to his position as a science writer. He clearly has experience in this field and has conducted large amounts of research. The research that Jaffe has carried out has taken place in different parts of the world, so we are given a global view of the various effects of ecotourism. Jaffe's studies do not limit us to one certain place, and he includes the human effect on animals in these areas. Yet, his article lacks credibility in the sense that he does not distinguish the difference between ecotourism and traditional tourism. He makes it appear as though the two types of tourism produce the same outcomes, which doesn't help us to differentiate their individual effects.

Furthermore, Ralf Buckley, director of the International Centre for Ecotourism Research in the School of Environmental and Applied Science at Griffith University, utilizes the data from different case studies conducted throughout various parts of the world to examine certain issues regarding ecotourism. Buckley acknowledges that in order to implement sustainable development there is a requirement of unprecedented changes to human population, lifestyle and behavior (219). Through all of his case studies, Buckley was able to determine that ecotourism certainly is a good starting point to helping preserve the natural world. In his own words he says, "Ecotourism is a potential tool to improve sustainability by modifying human social behavior in regard to environmental conservation" (219). In his research he acknowledges that regular tourism has detrimental impacts on the environment, but feels that "ecotourism may be able to provide models to reduce these impacts" (219). Buckley also makes the realization that even though ecotourism may be successful on a local level in terms of economic, social, and environmental matters, it sometimes has no effect globally. The predominant strength that is present in Buckley's article is his ability to remain neutral. He does not reveal a bias toward any particular side and offers explanations for both types of tourism. Through his research we are exposed to both the positive and negative effects of ecotourism, which are supported by his own professional investigations. Buckley also establishes dependability through his assortment of case studies and his extensive background on the subject. Since he conducts these studies in various parts of the world, there is diversity in his research.

Overall, it is evident that there is an ongoing debate on the topic of ecotourism. We have observed that there are some individuals who strongly believe in ecotourism as a mechanism to conserve the environment, and there are also individuals who believe the exact opposite. There are many different perspectives that have been uncovered in my research, and each perspective has its own individual strong points and its own individual flaws. Ralf Buckley's research proved to have the most integrity, deeming it the most reliable and successful source. Since Buckley was able to combine his scientific background with his ability to remain impartial, his book provided consistent conclusions. He didn't take his investigation to the extreme by creating a one-sided argument; instead, he offered justifications from multiple standpoints. Buckley allowed us as readers to maintain open minds and decide ecotourism's degree of benefit for ourselves. He did not attempt to compel us to his ways of thinking by swarming us with his own personal opinions. In this sense, Buckley presented us with logical rationalizations that ecotourism can certainly be of assistance on a local level, but does not produce the same effect on an international level.

Works Cited

Buckley, Ralf. "Significance and Context: Ecotourism and Sustainability." *Case Studies in Ecotourism*. Cambridge, MA: CABI Publishing, 2003. 219–250. Netlibrary.com: University Of Arizona Library eContent Collection. Web. 15 March 2010.

Gutierrez, Eva A., and Genoveva Millan Vasquez de la Torre. *Tourism Development: Growth, Myths and Inequalities*. Ed. Peter M. Burns and Marina Novelli. Cambridge, MA: CAB International, 2008. Print.

Honey, Martha. "Giving a Grade to Costa Rica's Green Tourism." *NACLA Report on the Americas* 36.6 (May/June 2003): 39–47. Web. 15 March 2010.

Jaffe, Eric. *What Is the Impact of Tourism?* Ed. Roman Espejo. Farmington Hills, MI: Greenhaven Press, 2009. Print.

What Is Ecotourism? The International Ecotourism Society. 6 April 2010. Web. 15 March 2010.

Kristi Kawamoto
Carol Nowotny-Young
English 102–107
7 April 2010

Cell Phones: A Potentially Fatal Means of Communication?

With 225 million Americans using cell phones (Goldman), it is crucial to understand what impacts they can have on health. As part of the American culture, it seems as if cell phones are appearing in more places to allow us to communicate with one another. However, with the increase of technology use, are there any major disadvantages? In recent years, many people have debated whether or not cell phone use causes cancer. Although many studies have been conducted, there has been no proven definitive answer as to how cell phones impact the user's health. In addition, it is difficult to test the effects of cell phones on the human body because testing is limited to short-term effects due to the fact that cell phones were not largely used in the United States until the 1990's (American Cancer Society). Nonetheless, many people are still wary of using cell phones even with the remote possibility that they could cause cancer. Does the need to be technologically connected outweigh the risk of there being a correlation between cell phones and cancer? With technology being used more and more every day, this controversy is an important topic that could heavily impact American society.

In an article titled "Cell-Phone Safety," Bryan Walsh explains the conflicting arguments as to whether or not cell phones are hazardous to the human body, but seems to think that they are generally unsafe. According to the article, there have been many studies that prove that cell phones are actually safe. However, scientists are still concerned because they feel that the studies "are inadequate and too often weighted toward the wireless industry's interests" (Walsh). Because this article was published in *Time* magazine, it is geared towards an educated American audience. In effect, many of the people who read this magazine probably have a cell phone and may be interested in what the author says. This article is effective due to its use of logical appeal, hard data and quotes from experts. By stating that people need to be careful with cell phones due to a cancer risk, the article is logically appealing to the audience. It leads the audience to wonder if they should continue using a cell phone if it is emitting dangerous waves. It employs scientific studies as a way of showing the audience that the topic is well researched and also includes an expert opinion so that the audience trusts the author. However, this article fails to give enough credit to studies that show a strong positive correlation between cell phones and cancer. Nearly all of the examples and scientific studies that were used state that the studies were inconclusive due the fact that brain tumors would take a much longer time to grow than what the studies allowed. In addition, many of the examples that were used did not have consistent results, which then led the scientists to believe that there is no correlation. The overall stance of the article is that although there has been no definitive answer as to whether or not cell phones negatively impact health, it is important to take precautions. This article is effective because it presents both sides of the controversy, but it is weakened by the lack of conclusive evidence.

On the other hand, *Popular Science* makes a strong link between cell phones and cancer. *Popular Science* published an article about a large study called Interphone showing a strong link between cell phones and cancer. The article by Melinda Wenner and titled "Last Call?" states that researchers in Israel "found that people who use cellphones regularly are 50 percent more likely than non-users to develop brain tumors" (Wenner). Although many scientists claim that it is impossible for cell phones to cause cancer due to the low amount of radiation, the researchers in the Interphone study realized that cell phones have the power to change cells into uncontrolled growths (Wenner). The article is very effective because there are statistics and the language is simple to understand. Because the audience is able to understand the article's wording while also being able to see hard evidence from the studies, they have a better understanding of the study. In addition, the article not only focuses on the positive points of the study, but it also identifies its weaknesses. By claiming that the study has imperfections, the author shows the audience that the viewpoint is not completely biased. This article appeals to the reader because it looks at the situation realistically by saying that even if there are proven risks, some people will simply not stop using their cell phones. Although this article is very strong in effectiveness, there is one main weakness. The Interphone study was conducted in a variety of different countries, but the article fails to point out the results of many of the countries. It gives only two of the results, which leads the audience to believe that the other results may not have shown any link between cell phones and cancer. The failure to address the results from the other countries is a major downfall for the article and gives less credibility to the study making it seem somewhat biased.

Both Wenner and Glazer lead the audience to think that cell phones are probably unsafe, but Glazer provides more circumstances under which they could possibly be harmful. According to "Do They Cause Cancer and Car Accidents?" by Sarah Glazer, the radiation limits can differ according to how the person holds the cell phone and how close the cell phone is to the person's head. The article claims, "A phone can pass the FCC's requirements when tested in one position but exceed those maximum levels when held in another position" (Glazer). The article doubts the safety of cell phones and leaves the audience unsure as to whether or not they should use a cell phone. The strengths of this article include using statistics and examples of people who believe that cancer is caused by cell phones. This article states how cell phones could possibly be safe under certain circumstances but be very dangerous when held in other positions. In addition, at the beginning of the article there is an example of how a man went to court claiming that a cell phone caused his wife's brain cancer that eventually lead to her death (Glazer). By appealing to the audience's emotions, the article is more effective and shows the effects that cell phones can have on relationships and families. A few of the weaknesses of the article include the lack of evidence that shows a negative relationship among cell phones and cancer and its limited examples. Nearly all of the examples that Glazer uses infer a positive correlation between cell phones and cancer, which leaves many of the audience's questions unanswered. The audience does not know of any studies which found no correlation, and the author does not address the objections of those who strongly believe that there is no link between cell phones and cancer. Although this article presents some strong facts, it is biased due to the lack of evidence strongly showing no relationship between cell phones and cancer, which therefore gives less credibility to the author. In addition, the article only has a few examples which supported the author's argument, thus leading the audience to believe that perhaps there is not enough evidence to definitively say that cell phones cause cancer. However, the author makes inferences within the article that cell phones do cause cancer. Although seemingly unbiased, due to the limited, one-sided view of the controversy Glazer appears to believe that cell phones do cause cancer. This article is effective in some points, but does not address a few important concerns.

In contrast, "Cell Phones and Brain Tumors: No Connection?" by Bill Hendrick explains a study that was conducted that showed no link between cell phones and cancer. The article states, "They could find no substantial change in the incidence trend of brain tumors among a study group of 60,000 people five to 10 years after cell phone usage rose sharply in the countries where they lived" (Hendrick). In addition, this article shows how the U.S. Food and Drug Administration and the American Cancer Society found no correlation between cell phones and cancer. However, the author suggests that people who use their cell phones frequently should be studied for more time. This article is strong in that it uses well-known organizations that support their claim. The author gains more credibility because the audience has most likely heard about the U.S. Food and Drug Administration and the American Cancer Society. Many people would find both the FDA and the American Cancer Society as reliable sources because they are responsible for ensuring public safety. Also, the reader's impression of these organizations would most likely be positive because oftentimes they conduct research and studies. Therefore, the audience would tend to agree with what the author says due to the sources he incorporates. In addition, one of the article's strengths is that it addresses how the two organizations could improve their studies. Because the article states that there are faults and ways to better the studies, the audience is more apt to believe the author. However, this article fails to give multiple examples that show a disassociation between cell phones and cancer. The author merely mentions one study and the claims of a few well-known organizations. Because the author limits the evidence to only one study, the article is somewhat ineffective in that it does not provide the audience with enough information on the topic. Also, the article is a bit confusing, and the organization and structure is not clearly defined. Therefore, it is difficult for the audience to follow what the author is saying. If the information and claims were constructed in an organized fashion, the article would be significantly more effective. Another main weakness is that one of the studies found that there was no link in data on over 59,000 men and women between the ages of 20–79 (Hendrick). This is a fault in the article because in the 21st century, many cell phone users are children under the age of 20. The author would lose credibility because the article does not address that more research is to be done with children and cell phones.

After reading several articles and researching this topic, I think that the evidence is stronger that cell phones may possibly be linked to cancer. Wenner's article seems to provide the best evidence that cell phones could cause cancer due to its overall effectiveness. The article employed claims from scientists while also addressing the faults in the research. Even though this article failed to give the results of the Interphone study in other countries, the findings that the author reveals strongly suggest a link between cell phones and cancer. It is also important to remember that not enough studies have been done on those who have used cell phones for more than 10 years. Therefore, it may be safe to use a cell phone for a few years, but the results may be very different for those who use a cell phone for 20 years. In addition, it appears that not enough studies took note of how heavily people use their cell phones. As cell phones become more popular as a means of communicating, people will most likely talk on their cell phones more, which is a factor that needs to be considered in studies. Even with the remote possibility of cell phones causing cancer, one would think that people would simply stop using their cell phones. However, as cell phones have become such an integral part of society, it is difficult for people to not have a way to communicate. Although cell phones may not seem harmful now, it may possibly be too late by the time scientists make new or more concrete discoveries. Other activities that scientists have linked to cancer still exist in the American society. For example, people still smoke and go to tanning salons (Reinberg). Therefore, do cell phones really pose enough of a problem that Americans would stop using them? Perhaps this question may be answered in the near future.

Works Cited

"ACS: Cellular Phones." *American Cancer Society*. Web. 9 Mar. 2010.

Glazer, Sarah. "Cell Phone Safety." *CQ Researcher* 11.10 (2001): 201-224. CQ Researcher. 16 Mar. 2001. Web. 5 Mar. 2010.

Goldman, Russell, and Matt Spector. "Cancer Controversy Causes Consumer Confusion." *ABC News*. 24 July 2008. Web. 27 Feb. 2010.

Hendrick, Bill. "Cell Phones and Brain Tumors: No Connection?" *WebMD*. 3 Dec. 2009. Web. 05 Mar. 2010.

Reinberg, Steven. "FDA Panel Weighs New Restrictions on Tanning Beds—Health News Health.com." *Health News*. 25 Mar. 2010. Web. 30 Mar. 2010.

Walsh, Bryan. "Cell-Phone Safety." *Time* 175.10 (2010): 47–49. Print.

Wenner, Melinda. "LAST CALL?" *Popular Science* 274.1 (2009): 46–47. Print.

Krystal Jenkins
ENG 102
4/05/10

Saving the Journalism Industry

The concept of the freedom of the press was established by the founding fathers of America long ago. Many people underestimate the importance of this section of the First Amendment, and in doing so they disregard the journalism industry as something that is dispensable. However, that is not the case because without journalism and journalists the public would remain largely uninformed about many issues that are central to living in a democracy. As stated in the book *The Elements of Journalism* by Bill Kovach and Tom Rosenstiel, "The purpose of journalism is to provide people with the information they need to be free and self-governing" (Kovach and Rosenstiel 5). This statement is the key to understanding how the journalism industry interacts with the public and the important role that they hold within American society. Today, there is a huge problem threatening the future of journalism as well as the future of America. With a decline in readership of print newspapers along with a lack of revenue from online advertising, there is an overall decline in profit for journalists. This means that newspapers all around the country are being forced to stop production, or at the very least lay off multiple employees; there are even some people who believe that eventually newspapers will all become extinct. While many economists thought that the industry would recover as the economy did, that is clearly not the case. If the crisis will not fix itself, then that means someone needs to take action. What are some of the possible solutions to the current crisis facing major newspapers such as *The New York Times* and *The Washington Post*, as well as the rest of the journalism industry?

One solution to the journalism crisis is that newspapers receive government subsidies. In an article written in *The Nation*, this solution is discussed. John Nichols and Robert W. McChesney support the idea that newspapers should be given government subsidies just as every other vital industry in America is. In their article, "How to Save Journalism," not only do the authors present the idea, they also explain how to do this, why it is necessary, and how it will be effective. By drawing a parallel to the use of government money in the journalism industry in America's past history, the authors shows a serious problem that could even be called an injustice. In the 1840's the subsidy for the journalism industry was around 30 billion dollars; today, it is only about 400 million dollars (Nichols and McChesney 14). Nichols and McChesney see that allocating more money for journalism would keep the industry alive because it can no longer support itself. Also, by showing the history of America and the importance of subsidies in journalism in the past, they strengthen the argument. Giving real-life examples as to why handing out subsidies to the journalism industry is responsible and important rather than just giving well-educated assumptions or suppositions gives the source credibility. Not only does this article discuss why using subsidies would work best, it also shows why other solutions are not as strong. For example, "Too many contemporary observers continue to fantasize that it is just a matter of time before a new generation of entrepreneurs creates a financially viable model of journalism using digital technologies"; the article then goes on to say that this solution is not a solution at all, but rather wishful thinking (Nichols and McChesney 13). By evaluating other solutions as well as their own the credibility of their argument is reinforced. This shows that they do not simply pay attention to their personal opinion of what the solution should be, but they also look at and explain the flaws of other sources' solutions, thus proving that theirs is a better option.

However, there is also a major weakness in their argument. The authors are opposed to giving the subsidies to commercialized and mainstream media and want to focus on the nonprofit sources of media more. When a resolution begins to leave out certain sections of the affected population, it could lead to a question of whether or not it is an act of discrimination or bias. The fact that the solution excludes some areas of the journalism industry makes the argument weaker.

Another solution to the journalism crisis is that with the support of Americans, not the government, newspapers will survive. However, they will not make the same amount of revenue that they are used to. This argument is presented in the article, "The Reconstruction of American Journalism." There are many strengths in this argument, such as a very detailed step-by-step way to support the original media that fosters democracy. By showing the public an exact way to execute the solution, the authors are more likely to elicit higher participation and feedback from their readers because in times of crisis people want to be told what to do and how it will fix the current problem. This step-by-step solution shows the people that this source is confident in its plan by telling the readers what their actions will accomplish. Using a cause-and-effect sort of situation will influence people to follow the set plan because they are able to see what the end result will be. Another strength in this article's argument is the fact that it mentions multiple solutions. The authors do not simply discount the other solutions, but they instead show how each solution could work and compare it to the one they are advocating for. For example, this article talks about how the technology revolution changed the journalism industry for the worse, and that if newspapers stopped posting an online publication, Americans would be forced to read print papers. The authors show that while this sounds easy and credible, it is actually quite unrealistic (Downie and Schudson 31). According to another source, *New Media & Society*, "A recent study by the Pew Research Center in Washington, DC, shows that a large (and apparently increasing) percentage of Americans are turning to the Internet for breaking news" (Pavlik 59). Such a large percentage of readers looking online makes it even more difficult for publications not to report news via the internet. One of the major weaknesses in this argument is the amount of effort it will require. Many of the actions the authors suggest are complicated and beyond the common person's level of interest. Therefore, people will be less inclined to participate, and the solution will ultimately fail.

One last solution to the crisis in the journalism industry is that there is no solution. In "Don't Blame the Journalism," Paul Farhi believes that there is nothing Americans can do to stop the failing print media: "Could smarter reporting, editing, and photojournalism have made a difference? Can a spiffy new Web site or paper design win the hearts of readers? Surely, they can't hurt. But if we, and our critics, were realistic, we'd admit that much is beyond our control" (Farhi 15). A strength in this article is that fact that the author uses ethos to appeal to the reader's emotions. Ethos is designed to make the reader feel included in the author's argument. This approach can cause the audience to feel more comforted and therefore more likely to agree with the solution Farhi is suggesting. For example, "I suspect someday our former readers will be peering forlornly towards their empty doorsteps and driveways and wondering where the paper they once loved has gone" (Farhi 15). By giving this image, Farhi makes his readers more inclined to agree with his opinion. A very big weakness in this argument is the fact that there are no facts to support the author's claims. It is almost as if the author is not sure himself that newspapers will disappear altogether. This makes Farhi's argument less credible.

Overall, each of the arguments has both strengths and weaknesses. All of the solutions are advocating and hoping for the same goal, to save the journalism industry and, through that, American democracy; their means of achieving it are just slightly different. The solution in the article "How to Save Journalism" by John Nichols and Robert W. McChesney is the one that seems the most credible and accomplishable. This article states that the journalism industry should receive subsidies in order to continue functioning properly. The authors show specific examples from the history of the United States that show the country has, in the past, supported the journalism industry with government subsidies. As well as examining their own solution, the authors also observed other proposed solutions and demonstrated why each was not as strong as the one that they presented.

Works Cited

Downie, Leonard, and Michael Schudson. "The Reconstruction of American Journalism." *Columbia Journalism Review* 48.4 (2009): 28–51. *Academic Search Complete*. Web. 10 Mar. 2010.

Farhi, Paul. "Don't Blame the Journalism." *American Journalism Review* 30.5 (2008): 14–15. *Academic Search Complete*. Web. 10 Mar. 2010.

Kovach, Bill, and Tom Rosenstiel. *The Elements of Journalism: What Newspeople Should Know and the Public Should Expect*. New York: Random House, 2001. Print.

Nichols, John, and Robert W. McChesney. "How to Save Journalism." *The Nation* 25 Jan. 2010: 11–16. *Academic Search Complete*. Web. 10 Mar. 2010.

Pavlik, John V. "New Media and News: Implications for the Future of Journalism." *New Media & Society* 1.1 (1999): 54–59. Print.

Michelle Faas
English 102
Controversy Analysis

Gun Rights or Gun Control?

Gun control has been considered an issue since the 1930's when the Bureau of Alcohol, Tobacco, and Firearms began regulating fully automatic weapons as a reaction to the Saint Valentine's Day Massacre in 1929. In recent decades, the issue of gun control has been considered a "hot button" issue. There are several different points of view on the subject; however, they all fit into either the gun rights or gun control categories. Gun rights advocates believe individuals have the right to bear arms, whereas gun control advocates believe there should be heavy regulation of the private ownership of firearms. Thus the question remains: what is the safest policy for private ownership and possession of firearms in the United States? Five different texts answer this question in various ways.

Joyce Lee Malcolm, author of *Guns & Violence*, is a gun rights advocate that has adopted the ideology that private ownership of guns and concealed weapons licenses invokes a sense of safety among citizens. Malcolm states, "Those who are armed protect themselves and others [...] simply knowing that some people are, and not knowing who, makes criminals hesitant to commit violent crimes" (252). Malcolm implies that people will feel safer knowing they or the people surrounding them are armed and ready to protect. This appeal to safety is an effective strategy to persuade people to support gun rights. Safety is an inherent issue most people are naturally concerned with; therefore by saying that guns provide safety, Malcolm is effectively appealing to her potential readers. Similarly, Malcolm points out, "In England fewer guns have meant more crime. In America more guns have meant less crime" (253). In this passage, Malcolm is providing somewhat of a cause-and-effect relationship for the reader. She tells the reader what happened in another country relatively similar to the United States when the opposite of her preferred policy is enacted. Again, she inspires fear in the reader by saying that a country that banned guns is less safe. This is effective because it ideally makes the reader desire the opposite policy of the country that is experiencing more crime. However, she also inspires hope in this passage by suggesting another cause-and-effect relationship to the reader: when people have guns, there is less crime. While there are very possibly other reasons for a reduction in crime, the reader doesn't think about that because she states the cause-and-effect relationship in such simple terms.

Although Malcolm effectively makes use of particular strategies, she also has some weaknesses. At particular spots in the text, her sentence structure makes it harder for the reader to understand. For example, she says, "Simply knowing that some people are, and not knowing who, makes criminals hesitant to commit violent crimes" (Malcolm 253). In this phrase she is referring to "knowing that some people are" carrying guns, but the way she words this is slightly awkward and not simple for the reader to understand. Another weakness Malcolm possesses is not addressing the opposite point of view, which in this case is support of gun control. She never presents potential counterarguments to her argument, which is ineffective because it indicates to the reader that she does not have an understanding of the other point of view. Also, by omitting potential counterarguments to her argument, it suggests that she may not feel confident enough that her argument would stand up in a debate.

James B. Jacobs, author of *Can Gun Control Work?* also believes in gun rights over gun control. Jacobs argues that private ownership of firearms is essential because it reduces crime, similarly to what Malcolm argued. According to Jacobs, "The private ownership of firearms provides a major social benefit if it deters crime. Even non gun owners benefit if potential criminals are dissuaded from committing crimes because they fear being shot by armed citizens" (15). Jacobs uses an appeal to safety here in order to persuade the reader to advocate for gun rights. Also, when Jacobs discusses the value of firearms, he effectively addresses potential counterarguments. First, he tells the reader what gun control advocates argue about private ownership of guns and their effect on crime (Jacobs 14), which is successful because it shows that he understands the opposite point of view and is confident enough with his argument to present opposing viewpoints. However, he takes this a step further by supplying the gun rights advocates' rebuttal to the gun control counterargument (Jacobs 15). This is highly effective because it shows the reader not only that he is confident in his argument, but also that to any challenge the opposing viewpoint may present, he can argue his point assertively. Another strategy Jacobs uses is definition of terms. He provides a definition of firearms, the different varieties of guns, and their uses (Jacobs 15). Defining terms is a great way to help the reader relate to the text and help increase their understanding. The final strategy Jacobs uses effectively is the use of statistics in his argument. Jacobs provides that "43 % of [interviewed inmates] reported that, at some point in their lives, they decided not to commit a crime because the victim possessed a weapon" (15). His use of statistics gives him credibility that the reader is likely to trust and therefore is more likely to believe his argument.

While Jacobs has many effective strategies, he has a weakness as well. Jacobs uses subtitles to "organize" his thoughts; however there really is no prominent theme within each subtitle. He jumps back and forth between topics in each subsection; therefore there is no actual organization. His use of subsections would be much more efficient if he stuck with a single theme, which would be advertized by the subtitle, because it would make his ideas easier to follow by the reader.

Warren Richey, writer for *The Christian Science Monitor*, wrote an article entitled "Supreme Court, Gun Control, and the Second Amendment: A Reckoning." Richey's argument, although subtle, is for gun rights. In the introduction of the article he states, "Gun-rights advocates are hoping for another landmark constitutional victory—this time extending an individual right to keep and bear arms in cities and towns across the country" (Richey). This is the only explicit indication as to what his point of view would be, since he omits the desires of gun control advocates in the introduction. To argue for gun rights, Richey examines past Supreme Court rulings and makes predictions on a current Supreme Court case that expects a ruling in June. He organizes his article by subsections, which is highly effective in this use. He defines standard of review in terms of gun rights in his first subsection. This is effective because it allows the reader to understand the references to cases he makes further on in the article. Also, in his subsections, he addresses what both gun rights advocates and gun control advocates want out of the case ruling. One major weakness of his argument is that it is almost too subtle. He spends most of his time talking about previous Supreme Court cases, and he writes about both arguments, but never passionately supports one. The fact that he only states what ruling gun rights advocates desire in his introduction and the fact that he only discusses Supreme Court case rulings that were in favor of gun rights advocates were the only indications of his stance on the issue. While his subtleness is a weakness, it is also somewhat effective only because many people do not like "in your face" arguments and people who are too aggressive; therefore, his argument is more of a suggestion, which many readers may feel more comfortable with.

"Something to Talk About," written by Eleanor Clift and Richard Wolffe, appeared in *Newsweek* in 2007. This article argues for gun control and states that a lack of gun regulation was a major reason for the Virginia Tech. shootings. Clift and Wolffe definitely use appeal to emotion in their article as an effective strategy. The article states that

> Hiring more cops wouldn't have stopped Cho Seung-Hui from purchasing the weapons he used in his shooting rampage—an uncomfortable fact that few people on Capitol Hill have rushed to point out. Democrats have been reluctant to even scold the president for allowing the assault ban to lapse, which enabled Cho to buy large capacity clips that were illegal under [a] previous law. (Clift and Wolffe)

The Virginia Tech. shootings are still a "fresh wound" in the United States, and referencing them as a result of a lack of gun control is a highly effective way to convince readers that gun control advocacy is the safe and right argument. Another strategy they use is invoking fear in the reader. They mention how easily someone with a mental illness could purchase firearms. Mentally ill people are highly unstable, and reminding the readers that unstable individuals can possess firearms as easily as "average" individuals is more than slightly scary. Invoking fear in the reader is extremely effective in getting the audience to act in the writers' favors. Readers will feel unsafe in their current situation and will therefore advocate for a change, which in this case would be to put more restrictions on the possession of firearms. Although Wolffe and Clift are effective in their strategy of emotional appeal, they have flaws in their argument. They never touch on what a gun rights advocate would argue about the shootings or gun control laws, which implies they are not familiar with the other argument and they are not confident in their argument.

The final text, written by Gregory Curfman, Stephen Morrissey, and Jeffrey Drazen, appeared in *The New England Journal of Medicine*. "Handgun Violence, Public Health, and the Law" argues that firearms commonly cause death and injury; therefore, the government should regulate in a way that is conducive to public safety. The writers of the article use three main strategies to effectively get their point across to the reader. First, they give a call to action: "By any standard, [the large number of firearm fatalities and injuries] constitutes a serious public health issue that demands a response... from law enforcement and the courts" (Curfman, Morrissey, and Drazen). In this phrase they demand that something needs to be done. The call-to-action approach is effective because it inspires a desire for change in the reader, which in this case would be to advocate for gun control. The second strategy is the use of appeal to public safety. They talk about how a lack of regulation of guns is a major cause for the extreme number of firearm deaths. This is successful because it inspires the reader to advocate for gun control in order to protect themselves and others. The final effective strategy they utilize is the use of statistics. The provide that "[There is] one death from firearms every 17 minutes and one death or nonfatal injury every 5 minutes" (Curfman, Morrissey, and Drazen). The use of statistics is greatly effective in supplying them with credibility on the subject by showing the facts. The statistics also invoke fear in the reader because, in less blunt terms, their content is implying that guns equal death.

The weakness of the argument is that there is absolutely no mention of any other viewpoints in the text. Again, this is a significant flaw because the reader is unsure as to whether or not the authors actually have a decent enough knowledge of the issue. The argument would be much more effective with mention of the other viewpoint and possible counterarguments.

While there are only two view points on the issue of firearms, gun control or gun rights, the authors all have a particular twist on their arguments that make them unique. Out of these five texts, James Jacobs' *Can Gun Control Work?* is by far the most effective argument presented. While all of the texts supply both effective and ineffective strategies, Jacobs has the largest number of effective strategies; therefore, he presents the most convincing and successful argument.

Works Cited

Clift, Eleanor, and Richard Wolffe. "Something to Talk About." *Newsweek*. Newsweek Magazine, 30 April 2007. Web. 27 March 2010.

Curfman, Gregory, Jeffrey Drazen, and Stephen Morrissey. "Handgun Violence, Public Health, and the Law." *The New England Journal of Medicine*. 358.14 (2008): 1503–1504. Web. 27 March 2010.

Jacobs, James. *Can Gun Control Work?* New York: Oxford University Press, 2002. Print.

Malcolm, Joyce. *Guns and Violence*. Cambridge, Massachusetts: Harvard University Press, 2002. Print

Richey, Warren. "Supreme Court, Gun Control, and the Second Amendment: A Reckoning." *The Christian Science Monitor* (2010). Web. 10 March 2010.

Readings in Controversy

Introduction

The following readings present two controversy clusters, one concerning the reason for the economic collapse of 2007–2008, and the other focused on the health care reform debate, as follows:

Controversy Cluster A: Economic Collapse of 2007–2008	Controversy Cluster B: Health Care Reform
"The Power of Negative Thinking"	"Change in Health Care: What It Means to You; and Now, the Battle to Define the Bill in the Public's Mind"
"A Cure for Greed"	"Health: After the Win, No Time to Lose"
"'Greed' Is Not Good"	"Investors Upbeat About Health Care Bill"
"The Economy Needs Corporate Governance Reform"	"Universal Health Insurance Coverage or Economic Relief— A False Choice"
"Where to Aim the Pitchforks"	"Lucrative Lies"
"Financial Crisis as a Learning Opportunity"	"A New Kind of Abortion Politics"
	"Not Covered"

When you are researching your chosen issue for your controversy analysis essay, you are going to discover clusters of readings like these. As you begin to focus on your issue, you will notice that the clusters tend to form around particular aspects of the debate. For example, if you were to research the recent economic collapse and resulting recession, you would find that various articles tend to cluster around a variety of aspects—not only what caused the collapse but also what areas of the economy suffered most, what the immediate results of the collapse were, what the more far-reaching and long-lasting impacts have been, individuals who figured prominently in the collapse, the effects of the economic stimulus package, and so forth. Since you couldn't discuss that many points in one paper, you would need to narrow your focus to one of those aspects. Thus, you might focus on various arguments about the main cause of the economic collapse—the focus of Cluster A.

Next, you might want to attempt a working thesis question to focus the rest of your research, something like "What was the main cause of the recent economic collapse?" At this point, remember that the thesis question is a *working* thesis question—that is, it will likely become more refined and specific as you continue researching and focusing more tightly on this aspect of the issue. It is too early in the research and writing process to become wedded to your thesis question; instead, use it to guide your research and allow it to evolve as your interest in and focus on the issue evolves.

Once you have a working thesis question, you want to take stock of your cluster of readings and plan where your research will take you next. One useful exercise is to make a cluster map of the readings and their answers the thesis question. A cluster map of Cluster A might look something like this:

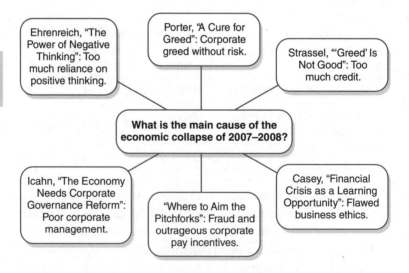

As we look at the previous cluster map, we can also see how the various readings relate to each other. Four of the six readings focus on similar answers to the question and relate to some aspect of corporate responsibility. A fifth reading stands in direct opposition to these four, and the sixth looks in a different direction altogether. It might be helpful to chart out these relationships, as follows:

As you can see from the chart, one reading, "'Greed' Is Not Good," which cites the easy availability of credit and those of us who overextended our credit as the main reason for the economic collapse, stands in direct opposition to "A Cure for Greed," "The Economy Needs Corporate Governance Reform," "Where to Aim the Pitchforks," and "Financial Crisis as a Learning Opportunity," which all look at the corporations in various ways for reasons for the economic collapse. The last reading, "The Power of Negative Thinking," stands by itself, linked to the others only by virtue of tackling the reason for the economic collapse, and does not much touch on the reasons the other readings focus on, even though it suggests that excessive positive thinking might lead corporations and individuals alike to make unwise financial decisions, creating a certain amount of agreement with the other five.

Making charts and maps like the ones above help you not only to see the range of arguments addressing the thesis question that you have so far and how they relate to each other, but also to discover where the holes in your research are. As we look at the above chart, we immediately see that the arguments are mostly one-sided: there are four readings looking at corporate responsibility, whereas only two suggest that perhaps the rest of us are to blame as well. The map shows that the four readings focusing on corporate responsibility all see corporate greed in one form or another as the main culprit. Are other arguments out there focusing on corporations arguing for

SECTION TWO

Readings

reasons besides greed? We also see that we need to look for arguments that assign blame elsewhere in order to create a more balanced analysis of the issue. Who or what else might be responsible? Is government to blame in any way? Are there other arguments looking at the role of individuals? Are there still other arguments that go in different directions than corporations or individuals? Try not to see the issue in polarized terms—either "this" or "that"—which might unnecessarily limit your presentation of the issue even in its narrowed aspect. Make a list of research questions as you consider your findings from the map and chart. These are the directions you will go in first to make sure you've considered as many "answers" to your thesis question as possible.

Once you are reasonably certain that you've made a fair and balanced search, then consider the sources themselves. Does each reading need more research in order to verify, support, or refute the claims it makes? In order to analyze each argument well, you will need to check out its claims. For example, let's look at "The Power of Negative Thinking" more closely. Ehrenreich's main claim in the article is that "the delusional optimism of mainstream, all-American, positive thinking" is as much to blame as greed and speculation. As the article continues, she gives examples of how this positive thinking manifests in our culture—self-help books, motivational speakers, Oprah Winfrey, "megachurch pastors," and corporate motivational retreats—and claims that focusing solely on the positive keeps both corporations and individuals from considering the possibilities of failure and preparing for bad times. But how pervasive is positive thinking? It might be useful to know if our society is as guided by positive thinking as she claims. Does the finance industry really practice the tenets of positive thinking to the extent that it could have blinded itself to the consequences of too much optimism? How much influence do popular figures like Tony Robbins and Oprah Winfrey really have? Ehrenreich is basing her argument on the premises that positive thinking has pervaded nearly every aspect of our society and that the purveyors of this philosophy have immense power over our decision-making. But if these premises are found to be flawed, Ehrenreich's argument is undermined, making it a fairly weak contender against the other arguments for the most convincing answer to your thesis question. Now you are armed with good information to support your analysis of the argument. As you

SECTION TWO
Readings

read through these six arguments, think about their main premises and consider what you need to find out in order to analyze them effectively.

Exercise with Cluster B readings: After you have discussed in class the eight readings in Cluster B, get into groups of three to five. In groups, do the following:

1. Do a cluster map of the readings with the apparent thesis question at the center. How do all the readings relate to the thesis question? Do they all neatly provide answers to this question, or do some appear to be answering a different question? Are they all focused on the same aspect of the issue of health care reform, or do some focus on different aspects? If you discover more than one aspect to the issue represented in this cluster, make a separate map for each aspect.

2. Then, chart out the relationships of the readings to each other. Again, if your group has found different aspects of the issue represented among the readings, make a separate chart for each aspect.

3. As you look at your map and chart, consider what they are showing you. If you have found different aspects, you might want to choose one grouping to focus on and eliminate the others (which is what you would need to do with your own groupings of sources). Are there holes in your research that you need to fill in, additional readings you would need to find in order to make your examination of the issue more balanced and representative? Make a list of research questions to guide this research.

SECTION TWO
Readings

4. Then consider the readings in your chosen grouping. Choose one of them and list its major premises. Consider how each premise is supported and if that support is sufficient to make the premise valid. What more do you need to find out to effectively analyze the reading's strengths and weaknesses? Make a list of information that you need to research.

5. Present your findings to the rest of the class for discussion.

Controversy Cluster A: Economic Collapse of 2007–2008

Barbara Ehrenreich—The Power of Negative Thinking

New York Times. September 24, 2008. Reprinted with permission of PARS International Corp.

 GREED—and its crafty sibling, speculation—are the designated culprits for the financial crisis. But another, much admired, habit of mind should get its share of the blame: the delusional optimism of mainstream, all-American, positive thinking.

As promoted by Oprah Winfrey, scores of megachurch pastors and an endless flow of self-help best sellers, the idea is to firmly believe that you will get what you want, not only because it will make you feel better to do so, but because "visualizing" something—ardently and with concentration—actually makes it happen. You will be able to pay that adjustable-rate mortgage or, at the other end of the transaction, turn thousands of bad mortgages into giga-profits if only you believe that you can.

Positive thinking is endemic to American culture—from weight loss programs to cancer support groups—and in the last two decades it has put down deep roots in the corporate world as well. Everyone knows that you won't get a job paying more than $15 an hour unless you're a "positive person," and no one becomes a chief executive by issuing warnings of possible disaster.

The tomes in airport bookstores' business sections warn against "negativity" and advise the reader to be at all times upbeat, optimistic, brimming with confidence. It's a message companies relentlessly reinforced—treating their white-collar employees to manic motivational speakers and revival-like motivational events, while sending the top guys off to exotic locales to get pumped by the likes of Tony Robbins and other success gurus. Those who failed to get with the program would be subjected to personal "coaching" or shown the door.

The once-sober finance industry was not immune. On their Web sites, motivational speakers proudly list companies like Lehman Brothers and Merrill Lynch among their clients. What's more, for those at the very top of the corporate hierarchy, all this positive thinking must not have seemed delusional at all. With the rise in executive compensation, bosses could have almost anything they wanted, just by expressing the desire. No one was psychologically prepared for hard times when they hit, because, according to the tenets of positive thinking, even to think of trouble is to bring it on.

Americans did not start out as deluded optimists. The original ethos, at least of white Protestant settlers and their descendants, was a grim Calvinism that offered wealth only through hard work and savings, and even then made no promises at all. You might work hard and still fail; you certainly wouldn't get anywhere by adjusting your attitude or dreamily "visualizing" success.

Calvinists thought "negatively," as we would say today, carrying a weight of guilt and foreboding that sometimes broke their spirits. It was in response to this harsh attitude that positive thinking arose—among mystics, lay healers and transcendentalists—in the 19th century, with its crowd-pleasing message that God, or the universe, is really on your side, that you can actually have whatever you want, if the wanting is focused enough.

When it comes to how we think, "negative" is not the only alternative to "positive." As the case histories of depressives show, consistent pessimism can be just as baseless and deluded as its opposite. The alternative to both is realism—seeing the risks, having the courage to bear bad news and being prepared for famine as well as plenty. We ought to give it a try.

SECTION TWO
Readings

Eduardo Porter—A Cure for Greed

New York Times. September 28, 2008. Reprinted with permission of PARS International Corp.

 Of course, it's all Gordon Gekko's fault! "Greed and irresponsibility," blasted Barack Obama. "Greed and excess and corruption," charged John McCain. President Luiz Ignacio Lula da Silva could tell from as far away as Brazil that the "boundless greed of a few" blew up the American financial system. Why didn't I think of that?

With the eureka moment behind us, I would suggest that this insight offers a way to try to restore the abused financial markets to health. If greed is to blame, the question is whether we can line up a reasonable array of alternative incentives—and disincentives—to do away with greed for good.

This will be no easy task. From populist opprobrium to elitist disdain—standard social behavioral devices have proved unable to dent humanity's greedy nature.

The Soviet Union deployed the entire power of the state to stamp out greed—and ensured that the state was the greediest actor of all. Even religion's not insubstantial powers of persuasion (think Hell) and coercion (think Inquisition) have proved insufficient to blot out this insidious sin.

The free market, it should be obvious by now, hasn't been up to the task either. Capitalism, in all its cleverness, decided that what you can't beat, you should use. It worked to harness greed. To be able to discuss it in polite company, economists renamed it "maximization of utility," and built a theory of the world that everyone benefits when we seek to maximize our own individual welfare.

Greed reached its zenith in the 1980s, when the Reagan Revolution brought us supply-side economics and its bedrock belief that the path to prosperity for all required removing every obstacle to utility maximization, including most regulations and taxes. Then financial markets crashed. On the campaign trail, the Rev. Jesse Jackson lambasted America's greedy corporations. And one survey found that 83 percent of Americans blamed "unmitigated greed" for the financial crisis. A few years later the markets were again soaring; greed was back in style.

SECTION TWO

Readings

Yet despite the consistent failure to temper our greedy nature, I still have hopes. Because there is a crucial brake that has been missing from the edifice of high-tech financial capitalism—a counterbalance at the other end of the scale from where utility gets maximized. That piece is fear. My suggestion, then, is to put fear back in the picture. When the banker who loses his or her bank also loses his or her shirt, greed will be tempered. At least for a while.

SECTION TWO

Readings

Kimberley A. Strassel—"Greed" Is Not Good

 Once upon a time, Washington told the nation a story. It was a dark tale of economic distress brought on by villainous, greedy Wall Street bankers.

The storytellers loved this yarn. The public wanted some one to blame for their unemployment, their foreclosures, their falling 401Ks, and Wall Street made an easy target. It was also so much simpler than the real story of societal credit mania, in which the Federal Reserve, Congress, regulators, credit-rating agencies, Fannie and Freddie, Wall Street—and yes, many homeowners and consumers—were all complicit.

Besides, it was an election year! What politician could be expected to stand up and tell taxpayers they needed to fork over trillions to forestall an economic collapse that Washington had helped engineer?

The Beltway is now stuck with its creative history. And that populist fiction is, yet again, threatening to derail efforts to revive the economy. The banking system desperately needs capital. Washington has it. Yet to provide it, and to provide it in such a way that it works, Washington will be "rewarding" all those greedy bankers it spent the past year accusing of perfidy and malice. Talk about a quandary.

This week's AIG political maelstrom is only the latest example of how that greedy-banker story is undermining recovery.

The politicians and the press had already embedded the wicked-Wall-Street storyline into the public conscience by last September. This was when Hank Paulson was gravely telling Congress that if it did not act immediately to rescue the banking system, the financial panic would turn into a financial crash.

But Congress had bigger problems. Its phone lines were jammed with constituents screaming it had better not "bail out" the banks who—according to Congress, after all—had caused all this. So it didn't. The House sent the Paulson plan down in flames, in the process tanking the stock markets, and further seizing up the credit markets. It took that pain, and more, to finally get TARP passed.

The execution of TARP has also been held hostage to the greedy-banker line. The program was designed to provide the banking system—the heart of the problem—with the capital cushion necessary to revive lending and to work through toxic assets. What followed was nonetheless inevitable.

If we are giving money to greedy bankers, why not hardworking employees of GM and Chrysler and their parts suppliers? If we are stumping up for Wall Street, why shouldn't Barney Frank get to help his community bank? If we are doling out for lascivious New York, why not throw billions at homeowners, who were the "victims"? TARP really is now a bailout machine, spreading moral hazard, even as it misdirects money away from the vital purpose for which it was intended.

It was also inevitable that tales of greed would lead to a bonus blowup. Stoked by President Obama's frequent critiques of "shameful" Wall Street bonuses, public anger was again rising. Connecticut Sen. Chris Dodd saw his opening to play off this—and deflect attention away from his sweetheart mortgage deal and AIG fund raising—by inserting bonus caps into the stimulus bill. Even at the time, Treasury was starting to worry that these restrictions might derail TARP.

Not that this stopped the Obama administration from jumping on the "outrage" bandwagon this week over AIG bonuses. Greed, greed, greed, screamed Washington, hoping nobody would notice its own failure to supervise AIG over the years, its botched intervention, or the administration's refusal to come clean about where the AIG money was going.

This spectacle has left the financial community with one impression: Stay away. What healthy bank, what hedge fund, what private equity firm wants to take part in an Obama plan to sell off toxic assets, or to revive consumer lending, with the knowledge that they might be Washington's newest bonfire? Executives are already working to get out of TARP, fearful of political punishment. This despite a recession, falling house prices and growing bank losses.

As it happens, the administration has suggested the banks might need yet more public capital, not less. But just who in Congress is today prepared to vote to provide more funding, with greedy AIG on the public mind? It's too busy passing laws to levy 90% taxes on bank employees everywhere.

SECTION TWO
Readings

275

Washington does have its grown-ups: Those few Republicans who tried for years to reform Fannie and Freddie, but who also voted for a necessary banking rescue; those in Congress who have tried to explain that the goal is not to bail out bankers, but to bail out ourselves; those very few who have stood up to remind Americans that—as distasteful as some Wall Street bonuses have appeared—it is far more pernicious for Washington to start setting salary caps. Sadly, their reward for political courage has been to be labeled as stooges of ... greedy Wall Street.

That's right. Washington has its story, and it's sticking to it. Perhaps to the bitter end.

SECTION TWO

Readings

Carl C. Icahn—The Economy Needs Corporate Governance Reform

 In his inaugural address this week, President Barack Obama said "our economy is badly weakened, a consequence of greed and irresponsibility on the part of some," and due in part to "our collective failure to make hard choices."

He's offered few policy specifics other than saying we need to undertake massive new infrastructure and education programs. But he is right, there are a lot of hard choices we need to make. And one of them is the decision to fix the way public companies are managed.

Private enterprise forms the basis for our economy. It provides most of the jobs we enjoy and creates the wealth that raises living standards. New government spending can only do so much to repair the economy. Reshaping corporate management can do much more.

The problem with doing nothing is obvious. Faltering companies are now soaking up hundreds of billions of tax dollars, and they are not substantially changing their management structures as a price for taking this money.

How does it serve the economy when we subsidize managements that got their companies into trouble? Where is the accountability? More importantly, where are the results?

The economy continues to sink, jobs are being lost, the markets continue on a downward course. Changes are needed and can come if Congress insists on reforms that make corporate boards and managers more accountable to stakeholders.

First, Congress needs to pass legislation giving shareholders enhanced rights to elect new boards, submit resolutions for stockholder votes, and have far more input on executive compensation and other issues. As companion to these reforms, Congress needs to pass legislation that prevents managers from making it more difficult for shareholders to exercise their ownership rights.

Managers often come up with creative ways to perpetuate their reigns of error. These include myriad takeover obstacles like poison pills, bylaw provisions, and other devices that thwart shareholder efforts to hold managers accountable.

SECTION TWO
Readings

277

If Congress is reluctant to make wholesale changes at the federal level, it can enact one simple provision that would allow many of the needed changes to take place on the state level: It can give shareholders the right to vote to move a company's legal jurisdiction to a more shareholder-friendly state such as North Dakota. Currently that decision is in the hands of company boards.

It is not reasonable to expect managers with failing track records to improve their performance on their own. They will only improve if they are placed under greater pressure by shareholders empowered to exert more influence on management decisions. Nothing will do more to improve our economy than corporate governance changes.

What we need are measures that let the capitalist system produce jobs and economic activity, with minimal but effective government oversight. Government spending is an important catalyst to economic gains, but we need to focus on improving the way private companies are managed so private capital can flow into them.

Our private sector is the greatest wealth creation machine ever devised, far outperforming any other economic model. Still, major improvements could do a lot to mitigate what Mr. Obama calls "the sapping of confidence across our land."

Lax and ineffective boards, self-serving managements, and failed short-term strategies all contributed to the entirely preventable financial meltdown. It is time for battered shareholders to fight back.

Mr. Obama was right when he said that "it has been the risk-takers, the doers, the makers of things...who have carried us up the long, rugged path towards prosperity and freedom."

I hope this means that the day of reckoning has come for those executives who simply feed at public and private troughs, putting little or no capital of their own at risk, and who produce little of value for the national economy.

It is time for change and the place to start is in the corporate boardrooms of America.

SECTION TWO
Readings

Anonymous—Where to Aim the Pitchforks

Editorial. USA Today. *March 25, 2009, p. A10. Reprinted by permission,*
via RightsLink.

 Rage is all the rage toward financiers whose greed and stupidity helped wreck the economy and throw millions of people out of work. "People are right to be angry. I'm angry," President Obama said last week as the American International Group bonus scandal erupted. "What I want us to do is channel our anger in a constructive way."

Obama spoke the day before furious House members voted to tax back most of the bonuses paid to executives at AIG, which would no longer exist if not for $180 billion in government bailout funds. Americans and their representatives are justifiably looking for ways to strike back at such wretched excess, but undiluted anger is a dangerous force in a place with as much concentrated power as Washington. There are constructive ways to mete out punishment and, more important, try to make sure this doesn't happen again. Three targets of opportunity:

- Go after the crooks. Prosecutors have already taken down megafraudster Bernard Madoff, who pleaded guilty to defrauding clients of almost $65 billion. But a national financial disaster measured in the trillions had many greedy but less grandiose authors, some of whom cooked books or concocted phony mortgage documents. The FBI told Congress last week that it's pursuing so many financial fraud investigations that the agency's resources are strained. Putting the fraudsters in prison sends an important message and reassures the public that justice is being done. If investigators need more resources, they should get them.

- Find out what happened. Major national disasters often spawn serious-minded investigations that reveal what happened and show ways to prevent a repeat. Models include the 9/11 Commission and the Watergate investigation. The 1930s Pecora hearings, which investigated stock market manipulation and the 1929 crash, exposed Wall Street's excesses and led to the creation of the Securities and Exchange Commission. A reprise now could be useful, much in the way a National Transportation Safety Board probe identifies fault and recommends changes after crashes of a different sort.

SECTION TWO
Readings

- Fix crazy pay incentives. It makes no sense to pay huge bonuses to executives who drive up short-term profits with reckless gambles that wreck the company later on. Nor does it make sense to let wealthy hedge fund managers pay the 15% capital gains tax instead of the 35% income tax on earnings.

For the sake of social stability, shareholders and the government need to restore sanity to executive compensation. When CEOs make 300 to 400 times more than the average worker, up from 30 or 40 times a few decades ago, it's no wonder that so many people are apoplectic.

SECTION TWO
Readings

Eileen Casey—Financial Crisis as a Learning Opportunity

National Catholic Reporter. *November 14, 2008, Special Section.*
Reprinted with permission of Catholic News Service, 3211 Fourth Street,
NE, Washington, DC 20017. www.usccb.org

 Heads of leading master's programs in business at a number of U.S. Catholic universities say they see the current market meltdown as a valuable occasion to teach their students the consequences of imprudent business decisions.

Christopher Puto, dean of the University of St. Thomas' Opus College of Business in Minneapolis, remarked: "There are powerful lessons here on the issues of greed, selfishness and the need for sound moral judgment that offer great insight for young people at the start of their careers.

"We may be able to use this to guide the development of a new class of business leaders who genuinely understand that profit and the common good are not mutually exclusive ends," he said.

Puto was among several deans and professors Catholic News Service interviewed from the University of Notre Dame in Indiana; Boston College; Georgetown University in Washington; Villanova University in Pennsylvania; Marquette University in Milwaukee; the University of San Diego; and the University of St. Thomas.

All said their schools' business programs integrate the importance of business ethics and social justice into the curriculum.

In addition to core classes in philosophy and theology, embedded in many of the business courses are elements of corporate responsibility and Catholic social teaching, the affirmation of human dignity, the common good, solidarity with the poor and subsidiarity, which is the principle that things should be done at the simplest, most decentralized and most local level possible.

SECTION TWO
Readings

Since the slide on Wall Street began in late September, professors said, classroom debates on the crisis have been commonplace. Many said they use the beginning of class to reflect on what has been happening, and what this means to students who want to break into the financial industry.

Professor Ed Soule at Georgetown's McDonough School of Business said professors are just trying to make sense out of the economic situation by putting it into context since most students do not have a basis for comparison.

"One thing that can happen with students is that they can start to see business as mechanical. ... The human dimension is not always as emphasized as it should be," he said.

He also said that a factor in the upset on Wall Street is a lack of trust between trading partners. "Once there is a breach of trust, it is difficult to get [it] back," he said. "Those that spent their entire careers showing that they are trustworthy proved it saved them in the end. Times like this show how important character can be."

The economic situation "seems to be a constant source of conversation, in all departments," said Sarah Peck, chair of Marquette's business school and associate professor of finance.

This coming spring semester Peck is scheduled to teach an investment ethics class, which she said will be the first of its kind nationwide.

Currently, in conversations about Wall Street, "there is no doubt that we tie [the financial crisis] to economic principles," she said. "But rather than saying, 'Wow, these people were bad,' we are approaching it [by] trying to understand how this really happened: the way incentives were set up, the pressures, etc."

"It can be hard to detect the beginning of deviating ethical practices, and it can culminate in a culture that can be disastrous," she added. "Because of the nature of the profession, it is not always black and white. In the business environment there is always a conflict of interest because both parties are trying to make money."

Notre Dame's Mendoza College of Business and its Institute for Ethical Business Worldwide emphasize values-based leadership and weave social issues and environmental stewardship into the curriculum. Dean Carolyn Woo believes this approach will prepare students to practice moral courage in times of frequent business judgment lapses.

"I think [the crisis] is a very teachable moment," said Woo. "It's an example of each person looking out for their own self-interest, not human charity—a graphic illustration of the harm that can be done, of what we as humans subconsciously do."

Controversy Cluster B: Health Care Reform

Susan Page and Mimi Hall—Change in Health Care: What It Means to You; and Now, the Battle to Define the Bill in the Public's Mind

USA Today, *23 March 2010, p. A1. Reprinted by permission obtained via RightsLink.*

WASHINGTON—The vote is over. The fight is just beginning.

In the East Room this morning, President Obama will sign the most comprehensive changes to the health care system in American history—and with that launch a fierce battle leading up to November's elections to define the law as either a crucial, overdue reform or a dangerous, Big Government power grab.

The president flies to Iowa on Thursday on the first of several cross-country trips to tout popular benefits in the bill that go into effect almost immediately. One advocacy group Monday began making 700,000 recorded phone calls to voters in a dozen congressional districts, blasting Republicans who voted against it.

Meanwhile, conservative talk-show host Rush Limbaugh told listeners that Democrats who voted for it should "be hounded out of office" and GOP officeholders promised repeal efforts, state-by-state resistance to key provisions and court challenges.

"The task now shifts from legislation to persuasion," says William Galston, a White House domestic policy adviser in the Clinton administration. Obama communications director Dan Pfeiffer says Obama plans "a sustained campaign to educate the public about the immediate benefits of health reforms."

The White House and Democratic congressional leaders also hope the health care victory will give them the political momentum and partisan unity to move forward on other issues—and a clear opening to focus more sharply on economic concerns, including unemployment, that Americans rank as their top priorities.

"Washington is a place that likes winners," says Lawrence Jacobs, director of the Center for the Study of Politics and Governance at the University of Minnesota. "When a president gets on a roll and gets a win like this, it snowballs."

SECTION TWO
Readings

Some changes in the bill demanded by the House and included in a separate measure have gone to the Senate for action as soon as this week.

Repercussions from the 219-to-212 vote late Sunday in favor of the Senate's original health care bill could be enormous.

Republicans see opposition to the bill and concern about its reach and price tag as issues that might enable the GOP to regain control of the House in the Nov. 2 congressional elections. Democrats hope to turn the issue into a positive for them.

And Obama has seen his approval rating erode as the health care debate has dragged on. In the past few days, as victory seemed increasingly likely, his standing rose to 50% approve vs. 43% disapprove in daily Gallup polling. Last week his rating was 46%–47%, the first time during his tenure that more Americans disapproved than approved of the job he was doing.

For the White House and Republicans, the target is no longer a few dozen undecided House members—abortion opponents, fiscal conservatives and liberals backing a government-run public option—who were furiously courted to approve the Senate version of the health care bill.

Now the target shifts to millions of Americans, including many who remain uncertain about what the 2,562-page bill means to them.

In the seven-month sprint to Election Day, some of them will continue to be bombarded by ads from both sides of the issue, invited to rallies and protests and encouraged to sign up for benefits in the plan.

"The prime question today is: What price victory?" says Robert Schmuhl, chairman of the American Studies Department at Notre Dame. "Passage of the bill is certainly historic, but its complexity and the enormous effort to get it to the finish line are bound to produce aftershocks long into the future.

"How it all plays out could well determine whether Barack Obama can win re-election in 2012."

Strategies in play.

After a year of debate, the *USA TODAY*/Gallup Poll and other national surveys showed neither side convinced a solid majority of Americans that they were right. With a bill enacted and taking effect, the effort to define the legislation may only intensify.

SECTION TWO
Readings

"There's a moment here where there will be a set of decisions made in voters' minds about, was this about me and my family?" says Andrew Stern, head of the SEIU, a major supporter. "Or was this about doctors and hospitals and the government?"

Strategies for both sides to make their cases:

Accentuate the immediate.

Some of the legislation doesn't go into effect for years, but Obama insisted that it include some steps that could demonstrate the bill's positive impact right away, says Neera Tanden, who until last month was one of his advisers on health care.

"Look, there's an essential quandary," Tanden says. "It does take awhile to get change like this up and running. But people deserve to see benefits relatively quickly."

Events featuring Obama and other administration officials will spotlight a prohibition on insurance companies denying coverage for children because they have pre-existing medical conditions, in effect in six months. At that point, the law also will allow parents to provide coverage on their insurance plans for their children up to age 26.

And seniors who are paying full prescription prices because they're caught in the "doughnut hole" of Medicare's drug coverage will get a $250 check in the mail this spring.

Play the expectations game.

Both sides have emphasized the historic nature of the health care bill. Democrat John Lewis of Georgia, a civil rights pioneer, said during the closing House debate that the legislation was as monumental as the Civil Rights Act. Republican leader John Boehner predicted an "Armageddon" from a measure he said would "ruin our nation."

Democrats say the most fevered predictions by opponents— warnings that passing the bill will bring a move toward socialism and a loss of liberty—will help them win over voters when catastrophe doesn't develop.

"There are not going to be 'death panels' sprouting up," says Rep. Chris Van Hollen, D-Md., head of the Democratic Congressional Campaign Committee. "There's going to be a huge credibility gap on the other side."

SECTION TWO
Readings

"It's much easier to sell something that's real and tangible than defend against a caricature," White House senior adviser David Axelrod says.

Republicans say they can focus on the expectations Democrats outlined, too.

"The challenge the Democrats have is people are going to expect these major changes to health care now and maybe wondering, what was all the hullabaloo?" says Republican pollster Glen Bolger. "They're the ones promising everything, to solve all the health care problems."

Sign them up.

Advocates want to encourage those who under the provisions of the bill are newly eligible for Medicaid and the insurance exchanges to enroll.

Ron Pollack, executive director of Families USA, says a new non-profit group would work with hospitals, pharmacies, doctors and community health centers.

The campaign is based in part on the early confusion and suspicion among some seniors toward the Medicare prescription drug benefit program when it was passed by Republicans in 2003 and took effect in 2006. Drugmakers and insurance companies financed an education campaign that encouraged seniors to enroll and, in the process, built political support for it.

Energize your base.

Groups that tried to influence the vote in Congress are now turning to the midterm elections.

Americans United for Change, which supports the health care bill, begins airing TV ads in the Twin Cities today that denounce Rep. Michele Bachmann, R-Minn., for her vote against the bill. More ads and automated calls targeting a dozen vulnerable Republicans will follow.

"Finally, Congress passed the health reform bill to rein in the power of the big insurance companies and guarantee that all Minnesotans can get the same kind of health insurance as members of Congress," the ad says. "But our congresswoman, Michele Bachmann, voted against that."

The SEW will air TV ads in a half-dozen districts thanking vulnerable Democrats who voted for the bill. And Organizing for America, a Democratic group that helped elect Obama, said supporters had committed to 9.3 million hours to work for Democratic candidates in the fall.

Republican stalwarts are energized, too.

The Republican National Committee has launched a fundraising appeal called "Fire Pelosi: 40 Seats Means No More Madam Speaker." Arizona Sen. John McCain, the party's 2008 presidential nominee who faces a primary challenge from conservative J.D. Hayworth, sent out his own fundraising appeal Monday headlined "Repeal the bill."

Not every critic is pushing for repeal, however.

The U.S. Chamber of Commerce, which spent $144 million on ads and lobbying against the bill, will work instead to fix the bill's flaws and "minimize its potential harmful impacts," Chamber CEO Thomas Donohue says.

Changing the subject.

Health care may be Obama's biggest achievement to date, but aides say the president will work just as hard in coming months on the economy.

Sunday's victory will give those efforts a boost. "There's no doubt the Democrats and President Obama are stronger today than they were yesterday," says Jacobs, the political scientist.

Facing high unemployment and polls that show voters angry about the bank bailouts, Obama will focus on "continuing to get the economy back on track," Pfeiffer says. That means job creation and Wall Street accountability in the form of financial regulations now being considered in the Senate.

Last week, Obama signed an $18 billion jobs bill that passed with some Republican support in the House and Senate. Now, the president will push relatively small-scale initiatives to spur lending to small businesses, promote weatherization of homes and more.

He'll also promote "common sense rules" to govern the nation's financial institutions and protect consumers from predatory, and financially ruinous, lending and credit practices, Pfeiffer says.

Pfeiffer jokes that the State Department also may help fill Obama's plate.

SECTION TWO

Readings

The president will have some tricky foreign policy issues to tackle. Even as he continues the planned withdrawal of U.S. troops from Iraq and preside over the troop buildup he has ordered in Afghanistan, Obama faces other challenges: seeking international sanctions on Iran to try to check its nuclear ambitions; negotiating with Russia to reduce nuclear weapons stockpiles; trying to restart peace talks between Israelis and Palestinians.

He meets today at the White House with Israeli Prime Minister Benjamin Netanyahu,

Obama also has promised to work on an energy bill, now stalled in Congress, and immigration changes. Last week, he praised efforts in the Senate by Democrat Charles Schumer of New York and Republican Lindsey Graham of South Carolina to tackle the controversial issue. But the odds are slim that Congress could get a bill through this year—and the White House isn't inclined to ask vulnerable Democrats to take another very difficult vote right before voters go to the polls.

If there are other issues the White House would like to pursue, aides are reluctant to talk about them. Asked to rank those issues at Monday's press briefing, spokesman Robert Gibbs demurred.

"I picked Kansas to win the bracket," he said, citing the loss by the top-seeded Jayhawks in the NCAA basketball tournament, "so I don't see any reason for me to begin ranking said priorities."

SECTION TWO
Readings

John Reichard—Health: After the Win, No Time to Lose

CQ Weekly, *5 April 2010, p. 814. Reprinted by permission obtained via The Copyright Clearance Center.*

After the past 14 months, no one can doubt the resolve of Democrats to shape the nation's health care system the way they want it. They have pushed the biggest overhaul ever through Congress and are baffle-tested and brimming with confidence that what is now Public Law 111-148 will firmly take hold across several agencies in the federal government.

But they face years of hard work—in a harsh political environment—both to get the law implemented and to sell it to a skeptical public at the same time.

Never mind that they face elections in 2010 and 2012 that could erode Democratic power enough to wash away big chunks of the law and its unprecedented coverage expansion before it takes hold fully in 2014. And never mind that Republican-appointed judges could yet upend the law on constitutional grounds, even if voters do defy conservative pundits, keep Democrats in charge of Congress and give President Obama a second term in office.

Just the sheer volume of regulations that agencies must issue and enforce and the number of new programs and payment systems they must create and test is reason enough to raise questions about how they can get the job done, And as with any law, the agencies have wide latitude in the implementation.

In fact, most prominent among the complaints from critics of the overhaul is the degree of discretion handed to Health and Human Services Secretary Kathleen Sebelius and to multiple divisions in her department. That's not to mention agencies ranging from the Department of Labor to the Internal Revenue Service, which will decide exactly how to implement the law's many provisions.

Some critics point to the frequent use of the phrase "the Secretary shall," which appears 1,045 times in the two bills. (On its own, "shall" appears 4,383 times.) There are multiple other instances of "the Secretary may," "the Secretary determines," "the Secretary has the authority" and similar formulations—which underscore the degree of administrative decision-making and rule-writing that will be required beginning immediately and extending over the next half-dozen years.

SECTION TWO

Readings

Among the questions: Is HHS up to the task of creating within the next three months a nationwide system for insurers to cover sick adults who today cannot qualify for insurance because of their pre-existing conditions? Can the 50 states find ways over the next three years to create workable exchanges in which uninsured Americans can purchase health coverage, with a government subsidy if necessary, while also handling the heavier administrative burdens of expanding Medicaid?

Without imposing more onerous paperwork on taxpayers, how is the IRS going to test whether every American has acquired health insurance and assess fines against those who haven't and who aren't somehow exempt from the process?

Meanwhile, savings will have to be squeezed from doctors, hospitals, nurses, drug companies and other parts of the health system with no organizational culture of working together to streamline care.

And with hundreds of billions of dollars in taxpayer money on the line and enormous expectations created by the legislation, Obama's agency heads must move quickly and competently. Otherwise, they'll give ground to Republicans who are determined to blow the whole thing up.

"In many respects, the implementation challenges are unprecedented, not only due to the breadth of the act but because so many of the key decisions will be made by the secretary," says Patrick Morrisey, now a partner at Sidley Austin and formerly chief health counsel to the House Energy and Commerce Committee.

Morrisey was one of the principal staff authors of the Medicare prescription drug law of 2003, which is probably the closest parallel process in terms of the implementation challenge. But even that law paled in comparison, Morrisey says, "because of the length of the new law, the extensive interplay between multiple federal and state laws, and the extent to which key terms are still undefined."

That law, like the new one, involved hundreds of billions in new federal spending and new systems to pay health plans, employers, drug companies and pharmacists. As will be the case with the new law, it also required an effort to teach millions of Americans about new ways to pay and shop for health care.

Starting "Yesterday"

As overwhelming as the job might seem, it's manageable if agency heads began the planning "yesterday," says Mark McClellan, who led the implementation of the Medicare overhaul in the Bush administration.

McClellan, now director of the Engleberg Center for Health Reform at the Brookings Institution, thinks one of the most important challenges will be establishing the program for people to purchase subsidized coverage through insurance exchanges, which are expected to be up and running in every state by 2014.

Getting regulations in place to create the e will take up to two years even under an accelerated timetable—"and that's just to lay out a clear understanding what needs to be done," he says.

The effort to expand coverage will be a strenuous one that will require 50 state governments and their Medicaid agencies to be yoked together into a single system. States are at the heart of the effort to cover 32 million uninsured people under the law, either through the exchanges selling subsidized coverage to individuals and small businesses or by expanding Medicaid eligibility in 2014 to households with incomes up to 133 percent of the federal poverty line.

But "given what we know about the political differences around the country, you can imagine that there are a number of states that may not jump on board real quickly," drily observes Urban Institute analyst John Holahan. Richard Curtis, an expert on insurance exchanges, also sees a risk that some states won't move quickly enough.

States have the option of creating one exchange for individuals and another for small businesses that gives workers a choice of competing plans, or they could create a single exchange for both, says Curtis, president of the Washington-based Institute for Health Policy Solutions. While he doesn't think creating exchanges for individuals will be difficult, Curtis says states may underestimate the work involved in making the exchanges a one-stop shop for small businesses that will qualify for a 50 percent tax credit in 2014 for buying coverage through exchanges.

The current budget crisis has left state agencies with virtual "skeleton operations" and "just gasping" to do their existing work, says Curtis. States can use federal startup money to create or designate separate organizations to run exchanges, but some policy analysts advocate using Medicaid agencies instead. "In most states that would be a mistake," Curtis says.

SECTION TWO
Readings

Each of the state exchanges will have the advantage of being able to offer small businesses two or more national plans that contract with the Federal Employees Health Benefit Program. Walton Francis, an expert on FEHBP who writes a guidebook to its plans for federal workers, says it will be no problem for the staff of the Office of Personnel Management to do the contracting. "It's what they do," he says. But OPM will have many politicians looking over its shoulder and will face a level of scrutiny it's not accustomed to, he adds.

Getting the Medicaid piece of the coverage expansion in place will be a challenge, too. McClellan notes that some states are suing to scale back their programs, which already heavily strain state budgets. While expansion costs for those newly eligible for Medicaid will be fully funded by the federal government from 2014 through 2016, states will have to pick up 5 percent of the costs in 2017, 6 percent in 2018, 7 percent in 2019 and 10 percent thereafter—which could mean anemic "outreach" to a population that can be tough to enroll.

Another financing problem for states is that "full" federal funding does not apply to currently eligible people who aren't enrolled in Medicaid but sign up because of publicity about the expansion.

Even if enrollment efforts aren't what overhaul supporters want, Medicaid rolls will grow, and finding more doctors and hospitals to treat Medicaid patients could be difficult even with improved payment rates for primary care physicians. Those rates will match those of Medicare, but only in 2013 and 2014.

Readying the Agencies

Federal agencies could also sag under the burden of their new responsibilities if their funding is neglected. The Internal Revenue Service will have to calculate and pay insurers income-based tax credits for individuals and small businesses buying coverage through the exchanges. While it has developed systems for doing so because of premium subsidies provided to laid-off workers under a 2002 law, "the way you do that for 100,000 people is going to be quite different than for millions," says McClellan, who also served as a senior Treasury official under the Clinton administration.

Iowa Republican Sen. Charles E. Grassley notes that the IRS will also have to enforce penalties for individuals who fail to carry coverage as mandated under the overhaul law and enforce "free rider" penalties on employers whose uninsured workers go to exchanges and get subsidized coverage. Still other new IRS tasks include administering small-business tax credits and calculating and collecting new fees on drug and device companies and insurers.

Grassley is afraid IRS functions such as answering taxpayer questions and enforcing current law will suffer. With 50 percent of the IRS workforce expected to retire soon, "it doesn't have the resources it needs to do its presently described job, never mind a whole new one such as administering health care reform," Grassley said in a floor statement Nov. 18.

Meanwhile, the Centers for Medicare and Medicaid Services (CMS) also has a tremendous amount of work to do administering almost half a trillion dollars in Medicare cuts; developing new forms of payment to spur better, more efficient care; and testing and scaling up other new payment approaches.

The cuts are important because they are needed to fund a wider expansion. At the same time, however, CMS will have to monitor the system to ensure that the cuts aren't denying seniors care or reducing its quality, McClellan says.

While the Congressional Budget Office assumes that the health overhaul law includes some $1 billion to $2 billion a year in "implicit authorizations" for the CMS and an equal amount for the IRS to handle these added responsibilities, that money must be obtained through the appropriations process.

No less critical is mastering the near-term provisions of the law. Tight procedures must be developed for payouts of billions of dollars through a new "risk pool" to provide affordable coverage to hard-to-insure Americans and "reinsurance" payments to bring down premium costs for older Americans.

SECTION TWO
Readings

The administration must also quickly write regulations for features of the overhaul law that Obama is busy promoting as starting this year. Those regulations "have to be done well," McClellan notes. "That is going to be what people notice between now and the election."

As Morrisey puts it: "Sadly, this is a regulatory lawyer's dream."

Already the process is off to a rocky start. Democrats insist that insurers under the new law must accept all applications for coverage of children with pre-existing medical conditions. Insurers initially balked, saying they could offer such coverage only to the entire family. They have since reversed that hard stance, however. Other regulations due out this year end lifetime caps on benefits and bar "rescissions" that cancel benefits when the policyholder gets sick.

A key piece of the planning effort is having the right people involved, McClellan emphasizes. "Personnel is just absolutely key." While implementing the 2003 Medicare law, McClellan says, CMS had special hiring authority to get private industry experts on board quickly with special areas of expertise, such as pharmacy operations, insurance benefit design, actuarial analysis, development of Web-based information tools and community outreach.

"Most important was actually educating the public and supporting them in taking steps to take advantage of the new benefits. And I think that's going to be the same thing here," McClellan says. "People don't know really how this is going to affect them and when, what new opportunities they have to get coverage, what kind of subsidies they're going to get, what their costs will be, and what kind of penalties they may have to face down the road if they don't get coverage."

"The real work here is by the senior managers in the agencies and their technical staffs," McClellan adds. Relative to agency legislative staffs and congressional aides, they should be well rested and ready to go, he says.

Indeed, they had better be, given the enormity of the job. What follows is a look at six of the top challenges ahead for the government in implementing the law.

John Reichard is editor of CQ HealthBeat.

SECTION TWO

Readings

Adam Shell—Investors Upbeat About Health Care Bill

USA Today, *23 March 2010. Reprinted by permission obtained via RightsLink.*

 NEW YORK—Costly health care reform was supposed to kill the Wall Street bull market. But there were more winners than losers on the first trading day after the House passed the landmark bill. The initial takeaway from investors is that President Obama's 10-year, $940 billion plan will not act as a profit-killing drug for the hospitals, insurers, pharmaceutical companies and medical device makers affected by the changes.

As Wall Street sees it, the bill, which will provide health insurance to an additional 32 million Americans, will result in greater demand for prescription drug purchases and medical care at doctors' offices from a new customer base with the ability to pay for their care. That revenue will offset the tens of billions in fees and taxes health care firms will pay to subsidize the plan.

"The more people insured, the greater demand there is for health care and more customers that can pay," says Jack Ablin, chief investment officer at Harris Private Bank.

While the longer-term impact of the bill might not be known for years, given that many key provisions don't take effect until 2014, investors reacted positively Monday. The Dow Jones industrials rose 44 points to 10,786, and the S&P Health Care index rose 0.6%.

But some health sectors fared better than others. The big winners were:

- Hospitals. For years, emergency rooms were the health provider of last resort for the uninsured, which left hospitals footing the bill for services patients couldn't afford. Now, there's a belief that hospitals will suffer smaller losses from the uninsured and see their revenue rise from payments received from insurance companies that will be covering more people.

  Says Dave Shove, senior health analyst at BMO: "Any money that helps cover bad debt from the uninsured helps hospitals."

- Drugmakers. The feared price controls were absent from the final bill, allowing pharmaceutical companies to benefit from increased demand for their prescription drugs from newly insured

SECTION TWO
Readings

295

patients. And while manufacturers and importers of branded drugs will have to pay annual fees ranging from $2.5 billion to $4.1 billion over 10 years, those costs should be offset by increased sales at pharmacies.

Medical device makers would benefit in similar ways as drug companies, despite being hit with a 2.3% excise tax.

While it might be too strong to label health insurance providers a loser, that sector is likely to benefit the least.

While the insurers will not have to compete with a government-sponsored health insurance option as feared, they, too, will face annual fees, starting at $8 billion beginning in 2014.

While insurers will also benefit from a new customer base, they'll also have to cover people with pre-existing conditions, which will result in increased payouts. "We believe it is a net neutral for the insurers," Shove says.

SECTION TWO
Readings

Jonathan Gruber, Ph.D.—Universal Health Insurance Coverage or Economic Relief—A False Choice

Perspective. The New England Journal of Medicine, *360.5 (January 29, 2009) 437–439. Copyright © 2009 Massachusetts Medical Society. All rights reserved.*

These are exciting times for advocates of universal health care coverage, with sizable Democratic majorities in both houses of Congress and a Democratic president who made universal coverage a central pledge of his campaign. Indeed, Senators Max Baucus (D-MT) and Edward Kennedy (D-MA) are hard at work on universal-coverage legislation, and Senators Ron Wyden (D-OR) and Robert Bennett (R-UT) have already submitted a bipartisan bill that would accomplish that goal. But despite this enthusiasm, many observers are skeptical that the United States can foot the bill for universal coverage in such economically trying times. Universal coverage, their argument runs, is a luxury that we must do without in order to make way for other programs that will stimulate the economy.

This argument presents a false choice. Indeed, I would counter that now is exactly the right time for universal coverage, because it can play such an important role in growing our economy, while also enabling us to shift the focus of health policy discussions to approaches for addressing our largest long-term fiscal challenge: escalating health care costs.

The first step toward universal coverage would be to send resources to the states for maintaining and expanding their public insurance programs. For example, the recent legislation reauthorizing the State Children's Health Insurance Program (SCHIP), which was vetoed by President George W. Bush, included large incentive payments to states for enrolling children who were already eligible for, but were not yet enrolled in, state public insurance programs. These bonus payments would have offset much of the cost that states would have incurred for the newly insured children, providing a major source of federal funds to cash-strapped states.

More generally, broad subsidies that make affordable health insurance available to lower-income families would improve not only the health of these families but also the health of our economy, by freeing up funds that the families could spend on other consumer goods. Indeed, this dynamic is exactly what we saw when Medicaid

SECTION TWO
Readings

was expanded to cover additional low-income children and pregnant women in the late 1980s and early 1990s. My colleague Aaron Yelowitz and I found that the families that gained insurance coverage through these expansions substantially increased their spending on other consumer goods[1]—by an average of about $800 per year in today's dollars. This sizable effect could go a long way toward offsetting the decline in consumer spending that is marring the current economic landscape.

Another major benefit of universal coverage would accrue to the labor market. A fundamental problem with our employment-based health insurance system is that Americans are afraid to leave jobs that come with health insurance for those that do not. Colleagues and I have documented the empirical importance of such "job lock," estimating that this fear reduces job-to-job mobility among the employer-insured by as much as 25%.[2] If workers are afraid to leave their jobs, they will not move to the most productive positions, and economic growth will suffer. Universal coverage that moves beyond the restrictions of the employer-sponsored system would end job lock and increase the productivity of our labor force.

If it were part of a comprehensive reform package, universal health insurance coverage could also be a source of growth for high-quality jobs. A key aspect of most reform plans is major new investments in information technology that is necessary to bring our health care system into the 21st century. For example, during his campaign, President Barack Obama called for investing $10 billion per year over 5 years to move the country toward the use of electronic health records. Such investments are central to the delivery of coordinated care that can improve the quality of health care and reveal opportunities for system-wide savings. But the economy would benefit as well, since this plan would require the creation and implementation of a vast new computer infrastructure for collecting and sharing medical information—which would, in turn, mean filling a large number of well-paid high-technology positions.

Moreover, making coverage universal will necessitate expanding the medical sector to meet the needs of a larger population. If this expansion were done right, it could be a huge jobs program. For example, the white paper issued by Senator Baucus in November focuses on the need for dramatic investment in the delivery of primary and preventive care.[3] His plan calls for improved payments to primary care providers and community health centers, for instance, and increased reliance on "patient-centered medical homes." Such an approach would shift the focus of the healthcare system from specialists to preventive care practitioners with much lower barriers to entry, such as those for nurse practitioners and registered nurses. Such rewarding, high-paying jobs could provide a landing spot for workers displaced from other sectors of our economy.

Finally, providing universal coverage represents an important prerequisite to addressing the most important fiscal issue facing the U.S. government: the enormous future promises made through our public insurance programs, Medicare and Medicaid. Recent estimates suggest that the future obligations of the U.S. government for the Medicare program alone, minus any Medicare payroll taxes collected, will be more than $70 trillion—an amount that is seven times that of our national debt. Closing this gap, along with the $15 trillion gap in the Social Security program, would require roughly a tripling of the existing payroll tax on firms and workers[4]—clearly an unsustainable fiscal burden for the country and its taxpayers.

The primary driver of this burden is not the aging of our society or the specifics of eligibility for these entitlements, but rather the uncontained underlying growth in health care costs. These costs have more than tripled as a share of our economy since 1950, and their escalation shows no signs of abating. The Congressional Budget Office recently projected that the share of the economy devoted to health care will double by 2050.[5] Thus, the sustainability of our public insurance programs depends on reining in health care costs.

Designing, passing, and implementing policies that will bring health care costs under control, however, will require herculean efforts on the part of U.S. policymakers. Universal health insurance coverage is, in a sense, central to these efforts, because squaring away a baseline level of coverage will allow policymakers to focus their energies on cost control. The health policy community has long been fighting a two-front war, and the goals of universal coverage and cost control can sometimes conflict. Having everyone pulling in the same direction—with the recognition that certain financial limits will be required to ensure ongoing health care for all—is key to developing the consensus necessary for cost control. I have witnessed

SECTION TWO
Readings

299

this effect firsthand in Massachusetts, where for years our advocacy community focused exclusively on expanding coverage for medical expenditures and therefore opposed most initiatives that might have put that goal at risk, even those that might have meant controlling costs. Since Massachusetts passed its universal-coverage plan, this powerful advocacy community has shifted its attention to controlling costs as a means of preserving the program's affordability to the state. The result was the passage last year of an opening salvo in the cost-control wars here in Massachusetts—Senate bill 2526, An Act to Promote Cost Containment, Transparency and Efficiency in the Delivery of Quality Health Care. Other countries, such as the Netherlands and Switzerland, have demonstrated that it is possible to have both universal coverage (even coverage provided through private insurance companies) and much lower health care spending.

Thus, the choice between fixing our health insurance system and fixing our economy is a false one. A smart health care reform bill, which has at its center universal health insurance coverage for our citizens, can improve both individual health and the economy's health, both today and in the long run.

No potential conflict of interest relevant to this article was reported.

Dr. Gruber is a professor of economics at the Massachusetts Institute of Technology, Cambridge.

1. Gruber J, Yelowitz A. Public health insurance and private savings. *J Polit Econ* 1999; 107:1249–74.

2. Gruber J, Madrian B. Health insurance, labor supply and job mobility: a critical review of the literature. In: McLaughlin CG, ed. *Health policy and the uninsured*. Washington, DC: Urban Institute Press, 2004:97–178.

3. Baucus M. Call to action: health reform 2009. November 2008. (Accessed January 9, 2009, at http://finance.senate.gov/healthreform2009/finalwhitepaper.pdf.)

4. Gruber J. *Public finance and public policy*. 2nd ed. New York: Worth, 2007.

SECTION TWO

Readings

5. Congressional Budget Office. The long-term budget outlook and options for slowing the growth of health care costs. Testimony of Peter Orszag before the Senate Finance Committee. June 17, 2008. (Accessed January 9, 2009, at http://www.cbo.gov/ftpdocs/93xx/doc9385/06-17-LTBO_Testimony.pdf.)

SECTION TWO
Readings

Elisabeth Garber-Paul—Lucrative Lies

The Nation, 5 May 2009, p. 5. Copyright © 2009 The Nation.
Reprinted with permission from the May 10, 2009 issue of The Nation.

South Carolina Congressman Joe Wilson's infamous outburst during President Obama's healthcare speech may not have endeared him to his Democratic colleagues, who voted overwhelmingly on September 15 to reprimand him, but it (and the blogosphere campaign against him) has made him a cause célèbre of the right wing. As Michael Kinsley noted in the *Washington Post*, "The more times he is required to write 'I will not call the President a liar' on a special blackboard set up in the well of the House, the bigger hero he will become to a large chunk of the population."

At press time, Wilson has raised more than $1.7 million since September 9—$750,000 of which came in within forty-eight hours of his eruption—outstripping the nearly $1.2 million he raised for his entire 2008 race. Wilson's Democratic rival, Rob Miller, hasn't fared too badly either. Since Obama's speech, his campaign has netted more than $1.5 million, in large part through a fundraising drive on ActBlue.com, whose members gave in hopes of "defeating the man who yelled 'liar' at Obama" or, as one donor put it, "retiring ass clown Joe Wilson."

Miller, a former marine, lost the 2008 Congressional contest to Wilson in a 45–55 percent split, having spent just $614,487, $220,000 of which came from his own pocket; so the incident as a whole has certainly helped to even the campaign-cash gap. Still, it's premature to conclude that Wilson's heckling will lead to a Miller victory in 2010.

"Folks are making Wilson a hero," says Kevin Gray, a civil rights organizer from South Carolina, who also noted that his state is "the ideological home of white supremacy in the country." Despite the Miller campaign's growing pocketbook, Gray believes that Wilson's constituents will continue to mobilize, making Miller's chances slim. "It won't be against Miller," he says. "It will be against Obama. The black guy."

SECTION TWO
Readings

Clea Benson—A New Kind of Abortion Politics

CQ Weekly, 29 March 2010, p. 740. Reprinted by permission obtained via The Copyright Clearance Center.

In the days just before the House voted on overhauling the nation's health care system earlier this month, Bart Stupak, an otherwise low-profile member of Congress from Michigan's Upper Peninsula, found himself being chased through the hallways and into jammed elevators by reporters waving digital recorders and shouting questions.

As the organizer of a group of as many as a dozen Democratic holdouts who refused to commit their votes until they received a guarantee that no tax dollars would pay for abortions, Stupak was blocking the leaders of his own party, including the president, from achieving victory on the centerpiece of their political agenda.

Despite the cards he held, the 6-foot, 2-inch, iron-haired former state trooper tried to stay out of the spotlight, but he was not terribly successful in outpacing the media scrums. At some point, it became clear he had reached his limit.

"Just relax," he said curtly. "We're going to get this done."

What he got done in the end was to broker a deal under which the House would send to President Obama a health care bill without what is known as the "Stupak amendment," anti-abortion language that was in the measure passed by the House last November but was not included in the Senate bill. In return, Stupak was able to secure a last-minute promise from Obama to issue an executive order essentially reaffirming the long-standing principle that federal dollars should not pay for abortions.

But it all came with a cost. In striking the deal, Stupak went from being the hero of the anti-abortion movement to a pariah, as evidenced by the now-famous 'baby killer" remark uttered by Texas Republican Rep. Randy Neugebauer as Stupak discussed the provisions of the deal on the House floor March 21.

By the time it was all over, Stupak was simultaneously fielding anonymous death threats from abortion opponents on his office voice mail and facing a primary challenge from an abortion rights supporter.

Combatants in the abortion wars will argue for years about the effect of the new health care law on abortion policy, and the degree to which federal dollars end up subsidizing abortions.

SECTION TWO

Readings

But in political terms, what the Stupak episode showed, say analysts and people who were involved in the fight, is that the abortion issue remains a potent weapon in legislative battles such as health care—and one that can be wielded by an atypical breed of lawmaker: a Democrat who shares an opposition to abortion with many Republicans, yet hews to the party's mainstream in most other ways.

The events of the past months, and especially in recent weeks, upended an established order in which anti-abortion lawmakers could usually be counted on to embrace the rest of the conservative agenda, such as an opposition to expanding the federal role in medical care. This has deeply upset adherents of both sides, as the threats to Stupak from both sides of the issue demonstrate.

"A strong pro-life Democrat voice is a threat to both the Republican party and to also the pro-choice hold over the Democratic party," said Kristen Day, executive director of Democrats For Life of America, a group that organizes grass-roots support for Democrats opposed to abortion. "And I haven't seen this strong of a group in a long time."

While the abortion issue has never been a strictly partisan one, divisions between anti-abortion Democrats and anti-abortion Republicans emerged more clearly than ever in this debate, as was made clear during the struggles of Stupak and his allies to find a way to support the Democrats' health care bill while preserving three decades of policies that barred the use of taxpayer money in the financing of abortions.

The debate, for example, has threatened to drive a partisan wedge in the Congressional Pro-Life Caucus, which has long been a strongly two-party endeavor on Capitol Hill.

The degree to which this shift in the politics of abortion really manifests itself will become clear in the coming months, as both sides are now vowing to increase their clout in Congress.

Anti-abortion groups say they are looking ahead to the midterm elections and planning to reach out to voters, particularly in districts where Democrats who oppose abortion rights voted for the health care bill. Organizations supporting abortion rights are doing the same.

"Our experience with the Stupak debacle this year illustrates our numerical challenge," said Donna Crane, policy director at the National Abortion Rights Action League (NARAL). "The numbers in Congress are not where we want them. And we've been flooded with interest from pro-choice supporters."

Hyde Amendment Lives

For more than a quarter of a century, federal policy on abortion has been defined by the Hyde Amendment, an annual addition to an appropriations bill that says tax dollars can't cover pregnancy terminations except in cases of rape, incest or danger to the mother's life. It's been renewed every year since 1976, when it was first introduced by Illinois Republican Henry J. Hyde, who served in the House from 1975 until 2007.

But the health care overhaul that has now been enacted significantly expands the government's role in the health care system, including providing tax credits and direct subsidies for people to buy coverage. Anti-abortion forces wanted to make sure the intent of the Hyde amendment is imprinted on the new coverage in the overhaul, and to eliminate the need to renew the Hyde prohibition every year in spending law.

From Stupak's perspective, it fell to him as the co-chairman of the Congressional Pro-Life Caucus and a member of the Energy and Commerce Committee to respond last summer when the House health care bill was introduced—and didn't mention abortion.

Now in his ninth term, Stupak had never been much of a national figure. His most high-profile public crusade before this was an effort to press for tighter controls on the acne drug Accutane, which he blamed for the suicide of his 17-year-old son, B.J., in 2000. As chairman of the Oversight subcommittee on Energy and Commerce, he was more likely to be seen on television grilling Toyota executives about faulty acceleration systems than talking about social issues.

SECTION TWO
Readings

But their own legal analysis and that of groups such as the U.S. Conference of Catholic Bishops convinced lawmakers in Stupak's caucus that the health care bill's silence on abortion would have allowed federal money to pay to terminate pregnancies.

Stupak quickly found himself at the epicenter of a roiling debate—or, as he put it, "thrust into this role."

"I don't go searching out these issues," Stupak, a Roman Catholic, said in an interview the week before the vote. "I never thought it would take on the life of its own that it has."

His perspective, he said, simply reflects that of his culturally conservative district, a vast and sparsely populated area where the economic engines are timber, mining and tourism. A working-class area, it's also pro-union and pro-gun. "Seldom do we get a non-pro-life person up there," he said. "For us, it's not a big deal."

In many ways, Stupak is characteristic of the type of Democratic lawmaker who holds anti-abortion views. For years, Democrats from anti-abortion districts were able to go about their business without much drama, allowing Republicans to carry the water on the issue and joining in for the occasional vote.

But now that their party is in the majority, all that has changed.

"When we had control of not only Congress but the White House, it really in the past year and three months has become more and more of an issue," said Daniel Lipinski of Illinois, a former political science professor. Lipinski was one of the few Democratic anti-abortion holdouts who ended up voting against the health care bill, in part because of the abortion language and in part because he had other concerns, including that it was not fiscally sustainable and did not do enough to constrain costs.

Lipinski noted that he is "very comfortable back home" in his district on the southwest side of Chicago, a heavily Catholic working-class enclave. But among other Democrats in Congress, he said, "It always causes problems with others who do not agree with the position."

Day, of Democrats For Life, says her organization exists because anti-abortion Democrats are in a tough spot.

"The pro-life community generally doesn't trust them because they're Democrats," she said. "The Democrats say, 'You can't be part of our party because you're pro-life.' "

Nonetheless, these political outliers took on a newly central role in November when, suddenly, the Democratic leadership needed them. With Republicans committed to voting against the House version of the health care legislation and bands of Democrats defecting for various reasons on the right and left, House Speaker Nancy Pelosi of California was scrounging for every vote she could find, including those in the Pro-Life Caucus. At Stupak's insistence, she allowed a vote on an abortion financing ban. It was adopted easily, 240-194, with yes votes from almost 25 percent of House Democrats.

Though many abortion rights supporters were caught off guard by the strength of anti-abortion sentiment within the ranks of Democrats in Congress, the vote on what became known as the Stupak amendment reflected a trend that had accelerated during the past two election cycles.

The anti-abortion component of the caucus still isn't as strong as it once was. In 1976, 107 Democrats voted for the original Hyde amendment. In November, just 64 voted for the Stupak amendment. But groups such as Democrats For Life see a growth trend: The party achieved its majority by taking seats in conservative districts and by encouraging candidates with conservative views to run on the Democratic ticket.

"To expand their coalition, the Democrats took in a fair number of people who are not going to be pro-choice, and they're living with the consequences," said Gary C. Jacobson, a political scientist at the University of California at San Diego who specializes in congressional politics. "I think they're happy to live with the consequences."

Exactly what those consequences are, as far as the health care bill goes, is still a matter of contentious debate.

Ultimately, the Senate, with fewer abortion opponents, passed the overhaul with language on abortion funding that was decried by opponents as less restrictive than the Stupak amendment. Nebraska Democrat Ben Nelson had tried to get the Senate to go along with Stupak's language last December, but the chamber killed his amendment on a tabling motion, 54–45. Nelson remained a holdout right until the end, and won concessions in the bill that passed on Dec. 24.

When the Senate measure reached the House earlier this month, the Stupak bloc once again pressed for changes. But this time their luck ran out. Pelosi was able to peel off enough of Stupak's holdouts that it appeared the bill would pass without concessions on abortion. The Sunday afternoon of the vote, Stupak and seven of his fellow anti-abortion Democrats announced they would accept the executive order as the best deal they could get and would vote for the bill. Later on March 21, it passed, 219-212.

In the days leading up to the vote, Stupak talked about wanting to support the health care overhaul. His concerns were the same as those of many Democrats. As Oversight chairman, he said, he had seen too many instances when insurance companies revoked poli-

SECTION TWO
Readings

cies of people who got sick. "As soon as a woman gets breast cancer, they're going to knock you off," he said. "Those are gut-wrenching deals."

As he stood up at a press conference on the afternoon of the vote, Stupak said he and his colleagues were comfortable that the president's executive order would allow "standing on our principle of protecting the sanctity of life in health care reform."

But it was clear, at the same time, that Stupak and the members who stood on the dais with him were relieved that they were able to cast their votes in favor of the bill.

"It is just so profound to be part of a moment when we truly move America into the 21st century," Ohio Democrat Marcy Kaptur said.

Then it was the anti-abortion movement's turn to be shocked. Some groups, such as the association representing Catholic hospitals, had already thrown their support behind the health care bill. But the mainstream of the anti-abortion movement, used to dealing with Republicans, had been sure that Stupak and company would hold out for nothing less than strict statutory language on abortion, even if it meant health care reform would die. They rejected the executive order as a weak alternative that was tantamount to allowing taxpayer dollars to pay for abortions outright.

Marjorie Dannenfelser, president of the Susan B. Anthony List, a group that promotes women who oppose abortion in politics, quickly revoked a "Defender of Life" award that the group had planned to give Stupak last week.

She described Stupak's final move as a betrayal, although she acknowledged that he and like-minded Democrats had been key in pushing abortion restrictions up to that moment.

"Certainly their votes have always been helpful in protecting the status quo," she said."But if they had been upfront in the beginning in saying an executive order is exactly what we need to fix this problem, then we would have been able to have a debate about what an executive order does."

Still, it's clear that without the efforts of Stupak and his like-minded cohorts in alliance with their Republican colleagues, the policy under a Democratic administration and majority in both houses would likely have been more permissive of federal funding for abortion. During the campaign, Obama himself said he wanted to overturn the Hyde amendment. And that is a top agenda item for members of the House Pro-Choice Caucus.

"We don't like current law," said Colorado Democrat Diana DeGette, co-chairwoman of the caucus. "We would like to overturn the Hyde amendment. But we said we would compromise to current law in order to make this a health care bill, not an abortion bill."

In the view of Energy and Commerce Chairman Henry A. Waxman, a California Democrat, having a group of Democrats ally themselves with Republicans on abortion changes the components of the political equation, but the results are the same in the end.

"The Hyde amendment has not been changed in 30 years,' he said. "So it's not likely that it's going to change in the immediate future."

But that's precisely what both sides in the abortion debate don't want.

Nobody's Happy

As much as Pelosi may want to steer clear of social issues that may divide her increasingly conservative caucus, the health care overhaul may have set off a dormant volcano. Outside groups on both sides of the abortion issue are deeply unhappy with the way things played out, and they say their supporters are now fired up to boost their representation in Congress as the midterm elections loom.

"It's been essential to do that, and it's even more essential to do it now," said Marcia Greenberger, co-president of the National Women's Law Center.

Greenberger said abortion rights supporters are also planning to push back on interpretations of the current law that they believe are overly restrictive.

"I believe that there is not a majority in the House or Senate that would support the kinds of extreme exclusions that Hyde has now been interpreted to contain," she said, noting the 'examples of women who have been denied abortion care when their very health is at stake."

The day of the vote, Stupak recounted how hard it had been on his staff and his family to take a constant pounding from angry citizens on both sides of the issue. "Hopefully, that will all end, and we can get back to some normal lifestyle,' he said. As of last week, his office phones were still ringing off the hook.

Meanwhile, Marjorie Dannenfelser says she is preparing to embark on what she calls a "bittersweet project."

SECTION TWO
Readings

Her first target for the midterm elections: Stupak and the other Democratic lawmakers who oppose abortion funding but who voted for the health care bill.

"It doesn't give me any pleasure to go about the job of opposing some of those people who have been described as pro-life Democrats," she said. But there's no question in my mind it has to be done.'

Stupak, for his part, appears to want to wear the criticism as a badge of honor.

"I guess that must mean I did a good job," he told Fox News last Friday, a day after the drama in the House and Senate came to an end. "I got both sides mad at me."

SECTION TWO
Readings

Jeffrey Toobin—Not Covered

The New Yorker, 85.38 (November 23, 2009) 37–38. Copyright ©
Condé Nast. *Reprinted with permission.*

Abortion is almost as old as childbirth. There has always been a need for some women to end their pregnancies. In modern times, the law's attitude toward that need has varied. In the United States, at the time the Constitution was adopted, abortions before "quickening" were both legal and commonplace, often performed by midwives. In the nineteenth century, under the influence of the ascendant medical profession, which opposed abortion (and wanted to control health care), states began to outlaw the procedure, and by the turn of the twentieth century it was all but uniformly illegal. The rise of the feminist movement led to widespread efforts to decriminalize abortion, and in 1973 the Supreme Court found, in *Roe v. Wade*, that the Constitution prohibited the states from outlawing it.

Throughout this long legal history, the one constant has been that women have continued to have abortions. The rate has declined slightly in recent years, but, according to the Guttmacher Institute, thirty-five per cent of all women of reproductive age in America today will have had an abortion by the time they are forty-five. It might be assumed that such a common procedure would be included in a nation's plan to protect the health of its citizens. In fact, the story of abortion during the past decade has been its separation from other medical services available to women. Abortion, as the academics like to say, is being marginalized.

The latest evidence comes from the House of Representatives, which two weekends ago narrowly passed its health-care bill, by a vote of 220 to 215. One reason that the Democrats won back control of Congress is that the Party adopted a "big tent" philosophy on abortion. The implications of that approach became clear when, during the health-care vote, the House considered a last-minute amendment by Bart Stupak, a Michigan Democrat, which proposed scrubbing the bill of government subsidies for abortion procedures. It passed 240 to 194, with sixty-four Democrats voting in favor.

A clear understanding of the structure of the health-care proposals currently under consideration shows why the Stupak amendment is such a threat to abortion rights. At the heart of the proposals is the

SECTION TWO

Readings

idea of an exchange, where consumers will be able to select among competing insurance plans. Theoretically, the exchange will increase consumer choice, promote competition, and (somewhat more theoretically) lower costs for everyone. If there is a public option, it will be offered through the exchange. At first, many of the people using the exchange will be those who are unable to pay for health insurance on their own. For them, the government will offer a sliding scale of subsidies. It is largely these subsidies which will increase the availability of insurance; estimates of how many people will gain coverage vary, but it may be close to forty million.

Restrictions on the use of federal funds for abortion go back to the Hyde amendment, which became law more than thirty years ago; for example, there has long been a ban on abortions under Medicaid or in military hospitals. But the implications of the Stupak amendment are broader, because of the structure of the exchange. To start with, Stupak states that anyone who buys insurance with a government subsidy cannot choose a plan that covers abortion, even if that person receives only a small subsidy, and even if only a tiny portion of the full premium goes for abortion care. And the influence of the amendment reaches beyond the recipients of federal subsidies. Stupak would prohibit the public option from offering any plans that cover abortion. Further, it is expected that each year more Americans will use the exchange, including people who don't need subsidies, but under the Stupak amendment insurance companies would have no incentive to offer those people coverage for abortion services, since doing so might cost them the business of subsidized customers. Today, most policies cover abortion; in a post-Stupak world, they probably won't. With a health-care plan that is supposed to increase access and lower costs, the opposite would be true with respect to abortion. And that, of course, is what legislators like Stupak want—to make abortions harder, and more expensive, to obtain. Stupak and his allies were willing to kill the whole bill to get their way; the liberals in the House were not.

It may be that the endurance of Roe and Democratic control of the federal government have led to a certain complacency among abortion-rights supporters. Yet it's not only with regard to insurance that abortion services are being treated like a second-class form of medicine. There is, for instance, the proliferation of "conscience clauses," which allow medical professionals to refuse to conduct procedures that they disapprove of. Shortly after Roe, Congress passed the first major conscience clause, which stated that medical professionals and hospitals that receive certain federal funds did not have to provide abortions or sterilizations if they objected on "the basis of religious beliefs or moral convictions." The Bush Administration sought to dramatically expand the clauses to cover not only doctors and nurses but anyone who works in a hospital, including pharmacists, and to increase the range of practices that might be rejected—a step that could potentially include such services as the dispensing of birth control. President Obama has said that he will revise or overturn the policy.

The President is pro-choice, and he has signalled some misgivings about the Stupak amendment. But, like many modern pro-choice Democrats, he has worked so hard to be respectful of his opponents on this issue that he sometimes seems to cede them the moral high ground. In his book "The Audacity of Hope," he describes the "undeniably difficult issue of abortion" and ponders "the middle-aged feminist who still mourns her abortion." Elsewhere, he announces, "Abortion vexes." The opponents of abortion aren't vexed—they are mobilized, focussed, and driven to succeed. The Catholic bishops took the lead in pushing for the Stupak amendment, and they squeezed legislators in a way that would do any K Street lobbyist proud. (One never sees that kind of effort on behalf of other aspects of Catholic teaching, like opposition to the death penalty.) Meanwhile, the pro-choice forces temporized. But, as Supreme Court Justice Ruth Bader Ginsburg observed not long ago, abortion rights "center on a woman's autonomy to determine her life's course, and thus to enjoy equal citizenship stature." Every diminishment of that right diminishes women. With stakes of such magnitude, it is wise to weigh carefully the difference between compromise and surrender.

SECTION TWO
Readings

SECTION TWO
Readings

Section Three

Public Argument

Introduction: Writing Outside of the Classroom Box: Academic and Public Audiences

By Christopher Minnix

 By this time in your life, you have written more than a few papers for what we call academic audiences, or audiences that are set in the academic context of school or the university. From your first essays about your summer vacation, you probably progressed to larger projects such as reports and then to writing your first academic essays in college. Each of these genres has challenged you to envision your audience, and by now you can probably conjure up an audience in your head when a teacher begins to talk about "academic writing." As one influential writing researcher has put it, when we sit down to write in our college classes we "invent the university" (Bartholomae 24). This means that we envision or invent our university audiences and their potential reactions. We also invent our expectations for the type of writing or research that would pass as academic and even the purpose of our writing for a specific class. The tricky part is often matching up the knowledge we use to invent the university or the rhetorical situations we encounter as students with the actual expectations of academic audiences.

Learning to write in academic contexts and using academic genres is an ongoing process, one that changes as you move to and from different academic contexts and disciplines. The understanding of rhetoric and the skills that you have developed for analyzing rhetorical situations are vitally important because they give you strategies for sizing up each of these new situations. You may not have experience writing in the genre that a teacher in an elective course on anthropology asks you to use, but you have methods for analyzing this genre and the rhetorical strategies of the genre. This is powerful knowledge.

But is this knowledge just useful for figuring out how to attain good grades on academic papers? Only if you choose to stop thinking rhetorically when you walk out of the door of your classroom. What we hope is apparent at this point in this book is that rhetoric is not simply a school-room subject, but a human capacity for persuasion, one that has deep roots in all of human activity and in all fields of human study, even the sciences. As you read through this section, you will be challenged to think about opportunities for going public with your writing. What you will find in this section are advanced strategies for analyzing audiences, making strong, persuasive arguments, and developing spatial-visual arguments. But you will find more than just strategies here. As you read this section, you will also find examples of how people, some of them students just like yourselves, took their own interests and writing public.

Can Student Writing Really Become Effective Public Writing?

As a student in a college class you are busy but lucky. Lucky in the sense that you have the opportunity to find issues and subjects that inspire passionate interest. These are subjects that you will probably continue to read about or even research for many years to come. This has been our experience, and as educators we hope that it is your experience as well. In addition, however, we hope that you will also be inspired to write about these issues for a variety of audiences, not just academic audiences. As you begin to find issues and ideas that interest you, we encourage you to think not only about the papers you would like to write in class, but of **potential public audiences** for your work. We will learn in this section that writing for the public does not mean writing for an undefined group of people, or everyone. Instead, when we write for public audiences *we write for a group of people who are involved in an ongoing discussion about an issue of public concern; or, we take on the task of trying to create an audience interested in addressing an issue by bringing a problem or issue to public attention.*

We will define and explain "public audience" more fully in the chapters that follow. We will also explain the connections and overlap between academic contexts and public contexts and discuss how your own academic research and work can speak to both of these contexts. You may find that the issues or ideas you are passionate about might have more local audiences than you think, even if they are issues or ideas that have their origins in places far from where you live. You may also find yourself writing about issues that have both international and local consequences, such as issues like climate change, immigrant rights, or even the development of social network technologies. What we hope you will see in this section is that the academic research and writing that you do has real-world consequences, both for your own growth, the ongoing discussion in the field you study, and for the public audiences that might benefit from your research and writing.

Arguing about Public Issues

Argument is often discussed by using metaphors of war and arguing in public can sometimes seem like a treacherous enterprise. Here are a few examples of the bellicose or war-like metaphors we use for argument taken from George Lakoff and Mark Johnson's book *Metaphors We Live By*:

> He *attacked every weak point* in my argument.
>
> I *demolished* his argument.
>
> If you use that *strategy*, he'll *wipe you out*. (5).

These examples show us that argument is often thought of as a hostile activity, one where we mobilize our arguments like a general mobilizes troops. This orientation does exist, and we can see it play out in debates on political talk shows. But does this mean that we can expect all argument to be a hostile activity? No. Like all rhetoric, the rhetoric of public argument changes in tone based upon the rhetorical situation. If you write publicly long enough, people will disagree with your ideas. This does not necessarily mean that you have failed rhetorically, however. Instead, it probably means that you have probably located a **point of controversy** in the public discussion about the issue you are writing about. As you continue to discuss this issue in your writing, you will find that responding to and thinking through this point of controversy becomes a key part of your writing or invention process.

We must be careful as writers not to let these points of conflict become discouraging, as they can do so in two damaging ways. First, they can leave us feeling as though we should refrain from writing about an issue. This happens quite a bit when we begin writing publicly as students, as we often have trouble mustering the confidence to write for a public audience, especially audiences that value expertise. Second, we can sometimes act on our discouragement by reacting sharply to our audience, concluding that they are simply "wrong" and that there is no need in discussing the matter further.

In the last section of this book, you learned to analyze controversial issues and to map out the varying rhetorical perspectives that shape the debate over these issues. As you begin to write your own responses to issues of public controversy, these tools of analysis will be invaluable. You have seen that arguments over public issues often respond to an ongoing debate. To respond to these debates authors often internalize and respond to the criticisms of others. These authors incorporate the arguments of their opposition into their own writing and draw from this knowledge to make their work more persuasive. Some attempt to find **common ground** on an issue, some attempt to respond directly to criticism with a **counterargument** or **rebuttal**, and others might have even sought to **shift the grounds of discussion** by arguing that the criticism is not focused on the important issues of the debate.

What is important to realize here is not just that we should have a thick skin as writers, but that **the process of public writing is dialectical**. This means that there is a healthy give and take of opinions. The result of this give and take is often not a clattering of voices but an ongoing conversation that is shaped by the different concerns, criticisms, ideas, and positions that public writers take up in these debates. In a famous passage, a scholar of rhetoric and literature, Kenneth Burke, described this process like a conversation that occurs in a parlor:

> Imagine that you enter a parlor. You come late. When you arrive, others have long preceded you, and they are engaged in a heated discussion, a discussion too heated for them to pause and tell you exactly what it is about. In fact, the discussion had already begun long before any of them got there, so that no one present is qualified to retrace for you all the steps that had gone before. You listen for a while, until you decide that you have caught the tenor of the argument; then you put in your oar. Someone answers; you answer him; another comes to your defense; another aligns himself against you, to either the embarrassment or gratification of your opponent, depending upon the quality of your ally's assistance. However, the discussion is interminable. The hour grows late, you must depart. And you do depart, with the discussion still vigorously in progress. (110–111).

In our networked age, we might imagine this parlor as a thread on a blog, or as posts on someone's wall on *Facebook* or *MySpace*. We have probably all had experience with this latter example, engaging back in forth in a conversation about something that happened, or even about an idea or issue. Notice, however, that in the parlor example, the conversation never ends. It outlasts not only our speech or writing, but also our own lives. Another thing that you might notice is that for all the people who disagree with you in this conversation "another comes to your defense." As you write for public audiences, you will find that this does indeed occur and that you will often draw on the arguments of these allies to continue to develop and defend your position.

The strategies that you will learn in the following chapters are thus strategies for sizing up the conversation, developing your arguments, and then adapting to the give and take of public argument. You will also learn to internalize or take in the critiques and support of others and use them to develop your positions further. You may also find that, unlike the parlor or the argument as war metaphors above, sometimes the discussion is less about winning and losing and more about finding common ground or seeking a common solution to an ongoing problem. These types of arguments are based on what can be called **assent**, or the ability to establish mutual agreement on a public issue or at least an agreement on a way to address the issue that is fair for all of those involved. Think of the debates that happen in your city councils where you live, debates about road construction, zoning, etc. These can be hotly debated contests that must be solved by voting and where one advocate wins and the other loses. Alternatively, though, there can also be decisions that are based upon seeking common ground or assent, such as the decision to name a street after a famous civil rights leader.

The type of argument you develop will depend on the rhetorical situation you enter. It will also depend upon the potential and plausible action that you would like your audience to take on an issue. It is important to remember that people will disagree, sometimes sharply, with you, whether you are seeking assent or seeking to directly rebut the argument of one of your opponents. In this sense, the skills of analysis that you have developed will help you determine not only the different parties involved in the debate, but potential allies and potential colleagues in the conversation about the issue you are writing about.

Conclusion

As you begin to take your writing and research public, I would like to leave you with a few ideas to pursue and a few questions.

First, I would encourage you to think about the different public communities that you are tied to in your own life. These can be communities that shape or share your values (both local, national, and international). They are communities that you work with to achieve common goals, communities with which you identify, and even communities that you just find interesting. Take out a sheet of paper and try to list down as many as you can think of and explain your connection to them. Now, I would like you to look over your list and determine how many of the communities you listed have actual physical contact with you. You may be shocked to find that many of the communities that you listed you know rhetorically, through public arguments, rather than through physical contact. They are no less important to us though.

Second, do some freewriting about an issue of public concern that you would like to address to a public audience. Try to write down our position or argument about the issue. Then, exchange this writing with one of your classmates and have them write a response to your writing from the perspective of someone who is least likely to agree with your position. In other words, ask them to write a rebuttal to your argument. Then, read their rebuttal and take a moment and think about how you might internalize your response to their objections. Write down your response to the rebuttal and examine how you might respond to it in order to strengthen your argument. I encourage you to have a conversation with your partner as you do this, as they will be able to explain their logic and give you a chance to try out some of your own counterarguments.

Finally, here are some questions to think about as you work through the chapters in this section:

1. *What are the differences and similarities between writing in a classroom and writing for a public audience?*

2. *How do you see academic research and writing connecting to public issues and public controversies?*

3. *What are some common rhetorical strategies of public arguments, strategies that you are familiar with from watching and reading public debates or controversies?*

4. *What are some examples of rhetorical strategies that you have observed working and not working for public audiences?*

5. *How do you see your own writing? Do you see potential for your writing to address an issue of public concern or to make a persuasive public statement about a public issue?*

Works Cited

Bartholomae, David. "Inventing the University." *Cross-Talk in Comp Theory: A Reader.* 2nd Edition. Ed. Victor Villaneuva. Urbana, Illinois: NCTE Press, 2003. 623–654. Print.

Burke, Kenneth. *The Philosophy of Literary Form.* Berkeley: University of California P. 1974. Print.

Lakoff, George and Mark Johnson. *Metaphors We Live By.* Chicago: University of Chicago P, 1980. Print.

Chapter 12

Audiences and Opportunities: How to Use Research and Rhetorical Analysis to Get Your Voice Heard

By Christopher Minnix

For many of us, the idea of making a public argument on an important social issue seems, at first, unrealistic and daunting. We often compare ourselves and our writing to the experts and commentators that we read, or maybe even to the professors that teach our classes. In doing this, we find ourselves feeling as though we lack the knowledge and authority to address the issue. We might even fear that we will not find an audience for our ideas. In one sense, this is a consequence of the fact that knowledge is very specialized in our society. Think, for example, of the many, many specialties and subspecialties in the departments at your university. This specialization means that we might not be able to contribute to some conversations about the issues that interest us because they are conversations among experts in a specific field of study. However, while these expert conversations are important, they account for only one part of public conversation about an issue. Your continued study in a field may place you in these conversations in the future, but there is an important conversation that you can take part in right now: a public conversation about issues of public controversy and concern and the consequences that they have on the lives of your fellow citizens.

Think for a moment about an important public issue such as stem cell research. While scientists and experts debate the technical benefits and drawbacks of this research, they are certainly not the only voice in the conversation. In fact, even if the scientific community were to reach unanimous or complete agreement on the practice of stem cell research, such agreement alone would not result in law and policy being passed on the issue. In a democracy like our own, public issues, even those that are highly scientific, depend upon their acceptance by a majority of citizens. While we do not vote on each of these issues, we do vote for the legislators (congressmen and senators in our case) that do. In addition, citizens voice their concern, outrage, and agreement with these policies in a way that challenges legislators to act. It is in this sense that your public voice becomes vitally important to the issues that affect your life and the lives of those around you. Public rhetoric is not only about writing our legislators, though. It is a process of bringing new ideas, arguments, and issues to the awareness of our fellow citizens in local, national, and even international communities. By doing so, we can take part in supporting or developing support for the policy, program, or idea that we are advocating and bring them to the attention of local, national, and international governments.

Consider, for instance, the example of *The Genocide Intervention Network*. In 2004, several students of international politics at Swarthmore College looked at the genocide that was taking place in Darfur, in Western Sudan and started thinking about strategies for intervention. These students ended up founding *The Genocide Intervention Fund*, which later became a powerful Non Governmental Organization called *The Genocide Intervention Network*. The beginnings of this organization can be traced back to the public argument of another writer several years earlier. Samantha Power, a young professor who would later become the Pulitzer Prize-winning author of *A Problem from Hell: America and the Age of Genocide*, gave a graduation speech at Swarthmore in 2002 asking Swarthmore students to change their world for the better. Two of the students who founded *The Genocide Intervention Network*, Mark Hanis and Andrew Sniderman, heard the speech and showed up at Power's office to ask how they could apply the lessons of the speech to stopping the Darfur genocide. From this meeting, they began writing up the materials that would form the basis of their public activism to stop the genocide in Darfur.

All this might not have happened, however, if Power had not written a paper for a law school class about genocide. According to Power, "*A Problem From Hell* began as a paper for a class I took in law school. Its publication changed my life. Unfortunately, my aim in writing the book had never been to change my life. I had set out,

far more humbly, to transform the way the United States conducted
its foreign policy around the world" (Power, "Why Can't We?").
Power took her academic research and translated it into a book for a
public audience. The scholarship in her book is excellent, but it is not
written for a specialized audience. Instead, Power made the choice
to address her book to a non-specialized audience, or public audience. The book became a New York Times Best Seller, and brought
the problem of genocide—both past and present—back to public
awareness.

Drawing inspiration from Power, the students began making
public arguments of their own to the students on Swarthmore's campus. In doing so, they persuaded students to lobby the university administration to "divest" or withdraw any investments that the university had with Sudanese industries, and they began raising funds
to support peacekeeping troops from the African Union to help stop
the violence. From this local beginning, they have attracted the attention of high-level politicians, celebrities, and public intellectuals
who have lent support to their cause. They are now considered a
leading activist organization for stopping genocide.

These students were in a position much like your own. They were
writing about an issue that was heavily discussed by experts without
being experts on the issue themselves, they were addressing an international issue in a local context, and they were using their intelligent
ideas to motivate a public audience to action. This chapter is designed
to help you do the same, to help you think through the process of
taking an active role in this conversation. As you will learn, there are
many, many audiences for your public arguments, and public argument is about much more than simply writing a letter to a legislator.
This will require you to learn to research and analyze the different
audiences, groups and organizations, and rhetorical strategies that
are used to engage your issue.

Brainstorming Public Audiences for Your Writing

Finding a public audience for our writing begins with thinking
through the purpose of our writing, or what we want to accomplish
through our writing. For example, let's say that you were interested
in developing a public argument against the heavy weight placed on
standardized test scores for college admissions. You researched the
controversy over this issue and found a variety of different arguments

for and against the use of standardized tests and developed a controversy analysis of these major arguments. Now, you want to raise public awareness about this issue and develop a public argument that calls on your fellow citizens to advocate against standardized testing. This is just the type of general starting point that most of us have after we research and read about a controversy. The next step to developing a public argument is to develop and define our argument more specifically for a particular audience.

Since your public argument is supposed to influence your audience to act in a certain way—even if it is simply considering a change in belief or attitude—you can begin thinking about your potential audiences by thinking about how you would like them to act. This is the purpose of your public argument. To get started, take out a piece of paper, if you like, and use the following activities to guide you.

Thinking through the Purpose of Your Public Argument

1. Freewrite for a few minutes on the goal of your public argument, or what you would like to see happen as a result of your argument. What do you want your readers to do, feel, think, believe, etc. as a result of reading it?

2. Now that you have an idea of what you want to accomplish, draw a line down the center of a piece of paper. Label the left side "Plausible Actions/Reactions" and the right side "Not Plausible." Then, fill these categories with likely and unlikely results of reading your analysis.

3. From your freewriting and list, we can now build a chain of likely consequences for your public argument. Take a plausible action from your list and then trace out the possible effects of it. For example, if you said "raise awareness about issue," draw a line beside it and then state what raising awareness might accomplish. Let's say that awareness might motivate the public to act. Draw lines outward from that for the possible actions the public might take.

4. Now, think through the possible audiences that you might want to address. You want to think about the people who are most likely to move towards achieving your goal. Draft out a paragraph that describes the groups of people who are most likely to advance your cause.

With this as your starting point, you are ready to begin researching the possibilities of your argument.

Researching Public Audiences

Public writing requires us to actively seek out the different audiences and types of writing available to us. In Chapter 9, you learned how to conduct library and field research on a controversial issue, and you will continue to use these research skills as you develop your public argument. To write a public argument, you will need to conduct a different type of research: research into the audiences, genres, and communities that surround your issue. You may find that you are familiar with some genres of public argument already, such as letters to the editor of a newspaper, letters to congressmen, petitions, even the websites of activist groups. While these are available to you on many issues, a bit of research can reveal that the individuals and groups debating your issue argue for many different audiences and use many different genres.

The process below will help you visualize the process of researching the different audiences, genres, and outcomes of your public rhetoric. Like any process, you may adapt it to the needs of your own particular project.

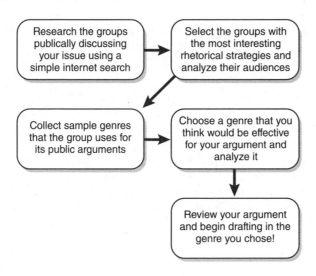

Research the Groups Publically Discussing Your Issue

In order to know how to address your issue persuasively, it is immensely helpful to analyze how others are addressing this issue or an issue like it in a public context. You can begin doing so by using a basic internet search. Scholarly research requires us to use library databases and peer-reviewed sources, but we are not looking for scholarly information in this search. Instead, we are looking for public rhetoric as your issue in the public space of the internet. Here are a few tips for making your searches efficient and productive. Like the library research that you learned for your controversy analysis, this research will require you to use effective keywords to filter the information.

Developing Effective Internet Searches for Examples of Public Rhetoric

1. Begin with a simple search. Type in the issue or topic that you are addressing and see what pops up. Ignore the encyclopedia articles at this point, and scroll through the first couple of pages of results to see if any activist groups on your issue pop up. Bookmark or note any groups that seem interesting.

2. While still looking at these pages, take out a sheet of blank paper or open a blank document on your computer. As you read through the first five or six pages of results, list any important words, terms, events, or ideas about your issue that keep popping up.

3. Now that you have some keywords to begin with, you can try an advanced search. Select the advanced search option of your search engine and look over the options. Then type in your topic and any keywords that you found from your simple search.

4. If these words do not yield any examples of groups debating your issue, then try typing in your topic or subject and adding in the following keywords: *controversy*, *debate*, *protest*, or *take action*.

5. If there is little information out there on your issue, consider looking up a more popular issue for examples of public rhetoric to model your writing upon.

Select the Groups with the Most Interesting Rhetorical Strategies and Analyze Their Audiences

Now that you have a few examples bookmarked or noted, it is time to get selective. You might look for groups that hold positions most like your own, but you do not need to limit yourself to these groups. Instead, look for the groups, organizations, or individuals who have what you feel are the most effective rhetorical strategies. As you study these groups, you will probably find that they seek to reach a diverse range of audiences. Think about the audience for your own work and the strategies you might utilize to reach them. Here are a few aspects of public audience to look for as you analyze.

Analyzing Public Audiences

1. Take a look at the main organizational webpage of the group. First, click on and read any links that say "About," "Mission," or that make any other references to the main focus of the group. This will give you a good overview of the types of audiences they might be seeking to persuade.

2. Click though the links in the webpage's menu and try to get an idea of the purpose of the group's website. Does the group provide opportunities for you to take action? If so, what types of action? Or, is the site mainly there to inform or raise awareness? If so, what is the goal of informing the audience or raising awareness about the issue? Look for purposes other than these as well.

3. Now, looking back through the same pages, note the language that each page uses. Does it use a lot of technical keywords or jargon? What does the reading level of the text say about the audience of the site? Does it differ from page to page or is the language consistent throughout the site?

4. Finally, look for bias. Does the page seek to include some readers in the groups' activities and exclude others? What biases do you detect and how do they help you understand the audience of the site?

Collect Samples That the Group Uses for Their Public Arguments

As you looked through the webpages of a few different activist groups, you more than likely noticed a variety of different types of communication that were used. You probably noticed a mixture of video, audio, textual, and even hybrid or multimodal (containing blends of visual images and text) texts. Look back through the site now and collect at least four different samples of these types of writing. You could bookmark these samples in your web browser, but you may find it easier to print them and annotate them with a pen as you analyze them. You will likely encounter more than four types of writing, so you will want to select those that you find most effective or persuasive. Once you have collected these genres, take a moment and try to answer the questions below. Then, save these samples and use the more detailed explanation of genre analysis in the next chapter to help you understand them more fully.

Some Steps for Collecting Genres

1. Begin by looking for different types of writing on the main organizational webpage of the group. Look first to the navigation menu of the webpage. As you click on the links, look for the different types of media and writing that are used to communicate the group's main points.
2. Now that you have surveyed the page, list the different types of writing and media that the group uses to persuade their audiences.
3. From this list, choose four different genres that you think are the most persuasive or interesting and circle them. Then, look at a few samples and try to determine who their audience might be.

Choose a Genre That You Think Would Be Effective for Your Argument and Analyze It

By now you have located some sample genres and have thought through the purpose that they might serve for their audience. Now, the key is to shift focus from finding examples to thinking through the type of genre that you might want to use for your own argument. Looking at your samples, choose a genre that you feel would communicate effectively to your audience. This means thinking through the relationship between audience and genre. If you would like to reach an audience of middle-school students for example, a public letter or even a PowerPoint presentation would probably not hold their attention. These middle-school students are simply not used to reading and using that genre. If you wanted to reach a group of students on your college campus, you might find that a genre like a speech may or may not work. If there is a forum for giving speeches on your campus, a campus protest for instance, you may reach your audience. If not, then you might seek out another way to reach students, such as through a video podcast posted on the school newspaper's website or even an article or well-placed letter in the school newspaper. You will learn much more about analyzing and writing public genres in the next chapter. For now, here are a few points to consider:

Some Questions for Analyzing Your Genre

1. Who writes or uses the genre? Think about yourself using the genre. Is it a genre that you can realistically see yourself using?
2. What purpose or function does the genre serve? Think about how the reader is asked to respond to it, or what types of action it moves them to take. What roles are the readers asked to play? What do you want to accomplish by using the genre?
3. How is the language of the genre connected to its audience? Think about the formality or informality of the language and why the language is formal or informal.
4. What different types of communication and media does the genre employ? Is it a print text or does it combine print with different mediums such as graphics or video? If so, how are the different mediums of communication connected?

Review Your Argument and Begin Drafting in the Genre You Chose

You have now analyzed how a group of people are debating and acting upon your issue. At this point, you are ready to begin shaping and drafting your own public argument. As you do so, you will probably look back to the sample genre you have analyzed in order to understand the different strategies and conventions that it uses. The key point to remember is that your writing need not be exactly like that of your sample. Using a genre does not mean saying the same thing in the same way. Instead, your task is to think through how you can communicate your point in a way that fulfills your readers' expectations. Your analysis of the genre samples helps you understand what the expectations of this audience are. Before you begin drafting, however, there is one more consideration to take into account: the fit between the genre you have chosen and the audience or community that you are addressing. The next section will walk you through this process of seeking the right fit between genre and audience.

Putting the Process Together: A Sample

Now let's put this process to work by looking at a sample search for public rhetoric on the issue of child soldiers in armed conflicts. This issue is one that we might of heard about through a film like *Invisible Children*, or even one that we learned about in an elective course on world politics. Let's say that I developed quite a bit of factual research on this topic through writing a controversy analysis. After this project, I began to think about ways that I could raise public awareness of this issue among my fellow students at my university. I started by thinking through the possibilities of this argument. In my freewriting, I found myself repeating the idea that students often feel as though they do not have a voice in international issues such as this one, and I wanted to find a way to give them a voice. I kept thinking through the different ways that students might act on this issue, and I thought through how they might attract the attention of the university and our state and federal congressmen. I then began to list out the plausible and implausible outcomes of my argument. Among the ideas I listed as plausible, one stood out to me: submitting a student-signed petition to my congressmen asking them to take action on the issue. I wasn't sure just yet what type of action I wanted my legislators to take, but as I listed the possible consequences of my argument, I found myself thinking about the fact that they could raise this issue in congress and perhaps internationally. Mostly, however, I kept wondering if there were any opportunities that students could use to act on the issue rather than just feeling guilty about it.

I started with a basic web search and used the keyword: "Child Soldiers." This produced a range of different results. Some were advertisements for the film *Invisible Children*, others were news ar-

ticles, and others still were blog posts on the crisis in Uganda. I then
decided to add the keywords "take action" and "get involved" to my
search to see if there were any organizations that were arguing publi-
cally about the issue. These simple additions brought up the pages of
many different groups who were active in campaigning against the
use of child soldiers. After clicking on a few of their links, I chose
an organization called *The Coalition to Stop the Use of Child Soldiers*.
I chose this group because it seemed to have the most developed
materials on child soldiers and the credentials of the organization let
me know that it was a valid site on this issue. In addition, this group
used a variety of engaging multimedia texts to move their audience
to action, and these texts looked most like the type of genre that I
wanted to choose for my project. After clicking through the different links on the site, I noticed that the organization spoke to several
different audiences. Some of its program links, such as the "Psycho-
Social Forum," were clearly written for professionals and experts.
The "Library" link led me to many different types of genres—from
reports that were written for and by experts to summaries of these
reports that were written for people like myself. When I clicked on
the menu link entitled "Get Involved," however, I found a variety of
different letter-writing opportunities and public petitions.

Having looked over the different links in the site, and noted the
different types of audiences, I chose four different types of genres
to analyze: (1) an introductory message on the homepage (in case I
decided to build a webpage), (2) a newspaper editorial letter (in case
I decided to write to my school paper), (3) a short video that documented the conflict and that was linked to a public petition, and (4)
a sample letter to a congressman about the issue. When I analyzed
these genres, I noticed that each genre was not only organized differently, but also had a different voice or tone, and supported and developed their argument differently. I then began to think about the
best choice for my own argument on this issue, and I remembered
that I had read quite a few interesting editorial articles in my university's student newspaper. I had even heard my classmates discussing
these editorials from time to time, so I knew that there was an active
audience for them. I also knew that there was an upcoming event
called *Red Hand Day* on my campus. This event was a chance to stop
by and write a letter to my local legislators about the importance of
addressing the problem of child soldiers. Students would dip their

hand in red paint, making their red handprint, and then write a letter beside or around the handprint and address it to our representatives. This event could provide me with a clear plan of action for my editorial, or a clear step that my audience could take to respond to it.

I downloaded a copy of an editorial letter sent to a national newspaper by *The Coalition to Stop the Use Child Soldiers*. I also analyzed a few more samples of editorials sent by other activist organizations. As I looked closely at the genre, it occurred to me that several of the samples drew upon the first-person testimony of activists and researchers in areas where child soldiers are used. I knew that I would not have access to this type of observation, and I began to wonder if the lack of this ethos might hurt my case. Then I thought back to the idea that I had started with: the feeling that students like myself could not do anything to address a tragic issue like child soldiers. I may not be able to go to the Democratic Republic of Congo or Uganda, but neither could many of the students that made up my audience. This gave me the opportunity to address my audience by tapping into their experiences and concerns. I even thought about the possibility of interviewing fellow students, asking them if they felt that they could do something constructive about the issue. I quickly brainstormed a series of questions that I might use as I interviewed students at my university and then began to list the different points of factual information that I wanted to present as well. From here, I began to think through how I might organize the editorial and weave the interviews and factual information together. In addition, I conducted some quick research to get the office address of my local congressman and the other materials that I would need to advertize the *Red Hand* event that was connected to my article. I also contacted the online editor of my school newspaper and asked if there was a way to connect an online petition to my editorial, which there was. At this point, I was ready for drafting. To see what my editorial ended up looking like, look to page 422 in Chapter 17.

Conclusion

Hopefully, this chapter has illustrated the process of using research
and rhetorical analysis to make your voice heard. Rhetorical analysis, as we have seen, means more than just learning how to analyze
texts written by others; it also means learning how we can effectively
analyze our own rhetorical situations. As you read on in this section, you will learn about argumentation in public writing, how to
analyze and construct several popular public genres, and even how
to create a visual-spatial public argument. We live in a society that
is made up of many different networks that link us together, and we
know that ideas can travel rapidly through these networks. As a public writer, you never need feel that you cannot address an issue that
you are passionate about. Instead, your skills of research and analysis
can help you find and even create new forums for your ideas.

Works Cited

Power, Samantha. "Why Can't We?" *The Nation*. 23 May 2006.
    Web. 10 June 2009.

Chapter 13

Persuasive Possibilities: Thinking through the Audience and Genre of Your Public Argument

By Christopher Minnix

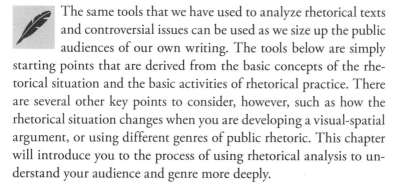

The same tools that we have used to analyze rhetorical texts and controversial issues can be used as we size up the public audiences of our own writing. The tools below are simply starting points that are derived from the basic concepts of the rhetorical situation and the basic activities of rhetorical practice. There are several other key points to consider, however, such as how the rhetorical situation changes when you are developing a visual-spatial argument, or using different genres of public rhetoric. This chapter will introduce you to the process of using rhetorical analysis to understand your audience and genre more deeply.

Analyzing Your Audience and Developing Your Purpose

We return here to the key question we asked in the introduction to this section: what do you want your writing to persuade your audience to do, think, feel, or say about your issue? When we analyze the purpose of our public arguments, we often have to analyze the possibilities of persuasion. This means thinking through the types of audiences we might persuade to consider our position and the plausible actions that they might take after being persuaded by our rhetoric.

Let's say that we are writing on media and eating disorders and arguing that there is a causal relationship between the media portrayal of adolescent girls and the rise in eating disorders over the past decade. We might think about writing a magazine article on this issue for a publication like *Time*. Is this plausible for us, though? There are actually many articles in the media that make this claim, and quite a few articles in *Time* that do. What would distinguish our article? We have to consider whether this publication would find our particular perspective interesting for its readers. In this case, *Time* might be more apt to publish a story or narrative of a personal experience with media and eating disorders, or an explanatory article about current scientific research on the subject written by a researcher or science writer. Is this to say that we should never try to publish for a popular magazine? Not at all! The key is to think about the possibilities for persuasion, or the types of audiences that would be interested in our research. Some subjects and genres might raise the chances of a popular magazine wanting to publish our views for its readers. We would need to analyze the audience of this magazine closely and think about whether or not our perspective and argument are the right fit. Then we might send it off and let the editor decide, or we may decide that this publication is not the best audience for our ideas.

So let's say that we think through the persuasive possibilities and decide that a popular magazine is not the right fit. We might make a quick list of public audiences: children, parents, educators, advertisers, and governmental agencies. Not a bad start, but as we make them more specific, we will once again have to think through the possibilities for persuading these audiences to take specific action. Writing to a government agency is a possibility, but we would have to pick a specific agency to address. We could select the Federal Communications Commission, but we would have to do further research to understand who we should contact there. We might find that we only get a form letter response if we send an individual letter rather than writing with a group of concerned citizens or activists. Let's say we pass on this example. We might address our paper to parents, but we have to be much more specific here as well, looking for a group of parents or even a parenting organization that we could address. We might think about a local group, such as a church group, that we could address in a speech or letter. We could also try to address educators, perhaps contacting our alma mater and seeing if we could return as a former student to present the topic to a few classes. Or, we could target the corporations who use the offensive ads by writing a letter of protest, or writing letters to members of our local community that ask them to boycott the products of the company. These are all possibilities, but they require us to keep the

potential persuasiveness of our writing in mind. In other words, we
have to analyze our persuasive goals and the plausibility of achieving
them by persuading the specific audience.

You can measure the persuasive possibilities of your writing by
looking at the following questions.

Persuasive Possibility Questions

1. Is the audience accessible or open to you as a writer? What is the
    likelihood of your work getting published or being used by your
    audience?

2. Is the action you want the audience to take or attitude you want
    the audience to form specific?

3. Is the action you would like them to take plausible? Do they have
    the power to act effectively on your issue?

4. What rhetorical strategies do you feel could possibly persuade
    this audience?

5. What are the potential outcomes of persuading the audience?
    How could the action that the audience takes address the issue or
    problem you are writing about?

Context

Our understanding of a public debate is shaped by the texts that
make up that debate. We interpret these public texts, connecting
them to our experiences and knowledge and use them to understand
how we might persuade our own public audiences. It is important
to remember that your goal is not to formulate a simple pro or con
summary of a public issue, as there are often many more than two
perspectives on the issue. At the same time, you do not want to try to
cover every single perspective. You are looking for those perspectives
that are the most prevalent in the debate.

Reading the Context of Your Public Debate

1. What are the key perspectives or schools of thought on the debate that you are studying?
2. What are the major points of contention or major disagreements among these perspectives?
3. What are the possible points of agreement, or the possible common ground between these perspectives?
4. What are the ideological differences, if any, between the perspectives?
5. What specific actions do their perspectives or texts ask their audience to take?
6. What perspectives are useful in supporting your own arguments about the issue? Why did you choose these?
7. What perspectives do you think will be the greatest threat to your argument? Why so?

In addition to these questions, it is also important to consider the **contexts of culture**, **contemporary history**, and **discourse** that shape the way specific audiences address issues. Contexts of culture are made up of the cultural ideas, values, ideographs, and beliefs that shape the worldviews of specific audiences or publics. These may be traditional values, religious or philosophical values, political values, or any other beliefs that are common to the audience or public you are addressing. Contexts of contemporary history are made up not only of the current events surrounding the debate on an issue, but also the history of the public's involvement with the issue. This contemporary history often shapes the **kairos** of your public rhetoric, or the way you characterize the moment you write or speak as the opportune or important moment to do so. Finally, the context of discourse can be thought of as the different forms of writing or genres that a public uses to address the issue that they write about. Knowing the forms of writing that your audience uses enables you to adapt your rhetoric more effectively to persuade them and even work alongside them in order to reach a common goal.

The following questions are focused on these contexts and are good starting points for thinking through how your own rhetoric will connect to the context or public debate about the issue.

> **Questions for Specific Publics**
>
> 1. Are there cultural or community values that shape your audience's view of the public issue?
> 2. What important, current events make up the current context of your audience?
> 3. What is your audience's position or role in the current debate over the public issue?
> 4. How much influence do they have on the debate?
> 5. What forms of writing or genres does the audience associate with the debate? What forms do they use when writing about it and what genres are they used to reading about it?
> 6. What is the history of your audience's interest in the issue?

These questions are often very important for local audiences, as they help you understand the role that your audience plays in the ongoing debate. As you choose or encounter audiences for your writing, you will develop more questions that are specific to the situation.

Analyzing the Genres of Public Writing

We learned in the last chapter that part of the process of getting our voice heard on a public issue is learning about the genres of public argument that different groups use to communicate to their audiences. Genres present us with certain ways of thinking about the public and certain forms of acting socially on public issues. When you write a letter to your congressman, for example, you use a genre that not only has certain conventions—such as a formal greeting, a description of a specific problem, and a call for a specific action (such as voting on a certain bill)—but also has a certain goal or purpose. This goal or purpose tells us quite a bit about how we view the public. By writing a letter, we assume that our legislators will take our request seriously, that others could write alongside us in such quantity that the legislator will be forced to notice, and that our voices as citizens have the power to move our legislators to vote in a certain way. We write in certain genres to achieve certain social goals and actions. This means that as we write in public genres we are envisioning the ability of the public to respond to our writing in a way that achieves our goals.

Earlier in this book, in Chapter 6, we learned the key questions to ask when analyzing a genre. Here is a quick review:

Questions for Genre Analysis from Chapter 6

Social Context
- Where is the genre typically set?
- What is the subject of the genre?
- Who uses the genre?
- When and why is the genre used? What purposes does the genre serve for the people who use it?

Rhetorical Patterns of the Genre
- What type of content is usually included and excluded?
- What rhetorical appeals are used most often? Do you notice any patterns in the appeals to logos, pathos, or ethos?
- How are the texts organized? Do they generally open in similar ways? Conclude in similar ways? What common parts do the samples share?
- Do sentences in the genre share a certain style? Are they mostly active, passive, simple, or complex? Is there an abundance or lack of questions, exclamation points, or semicolons?
- What type of word choice is used? Do many of the words fit in a particular category of jargon or slang? Is the overall effect of the word choice formal, informal, humorous, or academic?

Analyze What those Patterns Reveal about the Social Context of the Genre
- Who does the genre include and who does it exclude?
- What roles for writers and readers does the genre encourage?
- What values and beliefs are assumed about or encouraged from users of the genre?
- What content does the genre treat as most valuable? Least *valuable?*

These questions are important for understanding any genre that we encounter. In the last chapter, you were asked to research groups that are actively engaging in argument and activism about your issue. A key part of that process was collecting and analyzing sample genres of public argument. Now, using the key questions about

genre above, the rest of this chapter is going to walk you through a
genre analysis of a public argument. Then, it's your turn. Take the
sample genres you have collected and begin to apply these questions
to them. When you have finished analyzing your genres, you will
find that you have a firm grasp on the different conventions or strategies you will need to use as you create your own public argument.

A Genre Analysis of a Public Argument

Many different types of articles are utilized for public arguments.
Some of these genres are print, some visual, and some hybrids of
textual and visual that we call **multimodal texts**. You will likely
encounter many different types of genres even within a single group
or organization. Your choice of genre is limited only by how well it
serves the needs of your audience. You might, for example, decide to
write an editorial for your local or school newspaper, write a magazine article for an online magazine or zine, or even write a speech
to be given to a committee in your local government. These are all
genres that we might call **print genres**, meaning that they often
are not image-based and use only words to convey their message.
However, you may decide that your audience may respond better
to a genre that blends different modes of communication, such as
print and visual images, audio, or video. Whatever genre you use,
it is important to keep coming back to your analysis of your audience, asking yourself whether or not the genre is both used by and
effective for that audience. As with all things in rhetoric and writing,
audience is key.

We will discuss some of the key conventions of multimodal or
visual texts in Chapter 16. The genre that we will analyze on the
following pages is a print genre, a magazine article written about the
issue of global poverty by one of the leading voices on the subject,
Peter Singer. As we analyze this genre, think about the relationship
between the text and the reader, or what the text is asking of the
reader. Think through who the ideal audience of this text might
be and the action they could take on the issue. Look for the call to
action in the text and then look closely at the rhetorical strategies
utilized to move the audience to act.

Social Context: **Setting of the Genre and Audience:** The publication information lets us know quite a bit about the type of audience that might read or be exposed to the article. Articles in the *New York Times Magazine* are written for a public audience, but one that has a high degree of cultural literacy. As you read this article, try to get a sense of the demographics of its audience. This is important, as it helps us understand who Singer is asking to give.

Rhetorical Patterns:
Organization: Notice how the essay begins with a lengthy example, rather than a short introduction and then a thesis. As you read through the example, notice how it is used in the fourth paragraph to set up the major problem that the public argument is addressing. This is a common strategy in the genre of magazine essays. An example, narrative, or current event is utilized to connect the issue to the audience and then set up the main problem. If we look at several different articles, we will find that not all authors set up scenarios like Singer does. They do, however, often set up a problem in their introductions and offer arguments for solving it.

The Singer Solution To World Poverty by Peter Singer

New York Times Sunday Magazine, *September 5, 1999, pp. 60–63. Reprinted by permission obtained via PARS International.*

In the Brazilian film "Central Station," Dora is a retired schoolteacher who makes ends meet by sitting at the station writing letters for illiterate people. Suddenly she has an opportunity to pocket $1,000. All she has to do is persuade a homeless 9-year-old boy to follow her to an address she has been given. (She is told he will be adopted by wealthy foreigners.) She delivers the boy, gets the money, spends some of it on a television set and settles down to enjoy her new acquisition. Her neighbor spoils the fun, however, by telling her that the boy was too old to be adopted—he will be killed and his organs sold for transplantation. Perhaps Dora knew this all along, but after her neighbor's plain speaking, she spends a troubled night. In the morning Dora resolves to take the boy back.

Suppose Dora had told her neighbor that it is a tough world, other people have nice new TV's too, and if selling the kid is the only way she can get one, well, he was only a street kid. She would then have become, in the eyes of the audience, a monster. She redeems herself only by being prepared to bear considerable risks to save the boy.

At the end of the movie, in cinemas in the affluent nations of the world, people who would have been quick to condemn Dora if she had not rescued the boy go home to places far more comfortable than her apartment. In fact, the average family in the United States spends almost one-third of its income on things that are no more necessary to them than Dora's new TV was to her. Going out to nice restaurants, buying new clothes because the old ones are no longer stylish, vacationing at beach resorts—so much of our income is spent on things not essential to the preservation of our lives and health. Donated to one of a number of charitable agencies, that money could mean the difference between life and death for children in need.

All of which raises a question: In the end, what is the ethical distinction between a Brazilian who sells a homeless child to organ peddlers and an American who already has a TV and upgrades to a better one—knowing that the money could be donated to an organization that would use it to save the lives of kids in need?

Rhetorical Patterns: Notice how Singer uses logos or logical argumentation in this paragraph. He sets up the example of Dora and then draws a direct comparison to American consumers like ourselves. His logic, that we judge acts by their consequences, lead us to ponder whether or not our actions or inactions as consumers lead to the same end as Dora's, if she had not saved the child.

Of course, there are several differences between the two situations that could support different moral judgments about them. For one thing, to be able to consign a child to death when he is standing right in front of you takes a chilling kind of heartlessness; it is much easier to ignore an appeal for money to help children you will never meet. Yet for a utilitarian philosopher like myself—that is, one who judges whether acts are right or wrong by their consequences—if the upshot of the American's failure to donate the money is that one more kid dies on the streets of a Brazilian city, then it is, in some sense, just as bad as selling the kid to the organ peddlers. But one doesn't need to embrace my utilitarian ethic to see that, at the very least, there is a troubling incongruity in being so quick to condemn Dora for taking the child to the organ peddlers while, at the same time, not regarding the American consumer's behavior as raising a serious moral issue.

In his 1996 book, "Living High and Letting Die," the New York University philosopher Peter Unger presented an ingenious series of imaginary examples designed to probe our intuitions about whether it is wrong to live well without giving substantial amounts of money to help people who are hungry, malnourished or dying from easily treatable illnesses like diarrhea. Here's my paraphrase of one of these examples: Bob is close to retirement. He has invested most of his savings in a very rare and valuable old car, a Bugatti, which he has not been able to insure. The Bugatti is his pride and joy. In addition to the pleasure he gets from driving and caring for his car, Bob knows that its rising market value means that he will always be able to sell it and live comfortably after retirement. One day when Bob is out for a drive, he parks the Bugatti near the end of a railway siding and goes for a walk up the track. As he does so, he sees that a runaway train, with no one aboard, is running down the railway track. Looking farther down the track, he sees the small figure of a child very likely to be killed by the runaway train. He can't stop the train and the child is too far away to warn of the danger, but he can throw a switch that will divert the train down the siding where his Bugatti is parked. Then nobody will be killed—but the train

Social Context: Notice how Singer defines what a utilitarian philosopher is here. He would not have to do this if he were writing an article for a philosophy journal. For a public audience, however, he briefly defines the central tenant of his philosophy. He gives the audience just enough information, without losing them in the details of his philosophical theory.

Social Context: Magazine essays like this one offer extended coverage of an issue that short editorials or newspaper articles cannot. The length of this genre allows Singer to introduce, develop, and support his arguments in great depth. This clues us in to one of the purposes of this genre, which is to lead us through a careful, reasoned argument that might convince us to act or respond by reflecting upon our own relationship to the issue.

Rhetorical Patterns: Notice Singer's thesis here. He develops the main argument of his paragraph, but does not state his call for action yet. He saves it for the end of the essay. Many public arguments and magazine essays like this one do this in order to emphasize that readers should conclude by taking action on the specific issue.

Rhetorical Patterns: Notice that examples and arguments from other philosophers are included to support Singer's analysis. This tells us that this public genre draws upon academic writing and research in order to support its claims.

345

will destroy his Bugatti. Thinking of his joy in owning the car and the financial security it represents, Bob decides not to throw the switch. The child is killed. For many years to come, Bob enjoys owning his Bugatti and the financial security it represents.

Bob's conduct, most of us will immediately respond, was gravely wrong. Unger agrees. But then he reminds us that we, too, have op-portunities to save the lives of children. We can give to organizations like Unicef or Oxfam America. How much would we have to give one of these organizations to have a high probability of saving the life of a child threatened by easily preventable diseases? (I do not believe that children are more worth saving than adults, but since no one can ar-gue that children have brought their poverty on themselves, focusing on them simplifies the issues.) Unger called up some experts and used the information they provided to offer some plausible estimates that include the cost of raising money, administrative expenses and the cost of delivering aid where it is most needed. By his calculation, $200 in do-nations would help a sickly 2-year-old transform into a healthy 6-year-old—offering safe passage through childhood's most dangerous years. To show how practical philosophical argument can be, Unger even tells his readers that they can easily donate funds by using their credit card and calling one of these toll-free numbers: (800) 367-5437 for Unicef; (800) 693-2687 for Oxfam America.

Now you, too, have the information you need to save a child's life. How should you judge yourself if you don't do it? Think again about Bob and his Bugatti. Unlike Dora, Bob did not have to look into the eyes of the child he was sacrificing for his own material comfort. The child was a complete stranger to him and too far away to relate to in an intimate, personal way. Unlike Dora, too, he did not mislead the child or initiate the chain of events imperiling him. In all these respects, Bob's situation resembles that of people able but unwilling to donate to over-seas aid and differs from Dora's situation.

If you still think that it was very wrong of Bob not to throw the switch that would have diverted the train and saved the child's life, then it is hard to see how you could deny that it is also very wrong not to send money to one of the organizations listed above. Unless, that is, there is some morally important difference between the two situations that I have overlooked.

Is it the practical uncertainties about whether aid will really reach the people who need it? Nobody who knows the world of overseas aid can doubt that such uncertainties exist. But Unger's figure of $200 to save a child's life was reached after he had made conservative assumptions about the proportion of the money donated that will actually reach its target.

One genuine difference between Bob and those who can afford to donate to overseas aid organizations but don't is that only Bob can save the child on the tracks, whereas there are hundreds of millions of people who can give $200 to overseas aid organizations. The problem is that most of them aren't doing it. Does this mean that it is all right for you not to do it?

Suppose that there were more owners of priceless vintage cars—Carol, Dave, Emma, Fred and so on, down to Ziggy—all in exactly the same situation as Bob, with their own siding and their own switch, all sacrificing the child in order to preserve their own cherished car. Would that make it all right for Bob to do the same? To answer this question affirmatively is to endorse follow-the-crowd ethics—the kind of ethics that led many Germans to look away when the Nazi atrocities were being committed. We do not excuse them because others were behaving no better.

We seem to lack a sound basis for drawing a clear moral line between Bob's situation and that of any reader of this article with $200 to spare who does not donate it to an overseas aid agency. These readers seem to be acting at least as badly as Bob was acting when he chose to let the runaway train hurtle toward the unsuspecting child. In the light of this conclusion, I trust that many readers will reach for the phone and donate that $200. Perhaps you should do it before reading further.

Now that you have distinguished yourself morally from people who put their vintage cars ahead of a child's life, how about treating yourself and your partner to dinner at your favorite restaurant? But wait. The money you will spend at the restaurant could also help save the lives of children overseas! True, you weren't planning to blow $200 tonight, but if you were to give up dining out just for one month, you would easily save that amount. And what is one month's dining out, compared to a child's life? There's the rub. Since there are a lot of desperately needy children in the world, there will always be another child whose life you could save for another $200. Are you therefore obliged to keep giving until you have nothing left? At what point can you stop?

Rhetorical Patterns: Logos: Here again Singer takes on the counterarguments that he feels his audience might make. This argument, an argument from self-interest, is countered in the paragraph below with another scenario. By utilizing these thought-experiments or scenarios, Singer attempts to show how we might condemn not helping others in immediate contexts, but how we often fail to condemn or rationalize our unwillingness to help others in distant countries. He moves us to agree or negatively judge a local scenario, and then shows how this scenario is logically similar to our willingness or unwillingness to assist with global poverty.

Social Context: Notice how Singer's public argument calls for specific action from his readers. He transforms the role of the reader into the role of giver, or philanthropist. This might be thought of as his "call to action," which is a typical convention or strategy of public arguments like Singer's. Magazine articles like his often place readers in this role, asking them to at the very least act by rethinking the way they understand an issue. Other times, as in Singer's case, they call for direct action.

347

Rhetorical Patterns:
Notice again how
Singer takes on the
assumptions that he
perceives his audi-
ence to have. Here,
he assumes that his
audience may be
growing tired of the
different examples
that he gives and
may even question
whether or not they
are truly relevant to
the realities of global
poverty and his call
to give. By taking on
these assumptions,
he is able to assure
his readers that these
scenarios are useful to
his argument.

Social Context: No-
tice how he assumes
this belief on the part
of his readers. Singer
assumes that we will
accept the moral situ-
ations he presents as
examples of situations
that are roughly equal
to the choices that we
make. Some readers
might ask whether
this is true. We might,
for example, agree
that Bob acts unethi-
cally if he does not
throw the switch, but
argue that the situa-
tion is not the same
as our choice to go
out to dinner.

Hypothetical examples can easily become farcical. Consider Bob. How far past losing the Bugatti should he go? Imagine that Bob had got his foot stuck in the track of the siding, and if he diverted the train, then before it rammed the car it would also amputate his big toe. Should he still throw the switch? What if it would amputate his foot? His entire leg?

As absurd as the Bugatti scenario gets when pushed to extremes, the point it raises is a serious one: only when the sacrifices become very significant indeed would most people be prepared to say that Bob does nothing wrong when he decides not to throw the switch. Of course, most people could be wrong; we can't decide moral issues by taking opinion polls. But consider for yourself the level of sacrifice that you would demand of Bob, and then think about how much money you would have to give away in order to make a sacrifice that is roughly equal to that. It's almost certainly much, much more than $200. For most middle-class Americans, it could easily be more like $200,000.

Isn't it counterproductive to ask people to do so much? Don't we run the risk that many will shrug their shoulders and say that morality, so conceived, is fine for saints but not for them? I accept that we are un-likely to see, in the near or even medium-term future, a world in which it is normal for wealthy Americans to give the bulk of their wealth to strangers. When it comes to praising or blaming people for what they do, we tend to use a standard that is relative to some conception of normal behavior. Comfortably off Americans who give, say, 10 percent of their income to overseas aid organizations are so far ahead of most of their equally comfortable fellow citizens that I wouldn't go out of my way to chastise them for not doing more. Nevertheless, they should be doing much more, and they are in no position to criticize Bob for failing to make the much greater sacrifice of his Bugatti.

At this point various objections may crop up. Someone may say: "If every citizen living in the affluent nations contributed his or her share I wouldn't have to make such a drastic sacrifice, because long before such levels were reached, the resources would have been there to save the lives of all those children dying from lack of food or medical care. So why should I give more than my fair share?" Another, related, objection is that the Government ought to increase its overseas aid allocations, since that would spread the burden more equitably across all taxpayers.

Yet the question of how much we ought to give is a matter to be decided in the real world—and that, sadly, is a world in which we know that most people do not, and in the immediate future will not, give substantial amounts to overseas aid agencies. We know, too, that at least in the next year, the United States Government is not going to meet even the very modest United Nations-recommended target of 0.7 percent of gross national product; at the moment it lags far below that, at 0.09 percent, not even half of Japan's 0.22 percent or a tenth of Denmark's 0.97 percent. Thus, we know that the money we can give beyond that theoretical "fair share" is still going to save lives that would otherwise be lost. While the idea that no one need do more than his or her fair share is a powerful one, should it prevail if we know that others are not doing their fair share and that children will die preventable deaths unless we do more than our fair share? That would be taking fairness too far.

Thus, this ground for limiting how much we ought to give also fails. In the world as it is now, I can see no escape from the conclusion that each one of us with wealth surplus to his or her essential needs should be giving most of it to help people suffering from poverty so dire as to be life-threatening. That's right: I'm saying that you shouldn't buy that new car, take that cruise, redecorate the house or get that pricey new suit. After all, a $1,000 suit could save five children's lives.

So how does my philosophy break down in dollars and cents? An American household with an income of $50,000 spends around $30,000 annually on necessities, according to the Conference Board, a nonprofit economic research organization. Therefore, for a household bringing in $50,000 a year, donations to help the world's poor should be as close as possible to $20,000. The $30,000 required for necessities holds for higher incomes as well. So a household making $100,000 could cut a yearly check for $70,000. Again, the formula is simple: whatever money you're spending on luxuries, not necessities, should be given away.

Now, evolutionary psychologists tell us that human nature just isn't sufficiently altruistic to make it plausible that many people will sacrifice so much for strangers. On the facts of human nature, they might be right, but they would be wrong to draw a moral conclusion from those facts. If it is the case that we ought to do things that, predictably, most of us won't do, then let's face that fact head-on. Then, if we value the life of a child more than going to fancy restaurants, the next time we dine out we will know that we could have done something better with our money. If that makes living a morally decent life extremely arduous, well, then that is the way things are. If we don't do it, then we should at least know that we are failing to live a morally decent life—not because

Rhetorical Patterns: Singer takes on one of the most significant rebuttals to his argument here: the defeatist feeling that most people will not give and that they will wait for the government to address the problem. Notice in the paragraphs below how he uses the idea that the government will not address the problem as a basis for his argument for individual giving. In this way, he turns the argument of his opposition on itself.

Rhetorical Patterns: Notice Singer's provocative ethos again. He is deliberately provoking his audience here. Someone might respond while reading by asking why the solution to global poverty should demand them to give up their own lifestyle. If someone were to ask this question, they would do so in the context of the various arguments that Singer has already given, and they may find it hard to defend their choice not to give.

Rhetorical Patterns: Singer takes on the opposition to his argument right up until his conclusion. Notice here how he takes the logical arguments of evolutionary psychology and argues that they do not outweigh our moral responsibilities.

it is good to wallow in guilt but because knowing where we should be going is the first step toward heading in that direction.

When Bob first grasped the dilemma that faced him as he stood by that railway switch, he must have thought how extraordinarily unlucky he was to be placed in a situation in which he must choose between the life of an innocent child and the sacrifice of most of his savings. But he was not unlucky at all. We are all in that situation.

Our analysis of Singer's magazine article helps us understand that the purpose of his argument and the genre that he chose work hand in hand. If he had chosen to create a poster or brochure on this topic, he would not have had the space that he needed to lead readers through the examples he presented. These examples were important because he utilized them to develop his forceful argument. Singer leads us through moral situations or examples that we find disagreeable, even repugnant, and then carefully links these situations to situations from our everyday lives. Our choice to buy a new iPod, for example, becomes a choice not to help a starving child. In order to do this, he needed space to develop his examples and support his argument, so this longer genre was a strong choice.

Analyzing a sample genre like this one tells us more than what the author is saying about the issue, though. You will remember from the previous chapter that the example we discussed was writing an editorial letter in the student newspaper that called upon students to take part in a letter-writing campaign against the use of child soldiers. By comparing Singer's article to articles on social issues in the student newspaper, we can see several striking similarities and differences.

Genre Questions	Singer's Editorial	Editorials in Student Newspaper
Social Context	Written for a popular newspaper.	Written for a smaller audience—for a newspaper that focuses on the local campus context.
	Addressed by public intellectuals to Americans.	Most editorials are addressed to students and are written by students.
	Editorial genre is utilized to pose public arguments on social issues to a broad public audience.	Student editorials predominantly address local, national, and international issues that students find important and pose arguments for addressing or solving these issues.
	Addressed to the values and common assumptions of a broad range of Americans.	Addressed to the values and common assumptions or a broad range of university students.
	Function is to provoke action, change attitudes, or refute opposing arguments.	Function is to raise awareness, provoke action, change attitudes, and refute opposing arguments on important issues to students.
Rhetorical Patterns	Editorials include research along with logical arguments, ethical (ethos) arguments, and emotional or value (pathos) arguments. Each of these arguments is designed to speak to the values and logic of a broad audience.	Student editorials often include research and utilize appeals to logos, pathos, and ethos that are designed to speak to student concerns, values, and experiences. In addition, student narratives are often used to frame issues important to students.
	Lengthy explanations of research are most often excluded from newspaper editorials.	Lengthy explanations of research are also excluded from student editorials.
	Newspaper editorials open in different ways—some use a narrative, others (like Singer) use a scenario from popular culture, and others pose questions.	Student editorials often begin with scenarios, questions, and narratives, but have a more narrowly defined context. Most often they seem to relate the issue to the experience of students or to student concerns.

Rhetorical Patterns	Newspaper editorials often state a general thesis in their opening paragraphs, but lead to a more specific call to action, proposal, or thesis in their conclusions.	Many student editorials follow this same pattern, and student editorials often conclude with a more specific call to action, proposal, or more specific thesis.
	Newspaper editorials develop body paragraphs that serve to support or lead to their thesis. Body paragraphs serve as evidence and examples to support a main thesis, rather than covering different topics related to the issue. In addition, authors often use body paragraphs to provide background on new or difficult concepts and to refute arguments against their position.	Student editorials also follow this model. Body paragraphs are supporting evidence for the main argument of the editorial. Students also use body paragraphs to offer background on difficult or new concepts and to refute the arguments against their position.
	The tone of newspaper editorials varies from provocative to concerned or even critical. It is a genre of argument, so provocative statements are allowed and common.	Student editorials also vary from provocative to concerned or critical.
What Rhetorical Patterns Say about Social Context	Newspaper editorials are theoretically written for everyone, but in practice are used by those who have a strong degree of knowledge in current events and politics.	Student editorials encourage readers to play the role of a concerned or active student who is able to work to solve issues on and off campus.
	Newspaper editorials often encourage readers to play the role of an active citizen or a citizen who is able to take action that can help to change a social issue or resolve a social problem.	Student editorials often address issues that are or should be important to all students. Users often have a knowledge of contemporary events and campus events.
	Newspaper editorials assume their readers to have a wide range of differences in belief, but often assume and encourage basic moral values of concern for others, foundational American values such as justice and equality, and the values of a democratic society.	Student editorials assume these values, but add the values and experiences of students their campus. In addition, they also point to the values of the university, the values of education, and the economic values that students have towards education.

From this comparison, we can see that student newspaper editorials are part of the larger genre of editorial writing that is used in public forums such as newspapers. In this sense, the genres share quite a bit with one another, as student editorials come from the older, and more widely read genre of newspaper editorials. However, by contrasting the genres, we can also see that student editorials most often place the issues they are taking on in the context of student life. This requires them to adjust the strategies and convention of the typical newspaper editorial. In doing so, they take national, international, and local issues and make them meaningful to the students who read the editorials.

Conclusion

Hopefully, this chapter has equipped you with a set of questions to apply to your own audience and genre. By taking the time to analyze your audience and the genres they use, you give yourself the best possible chance of persuading your audience and moving them to act upon your issue. With these important aspects of the rhetorical situation under your belt, we now turn to the process of thinking through your argumentation. The next chapter will provide you with an opportunity to imagine yourself in conversation with others on your issue and to develop arguments and counterarguments to their reactions. As you do so, knowing your audience and your genre will be invaluable. For example, by knowing your genre, you know the types of research that are used for evidence and the types that are irrelevant for your audience. You also have an excellent understanding of the rhetorical strategies that are utilized in each genre, which helps you understand not only your logical arguments and arguments from your sources, but also your ethos or public character and the emotional and value-based (pathos) arguments that will work and not work for your audience.

Chapter 14

Writing for the Public: Argumentation and Imagination

By Jessica Shumake

 Writing an argumentative essay is frequently misunderstood to be solely an act of persuasion. We tend to think that we need to advocate for our position to change readers' minds and to perhaps move them to take action or adopt some belief. Argumentative writers, however, understand that demonstrating their ability to consider other perspectives, imagine alternatives, and write critically is required in all situations where opinions differ. Argumentative writing is more than simple pro-con writing, showing that you understand course content, or the presentation of research and facts: argumentation is a dialectical activity that helps you imagine, analyze, and evaluate your position by internalizing interested critics. Argumentative writers view contradictory positions **dialectically**. Thinking about your topic dialectically means that, as a writer, you have more tools to help you discover how to begin an argument.

Dialectical thinking requires considering and responding to different viewpoints. A dialectical thinker is someone on the lookout for opposing or contradictory arguments. He or she uses counterarguments as tools for gaining familiarity with a topic.

Coming up with an argument and identifying counterarguments does more than help a writer find things about which to write. The benefit of considering multiple sides of a position is that you can demonstrate to readers, who do not necessarily share your perspective, that you are a thoughtful person who is willing to approach a controversial topic with an open mind. An argumentative essay, then, is a written record of intellectual inquiry into some controversy that interests you. Argumentative writing also helps you probe an argument's strengths and weaknesses, weighing it against alternatives. This is not an exercise for those who are comfortable parroting authorities or treading paths of least resistance. In other words, argumentative writing is not about determining what some authority figure believes to demonstrate that you share his or her position. Argumentative writing is about entering a real-world controversy to assess which set of reasons you find most persuasive and then articulating why you are persuaded. You have to reengage the child within who continually asks "Why?" Then, you must be open to an array of "becauses" that arise as you engage with imagined interlocutors. You have to put yourself out there to support an argument, about which you would be willing to change your mind, upon reading the available research and thinking things through.

Imagining Interlocutors

When thinking about the abilities citizens need to flourish in a democracy or friends need to understand each other's differences, the capacity to think **dialectically** and engage with interlocutors tops the list. An **interlocutor** is someone with whom one engages in a back and forth conversational exchange, but with whom one disagrees. Ultimately, an interlocutor's viewpoint alters the ground of a discussion because the writer must make an effort to understand why the interlocutor believes what he or she does. The following is a conversational exchange between three friends (Harman, Sahar, and Elba) and an absent interlocutor (Harman's roommate):

An interlocutor is someone with whom you disagree, but with whom you nonetheless engage in a back and forth exchange.

> *Harman*: I'm so annoyed with my roommate. No matter how much evidence I muster he remains unconvinced that capital punishment does not act as a deterrent against violent crime.

> *Sahar*: My mom's the same way when we talk about religion.

> *Elba*: I find that most people I talk with are more open-minded when I show them that I am listening to them and looking for points where we both agree.

> *Sahar*: Can you tell us more about why your roommate holds the position he does?

> *Harman*: His uncle was a police officer who was killed in the line of duty, so he's very emotional about the topic.

Sahar: Wow! What happened?

Harman: His uncle was working undercover at the time. The guy who shot him was involved in organized crime.

Elba: Are you saying the guy who killed his uncle was a career criminal?

Harman: Yes. My roommate keeps arguing that all executions should be televised because he thinks that would dissuade people from becoming involved in nefarious activities.

Sahar: A public execution isn't something I'd like my younger brother to see on TV.

Elba: I think that your roommate's anger toward criminals makes perfect sense given his life experience. Gang members do operate as though they are above the law and that threatens public safety. Could you try to communicate to your roommate that you do agree that some kind of punishment should be incorporated into our legal system even though you disagree with televised executions?

Sahar: Your roommate might never agree with your position that the death penalty is barbaric, Harman, but you can both agree that our society needs laws to protect public safety.

Harman: My roommate and I both agree that living in society where people can commit crimes without consequence is undesirable. Next time we talk I'm going to start with where we both agree so that he's aware I'm considering his point of view. He disagrees with me about putting more public resources into rehabilitating offenders. He believes that the man who shot his uncle does not deserve access to education and counseling.

Just as in conversations on controversial topics with friends, when we witness a court proceeding or hear a politician give a speech we comprehend that the words uttered are shaped by situational factors and governed by conventions. Lawyers and politicians have to deal with criticisms, objections, and alternative standpoints as part of the rhetorical situation in which they find themselves: they have dialectical obligations. In writing for public audiences, the most valuable device in your toolkit is showing your audience that you respect them enough to take their objections seriously. Anticipating objections and alternatives to your position is the primary way you can demonstrate to any audience that you are well informed, inquisitive, and willing to reconsider your own personal biases. The most important rule to remember when writing for a public audience is to internalize an interested critic of your position so that you can assess whether the thesis you have provisionally adopted on a controversial topic can withstand scrutiny.

An arguer discharges his or her dialectical obligations by considering alternative positions, objections, and criticisms.

A public audience's interpretation of your argument is viewed through the worldviews, beliefs, and life experiences they carry with them. To effectively advance an argument that has the power to reach a public audience, you need imagine that you have dialectical obligations to other people. In other words, you need to imagine a community of critical interlocutors while simultaneously keeping in touch with your actual audience by shoring up concerns they expect you to address. You need to imagine yourself engaged in a discussion with people who will consider the justifications and refutations you offer, even though they have a different standpoint from yours.

Argumentation and Audience

Argumentation is an audience-oriented activity. The audience a writer imagines influences the choices he or she makes, particularly when the writer's imagined audience and actual audience have conflicting expectations. Conflicting expectations from an imagined and actual audience is why feedback from interested readers is so integral to developing a strong argument. Arguments that invite readers to participate in the process of thinking through a controversy demonstrate dialectical awareness. **Dialectical awareness** is a skill a writer develops to identify and anticipate the challenges, criticisms, alternative positions, and objections from audience members. No writer interested in rational persuasion can ignore his or her audience. For example, since Harman knows that his roommate disagrees with him about the death penalty, his roommate's objections ought to influence the way he approaches the topic. Accomplished writers know that arguments develop in tandem with the demands of an audience. Anticipating how an audience will respond to an

Dialectical awareness is a skill a writer develops to identify and anticipate the challenges, criticisms, alternative positions, and objections from audience members.

argument is a key facet of dialectical awareness. When approaching argumentation as an audience-oriented practice the following questions arise:

- To whom is my argument addressed?

- What does my audience think, know, and/or believe?

- Does my argument invite my audience to collaborate with me as I reason through ideas?

- Is my argument responsive to audience criticism?

As a writer struggles to make sense of the disputes that emerge between various groups and individuals it is helpful to consider a couple of key terms that help a writer adapt his or her argument to accommodate the demands of a sympathetic audience and an audience of interested critics. The term **stakeholder** is a shorthand term used in argumentation for an interested audience member who has made up his or her mind about some aspect of a controversy. The term **constituency** is another useful term that helps a writer consider audience members who are bound by shared goals and motivated to achieve these goals above all. Since the effectiveness of an argument is measured by the response of sympathetic constituencies or stakeholders *and* critical interlocutors, argumentative writers must understand the needs of both audiences. When dealing with an audience made up of both supporters and critics, a writer should communicate that he or she approaches argumentation as an exercise in reasoning with a diverse range of people. When a writer communicates that he or she understands argumentation to be a cooperative undertaking, his or her audience is more likely to be open to that argument because the audience will recognize the writer respects their autonomy to decide from themselves what to believe.

Given that the purpose of an argumentative inquiry is to assess whether a controversial position is worth accepting in the first place, a writer will have to make choices about which arguments to present. Of the available arguments some will be strong and others weak. It is best to avoid using weak arguments because ignoring significant objections demonstrates a refusal to collaborate dialectically with the audience in an intellectually honest manner and will decrease the effectiveness of an argument.

A stakeholder is a shorthand term used in argumentation for an interested audience member who has made up his or her mind about some aspect of a controversy.

The term constituency is another useful term that helps a writer consider audience members who are bound by shared goals and motivated to achieve these goals above all.

359

Imagine that your friend Harman asks for your advice about the argumentative essay he is writing for his English class. He just watched the movie *Dead Man Walking*, which advocates for the abolishment of the death penalty. The movie inspired Harman to pursue the topic further on his own. Harman is a leader in the local Quaker youth group and volunteers each week tutoring formerly incarcerated men for the GED test. Harman tells you, "Capital punishment should be abolished because theories of retributive (eye for an eye) justice are morally backward." You wonder, "What reasons, other than retributive justice being barbaric, supports the abolition of the death penalty?" Harman clearly believes the death penalty is morally wrong, yet he does not offer any reasons to abolish capital punishment. In other words, Harman has not yet presented a complete argument. In this situation, Harman must reply to an alternative position. The alternative position is that retributive justice does act to deter crime. "You are a person who is good at seeing both sides of an argument," Harman says. "What are some objections to the position that the death penalty deters crime?" He shows you his tentative outline:

Thesis: Abolish the death penalty! It's uncivilized!

- The threat of the punishment of death does not deter crime.

- Rehabilitate and educate.

- Many perfectly innocent people are executed each year.

- Canada, France, and many other countries around the world abolished it, so the U.S. should too.

Over lunch you ask Harman a list of questions to test his **dialectical awareness** of the multiple dimensions of the death penalty debate. He tells you that even though he believes strongly that the death penalty is unjust, he wants his essay to convey to readers that he cares about having a dialogue with people who disagree with him. He is committed to identifying viewpoints that differ from his own. Harman is inquisitive and he has spent substantial time doing library research to become more informed about the capital punishment debate. He plans to interview someone from his dorm, an international student born in Singapore, who he knows disagrees with him, to understand why she does not share his beliefs.

A writer develops dialectical awareness by identifying and anticipating the criticisms, challenges, and objections audience members may raise.

Based on these answers (and conversations you've had with people with whom you disagree), consider the chart on the following page. Each answer leads you to a decision about how Harman ought to proceed as he drafts his argument.

Questions to Test Dialectical Awareness Chart

Question	Answer	Implications for Your Public Argument
What assumptions do the stakeholders or constituencies in this dispute bring to it?	They don't all agree that capital punishment is wrong. Those who do think it's good don't all justify their beliefs on the grounds that it prevents future crimes.	Consider objections to your position. Look for the reasons people offer in support of their beliefs.
What's the difference between rational persuasion and preaching to the choir?	Rational persuasion requires internalizing the critic of one's position. If I'm at the Quaker house, most of my friends share my belief, so there's no need to argue. It makes sense to advance argumentation *only* when there are people who doubt the acceptability of your thesis.	When writing an argumentative essay you need to pose and respond to objections rather than assume you're writing for a friend who agrees with you. When you do this you are more likely to get people who do not agree with you to see that your perspective is at least reasonable. Maybe they will even change their minds.
Why should I address an objection that might damage my thesis?	If an objection creates difficulties for an arguer, then she or he is all the more obliged to deal with it.	From the perspective of covering all your bases, you want to refute strong objections. If you cannot deal with an objection then you need to modify your thesis on the basis of it.
How will I know if my thesis is arguable?	Arguable thesis statements tend to stick their necks out to answer a *why* or a *how* question.	Reasonable people disagree over claims all the time. Be bold in stating your provisional thesis, then evaluate whether you are justified in believing it. Always support your thesis with relevant evidence to justify why it is acceptable.
Why does failing to consider my dialectical obligations make my argument ineffective for a public audience?	If you do not consider counter-arguments, you cannot establish whether the position you've taken on a controversial topic is a reasonable one to take.	Your aim is to present yourself as a writer who is capable of correcting mistakenly held positions after reflecting upon and evaluating the evidence. You must probe your own position and be willing to reconsider it as the circumstances of your inquiry permit.

Harman gives you the draft below. It is meager in its dialectical awareness.

> Is capital punishment morally justifiable based on a theory of retributive justice? I take the position that *it is not*. Has anyone ever proven it to be ethical? No, they have not. Is there evidence that demonstrates that the death penalty prevents crime? No, there has not been even one shred of evidence. Can my audience prove to me that innocent people are not wrongfully convicted and sentenced to die each year? No, they cannot. Since I have established that capital punishment is morally wrong, based on that fact the death penalty doesn't prevent crime and results in innocent people receiving a death sentence, I have established my position.

Based on the **Questions to Test Dialectical Awareness Chart**, what problems can you identify with Harman's draft? How can Harman revise his draft to address a public audience? Why is it illegitimate for Harman to attempt to shift the burden of proof to his imagined audience? In what ways does his draft demonstrate that he has not been diligent in looking for opposing viewpoints? How do you think a critical audience would react if Harman told them he could not find one single argument against his thesis? Would an audience accept Harman's reasoning without any evidence of engaging opposing viewpoints?

When you argue in the public sphere you need to anticipate being asked to justify why your thesis is more convincing than an alternative thesis. At this point Harman asks you why writing for a community of model interlocutors—who do not agree with him—is preferable to writing for an audience who does share his view. You tell Harman, "it makes no sense to advance argumentation if your audience already agrees with your standpoint." Having solid answers to the **Questions to Test Dialectical Awareness Chart** enables Harman to justify why public audiences will inevitably baulk if he toes a particular party line, rather than considering and refuting objections to his position.

Harman asks you the following question: "if my position is eventually strong enough to withstand public scrutiny, will I be able to get others to agree with me that the death penalty should be repealed?" At this point it is clear to you that Harman has learned that establishing his *ethos* or rhetorical credibility with a public audience is achieved primarily through his responsiveness to their doubts about the acceptability of his position. Harman has learned that, in fact, being open to opposing viewpoints requires that he demonstrate a willingness to see the process of inquiry itself as one of rational persuasion whereby he considers audience expectations.

As you continue helping Harman develop an argumentative essay, revisit the **Questions to Test Dialectical Awareness Chart**. From the shortcomings of his first draft, Harman has learned that it is illegitimate to attempt to shift the burden of proof to readers who do not share his beliefs. Moreover, since Harman cannot possibly anticipate every objection to his position, he has prioritized the points of disagreement by refuting those that are the most damaging to his standpoint first.

Stasis Theory: A Heuristic for Inventing Arguments

Classical *stasis* theory—developed by the Greek rhetorician Hermagoras, in the late second century BCE, and expanded by Cicero, Quintilian, and Hermogenes—is an invention strategy. In antiquity *stasis* theory provided students with a concrete method for finding, comprehending, and handling argumentative topics. *Stasis* theory is useful today because it continues to help student writers identify the central issues in a controversy. Specifically, *stasis* theory helps Harman develop his argument against capital punishment because it gives him four stock points to address in order for his argument to more adequately satisfy the scrutiny of interested critics. Here are four questions Harman can use to locate opposition to his argument and seek to resolve it:

1. **Conjecture:** The *stasis* of conjecture concerns the existence of a fact. The focus of the argument is whether there is a cause for dispute? In his draft Harman states, "capital punishment is wrong because innocent people are sentenced to death." In reply, you argue, "The conviction and execution of innocent people is increasingly rare because of the advent of DNA testing and other standards of evidence collection." Now we have the following dispute: "Does capital punishment result in innocent people receiving death sentences or not?" If your argument is better justified than Harman's, then Harman must modify his stance.

If Harman's argument is better justified, then the dispute over whether or not capital punishment results in the death of innocent people will no longer be the focus of his argument since he will have placed the burden of proof on you through the giving of reasons and the presentation of evidence.

2. **Definition:** The *stasis* of definition concerns how something, typically some act, is defined. During this stage arguers disagree over the meaning of terms and what the defining features of the dispute are. In the above example, Harman's argument is: "the death penalty results in the death of innocent people." Harman offers an example of a man who was imprisoned and executed by lethal injection on the basis of false testimony from his brother. In reply, you offer "it is not the death penalty itself that causes wrongful conviction and punishment, but poor standards for what counts as adequate proof of guilt. Technically, an innocent person with a life sentence, who never gets paroled, can die while incarcerated too." Out of this dispute emerges an issue, "If the death penalty was abolished would people convicted on false testimony still be alive today?" If your argument is better justified than Harman's then he must modify his standpoint that capital punishment results in the wrongful conviction and death of innocent people. If Harman's argument is better justified than yours, then the dispute regarding whether we should say that the death penalty is the heart of the problem will no longer be the focus of his argument since he will have placed the burden of proof on you.

3. **Quality:** The *stasis* of quality concerns the seriousness of an act and the circumstantial evidence surrounding it. During this stage interlocutors try to determine the significance of an issue and settle it. Harman argues, "Since capital punishment has resulted in the wrongful death of innocent people, it is unjustifiable." In reply you argue "However, the wrongful conviction and punishment cases you cited all occurred before the advent of DNA testing and other advanced methods for collecting evidence from a crime scene." Out of the dispute arises an issue, "Do advanced methods of evidence collection today assure that only those who are truly guilty receive the death penalty?" If your argument is better justified than Harman's, he must modify

his position. If Harman's argument is better justified than yours, then the dispute over how serious of a problem wrongful conviction and execution is today will no longer be the focus of his argument. In other words, Harman will have placed the burden of proof on you through the giving of reasons and the presentation of evidence.

4. **Translation:** The *stasis* of translation concerns objections of a procedural nature. During this stage arguers try to determine whether or not a dispute is being argued properly and in the proper venue. Harman, for example, may argue that even though a convicted criminal is legally guilty of a heinous crime the death penalty is still wrong on religious grounds (it is Divine will and not human law that should determine when to end a person's life). In reply, you argue that theological arguments are irrelevant because of the separation of church and state in the U.S. Out of this dispute emerges an issue, "Are religious arguments valid when it comes to the punishment of violent offenders in a court of law?" If your argument is better justified than Harman's, he must modify his position. If Harman's argument is better justified than yours, then the dispute over the separation of church and state will no longer be the focus of his argument since he will have placed the burden of proof on you through the giving of reasons and the presentation of evidence.

As you can see, the four stock issues from *stasis* theory help Harman imagine a dialectical back and forth with a critical interlocutor. In this framework his argument will be stronger if it is more convincing than the alternatives that a critic advances in all four of the *stases*. Will all four *stases* need to be argued in every situation? Not necessarily. The number of *stases* will vary from one argumentative exchange to the next. Nonetheless, *stasis* theory offers Harman a method for anticipating important points of agreement and disagreement. In this way *stasis* theory helps him build, understand, and revise his own argument. Using *stasis* theory also helps Harman make rational appeals to a public audience who do not necessarily share his beliefs.

Formulating Arguments: The Controversial Folklorist Alan Dundes

How might a writer handle a public controversy that incites even stronger emotions than the topic of the death penalty? Let's consider another example.

Sahar just read Alan Dundes' controversial article about football. As she was reading she came up with several smart counterarguments against Dundes' thesis. She knows the content of Dundes' essay gave rise to ample public disagreement because he received numerous death threats after its publication. Sahar keeps returning to the following research question as she thinks about what she just read: "*Why* did Dundes' conclusion about the deeper meaning underlying how everyday people talk about football make so many people so livid?" After all, before the end of his life, Dundes tackled subjects like anti-Semitic jokes and the folkloristic content of the Koran in his writing, which are at least as controversial as whether football is a socially sanctioned space for the display of homosexual masculinity. Sahar wishes to respond fairly, though critically, to Dundes' thesis. Let's take a moment to read through Dundes' article before reading about Sahar's response.

Alan Dundes—Into the Endzone for a Touchdown: A Psychoanalytic Consideration of American Football

Alan Dundes. "Into the Endzone for a Touchdown: A Psychoanalytic Consideration of American Football." Western Folklore. Vol. 37, No. 2 (April 1978), pp. 75–88. Copyright © 1978 Western States Folklore Society. Reprinted with permission.

In college athletics it is abundantly clear that it is football which counts highest among both enrolled students and alumni. It is almost as though the masculinity of male alumni is at stake in a given game, especially when a hated rival school is the opponent. College fund-raisers are well aware that a winning football season may prove to be the key to a successful financial campaign to increase the school's endowment capital. The Rose Bowl and other post-season bowl games for colleges, plus the Super Bowl for professional football teams have come to rank as national festival occasions in the United States. All this makes it reasonable to assume that there is something about football which strikes a most responsive chord in the American psyche. No other American sport consistently draws fans in the numbers which are attracted to football. One need only compare the crowd-attendance statistics for college or professional baseball games with the analogous figures for football to see the enormous appeal of the latter. The question is: what is it about American football that could possibly account for its extraordinary popularity?

In the relatively meager scholarship devoted to football, one finds the usual array of theoretical approaches. The ancestral form of football, a game more like Rugby or soccer, was interpreted as a solar ritual—with a disc-shaped rock or object supposedly representing the sun and also as a fertility ritual intended to ensure agricultural abundance. It had been noted, for example, that in some parts of England and France, the rival teams consisted of married men playing against bachelors. In one custom, a newly-married woman would throw over the church a ball for which married men and bachelors fought. The distinction between the married and the unmarried suggests that the game might be a kind of ritual test or battle with marriage signifying socially sanctioned fertility.

The historical evolution of American football from English Rugby has been well documented, but the historical facts do not in and of themselves account for any psychological rationale leading to the unprecedented enthusiasm for the sport. It is insufficient to state that football offers an appropriate outlet for the expression of aggression. William Arens has rightly observed that it would be an oversimplification "to single out violence as the sole or even primary reason for the game's popularity." Many sports provide a similar outlet (e.g., wrestling, ice hockey, roller derby), but few of these come close to matching football as a spectacle for many Americans. Similarly, pointing to such features as a love of competition, or the admiration of coordinated teamwork, or the development of specialists (e.g., punters, punt returners, field goal kickers, etc.) is not convincing since such features occur in most if not all sports. Recently, studies of American football have suggested that the game serves as a male initiation ritual. Arens, for example, remarks that football is "a male preserve that manifests both the physical and cultural values of masculinity," a description which had previously been applied, aptly it would appear, to British Rugby. Arens points out that the equipment worn "accents the male physique" through the enlarged head and shoulders coupled with a narrowed waist. With the lower torso "poured into skin-tight pants accented only by a metal codpiece," Arens contends that the result "is not an expression but an exaggeration of maleness." He comments further: "Dressed in this manner, the players can engage in hand holding, hugging, and bottom patting, which would be disapproved of in any other context, but which is accepted on the gridiron without a second thought." Having said this much, Arens fails to draw any inferences about possible ritual homosexual aspects of football. Instead, he goes on to note that American football resembles male rituals in other cultures insofar as contact with females is discouraged if not forbidden. The argument usually given is one of "limited good." A man has only so much energy and if he uses it in sexual activity, he will have that much less to use in hunting, warfare, or in this case, football. I believe Arens and others are correct in calling attention to the ritual and symbolic dimensions of American football, but I think the psychological implications of the underlying symbolism have not been adequately explored.

Football is one of a large number of competitive games which involves the scoring of points by gaining access to a defended area in an opponent's territory. In basketball, one must throw a ball through a hoop (and net) attached to the other team's backboard. In ice hockey, one must hit the puck into the goal at the opponent's end of the rink. In football, the object is to move the ball across the opponent's goal into his endzone. It does not require a great deal of Freudian sophistication to see a possible sexual component in such acts as throwing a ball through a hoop, hitting a puck across a "crease" into an enclosed area bounded by nets or cage, and other structurally similar acts. But what is not so obvious is the connection of such sexual symbolism with an all-male group of participants.

I believe that a useful way to begin an attempt to understand the psychoanalytic significance of American football is through an examination of football folk speech. For it is precisely in the idioms and metaphors that a clear pattern of personal interaction is revealed. In this regard, it might be helpful first to briefly consider the slang employed in the verbal dueling of the American male. In effect, I am suggesting that American football is analogous to male verbal dueling. Football entails ritual and dramatic action while verbal dueling is more concerned with words. But structurally speaking, they are similar or at least functionally equivalent. In verbal dueling, it is common to speak about putting one's opponent "down." This could mean simply to topple an opponent figuratively, but it could also imply forcing one's adversary to assume a supine position, that is, the "female" position in typical Western sexual intercourse. It should also be noted that an equally humiliating experience for a male would be to serve as a passive receptacle for a male aggressor's phallic thrust. Numerous idioms attest to the widespread popularity of this pattern of imagery to describe a loser. One speaks of having been screwed by one's boss or of having been given the shaft. Submitting to anal intercourse is also implied in perhaps the most common single American folk gesture, the so-called *digitus impudicus*, better known in folk parlance as the "finger." Giving someone the finger is often accompanied by such unambiguous explanatory phrases as "Fuck you!," "Screw you!," "Up yours!," or "Up your ass!." Now what has all this to do with football? I believe that the same symbolic pattern is at work in both verbal dueling and much ritual play. Instead of scoring a putdown, one scores a touchdown. Certainly the terminology used in football is suggestive. One gains yardage, but it is not territory which is kept in the sense of being permanently acquired by the invading team. The territory invaded remains nominally under the proprietorship of the opponent. A sports announcer or fan might say, for example, "This is the deepest *penetration* into (opponent's team name) territory so far" [my emphasis]. Only if one gets into the endzone (or kicks a field goal through the uprights of the goalposts) does one earn points. The use of the term "end" is not accidental. Evidently there is a kind of structural isomorphism between the line (as opposed to the backfield) and the layout of the field of play. Each line has two ends (left end and right end) with a "center" in the middle. Similarly, each playing field has two ends (endzones) with a midfield line (the fifty yard-line). Ferril remarked on the parallel between the oval shape of the football and the oval shape of most football stadiums, but I submit it might be just as plausible to see the football shape as an elongated version of the earlier round soccer or Rugby ball, a shape which tends to produce two accentuated ends of the ball. Surely the distinctive difference between the shape of a football and the shape of the balls used in most other ballgames (e.g., baseball, basketball, soccer) is that it is not perfectly spherical. The notion that a football has two "ends" is found in the standard idiom used to describe a kick or punt in which the ball turns over and over from front to back during flight (as opposed to moving in a more direct, linear, spiraling pattern) as an "end over end" kick.

The object of the game, simply stated, is to get into the opponent's endzone while preventing the opponent from getting into one's own endzone. Structurally speaking, this is precisely what is involved in male verbal dueling. One wishes to put one's opponent down; to "screw" him while avoiding being screwed by him. We can now better understand the appropriateness of the "bottom patting" so often observed among football players. A good offensive or defensive play deserves a pat on the rear end. The recipient has held up his end and has thereby helped protect the collective "end" of the entire team. One pats one's teammates' ends, but one seeks to violate the endzone of one's opponents!

The trust one has for one's own teammates is perhaps signalled by the common postural stance of football players. The so-called three point stance involves bending over in a distinct stooped position with one's rear end exposed. It is an unusual position (in terms of normal life activities) and it does make one especially vulnerable to attack from behind, that is, vulnerable to a homosexual attack. In some ways, the posture might be likened to what is termed "presenting" among nonhuman primates. Presenting refers to a subordinate animal's turning its rump towards a higher ranking or dominant one. The center thus presents to the quarterback—just as linemen do to the backs in general. George Plimpton has described how the quarterback's "hand, the top of it, rests up against the center's backside as he bends over the ball—medically, against the perineum, the pelvic floor." We know that some dominant nonhuman primates will sometimes reach out to touch a presenting subordinate in similar fashion. In football, however, it is safe to present to one's teammates. Since one can trust one's teammates, one knows that one will be patted, not raped. The traditional joking admonitions of the locker room warning against "bending over in the shower" or "picking up the soap" (which would presumably offer an inviting target for homosexual attack) do not apply since one is among friends. "Grabass" among friends is understood as being harmless joking behavior.

The importance of the "ends" is signalled by the fact that they alone among linemen are eligible to receive a forward pass. In that sense, ends are equivalent to the "backs." In symbolic terms, I am arguing that the end is a kind of backside and that the endzone is a kind of erogenous zone. The relatively recently coined terms "tight end" and "split end" further demonstate the special emphasis upon this "position" on the team. The terms refer to whether the end stays close to his neighboring tackle, e.g., to block, or whether he moves well away from the normally adjacent tackle, e.g., to go out for a pass. However, both tight end and split end (cf. also wide receiver) could easily be understood as possessing an erotic nuance.

Additional football folk speech could be cited. The object of the game is to "score," a term which in standard slang means to engage in sexual intercourse with a member of the opposite sex. One "scores" by going "all the way." The latter phrase refers specifically to making a touchdown. In sexual slang, it alludes to indulging in intercourse as opposed to petting or necking. The offensive team may try to mount a "drive" in order to "penetrate" the other team's territory. A ball carrier might go "up the middle" or he might "go through a hole" (made by his linemen in the opposing defensive line). A particularly skillful runner might be able to make his own hole. The defense is equally determined to "close the hole." Linemen may encourage one another "to stick it to 'em," meaning to place their helmeted heads (with phallic-symbolic overtones) against the chests of their opposite numbers to drive them back or put them out of the play.

A player who scores a touchdown may elect to "spike" the ball by hurling it down towards the ground full force. This spiking movement confirms to all assembled that the enemy's endzone has been penetrated. The team scored upon is thus shamed and humiliated in front of an audience. In this regard, football is similar to verbal dueling inasmuch as dueling invariably takes place before one or more third parties. The term "spike" may also be germane. As a noun, it could refer to a sharp-pointed long slender part or projection. As a verb, it could mean either to mark or cut with a spike (the football would presumably be the phallic spike) or to thwart or to sabotage an enemy. In any event, the ritual act of spiking serves to prolongate and accentuate the all too short moment of triumph, the successful entry into the enemy's endzone.

The sexual connotations of football folk speech apply equally to players on defense. One goal of the defensive line is to penetrate the offensive line to get to the quarterback. Getting to the offensive quarterback and bringing him down to the ground is termed "sacking" the quarterback. The verb "sack" connotes plunder, ravage, and perhaps even rape. David Kopay, one of the few homosexuals participating in professional football willing to admit his preference for members of the same sex, specifically commented on the nature of typical exhortations made by coaches and others:

The whole language of football is involved in sexual allusions. We were told to go out and "fuck those guys"; to take that ball and "stick it up their asses" or "down their throats." The coaches would yell, "knock their dicks off," or more often than that, "knock their jocks off." They'd say, "Go out there and give it all you've got, a hundred and ten per cent, shoot your wad." You controlled their line and "knocked" 'em into submission. Over the years I've seen many a coach get emotionally aroused while he was diagramming a particular play into an imaginary hole on the blackboard. His face red, his voice rising, he would show the ball carrier how he wanted him to "stick it in the hole."

I have no doubt that a good many football players and fans will be sceptical (to say the least) of the analysis proposed here. Even academics with presumably less personal investment in football will probably find the idea implausible if not downright repugnant that American football could be a ritual combat between groups of males attempting to assert their masculinity by penetrating the endzones of their rivals. David Kopay, despite suggesting that for a long time football provided a kind of replacement for sex in his life and admitting that football is "a real outlet for repressed sexual energy," refuses to believe that "being able to hold hands in the huddle and to pat each other on the ass if we felt like it" is necessarily an overt show of homosexuality. Yet I think it is highly likely that the ritual aspect of football, providing as it does a socially sanctioned framework for male body contact—football, after all, is a so-called "body contact" sport—is a form of homosexual behavior. The unequivocal sexual symbolism of the game, as plainly evidenced in folk speech coupled with the fact that all of the participants are male, make it difficult to draw any other conclusion. Sexual acts carried out in thinly disguised symbolic form by, and directed towards, males and males only, would seem to constitute ritual homosexuality.

Evidence from other cultures indicates that male homosexual ritual combats are fairly common. Answering the question of who penetrates whom is a pretty standard means of testing masculinity cross-culturally. Interestingly enough, the word masculine itself seems to derive from Latin mas (male) and culus (anus). The implication might be that for a male to prove his masculinity with his peers, he would need to control or guard his buttocks area while at the same time threatening the posterior of another (weaker) male. A good many men's jokes in Mediterranean cultures (e.g., in Italy and in Spain) center on the culo.

That a mass spectacle could be based upon a ritual masculinity contest should not surprise anyone familiar with the bullfight. Without intending to reduce the complexity of the bullfight to a single factor, one could nonetheless observe that it is in part a battle between males attempting to penetrate one another. The one who is penetrated loses.

If it is the bull, he may be further feminized or emasculated by having various extremities cut off to reward the successful matador. In this context, we can see American football as a male activity (along with the Boy Scouts, fraternities and other exclusively male social organizations in American culture) as belonging to the general range of male rituals around the world in which masculinity is defined and affirmed. In American culture, women are permitted to be present as spectators or even cheerleaders, but they are not participants. Women resenting men's preoccupation with such male sports are commonly referred to as football widows (analogous to golf widows). This too suggests that the sport activity is in some sense a substitute for normal heterosexual relations. The men are "dead" as far as relationships with females are concerned. In sport and in ritual, men play both male and female parts. Whether it is the verbal dueling tradition of the circum-Mediterranean in which young men threaten to put opponents into a passive homosexual position, or the initiation rites in aboriginal Australia and New Guinea (and elsewhere) in which younger men are subjected to actual homosexual anal intercourse by older members of the male group, the underlying psychological rationale appears to be similar. Professional football's financial incentives may extend the playing years of individuals beyond late adolescence, but in its essence American football is an adolescent masculinity initiation ritual in which the winner gets into the loser's endzone more times than the loser gets into his!

University of California
Berkeley, California

Sahar decides that because she feels so strongly that Dundes' argument is misguided she'll need to step back to organize her thoughts. Taking some time to organize her thoughts is a strategy that allows Sahar to develop the disposition of a critical thinker, to understand the issues in an argumentative situation, and to invent adequate counterarguments in response rather than simply reacting to Dundes' argument hastily.

Reactionary Thought Filter Chart

Critical Thinking and Close Reading *require*:	Critical Thinking and Close Reading are *not*:
<ul><li>Fairly and accurately:</li><ul><li>Explaining the substance of the writer's argument</li><li>Explaining how the writer's disciplinary context, research, or worldview might have led him or her to take a position</li></ul><li>Granting that others have important and valid reasons for their beliefs and argument</li></ul>	<ul><li>Misrepresenting someone's argument</li><li>Taking an argumentative shortcut by attacking people (the *ad hominem fallacy*) then labeling them stupid or otherwise casting aspersions on their moral or intellectual character</li><li>Pretending to be convinced when you really are not Interjecting your own opinion to derail an interlocutor rather than asking critical questions that focus the inquiry</li></ul>

Here's how Sahar organizes her thoughts to demonstrate her ability to read closely and respond critically to Dundes' argument.

- She states Dundes' position.

- She makes the strongest counterarguments against Dundes' controversial position that she can imagine.

Argument Comprehension and Counterargument Chart

Nutshell of Dundes' Premises	Counterarguments
Premise 1: The idioms and metaphors we use to talk about football (i.e., football folk speech) are rife with sexual connotation.	If football were a homosexual ritual, then it wouldn't be as popular as it is with people who are prejudiced against gay people.
Premise 2: Football, as a contact sport, resembles other same-sex initiation rituals around the world where masculinity is demonstrated by penetrating into an opponent's end zone.	Most men who play football are heterosexual and hence the desire to display dominance over other male players is a way to show women that they are powerful. If it's a mating ritual, then it's a heterosexual one.
Premise 3: Football is an all-male sport, which gives it added same-sex erotic nuance.	The language we use in the games we play does not have the deep symbolic meaning Dundes believes it does. For example, Dundes is grasping for evidence of this so-called deeper meaning when he uses the Bible to support his interpretation of the word "touch."
Thesis/Conclusion: American football is a form of same-sex combat for young men to establish their virility and sexual dominance.	

Next, Sahar's English instructor asks her to write a two-page critique of Dundes' argument. Here are the first two paragraphs of Sahar's mini-argumentative essay:

Humans compete. Inherent to our nature is the endless struggle against the unpleasantness of defeat. As a consequence, even in our leisure time we enjoy watching struggles for dominance and cheering for our favorite team. Alan Dundes' exploration of the homosexual aspects of American football is amusing, but he overestimates the same-sex erotic aspects of the game. In this essay, I will argue that if football is a kind of dominance ritual it is one where women are presumed to be too frail to compete.

According to Dundes, "it is highly likely that the ritual aspect of football, providing as it does a socially sanctioned framework for male body contact…is a form of homosexual behavior" (87). Yes, football is an all-male full body contact sport. However, football is not sex-segregated so that ostensibly straight men can touch each other on the sly. Female athletes do not play football with men because of tradition and legitimate concerns that women may be injured on a co-ed team. The fact that nearly all contact sports are sex-segregated around the world has everything to do with our deep-seated beliefs that there are basic physical differences between women and men. Whether these differences actually exist, or to what extent, is a subject of much debate. However, Dundes ought to have taken perceptions of sexual difference into account because as it stands there is little evidence to support his claim that football is a socially sanctioned venue for men to touch each other.

What further evidence or support does Sahar need to make her case? What other counterarguments can you think of to make an argument against Dundes? Do you think his argument is strong? If so, what evidence can you provide that attests to its strength?

Writing Your Own Public Arguments

The example above shows how Sahar moves from posing a research question, to accurately summarizing Dundes' position, to coming up with counterarguments, to writing her own argumentative essay. In a longer public argument it is necessary to give your readers plenty of **signposts** to map out where you have been and where you are going. The following is an illustration of signposting for Sahar's mini-argumentative essay.

Now that we see that Dundes' claims that football is a form of ritualized same-sex combat, let me map out my argument so far. In supporting the thesis that football is a kind of dominance ritual, where women are assumed to be too physically weak to compete, I cited the sex-segregation of sports around the world. To the objection that homosexuality violates social norms and hence must operate beneath our conscious awareness in rituals like football, I responded that in a culture such as the U.S.—a culture where women and men are ostensibly equal—an abiding belief in men's physical superiority is not expressed as nonchalantly as it might have been in the past. After conceding that there is still a lot of discrimination against both sexual minorities *and* females in athletics, I now will argue that forms of ridicule such as, "you throw like a girl" demonstrate that a disdain for feminine or effeminate characteristics underlies both sex-segregation and homophobia in sports.

Public argumentation requires that we recognize that we have dialectical obligations, which make it necessary to imagine ourselves as engaged with a critic who challenges us with well-founded objections. Responding to critical readers creates opportunities for all writers to more effectively gain rational adherence from public audiences.

Questions and Prompts for Discussion

1. Who determines what is reasonable? What criteria can we use to assess whether an argument is justified adequately?

2. How might imagining a community of model interlocutors potentially cause an arguer to lose touch with her or his actual audience?

3. Give an example of how thinking solely in terms of your actual audience can limit your ability to think critically or creatively.

4. Why might imagining your audience as comprised of people who already support your position come across as dismissive to those readers who have not yet made up their minds?

5. Why is it helpful to conceptualize arguing as a practice that requires a good imagination?

6. List the invention strategies you use to locate a range of arguments on a controversial topic.

7. Write a paragraph or more that expresses a range of possible positions on an issue of public controversy.

8. What does rational persuasion mean to you? Give an example of a situation where you think rational persuasion may not be effective.

Chapter *15*

Analyzing Visual-Spatial Arguments for a Public Audience

By Jessica B. Burstrem

Rhetoric is text with a purpose. And **text** could mean anything: words, written or spoken; images, on paper, canvas, film, clothing, or any other medium; sound; sculpture; even hair. If you can "read" it—as you can read the expression on someone's face, for instance, or their "body language"—then it is a text.

As for the purpose, is there anything that does not have one? Even a photograph—which often seems innocent, since, we tend to think, it is supposed to capture what is "real"—always has a purpose. Someone has taken it for a reason. You might take pictures to document something (vandalism to your car, for instance, or a valuable collection, for insurance purposes) or to remember something (a family vacation, perhaps, or a fun night with friends) or to share what you see with someone else (the growth of a child who lives far away from some of his/her relatives, or a spectacular Arizona sunset). And in a professional photograph, every aspect of that photo is a choice, a design—the lighting, the angle, the distance, the tone, the focus, the horizon, etc. Not so "real" after all, huh?

Each of those choices also has a purpose, a rationale, an intended effect. In seeking to achieve that intended effect, the **rhetor**, or creator, needs to have in mind a particular **target audience**—the viewer(s) to whom s/he is hoping to appeal. Then, the **ideology**—or feelings, beliefs, customs, values, and experiences—of that audience should determine what choices would make the photo most effective at achieving its purpose. By noticing and thinking about those choices, we can identify the creator's likely purpose and target audience. That is **rhetorical analysis**.

379

But it is not enough to appeal to your target audience, or **second persona** (the theoretical ideal audience implied by a text).[3] You have to appeal to your actual audience as well, which probably does not exactly coincide with your target audience. You may still address your image to your **primary audience**, the part of your actual audience directly targeted by a text, but you also need to think about your **secondary audience**—the people who will still encounter the text or, in this case, who may see the image. If your appeal is too narrow, too specific to your primary audience, will you fail to achieve your purpose with—or maybe even offend—your secondary audience? On the other hand, if your appeal is too broad, will it become so unspecific, so un-targeted, that it fails with everyone? These are the types of decisions that a rhetor must make, the types of risks that s/he must consider and balance—and, when performing a rhetorical analysis, we want to think about those issues too.

Rhetorical Analysis of Images

A rhetorical analysis of a visual or spatial argument should address the following questions:

> What argument/message is the creator likely trying to make with the image? How do you know? How successful is s/he?
>
> What is his/her probable purpose? How do you know? Does the image help him/her achieve it? If so, how?
>
> Who is apparently the target audience? How do you know? Did the creator make the image appropriate to his/her likely intended audience? If so, how?
>
> It could also address these questions:
>
> What does the image seem to tell you about its creator? Is that an impression that adds to the creator's **ethos**? (An ethical appeal, you remember, functions through the power of credibility; in other words, it presents the rhetor as trustworthy.) If so, why/how?

---

3 **First persona**, on the other hand, is the image of the rhetor presented through the text. These are imaginary constructions: The rhetor may not "really" be who the text presents him/her to be, and there may not actually be any real audience that matches the target one, but both should be appealing to the audience—the first persona as someone trustworthy from whom to accept an argument, and the second persona as who an audience member would like to be him/herself.

In a visual argument, ethos could come, for instance, from the quality of the presentation. By demonstrating skill, you demonstrate expertise, and that increases your audience's approbation of you. If your viewers think well of you, then they are more likely to think highly of your message too, and that increases your chances of achieving your purpose with them.

Another ethical appeal in a visual argument could come from the depiction of a well-regarded or well-known person or symbol. A famous person in a public service announcement suggests his/her endorsement of the message; if that person is well-respected and/or well-liked, it can cause the viewers to consider that message more seriously than they might with someone unknown.

On the other hand, unless the person is famous for expertise in a relevant area, it could actually hurt the message. Just because someone is a home decorating diva, for instance, does not mean you should take her advice about, say, insider trading. And in commercial advertisements, the presence of a famous person generally indicates that the company behind the ad paid him/her to appear in the commercial—which means that s/he may not even like the product at all. Not much of an endorsement.

We all know that already, of course, but advertisers do it anyway. Why do you think that is so?

Celebrities in Images

The well-known "Got milk?" campaign has evolved over the years, but what has not evolved is its strategy. Generally the ads feature one celebrity with a milk moustache in front of a nondescript background. The celebrity *is* the ad, so little is allowed to distract from him/her. Which celebrity appears in the ad, though, can tell you something about the audience to whom the creators are trying to appeal with that particular version. In one ad, we have Kate Moss, super-thin supermodel, hence primarily targeting those who follow and value fashion and appearance—generally women—and who are young enough to know her—probably from Generation X and after, since she first became well-known in the early 1990s. Once the ad has gotten viewers' attention, the caption then utilizes humor (see relevant section on next page) to actually mock her trademark size and support the ad's purpose:

Bones. Bones. Bones. Maybe so, but unlike 75% of women today, there's one way I'm taking good care of mine. By getting lots of calcium. How? From drinking lots of milk. 1% ice cold. And besides, haven't you heard that the waif look is out?

The first part of the caption, "Bones. Bones. Bones," refers to early descriptions of her as little more than skin and bones, since she was so thin. But at the end, the suggestion that "the waif look is out," indicates that a healthy weight—and healthy bones—are the new fashion. The fact that Moss is posing with a glass of milk and a milk moustache also suggests that showing that you drink milk makes you appealing, as arguably all of the other "Got milk?" ads do too. In this case, viewers who want to be fashionable and who value the example of a supermodel to that effect might be more likely to drink milk as a result of this ad.

One ad, including the actress Glenn Close, appeals to a different audience. She is a talented actress best known for her role in the 1987 film *Fatal Attraction*, so those younger than Generation Xers may not be familiar with her. In this ad, she is in her early 60s, when women are still rarely depicted positively in film, television, or print; thus the ad particularly appeals to women in their 50s and 60s, who see so few women their age to admire in the popular media. Then, the caption promotes the ad's purpose with those viewers:

Look Close. To perform my best, I need to give my body the attention it deserves. That's why I eat right, exercise and drink milk. Studies suggest the nutrients in 3 glasses of lowfat or fat free milk a day can help you maintain a healthy weight. And the protein helps build muscle for a lean body. You'll see.

The emphasis in the ad **copy**, or the words that appear in the ad, is weight management, rather than what you might expect would best motivate women in their 60s to drink milk: preventing osteoporosis. But there are two reasons why not mentioning that condition is more effective here. First of all, we generally associate bone loss with old age, and treating Close as old here would weaken the celebration of her strength, beauty, and success that otherwise makes the ad appealing to its primary audience. Then, we already generally recognize that the calcium in milk helps prevent bone loss; instead, in both the Close and Moss ads, the milk producers are trying to combat the image of milk as fattening by associating it with thin, attractive women and even describing it as helping to "maintain a healthy weight." The creators realize that this new information is more important to achieving their purpose than reminders of what people generally already know.

After all, the purpose of these two ads is not to help women feel beautiful or healthy, no matter how much they may present themselves that way. The purpose is to increase milk sales. By making members of the primary audience feel good about themselves, the creators increase their ethos, which, like the presence of the well-respected celebrities, leads those viewers to trust the ad's messages as a whole. That is what makes each of these ads a successful visual argument.

Provoking Images

We are so used to advertisements in general these days that many times we flip or drive or walk past them without paying the least attention to them at all. But if no one notices your ad, not only will you not reach your target audience, but you will have effectively no audience at all.

Consequently, advertisers are taking different approaches to attract viewers' attention. For instance, you have most likely noticed **product placement** before. I remember one episode of the ABC television show *Ugly Betty* in which magazine editors are debating the layout of a fashion spread, and one man suggests that an ad for Cherry 7-UP with Antioxidants be moved to the middle of the spread. He even has a 12-pack of the product with him at the time, and one of the other editors dashes over to get a can, disrupting the meeting. When he is scolded—as if we didn't get the message already—he says, "But it has antioxidants!" and holds up the can.

Yet, would you believe that, even though as I watched it I thought the scene was awfully odd, I did not actually realize what it was—a product placement—until I saw a more typical advertisement for the product during the next commercial break? The creators got what they wanted: I could not avoid their ad while getting a snack in the kitchen or fast-forwarding with my Tivo. I was a captive audience as long as I wanted to keep watching the show.

They got even more than that too: my curiosity. A few months after that show, to a social gathering that I was attending, someone brought some Cherry 7-UP with antioxidants. I took the first one.

Another way that creators of visual rhetoric try to garner viewers is by making their images eye-catching. They could be horrifying or stunning or utterly bizarre—but they capture our attention.

Perhaps you've seen photos of the public displays staged by animal rights groups in which what appear to be bloody, dead, nearly naked white women lie sprawled on what resemble white Styrofoam trays wrapped in clear plastic with printed white labels, like the packaging for raw meat sold at the grocery story. These spatial displays are, probably more than anything else, shocking. They make you stop and stare. Each display is thus effective at getting its audience to pay attention. The question is, what does that attention achieve next?

The displays use **pathos**, or a pathetic appeal, which, you recall, means constructing an argument in accordance with your audience's values and emotions. As people ourselves, we generally value human life and feel horror and sadness at the loss of it. Such viewers would consequently have strong negative feelings about what they are seeing. Animal rights groups hope that viewers will transfer those feelings to nonhuman meat, such as chicken or beef, which connection the displays seek to evoke. Just like packaged meat at the grocery store, the women are on white trays wrapped in clear plastic. Like red meat, they are covered in what looks like their own blood. These groups are trying to make an **analogy**, which is a form of **logos**, or a logical appeal. The creators seek to compare the murder of animals to the murder of humans to get their audience to feel some of the same horror of the first practice that we already do of the second. But other reactions are possible as well. How else do you think viewers might respond? What impact could that have on their attitudes toward the images' message?

The images are desgined to shock viewers into according with the group's ideology. But, readers might respond in ways that the creators did not intend. As you review these images, think of the organization's ethos. How might this ethos work for some viewers and not for others? How might the images move some readers to join the group and others to resist their message? That is a risk that the creators of these displays have chosen to take by provoking their audience.

Of particular note are the gender, race, age, body type, and clothing of the models who typically appear in these exhibits. In some images, activists in the packaging are young, slender, light-skinned females, and they are either on display in their underwear or sometimes appear to be wearing nothing at all. Their flesh does resemble that of the chicken sold in this manner at your local grocery store. We might think through how other choices might make this image more effective or ineffective. How would using activists of other races, ages, and body types affect the meaning of the image? Consider using a white, young female. There are consequences to this choice. This choice might confirm the reality that the mainstream idea of an attractive white female—young, slender, etc.—seems uniquely relevant to all ages, races, sizes, and possibly even genders because that has for so long been the primary, if not the only, type of woman featured in television, film, fashion, advertisements, and the like. We have learned that the attractive white female is supposed to represent all of us...even though she does not. However, organizations also use activists of various genders, races, and body types. How might different choices impact the meaning of the image? Why do you think they make the decision to use various activists? What does this tell us about the rhetorical situation they encounter?

At the same time, we should consider that the characteristics of the participants may not have been an animal rights group's choice at all: The models are volunteers, and so they are self-selected to play a role in sending the organization's message. The commonalities among them may tell us just as much about the women who volunteered as about the organization they represent, then.

But—particularly because they are dressed only in their underwear or appear naked—they may also look to some viewers like bodies of raped and murdered women, as we see on television crime fighting shows like *Law & Order: Special Victims Unit* or *CSI*. The correspondence is even more noticeable since these displays are all positioned on the street, where such bodies are often found on those shows, rather than in a grocery store.

What do you think? How do the gender and other physical characteristics of the models—though possibly accidental—affect the images? Would they function differently with men in them, for instance? How could the shock value of images actually be counterproductive to their creator's purpose? These are all issues that creators must consider and risks they must take when constructing visual rhetorical arguments.

Humorous and Graphic Images

Figure 1. *Human Chicken ad: http://www.usdesignstudio.co.uk/ ImageHandler.ashx?ImageID=690&size=1 Reprinted with permission from us (design studio), Alex Wooley, Adam Mileusnic, Edward Heal, and Cilena Rojas.*

Figure 1 depicts a work from a graphic design studio which is similar to animal rights groups displays discussed above in that it takes the same basic approach of likening humans to chickens —but for a different purpose, and with a different tone.

The image is part of a two-part series. This one features the label "Free range Whole human" and the description "Free to roam on green pastures for health, happiness and recreation, with permi- nant [sic] access to over 60 free on-site classes and activities, ranging from yoga to guitar lessons. Unit 2, air-conditioned." The other im- age, which is not reproduced here, features the label "Office-grown Whole human. Reared in office conditions. Office 3, non-air-con- ditioned." Both labels also read, "Computer-literate. Once opened consume within 85 years. £18,350. 71.2kg." Unlike animal rights group ads, there is no fake blood here, and both models are male and appear to be wearing shorts. The "free-range" human also has slightly darker skin than the "office-grown" one. (In a rhetorical analysis essay, you must describe what you are discussing as though your readers are unfamiliar with it. Since only one of these images appears here and the label is difficult to read, I must do the same for you in this chapter.)

This series uses the stylistic device of **humor** to engage its audience and help to achieve its purpose. In general, humorous arguments can get your audience to like you (which builds your ethos), to open up to you, to want to be on your side, and to make a controversial idea seem more palatable. In this case, the creators are comparing the differences between "free-range" and caged chickens to the differences between humans living at a kind of recreation facility and working in an office. Perhaps it mocks the distinctions that make free-range chicken more appealing to consumers, and so in that respect it might offend some animal rights activists or people who believe strongly in that choice. But by avoiding the shocking nature of animal rights group displays, it is still less likely to offend its audience while nonetheless remaining eye-catching.

An Absolut advertisement also appeals to humor in order to make its target audience feel good about and therefore be more likely to purchase/consume its brand of vodka. It targets a particular type of woman: one who "wants it all," so to speak. This white heterosexual couple is in what appears to be a luxurious home, with ornate wallpaper and baseboards, a large floor plan, a fireplace, a marble floor in front of it, a stylish armchair, and white carpet throughout. They also have what must be a very well-behaved little dog. The woman is smiling, very thin, and dressed for a cocktail party with a martini in her hand. The man, on the other hand, is very pregnant and holding his back from the pain as a result. He is not smiling either, nor is he drinking, since the consumption of alcohol is generally frowned upon during pregnancy. The implication is a kind of role-reversal, since usually it is the woman who would be pregnant and not drinking. This woman gets to have her baby and her drink too. It is an ideal world for her, the ad argues, and so Absolut is ideal.

Certainly men are in the secondary audience here, and they may enjoy this ad too, since it is funny and also emphasizes what some may characterize as their privilege to never have to be pregnant and not drinking cocktails. But there are plenty of alcohol ads that target primarily men; instead, this Absolut ad is trying to get that 52% of the drinking age population that is female and yet often left out of advertising. It still leaves out gays and lesbians, though, and most likely everyone of a different race, although slim white women are often taken to represent all of us, even though they do not. The setting of the ad also has class implications, but some working and middle class people might aspire to that standard of living, so the approach might work for the secondary audience as well. This image is therefore an example of a targeted advertisement—think, aficionados of the nightclub scene in Scottsdale—that still has broader appeal.

One can do more than **classical**, or **Aristotelian**, rhetorical analysis—that is, focusing on ethos, pathos, and logos—of visual/spatial arguments. For instance, **ideological** rhetorical analysis, which involves mapping the ideological characteristics of the rhetor (and, perhaps, the implied audience), would be just as relevant to consideration of the images discussed in this chapter so far. This approach considers the effectiveness (for the argument that the rhetor appears to be trying to make and the audience to whom he or she is addressing it) of the ideology *behind* a text. In other words, what does a text tell us about its rhetor, and does that make the rhetor more credible and thus the text more successful at achieving his/her purpose for it? Does the get-the-message-across-at-any-cost approach evident in The animal rights group's displays hurt the argument because it might lead viewers to dislike the source of the argument? Does the exclusion of non-white non-heterosexual people make Absolut less likeable for those viewers as well?

Figure 2. *Absolute End ad: www.adbusters.org/gallery/spoofads/alcohol/ absoluteend 6/12/09 Reprinted with permission from Adbusters Media Foundation.*

Adbusters, an anti-corporate media organization, produced the **spoof ad** in Figure 2 to cause viewers to question alcohol advertising, particularly that of Absolut vodka. In this image, a chalk outline, which we associate with dead bodies at a crime scene, takes the characteristic shape of an Absolut bottle, thereby reminding viewers of the death toll of drinking and driving. Knowing Adbusters' stance, we can probably presume that it also seeks to blame alcohol advertising to some extent for that death toll.

But because the chalk outline is of the bottle rather than of a human, the ad lacks the chilling effect that could cause the outrage in viewers that, directed appropriately, could motivate them to try to change their lives or the world in which we live, as the creators hope they will. Adbusters chose to be light rather than explicit in this piece, and consequently the desired effects may not ever achieve their full realization.

At the same time, this light approach makes the ad more humorous than shocking, and so viewers—especially on the Internet—may be more likely to share it with their family, friends, and acquaintances for that reason than they would if it were really disturbing (consider, for instance, the drunk driving prevention ad discussed below). Sometimes it is actually better to not horrify your audience. Which approach do you think would be most effective here?

Commercial Advertisements *v.* Public Service Announcements

Perhaps you have also seen some of the ads in the Dove Campaign for Real Beauty series. They depict women of a variety of shapes, sizes, and colors, some with tattoos—which are generally absent from fashion magazines—and all smiling, though wearing nothing more than white cotton bras and underwear. Like the "Got milk?" ads, these Dove skin care ads were not actually created to help women feel beautiful or healthy, though, no matter how much they may seem to operate that way. In fact, their purpose is to sell a product—in my favorite example, a firming cream to reduce or eliminate cellulite, which depends on women's dissatisfaction with their bodies' appearances in order to sell at all. This ad, again like the milk ads, just presents itself as campaigning for "real beauty" to add to Dove's ethos with its audience. It certainly appeals to women of many races and colors by including such a variety of them in its image, and it appeals to women who dislike the limitations that the fashion industry seems to place on the mainstream standard of beauty. Here are women who do not have rail-thin bodies and large breasts, some of whom are not tall and tanned, and one of whom is displaying her tattoo. But they are smiling and showing comfort in their bodies, posing just in their underwear for the entire world to see. That is certainly affirming—until you think about the purpose that the ad is meant to help achieve. The power to dissect such rhetorical images is one of the goals and benefits of this course.

The Adbusters image in Figure 2 at first seems to resemble the Dove ad in that it also seeks to show its audience a different perspective on the world than one purportedly gets from most other advertising, but it is their purposes that distinguish them from one another. Adbusters is an organization, not a corporation, so it seeks to inform or alert the public rather than to convince people to buy something. Do you think that viewers would find an Adbusters ad more credible than a commercial one as a result of that concern for them? How about an animal rights ad?

Since Adbusters and animal rights groups are not just interested in helping the public but in advancing their own philosophies at the same time, they still do not have as much ethos as they could earn through showing concern for their audiences' interests above and beyond everything else. But there are some ads that do make what is arguably the ideal ethical appeal: public service announcements. These are advertisers who are spending money to inform the public, usually of ways to protect its own health and safety.

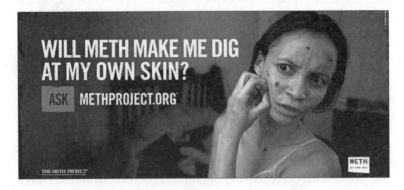

Figure 3. *The Meth Project ad. Reprinted with permission by The Meth Project.*

Anti-drug ads can have much credibility, pathetic appeal, and overall effectiveness because their images are realistic and shocking and their intentions as clear. An excellent example is the Meth Project ad in Figure 3. How does this image compare to the other advertisements reproduced in this chapter? What else should you consider if you were doing a rhetorical analysis of this image? How do the background, the race of the subject, the style of the text, and other details contribute to or detract from its effectiveness? Do you think the image is an actual photograph of a methamphetamine user? Why or why not? What impact does that have on the ad's success?

Creating a Visual/Spatial Public Argument

Rhetorically analyzing visual/spatial arguments does not only help you think more critically about what you see around you in the world: It also helps you think more about how you present your own arguments. If you plan to create a visual/spatial argument for this course—or for any other purpose—you need to determine what you want it to accomplish and with whom. What is your goal? What do you want your project to accomplish? Who is your target audience for that goal? How can you best reach that audience? What do you need to do to appeal to your secondary audience as well? How can you prepare against oppositional argument(s)? How can you make sure that your purpose is clear and convincing in your text?

Make sure that the purpose and audience that you select fit the assignment. Oftentimes the choice of topic is what determines how successful each student's project ultimately is. Pick something that you can accomplish effectively in light of the constraints and requirements of the assignment. Also pick something that works well with your strengths and preferences so that you enjoy this assignment and excel at it. That is part of considering how best to respond to a **rhetorical situation**, or the particular time and place and method and purpose and target audience of your text.

Chapter *16*

Designing and Writing Visual-Spatial Public Arguments

By Christopher Minnix

The last chapter introduced you to the effects and persuasiveness of visual arguments. This chapter is designed to lead you through a step-by-step process that helps you develop a visual-spatial argument. There are many directions that you could take, so the concepts here account for just the basic decisions that you will have to make. A visual-spatial argument adds elements of visual design, space, and image to your writing process, and this chapter is designed to help you think through these elements. Before we move on, we need to make a distinction between two different types of texts, or two options for your project:

Visual Compositions: texts that individuals or groups design/compose, primarily of visual elements and visual materials, for the purposes of communicating.

Multimodal Compositions: texts that blend visual and textual elements and materials in order to communicate or persuade.

Visual compositions, though they may not use large amounts of text, are still rhetorical and still have rhetorical strategies. For example, a visual composition could persuade us based upon the way that it juxtaposes certain images, portrays a particular person or event, or through its artistic design. Take a second look, for example at the Kehinde Wiley painting "Officer of the Hussars" on page 191 of this book, and contrast it to the original by Gericault. We can see that the painting has a rhetorical purpose through its substitution of the visual image of a soldier for an African-American man in regular clothes.

Think for a minute about why a soldier, a representative of valor, courage, and patriotism might be substituted in this way, and you begin to see the rhetorical purpose. By doing this, Wiley places human beings who are negatively stereotyped in our society with images of our highest cultural and artistic ideals. This is just one example, however, and you may find visual compositions everywhere around you in the shape of sculptures, posters, photographs, and collages.

Multimodal texts, while using powerful visual images, normally blend these visual elements with text and design elements. Multimodal texts can also be video texts, blending text with video, audio, and images. You encounter these texts quite often as well. Sometimes they come in the form of PowerPoint presentations, online videos (such as tutorials or activist videos), posters, advertisements, and websites. These texts require that their authors create clear and persuasive links between the images, design elements (backgrounds, colors, fonts, etc.), and words. They use a multiple number of modes (visual, textual, etc.) to communicate.

This chapter focuses primarily on multimodal texts, and walks you through the major decisions that you will have to make in order to craft an effective visual-spatial argument. The third chapter of this book introduced you to the elements of visual design in order to help you analyze visual-spatial arguments. This chapter will draw upon these terms again in order to help you think through the important decisions that you have to make. As you put your visual spatial argument together, you will want to consider each of the aspects below.

The Elements of Visual Design

Visual Coherence: The extent to which visual elements of a composition are tied together with color, shape image, lines of sight, theme, etc.

Visual Salience: Importance or prominence of a visual element in relation to the composition as a whole

Visual Organization: Pattern of arrangement that relates the elements of the visual essay to one another in a way that makes them easier for readers/viewers to comprehend.

Visual Impact: The overall effect and appeal that a visual composition has on an audience.

Visual Choices: Thinking through Your Visual Spatial Argument

As you read through this process, think about the genre you have chosen for your public argument. If it is a visual-spatial genre, get out a sheet of paper and answer each set of questions below as you read the chapter. Doing so will give you a blueprint for the design of your own project.

Creating Visual Coherence: When we think of visual coherence we are thinking of the various design elements that organize the visual spatial argument in a way that creates a clear and persuasive effect. As we work through the visual design of our public argument, we might keep one coherence question in mind: *How can I connect the different visual and textual elements of my composition?* Answering this question means thinking through the relationship of color, lines, image shapes, and font to your topic and argument. We might call this the **visual rhetorical tone** of your project. A whimsical font for a deadly serious issue like child soldiers would seem inappropriate and set the wrong rhetorical tone. In this sense, your entire argument can be undermined by any of these elements of design. In order to make sure your argument is persuasive, carefully consider the following questions.

Creating Visual Coherence

Color Choices:

What color choices best reflect the visual-rhetorical tone of my project?

If my project has a background, what color is the most appropriate for the project, or the most visually engaging?

Thinking of my background color, what color should the font be in order to be readable and appropriate to the message of the project?

Is the background and font color complementary to the visual images (such as photographs) being utilized for the project? Do they clash?

If the text is divided using text boxes or lines, are the colors appropriate to my visual-rhetorical tone and do they complement the other colors in my project?

> ### Creating Visual Coherence (*continued*)
>
> #### *Font Choices:*
>
> How might I vary the fonts used in my project for emphasis, such as in the title and body of my project?
>
> Are the different fonts I use complementary, or is the combination distracting?
>
> What types of text or associations do the font(s) produce? What type of text might my reader think of when they see the font?
>
> Are the fonts appropriate to the visual-rhetorical tone of my project?
>
> If my project is going to be displayed, are the fonts large enough to be read at the distance from which it will be viewed?
>
> What color do fonts need to be in order to stand out against the background(s) of my project?
>
> #### *Shapes, Text Boxes, Headings, and Lines*
>
> If my project uses graphics—such as Smart Art in Microsoft Word—are these graphics appropriate to the visual-rhetorical tone of my project?
>
> If my project uses text boxes to break up the text of my argument, do the text boxes effectively draw my audience's attention to the most important points of my argument?
>
> Is the color that my text boxes are filled with complementary to my background and font, or do they clash?
>
> If my project uses headings for different sections of my argument, do these headings stand out and break up the text clearly? Should another font or font color be used to make them more distinct?
>
> If lines are used to break up my text, are they clearly visible from the distance from which the project will be viewed?
>
> If lines are used, do they create a clear visual flow for my project?

Creating Visual Salience: Visual salience can be thought of as the relationship between the images you choose and the text and design elements of your public argument. We choose images for a reason, and we often select specific images because they capture and illustrate the major point that we are trying to make. In a visual-spatial argument, we want our images and our text to work together seamlessly in order to persuade our readers. This means that we not only have to think about what images we select, but also how they emphasize a certain point or argument that we are trying to make.

We might simply think of photographs when we think of visual images, but there are several other images that we need to consider.

Types of Images to Consider for Your Visual Spatial Argument

Photographs: perhaps the most obvious choice, photographs can often be used to powerfully capture the central points of our public arguments.

Video: in a webtext or even a short film, video images can be utilized to support and illustrate our arguments.

Graphs and Charts: graphs and charts can visually capture statistical information in a way that helps readers understand a complex issue in a short time. They can also underline or emphasize our arguments.

Visual Art and Cartoons: can be utilized to emphasize certain aspects of our arguments. Cartoons can often place the issue we are writing about in a satirical frame that can engage readers.

Screen Captures: screen shots or screen captures can also be effective for our public arguments, especially if we are engaging an issue with a significant presence on the web.

As you assemble the images for your visual-spatial argument, it is important to think through the roles that they will play in your project. We need to ask ourselves, *Are the visual images effective for my argument? How can I place the visual elements in a way that will make them more effective?* This is the important general question to keep coming back to, but there are more specific questions to consider also.

Creating Visual Salience

Image Selection

Is the theme or association that the image produces relevant to the theme of my argument?

Is the feeling or tone that the image invokes appropriate to the visual-rhetorical tone of my argument?

Does the image inform or emphasize my argument in an important way, or does it seem superficial or unrelated to my argument?

If the image is a graph or chart, does it clearly support a major point of my argument, or is it superfluous?

Image Framing or Anchoring

Is the image in close proximity to the argument that it is emphasizing or illustrating?

If the text is multimodal, is the image anchored or placed within the verbal text effectively? Is the verbal text in close proximity to the image that illustrates it?

If the visual image is used as part of a video, does the information or images that come before and after it clearly connect to the image?

Creating Visual Organization: One key aspect to consider before we learn how to use these elements is the way that our eyes scan a page of text. This sounds like a basic point, perhaps too basic, but keeping this in mind will help you think through the visual design and flow of your project. The following diagram illustrates how our eyes normally move left to right and top to bottom when we scan a text.

How Our Eyes Scan a Text

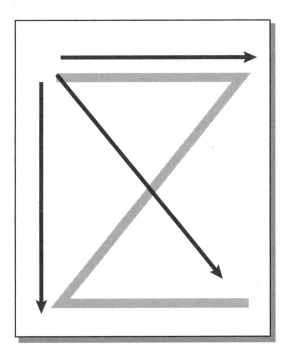

Unlike a work of art, such as a portrait, when we deal with multi-modal texts our eyes move as they do when we read a normal page of text. What does this mean for our projects? If you are working on a project like a poster, a project that uses PowerPoint slides, or even a website, then it means that you will want to think through where you place the most important points of information on the page.

For example, if I were working on a poster that gave an overview of the crisis of child soldiers and asked viewers or readers to contact their congressmen to raise awareness of the issue, my visual organization might look like this:

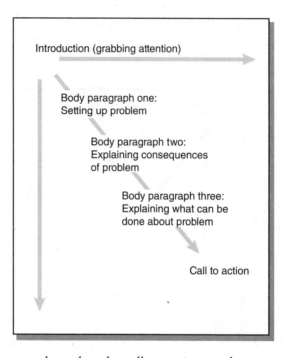

Introduction (grabbing attention)

Body paragraph one:
Setting up problem

Body paragraph two:
Explaining consequences
of problem

Body paragraph three:
Explaining what can be
done about problem

Call to action

We can see here that the call to action is what we are led to logically as a last step, a step that leaves readers with a concrete action that they can take on the issue. This is a typical organizational outline for a poster that is designed to move us to act on an issue. We move from introduction to call to action, but we can also say that we move from problem to, if not a solution, an action we can take to help solve the problem. Notice also that many types of visual spatial arguments, such as webpages, may not use the diagonal line, but may simply move from top to bottom. We can read in many different ways, so this diagram is not the only way to organize your project. However, it does point us to a concern that needs to be at the forefront of our mind:

> *We need to be constantly thinking about how our audience will move from one idea to the next in our project and the persuasive effect that this will have on our audience.*

We might think of this as the visual **flow** or organization of our project. This flow or organization is what we use to guide our audiences through our information and to the action that we would like them to take. In this sense, it requires us to think through the way we present each part of our argument in order to create the most persuasive effect.

Creating Visual Organization

Scan your public argument or your outline. Do your eyes move easily from section to section in the order that you intended?

If you are writing a multimodal argument, do the visual images help you move from point to point in the argument clearly?

If you are using design elements such as lines and section headings, do they create clear transitions from each major point in your argument?

If you are designing an audiovisual text, such as a short film, are the scenes ordered clearly?

If your project contains large blocks of text, could they be broken up more effectively using text boxes, lines, headings, or images?

Do too many visual images make your text busy or disorganized? If so, which images might you omit?

Creating Visual Impact: Now that you have thought through the major elements of visual coherence, salience, and organization, you have one more important step: considering the overall impact of your visual-spatial argument. This requires you to think through the relationship between the purpose of your argument and the different design elements we have discussed above.

Perhaps the most important question to consider is the way that your audience will take up the information and arguments you present. Are you asking them to take a specific action, change their attitude or beliefs, try something new, etc.? Think about the next step you would like your audience to take after viewing your project, then use the following questions to look at the overall visual impact of your project. Do you think that it produces the impact that you intended?

Before You Use Images in Your Project—Understanding Copyright Law

Creating a visual argument means that you will have to think deeply about the images you use. You have probably already spent time thinking about the rhetorical effect of the images in your project, but developing a visual argument also requires that you understand when you can use visual images (photographs, video, or other online materials) from a source and when they are off limits. Understanding the basics of *fair use* and *copyright* is particularly important for your public argument, as you may post this argument online through a variety of social media. Because your project bears your name, you have the responsibility to learn the basics of fair use and copyright and to ensure that the images and other content in your project are available for you to use and cited properly.

Given the complexity of the laws, you might find yourself asking whether or not developing a multimedia project is worth it. You might, for example, want to create a mashup of video and pictures that now seems impossible because of the laws. Do not let fear of copyright law keep you from creating your project. With the steps that follow, you can confidently develop your project without fear of breaking copyright. Luckily, you do not need a law degree to understand fair use. This section will explain what copyright and fair use mean from your perspective and will give you a set of steps you can follow to make sure that you are using images and other materials legally. As you work on your project, you should ask your instructors about any images or materials that you have questions about, as they will be able to help you think through this issue even further.

What Does Fair Use Mean for You?

Fair use is basically a term that defines how you can legally use information without violating copyright law. It is particularly important given the way in which writing is changing. For many of your projects in college, you will likely use a mix of traditional text, images, and even elements of digital and visual design. Knowing how to use information fairly and legally has simply become part of writing.

In developing a visual argument, you are producing your project in an educational context, and the fair use law allows students to use these materials in the context of a classroom, if they attribute them to the author or cite them. The moment that you put your work in a public context or share it online, however, it is no longer in a classroom or educational context.

As you develop your project, you will likely find yourself in one of the two scenarios below. The important thing to remember is whether you have to ask for permission to use images or materials or not, it is always vital that you cite the materials correctly. If neither of the scenarios listed below applies to your project, please discuss your options with your instructor.

Two of the Most Common Fair Use Situations for Students

1. If you are not going to display the project online and are **only** going to present it in class, then fair use covers the use of images in your project. However, you must cite them according to the style guide used for your class. In most English classes, the style guide will be Modern Language Association (MLA).

2. If you are going to display the project online or in another public context, then you will need to either receive permission to use the image or video, or choose another image from a source that has a Creative Commons license. Creative Commons images are often free for you to use without permission. Resources on Creative Commons images and video are presented on the following page.

We might ask, "If it's clear that my project is for a class, why should it matter if I post it on YouTube, or on a blog?" To answer this question, we need to think critically about the word "publishing." The word "publishing" does not just mean publishing in a magazine or publishing a book. If you place content on the web for everyone to see, you have "published" it, and you must follow the fair use guidelines. This is an important point because we do not often think of sharing information with others online as "publishing." However, anything that you put on the web is effectively published, even materials that you post on social network sites and other restricted social media.

How Can I Use Materials on the Internet without Violating Copyright or Fair Use?

If you use a search engine to find images on the internet, one of the first problems that you encounter is not everyone online follows copyright guidelines. People routinely copy and paste images into blogs, websites, documents, and other media without citing them or obtaining permission. However, *this does not mean that you can assume that since many are violating copyright it is alright for you to do so.* Content that you place online is your responsibility, so learning how to use materials on the web protects you from violating copyright.

As you find images, video, and other materials on the web, use the following guidelines to assist you:

Finding the Essential Information for Web Media

1. Find the original image information. Look at the website the image is located on and see if there is any citation information. Is the author's name mentioned, or the name of the publisher?
2. If you find the author's name or name of the publisher, do a quick internet search for their official website.
3. Once you find the official site, look for information on obtaining permission to use the image. This is sometimes called licensing. Read this information and determine if the image can be used with or without permission.
4. If you cannot find the author or permission information, you may want to consider looking for another image. In most cases, it is best to play it safe.

Once you have the information listed above, you are ready to start thinking about citing the image or requesting permission to use it. For many students, obtaining permission is a frustrating process, as it can take weeks. If you feel that you absolutely have to use an image or other media, then sending an email asking for permission may be useful, especially if there are several weeks before your project is due. Here is an example email which you may use for your own permissions:

10 January, 2011
Tucson Courier Times

Dear Tucson Courier Times:

I am writing you to request permission to use the image "Global Temperature," which was published with the article "Global Warming Debate Heating Up" on October 6, 2008. I would like to use this image as part of a short documentary film for my English 102 course at the University of Arizona. The image will be placed beside text that presents statistical information about rising ocean temperatures. I will be posting this documentary on You Tube as part of the assignment requirements. As my project is due in four weeks, I ask that you please contact me and let me know about permission as soon as possible.

Sincerely,
Jane Student.

If the permission process seems unlikely, then the next step is to begin looking for images from Creative Commons sites. The key thing to remember is time. Permissions may take longer than you have to complete your project. If your project is due in four weeks, and you do not receive a response to your email within a week, you may want to find other images.

Where Can I Find Images that I Do Not Have to Seek Permission to Use?

While all images need to be cited, there are places that you can go to find images that you can use without having to write for permission. Many creators of online content have begun to use *Creative Commons*

405

to license their work. Many Creative Commons licenses give all users the ability to use and reproduce the work without written permission. Many artists, musicians, and others are using Creative Commons, so finding images, music, and other media that you do not have to ask permission for is much easier than you think. However, not all Creative Commons licenses are the same, and some images may be used but not altered. Look for the symbols below to guide your choices.

Recognizing Creative Commons Images

Creative Commons images are most often Identified by the CC symbol. Below, you will see that the CC symbol is accompanied with other symbols. These tell you the type of Creative Commons license the owner of the image has and what you can do with the image. Some authors will allow you to use, share, or remix the work without permission, some will allow you only to reuse the work, and some have other important conditions, such as using the image non-commercially.

	CC Symbol	Description
1		**[BY] Attribution** Permits all uses of the original work, as long as it is attributed to the original author *Note: Attribution is in all six licenses.*
2		**[BY-SA] Attribution—Share Alike** As above, but any derivative work must also use a similar license, hence "Share Alike."
3		**[BY-ND] Attribution—No Derivatives** Licensed works are free to use/share with attribution, but does not permit derivative works from the original.
4		**[BY-NC] Attribution—Non-Commercial** Licensed works are free to use/share/remix with attribution, but does not permit commercial use of the original work.
5		**[BY-NC-SA] Attribution—Non-Commercial— Share Alike** Does not permit commercial use of the original work, and any derivatives from it must use a similar license.
6		**[BY-NC-ND] Attribution—Non-Commercial— No Derivatives** Does not permit any commercial use or derivatives of the original work. *Note: This is the most restrictive of CC licenses and is often regarded as a "free advertising" license.*

Figure 1. *Creative Commons Licenses. Source of CC License Symbol/ Images: http://creativecommons.org/licenses/.*

Some of the terms in the Creative Commons diagram are probably new to you, unless you have done some graphic or web design work. For your project, two of the most important terms are **derivative work** and **sharing**.

Sharing: This means using an image in your project without modifying it in any way. This is the typical way that you might use an image. You might, for example, paste an image into a poster or PowerPoint presentation. You must cite the image, but you are free to use it without permission if it has the appropriate Creative Commons BY emblem on the Creative Commons license.

Derivative Work: Derivative works are works that take an original work and modify it in some way. If you change an image, put a caption inside it, change its color or format, or do anything else to alter the original image, you will need to either get permission to do so or find an image with a Creative Commons license that allows you to do so. The most common is a license with the BY emblem.

While Creative Commons images can be found on various websites, such as Flickr, Google Images, and Wikipedia, perhaps the best starting point is the search engine found on the Creative Commons website: http://search.creativecommons.org/.

From this one website, you are able to search for images you can use and even adapt for your projects. This search engine pulls from popular sites such as Google Images, Flickr, YouTube, and others.

What Is Attribution?

Attribution, for our purposes, means "citing" your sources with the correct information.

Whether you are publishing your project online or simply presenting it in a class, you must cite the images and materials that you use correctly and make certain that you attribute them to the correct authors. This means that you will need to find the author and publishing information for the images that you are using. Bear in mind that this can take some time, so budget enough time to find this information.

Once you locate this information, the key is to make sure that each of your images is clearly cited. Where you place your citations will vary based upon the technology that you are using. For example, if you are creating a PowerPoint slideshow, the citations can be placed in small type below each image. However, some software does not allow for this, and you will want to spend time thinking about how you might make sure that your images are attributed to their authors. The tips below are for both cases.

You must cite every image that you utilize in your project. This is tricky, as you have probably never cited images before. Whether you find the images on the web, or in a print text, you must cite properly. To cite these images, you will want to follow two steps:

In-Text Citation

1. Label each image with the title "Figure," and number each image consecutively—"Figure 1," "Figure 2." Use a smaller font, so that you do not take up too much space in your project.

2. Give each image a short caption after the label "Figure 1." Here is a quick example of an image that might be used for a visual-spatial argument on nutrition.

Figure 1. A Healthy Nicoise Salad by John Doe.

This is the basic MLA format for a citation in the text. You can use this format for video that is embedded in a webpage or PowerPoint slide as well. Without these citations, readers may be left wondering where the image was found or, worse, mistake the image as your own, which is plagiarism.

Bibliographic Citation

Once you cite the image in the text, you will want to create a bibliographic entry for it on a Works Cited page. Below is an MLA entry for an image found on a website.

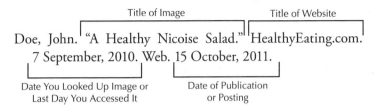

Note that you will want to give the title of the websites that the image is found on, even if you found them through a service such as Google Images. Your Works Cited page might be located on your last PowerPoint slide, the last frame of a video, or at the bottom of your poster. Depending upon the genre, you might also have a separate Works Cited page that accompanies your public argument.

Now that you know how to find images you can use and cite them in your work, you should feel more comfortable looking for them and utilizing them in your visual-spatial argument. We hope that you will find the process of creating a visual-spatial argument not only intellectually engaging, but also enjoyable.

Works Cited

Creative Commons. "About the Licenses." *Creative Commons.org.* 21 September, 2011. Web.

The author wishes to thank Professor Shelley Rodrigo for giving suggestions and pointing to sources for the development of this section. Any errors or omissions are solely the fault of the author.

Chapter 17

Writing Your Public Argument

By Christopher Minnix

The chapters in this section of the book have hopefully given you an important set of processes and tools that you can use to find an audience and develop your public voice. As you write your public argument, these processes and tools will help you adapt your ideas and voice to the genres you have chosen. Each genre will use different strategies, and it is up to you to analyze and think through the choices that you will have to make to communicate successfully. This chapter illustrates some general aspects of the public writing process. Your audience research, genre analysis, and critical reflection will bring up questions and ideas that are more specific.

Bringing the Ideas in This Section Together

In this section, you have learned to analyze the audiences and genres of public writing, to think critically through the logic of your public arguments, and to create compelling public arguments. As you have seen, crafting a successful public argument takes quite a bit of reflection and writing. The tools of *audience analysis*, *genre analysis*, and *logical argumentation* you have learned are not only tools for creating a strong public argument, but can also be thought of as tools for **revising** your public argument. While *composing*, you analyze your audience by analyzing sample genres, thinking through the various positions that respond to your argument, and thinking critically about the type of voice, information, and structure that might work for your audience. While *revising*, you analyze and evaluate how persuasively you have addressed your audience by looking at the strength of your argument, how well you used the genre you chose, and how appropriate and engaging your voice is. In this sense, we ask the same questions when we are writing a public argument as when we are revising it.

The activities below will lead you through the process of using your newly acquired skills to compose and revise your Public Argument.

Beginning: Develop a Rhetorical Action Plan

At this point, you have conducted research into your audience, genre, and issue. Now, we need to think through the purpose and action that our writing is meant to inspire. Use the questions below to help you develop a rhetorical action plan for your writing. Doing so will help you think through your persuasive strategies and the possible effects of your writing.

An action plan like the one below is important in public writing because it helps you think through the action that you would like your audience to take and the most effective strategies for persuading them to take this action.

Developing a Rhetorical Action Plan

1. Audience: Who are you going to try to persuade with your public argument? Describe the following aspects of your audience in a few sentences:
   - Knowledge: What does the audience know about the topic, text, or idea? How do they know the topic (where do they get their knowledge from)? Do they have certain predispositions or opinions about the topic that you will need to address?
   - Values: What do you know about how the values, ideals, principles, or norms (standards of conduct) that members of the audience might hold?
   - Standards of Argument: What type of research or evidence do you think will be persuasive for your audience? How might you have to translate this research for them?
   - Visual Elements: What visual images or elements might your audience respond to? Why?
   - Purpose: Why is your audience reading or listening to your argument? Are you trying to expand their understanding of an idea, encourage them to take action on an issue, challenge a long-held tradition or viewpoint, etc.? How likely is your argument to motivate your audience?

Defining Your Public Argument: Now that you have worked through your rhetorical action plan, it is time to consider the type of public argument you might develop.

Introduction

We have all heard that first impressions matter, but there are few places where they matter more than in public writing. This is because we find ourselves vying for the attention of people who are often saturated with different forms of media and information. Sometimes, we find ourselves in the position of illustrating a relatively unknown issue to readers, and we must illustrate the importance of this issue to our readers' lives. Other times, we find ourselves dealing with a well-discussed issue, and we are either bringing our own perspective to bear on the issue, or introducing the issue to a community that we believe needs to take part in the discussion. In each case, our object is to connect our readers to our ideas about the issue and to frame the need for them to act on the issue.

2. Genre: What form of writing will you use? After identifying your genre, list your answers for the following questions:
   - What is the function of the genre? What is it designed to do for your readers? Or, why did you choose it?
   - What is the setting of your genre? Where could you see it being used?
   - How might you use the rhetorical appeals we have studied—ethos (character), pathos (values/emotion), and logos (logical argumentation) in this genre?
   - What type of visual elements, if any, will you use in this genre?
   - What type of style (formal, informal, conversational, academic, etc.) will you use in this genre?
3. Responses/Actions: Explain the possible actions you would like your audience to take after they read or view your argument.
   - On a blank sheet of paper, make two columns: **Positive Support** and **Negative Rebuttals**. Then list out the potential positive and negative reactions to your argument.
   - Looking at this list, circle the negative rebuttals that you feel will be most important for you to address and briefly list your response to them.
   - Finally, trace out the potential chains of action that your writing might create. If for example, you wanted to "raise awareness" about an issue, draw a line from this point and list the potential actions that raising awareness might create.

Choosing a Type of Public Argument

In addition to understanding your public genre, you will also want to think through the type of public argument that you might develop. Here are five basic options. Note that there are many more types of arguments, so please feel free to modify these, or pursue other types for your project. You may also note how these options resemble the types of controversy that were introduced in the Controversy Analysis section.

Five Basic Types of Public Argument

Position Argument: You probably know this type of argument as a pro/con argument. In this argument, you would defend a specific policy, position, or idea in a controversial debate. Instead of just repeating what one side in the debate has already said, you would develop your own defenses of this position. A common example might be the debate over whether or not capital punishment deters violent crime. A position argument would defend either side of this issue with arguments that would work for a specific audience.

Casual Argument: This argument introduces your audience to the causes of a specific problem or phenomenon in our society. Causal arguments argue for one cause or one set of causes for a particular problem. By pointing to the cause, you are able to also help your audience understand the potential solutions to the controversy as well. Often, these arguments require you to rebut or contradict the arguments in favor of other causes. For example, in an argument on the stem cell debate, you might argue that lack of public understanding of the science of harvesting cell lines has led to the current controversy over the use of stem cells in research.

Evaluative Argument: This argument evaluates the successfulness of a specific policy, idea, solution to a problem, etc. Evaluative public arguments will often evaluate specific public policies and proposed solutions that have been developed or are being proposed. Your thesis would argue for the policy or solution's effectiveness, and you would give good reasons to support this thesis or solution. An example would be an analysis of the current health care bill's effectiveness in addressing a specific health care problem in this country.

Proposal Argument: This argument analyzes a particular problem and then develops a proposal for addressing the problem in its thesis. The bulk of the argument explains and defends this proposal. Proposal arguments map out their solutions step-by-step for their readers, introducing them to the proposal, explaining the logic of the proposal, discussing the steps for implementing the proposal, and pointing to the benefits of following the proposal. One example would be a student paper that developed a proposal for developing a program that provided safe rides back to the dorms from various locations on and off campus.

Refutation Argument: Though all of the arguments above will have an element of refutation, a refutation argument is devoted almost entirely to refuting an idea, opinion, or argument of another person or group. For a public argument, a refutation argument would point to the possible harmful public effects of the argument it is refuting and give good reasons to convince the audience not to follow this argument. An example would be an argument against the idea that tuition increases improve educational quality.

Each genre that you encounter will have different strategies for introductions, but you will find that there is quite a bit of room for you to make your introduction your own. Look at the introductions of your sample genres closely. In visual-spatial genres, you will find that the introduction may simply use an image that is paired with only a few lines of text to introduce the issue the writer is arguing about. Other genres, such as editorial essays, might utilize some of the strategies for introductions that are well known to us. They might begin by posing a question, using a quotation to spark discussion, or even by telling a story that captures the theme of their piece.

Each genre uses different strategies, so you will want to pay close attention to the strategies that your samples use. Here are a few general tips that can transfer across genres.

Introducing Your Public Argument

1. *Connect the Issue to Your Audience's World View*: You are out to show your audience that the issue has a bearing on their lives and that they should act upon it. As you think about your audience, look for key aspects of their values, ideals, politics, and current context that you might connect to your argument or issue.

2. *Think about Your Situation or Kairos*: You are moving the audience to act or think about your issue in a specific context. In this case, you may want to introduce the issue by drawing on current events or discussions concerning the issue. You might point to recent legislation on the issue, mentions of the issue in the news, or even recent protests or writing about the issue.

3. *Frame the Consequences*: One way to frame your introduction is to point to the consequences of the issue you are discussing. This enables your readers to understand why they might want to take the time to address your issue. Looking at long- and short-term consequences can help you frame not only your position on the issue but also your disagreements with other positions.

4. *Define or Narrow the Problem*: Nothing is more daunting for an audience than to feel that they cannot act upon a problem because it is too large. As you develop your introduction, think about developing a realistic plan of action for your audience. Focus on an aspect of the larger problem that you feel that your audience can actually address.

In addition to these basic tips, take the time to look at the different options that you have for introducing your ideas in the genre that you have chosen. Look for a wide variety of different samples to help you make your decision. Here are a few options that you might see.

Some Common Introduction Strategies for Public Arguments

Note: Some strategies are more appropriate for some genres than others!

Narrative: Develop or utilize a story that frames your discussion. The narrative might be real or imagined.

Scenario: Set up a scenario (real or imagined) that helps readers understand the importance of your point. You might use an example or develop an analogy.

Question: Pose a question that gets to the heart of your argument or position.

Context: Draw on a current event or discussion that sets up the context of your discussion.

Image: If you are developing a visual-spatial argument, you might combine any of the strategies above with an image that captures the importance of your argument.

History: You might draw on an important aspect of the history of your issue to set up the importance of your current discussion.

Remember, these are just a few quick examples. As you read and analyze samples of the genre you are using, you will find other options for introducing and framing the issue.

Developing an Argumentative Thesis

Now that you have thought through your introduction, you need to develop a strong thesis for your public argument. The thesis for this argument differs from the thesis in your rhetorical and controversy analysis. There, you focused on persuading your readers of your interpretation of a rhetorical text or controversy. Now, you need to develop a thesis that develops your own position in the controversy and supports this position with strong reasons. You are also drawing on the evidence that you have found from your research to support your claims and defend your argument. As the table below shows, you have three major elements of your thesis to contend with: claim, reason, and evidence.

Major Elements of an Argumentative Thesis

Claim: the major statement of your argument that will need to be explained, supported, and defended by good reasons.

Reasons: the supporting points or logic that persuade readers to back up or accept your claim.

Evidence: research and logical arguments that you can point to that supports your overall claim. Often evidence is given for the reasons that support the claim.

Example:

While our intuitions might lead us to believe differently, the deterrence effect theory of capital punishment is an unsubstantiated myth. There is no simple, causal link between states opting to use capital punishment and decreases in rates of violent crime. In fact, multiple studies over the past decade have shown that rates of violent crime have remained stable or increased in states that regularly employ capital punishment. In this sense, the causal link between capital punishment and deterrence is, while intuitive, simply a false perception with grave consequences.

In the example above, the author has set up their thesis as a rebuttal argument. We know this because they set up the argument that they are critiquing within the thesis. In this example, the claim is an argument against the position that capital punishment deters people from committing violent crimes. The reason suggests that there is no causal link between capital punishment and lower rates of violent crime. This reason is supported by the mention of many studies that point to the fact that crime has increased or remained stable in states that enforce capital punishment. In this case, each of the three elements work together to support the main point of the argument.

It is important to note, however, that this type of thesis is often the result of several revisions. As you draft your public argument, it is often good to develop a **tentative thesis** first and then continue to write out your draft. Once you are revising your essay, you can then strengthen the claim, reason, and evidence of your thesis.

Developing Strong Supporting Paragraphs

Way back when the five-paragraph essay was your go-to genre, you probably developed your thesis and listed three major points to support it. This genre, which often works well for essay tests and very short essays, can sometimes lead us to think that every piece of writing we undertake should list three major points. For your public argument, you will find that the different genres that you choose have different ways of arranging their major supporting points or arguments. Because of this, it is important to use your skills of genre analysis to figure out two important aspects of organization:

1. *The Order of Arguments*: Look closely at your sample genres for the order of their arguments. Some will begin with the thesis and then support and develop the thesis throughout the body of the genre. Many newspaper editorials that are written as rebuttal arguments or position arguments do this. Other genres will introduce a problem in the beginning and not work out the solution or thesis until later in the essay. Proposal arguments in magazines or newspapers sometimes do this, but we often see this in visual spatial texts. For example, a human rights group might lead you through video images and arguments for intervening in a genocide, and then develop their thesis or call to action at the end of the text.

2. *The Types of Arguments*: Look closely at the details about the audience that you have developed as part of your rhetorical action plan. Different audiences often require different types of information as proof of your argument. An audience made up of those who follow scientific news closely would require you to clearly utilize scientific studies to support a discussion of stem cell research. A community group addressing this issue may require scientific background, but may be persuaded less by lengthy treatment of specific studies. As you think through the types of

arguments that you will use, also don't neglect ethos, or character based arguments, and pathos, or emotional- and value-based arguments. These arguments complement your research and logical argumentation.

While every genre will organize and arrange its supporting paragraphs differently, the general principles below transfer well across many different types of writing or genres.

Developing Strong Supporting Paragraphs

1. *List Down the Major Supporting Arguments*: Before writing, list out as many important arguments that support your position as you can think of on one side of a blank sheet of paper.

2. *List Down the Major Criticisms*: Now list the major criticisms of your position on the other side of the same piece of paper.

3. *Select Your Key Support and Rebuttal Points*: Look at your lists and select the supporting points that are most important and relevant to your argument. Then, select the rebuttal points that are most necessary for you to address.

4. *Write Out a Tentative Topic Sentence for Each Support and Rebuttal Point*: Write out a sentence that states the main supporting argument or response to criticism on a new sheet of paper. Leave room for notes under each sentence.

5. *Gather Evidence*: Now that you have your key arguments and rebuttal points, it is time to go back to your research and find supporting evidence for each paragraph. Write down any key quotations, examples, or page numbers from your research beside each topic sentence or point you have developed.

6. *Develop a Map of Your Argument*: Outlines will change as you write, but in order to conceptualize your argument, it is helpful to think about how each point that you make will lead into the other. Use the example on the following page to make a map of your argument, taking care to write in the transitions between each of your major points.

Developing a Map of Your Public Argument

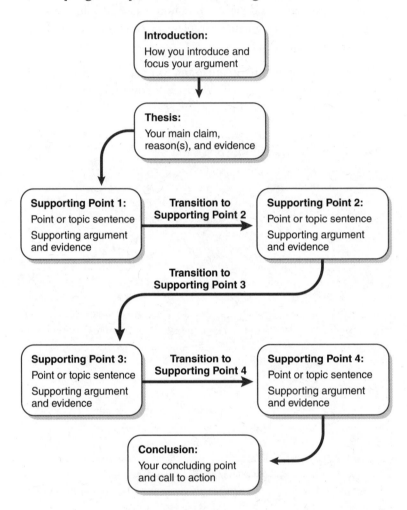

A map like this can be used as an outline before writing, or as an outline that can help you think through the revision of your draft. If you use this map as an outline, revisit it after you write your first full draft of your paper. You will find that some paragraphs and ideas have changed. As you revise your map, work through the transitions first, linking the major ideas in your paragraphs together. Focus on refining and revising these transitions until you have a clear trajectory from paragraph to paragraph.

Developing a Strong Conclusion

Conclusions can be horribly boring and repetitive if we approach them as just an opportunity to restate our thesis and main points. In a public argument, you are not out to recap what you have said, but use the last bit of space in your project to convince your readers to take the action you would like them to take. As you develop your conclusion, you might think of it as a chance to leave readers thinking about the implications or consequences of what you have argued. Here are a few ways that you might do this.

Concluding Strategies

1. *Call to Action*: If you do not do so earlier in your public argument, explain how your reader can act to address your issue.
2. *Negative Consequences*: Outline and explain the negative consequences of inaction on the issue. If readers do not take action on your issue, what might the harmful effects on society be?
3. *Positive Consequences*: You might also include or outline the positive benefits of taking action and how your readers' action might produce a positive effect on their society.
4. *Common Ground*: If your argument is a rebuttal of a position, or if your issue is particularly controversial, you might consider explaining the common ground for action, or the actions that can be agreed upon.
5. *Future of the Debate*: You might also point to the future of the debate over the issue. Even if you persuade readers to act, how will the debate continue? What issues remain to be explored? What problems remain to be solved?

These are just a few basic examples, so please do not feel that you have to follow them to the letter in your own paper. Look closely at the sample genres you collected. How do they normally conclude? Looking at your samples will provide you with even more options.

The sample public argument on the next page revisits the sample topic that was introduced in the first two chapters of this section: the use of child soldiers in armed combat. It is written for the campus newspaper of a large state university and is designed to move students to act by writing their state and federal representatives about this issue. As you read it, use your skills of analysis and annotation to circle and highlight its key features or genre conventions. Notice how it introduces its focus, sets up its problem, develops its thesis, organizes its supporting arguments, and concludes. Also, think through how its rhetorical strategies are used to persuade its audience. Notice its tone, the author's ethos, the emotional and logical arguments used and the overall effect they create. Finally, think about how you might approach the editorial differently, or revise it.

A Sample Public Argument

Children at War: What You Can Do about Child Soldiers and Why You Should Do It

Think back to the daily routines of your childhood. For me, this involved a hot breakfast prepared by my father, which I ate while furiously finishing my homework, a short bus ride to school, six mind-numbing hours of class, a bus ride home, and then some pickup basketball with my friends until dinner. There were variations, but most days went just like this. I had my problems and concerns—fitting in, making decent grades, getting a girlfriend at some point in my life. These were important to me, and I thought about them constantly. What I didn't ever have to think about, however, was trading in my backpack or my basketball for a gun. For many of us, this idea seems so far-fetched, so divorced from our daily realities, that we can barely envision it. For thousands of children in war-torn sections of Africa, however, trading their books and backpacks for an AK-47 is not merely a possibility but a reality.

The United Nations Children's Fund (UNICEF) reports that "some 300,000 children—boys and girls under the age of 18—are today involved in more than 30 conflicts worldwide. Children are used as combatants, messengers, porters and cooks and for forced sexual services. Some are abducted or forcibly recruited, others are driven to join by poverty, abuse and discrimination, or to seek revenge for violence enacted against them or their families" ("Fact Sheet: Child Soldiers"). For these children, all other opportunities are placed on hold indefinitely. Their educational and social advancement must wait as they go to war. Unlike our armed forces, where soldiers serve for fixed time periods or terms, there is no end other than death to their forced service. Stripped from their families, their classrooms, and their friends, child soldiers are also stripped of their futures.

In my classes, I am often told that I live in an information age, one where information from anywhere in the world can be instantly transmitted. We are becoming more and more interconnected, despite our borders. I hear this a lot. If this is true, then we have to ask ourselves how it is possible that 300,000 children are being used as soldiers and why this issue is not more prevalent in the media. A child abducted into the Mayi Mayi army in Congo described his life to *Amnesty International* as follows: "I had nowhere to go and no food to eat. In the mayi-mayi I thought I would be protected, but it was hard. I would see others die in front of me. I was hungry very often, and I was scared. Sometimes they would whip me, sometimes very hard. They used to say that it would make me a better fighter. One day, they whipped my [11-year-old] friend to death because he had not killed the enemy. Also, what I did not like is to hear the girls, our friends, crying because the soldiers would rape them" ("Stories"). Despite our interconnectedness, there is often little justice for these children. The 2008 *Child Soldiers Global Report* from The Coalition to Stop Child Soldiers, reminds us of this lack of justice, noting "With the exception of two cases in the DRC, no one is known to have been prosecuted by national-level courts for recruiting and using children" (11). Clearly, there is a long way to go towards developing international laws that are enforced to protect these children. Without this legal power, it may be the case that there is little or no incentive for those who force children into armed combat to stop. These are, after all, not the kind of governments, political groups, or people who would stop just because the rest of the world finds their behavior shameful or offensive.

This is not, however, to say that there has not been significant progress made on the issue. The few prosecutions at the International Criminal Court were historic and important. These prosecutions sent the message that those who deal in child soldiers can be held accountable in a world court. In our own country, President George W. Bush signed the *Child Soldiers Accountability Act* into law in 2008. This law allows the U.S. to prosecute people in the U.S. who have recruited child soldiers. In addition, the *Child Soldiers Prevention Act* was passed in 2009 as part of the William Wilberforce Trafficking Victims Protection Reauthorization Act (HR 7311). This act allows the U.S. government to restrict its military aid to any government that is shown to be using child soldiers. Even if they are explained in "legalese" and difficult to understand, these are significant achievements. Basically, this shows that our own government is committed to addressing this issue and to pressuring other governments to stop using children in combat.

But is this all that can be done? I do not doubt the potential of these acts. What I do doubt, however, is that they will be enforced without the vigilance of citizens consistently addressing this issue with their governments. We have the acts, and they are important, but we also still have over 300,000 highly traumatized children carrying guns in these war-torn areas. We have to face the possibility that this issue, like many others, could easily become just another "issue of the moment," or this year's human rights issue. If this happens, this problem, one that can be solved, will eventually be ignored.

So, what can we do? There are many opportunities to act, from writing a letter to our state representatives, donating to child soldier protection groups, and raising awareness about the issue through our local newspapers. These are tried and true methods, but you can also take action on this campus. In three weeks, on February 12, students on this campus will take part in the second annual *Red Hand Day* campaign. To participate, you simply need to stop by the Student Union and take ten minutes to create a message to our representatives asking them to continue to take up the issue of child soldiers in the House and Senate. By adding your handprint and message, you help send a message to our legislators that this issue will not be ignored, will not become simply another issue of the moment.

Like many of you, I am one of the lucky people. I was born in a place and time where I never had to contemplate the lives that these child soldiers lead. I even have the luxury of ignoring these children, as their life and death do not directly affect my own. You too may be tempted to ignore them. After all, our lives are filled with people that we "should be helping." Before you turn to the next article, however, consider the horror that you would feel if you were in their situation and knew that people in the most powerful country in the world, a country with more than enough influence and power to help them, simply didn't care. In his "Letter from a Birmingham Jail," Martin Luther King Jr. stated "that an injustice anywhere is a threat to justice everywhere." If we think about this statement, it means more than simply fighting injustice anywhere we find it. Instead, it makes us aware of the fact that turning a blind eye to injustice in any part of the world makes us part of that injustice. The ultimate horror is not that the child soldiers might perceive that we don't care, but that those who kidnap and recruit them might recognize that the rest of the world does not care. If this happens, our silence becomes an endorsement of their actions. If you, like me, feel that you cannot live with this, then come join us on February 12 and make your voice heard.

Conclusion

As you write your public argument, you will find many more options and strategies than could be covered in this chapter. Different genres utilize different strategies of argument, organization, and style, and all genres allow us to vary those strategies to fit our own voice and needs. As you move through the various drafts of your public argument, you will begin to develop your own voice on the issue as well. This is something that no list of strategies can give you. Instead, it comes from reflective writing, from thinking about how, out of all of the writing on your subject, you can make your own perspective on the issue stand out for your audience. This is a challenging aspect of public writing, but also an amazingly meaningful and satisfying aspect of public writing.

Readings in Public Argument

Introduction

As we have learned in this section, public writers often use their rhetoric in order to address matters of public concern. The readings in this section represent public arguments on three important issues: culture jamming, food, and bioethics and human dignity.

Culture jamming is a public argument against the ways that advertising and media shape the realities of our worlds. While many people make arguments against the negative influence of popular media, culture jammers create images and texts that use satire in order to "spoof" media images. By spoofing these images, culture jammers attempt to illustrate the problems with the ideologies and worldviews that popular media presents to us. Culture jammers view the media and advertisements of corporations—magazines, corporations, television stations, etc.—as forms of social propaganda that manipulate viewers into living a life based upon a media fantasy rather than reality.

The public arguments concerning food question the problems with genetic modification, the marketing of high-calorie foods to the poor, and the various proposals for improving our food supply. The authors of these arguments challenge us to think through the long-term consequences of our food industry and our personal responsibility to challenge this industry.

Finally, the two arguments concerning human dignity and bioethics offer direct rebuttals to each other's positions. These arguments question the ethical obligation of scientific research in human genetics to uphold the traditional concept of human dignity.

As you read these public arguments, look for the ways they organize, support, and defend their arguments. Also, note how their arguments are addressed to their audiences and the purpose(s) that they want to achieve.

Public Arguments on Consumer Culture

Kalle Lasn—Free to Be You and Meme

Utne Reader. *July/August 1990. Reprinted with permission from Adbusters Media Foundation.*

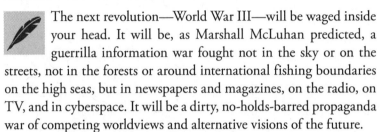 The next revolution—World War III—will be waged inside your head. It will be, as Marshall McLuhan predicted, a guerrilla information war fought not in the sky or on the streets, not in the forests or around international fishing boundaries on the high seas, but in newspapers and magazines, on the radio, on TV, and in cyberspace. It will be a dirty, no-holds-barred propaganda war of competing worldviews and alternative visions of the future.

We culture jammers can win this battle for ourselves and for planet Earth. Here's how: We build our own meme factory, put out a better product, and beat the corporations at their own game. We identify the macromemes and the metamemes—the core ideas without which a sustainable future is unthinkable—and deploy them. Here are the five most potent metamemes in the culture jammer's arsenal:

True cost: In the global marketplace of the future, the price of every product will tell the ecological truth.

Demarketing: It's time to unsell the product and turn the massive power of marketing against itself.

The doomsday machine: The global economy is a juggernaut that must be stopped and reprogrammed.

No corporate 'I': Corporations are not legal 'persons' with constitutional rights and freedoms of their own, but legal fictions that we created and must control.

Media Carta: Every human being has the right to communicate—to receive and impart information through any media.

Only the vigilant can maintain their liberties, and only those who are constantly and intelligently on the spot can hope to govern themselves effectively by democratic procedures. A society whose members spend a great deal of their time in the irrelevant worlds of sport and soap opera, of mythology and metaphysical fantasy, will find it hard to resist the encroachments of those who would manipulate and control it.

Aldous Huxley was on the spot in the foreword of his revised 1946 edition of *Brave New World*—which, perhaps more than any other 20th-century fiction work, predicted the psychological climate of our wired age. There's a clear parallel between 'soma'—the pleasure drug issued to BNW citizens—and the mass media as we know them. Both keep the hordes tranquilized and pacified, and maintain the social order. Both chase out reason in favor of entertainment and disjointed thought, encourage uniformity of behavior, and devalue the past in favor of sensory pleasures now. Residents of Huxley's realm willingly participate in being manipulated. Only you, the reader (and a couple of 'imperfect' book characters who somehow ended up with real personalities), know it's dystopia. It's a hell that can be recognized only by those outside the system.

Our own dystopia, too, can be detected only from the outside—by 'outsiders' who by some lucky twist of fate were not seduced by the Dream and recruited into the consumer cult of the insatiables. Although most of us are still stuck in the cult, our taste for soma is souring. Through the haze of manufactured happiness, we're realizing that our only escape is to stop the flow of soma, to break the global communication cartel's monopoly on the production of meaning.

Guy Debord, leader of the situationist movement in 1960s France, said, 'Revolution is not showing life to people, but making them live.' The desire to be free and unfettered is hardwired into each of us. It's a drive almost as strong as sex or hunger, an irresistible force that, once harnessed, is nearly impossible to stop. With that irresistible force on our side, we will strike. We will strike by smashing the postmodern hall of mirrors and redefining what it means to be alive. We will reframe the battle in the grandest terms. The old political battles that have consumed humankind during most of the 20th century—black vs. white, left vs. right, male vs. female—will fade into the background. The only battle still worth fighting and winning, the only one that can set us free, is the People vs. the Corporate Cool Machine.

First we kill all the economists (figuratively speaking). We prove that despite the almost religious deference society extends to them,

SECTION THREE
Readings

they are not untouchable. We launch a global media campaign to discredit them. We show how their economic models are fundamentally flawed, how their 'scientifically' managed cycles of 'growth' and 'progress' are wiping out the natural world. We reveal their science as a dangerous pseudoscience. We ridicule them on TV, in unexpected places: the local business news, commercial breaks during the midnight movie, national prime time.

At the same time, we lay a trap for the G-8 leaders. Our campaign paints them as Lears, deluded despots unaware of their deepening madness and the damage it does. We demand to know why overconsumption in the First World is not an issue on their agenda. In the weeks leading up to their yearly summit meeting, we buy TV spots on stations around the world: 'Is Economic Progress Killing the Planet?' In a worldwide press conference, we ask, 'Mr. President, how do you measure economic progress? How do you tell if the economy is robust or sick?' We wait for a pat answer about rising GDP. And that will be the decisive moment. We will have given our leaders a simple pop quiz and they will have flunked.

This escalating war of nerves with the heads of state is the top jaw of our strategic pincer. The bottom jaw is grassroots work at university economics departments, where neoclassical dogma is still being propagated every day. We must challenge the keepers of the neoclassical flame.

We must also challenge the idea that corporations have the same rights as a private citizen. A corporation has no soul, no morals. It is nothing but a process, an efficient way of generating revenue. We demonize corporations for their unwavering pursuit of growth, power, and wealth, but they are simply carrying out genetic orders. The only way to change the behavior of a corporation is to recode it, rewrite its charter, reprogram it.

In 1886 the U.S. Supreme Court handed down a decision that changed the course of American history. In Santa Clara County vs. Southern Pacific Railroad, a dispute over a railbed route, the justices ruled that a private corporation was a 'natural person' under the U.S. Constitution and therefore entitled to protection under the Bill of Rights.

SECTION THREE
Readings

The judgment was one of the great legal blunders of the century. Sixty years after it was inked, Supreme Court Justice William O. Douglas said of Santa Clara that it 'could not be supported by history, logic, or reason.' Yet, in a single legal stroke, the whole intent of the Constitution—that each citizen has one vote and exercises an equal voice in public debates—had been undermined. There is only one way to regain control. We must challenge the corporate 'I' in the courts, and ultimately reverse Santa Clara.

Let's send chills down the spine of corporate America by making an example of the world's biggest corporate criminal. Let's take on Philip Morris Inc., get the truth out, apply pressure until the state of New York revokes the company's charter.

This is how the revolution starts: A few people begin to break their old patterns, embrace what they love (and in the process discover what they hate), daydream, question, rebel. What happens naturally then, according to the situationists, is a groundswell of support for this new way of being; more and more people are empowered, 'unencumbered by history.'

If the old America was about prosperity, maybe the new America will be about spontaneity. The situationists maintained that ordinary people have all the tools they need for revolution. The only thing missing is a shift in perception—a tantalizing glimpse of a new way of being—that suddenly brings everything into focus.

Kalle Lasn is editor and publisher of Adbusters *magazine.*

SECTION THREE
Readings

Adbusters—Create Your Own Print Ad

From the website of Adbusters Magazine. *Reprinted with permission from* Adbusters Media Foundation.

1. Decide on your communication objective
2. Decide on your target audience
3. Decide on your format
4. Develop your concept
5. The visual
6. The headline
7. The copy
8. Mistakes to avoid

1. Decide on your communication objective

The communications objective is the essence of your message. If you want to tell people not to eat rutabagas because it's cruel, then that's your communications objective. A word of caution: though perhaps the most important of your 8 steps, this is also the one that beginners tend most to neglect. A precise and well-defined objective is crucial to a good ad. If your objective isn't right on, then everything that follows will be off as well.

2. Decide on your target audience

Who is your message intended for? If you're speaking to kids, then your language and arguments will have to be understandable to kids. On the other hand, if you're speaking to high income earners (for example, if you're writing an ad to dissuade people from wearing fur coats), then your language will have to be more sophisticated. So define who your target audience is, because that will decide how your message is conveyed.

3. Decide on your format

Is it going to be a poster, a half-page magazine ad, or a tiny box in the corner of a newspaper? Make this decision based on the target audience you're trying to reach, and the amount of money you can afford to spend. If you're talking to kids, a poster in one high school will not only cost less, it will actually reach more of your target audience than a full-page ad in the biggest paper in town. When it comes to deciding on the size of your ad, the more expensive it will be to produce and run. Don't let that discourage you. You can do a lot with a small ad so long as it's strong, clear, and properly targeted.

4. Develop your concept

The concept is the underlying creative idea that drives your message. Even in a big ad campaign, the concept will typically remain the same from one ad to another, and from one medium to another. Only the execution of that concept will change. So by developing a concept that is effective and powerful, you open the door to a number of very compelling ads. So take you time developing a concept that's strong. Typically, an ad is made up of a photograph or a drawing (the "visual"), a headline, and writing (the "copy"). Whether you think of your visual or your headline first makes little difference. However, here are a few guidelines worth following.

5. The visual

Though you don't absolutely require a visual, it will help draw attention to your ad. Research indicates that 70% of people will only look at the visual in an ad, whereas only 30% will read the headline. So if you use a visual, then you're already talking to twice as many people as you otherwise might. Another suggestion is to use photographs instead of illustrations whenever possible. People tend to relate to realistic photographs more easily than unrealistic ones. But whether you choose a photograph or an illustration, the most important criteria is that the image be the most interesting one possible and at least half your ad whenever possible.

SECTION THREE
Readings

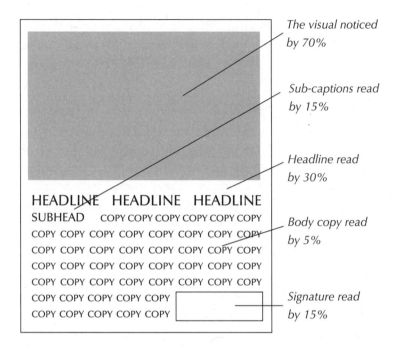

The visual noticed by 70%

Sub-captions read by 15%

Headline read by 30%

HEADLINE HEADLINE HEADLINE
SUBHEAD   COPY COPY COPY COPY COPY COPY
COPY COPY COPY COPY COPY COPY COPY COPY
COPY COPY COPY COPY COPY COPY COPY COPY
COPY COPY COPY COPY COPY COPY COPY COPY
COPY COPY COPY COPY COPY COPY COPY COPY
COPY COPY COPY COPY COPY
COPY COPY COPY COPY COPY

Body copy read by 5%

Signature read by 15%

6. The headline

The most important thing to remember here is that your head-line must be short, snappy and must touch the people that read it. Your headline must affect the reader emotionally, either by making them laugh, making them angry, making them curious or making them think. If you can't think of a headline that does one of these four things, then keep thinking. Here's a little tip that might help: try to find an insight or inner truth to the message that you're trying to convey, something that readers will easily relate to and be touched by. Taking the rutabagas example once again, it might be tempting to write a headline like: "Stop Exploiting These Migrant Workers." However, with a little thought, a more underlying truth might be revealed—that Migrant Workers are as human as we are, and that our actions do hurt them. From that inner truth, you might arrive at the headline: "Do unto others as you would have them do unto you." Of course, the headline doesn't have to be biblical, though that in itself will add meaning and power for many people. Finally, whenever possible, avoid a headline longer than fifteen words. People just don't read as much as they used to.

7. The copy

Here's where you make the case. If you have compelling arguments, make them. If you have persuasive facts, state them. But don't overwhelm with information. Two strong arguments will make more of an impression than a dozen weaker ones. Finally, be clear, be precise, and be honest. Any hint of deception will instantly detract from your entire message. Position your copy beneath the headline, laid out in two blocks two or three inches in length. Only about 5% of people will read your copy, whereas 30% will read your headline. By positioning your copy near your heading, you create a visual continuity which will draw more people to the information you want to convey. Use a serif typeface for your copy whenever possible. Those little lines and swiggles on the letters make the reading easier and more pleasing to the eye.

If you have lots of copy, break it up with interesting subheads, as we've done in the graphic above. This will make your ad more inviting, more organized, and easier to read.

8. The signature

This is where the name of the organization belongs, along with the address and phone number. If you don't have an organization, then think of a name that will help reinforce the message you're trying to convey. Perhaps "Citizens for Fairness to Migrant Rutabagas Pickers" would work for the example we've been using. This isn't dishonest. Your organization doesn't have to be incorporated or registered for it to be real.

9. Some mistakes to avoid

The single most common mistake is visual clutter. Less is always better than more. So if you're not certain whether something is worth including, then leave it out. If your ad is chaotic, people will simply turn the page, and your message will never be read. The second most common mistake is to have an ad that's unclear or not easily understood (haven't you ever looked at an ad and wondered what it was for?). The best way to safeguard against this is to do some rough sketches of your visual with the headline and show it around. If people aren't clear about your message, then it's probably because your message is unclear. And however tempting, don't argue with them or assume that they're wrong and that your ad is fine. You'll be in for an unpleasant surprise. Proofread your ad, then give it to others to proofread, then proofread it yet again. Typographical errors diminish your credibility and have an uncanny habit of creeping into ads when you least expect it.

SECTION THREE
Readings

Adbusters—Selected Spoof Ads

Nike Spoof Ad—Adbusters

Reprinted with permission from Adbusters Media Foundation.

Absolute Vodka Spoof Ad—Adbusters

Reprinted with permission from Adbusters Media Foundation.

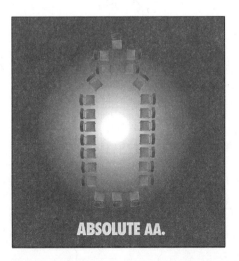

Marlboro Spoof Ad—Adbusters

Reprinted with permission from Adbusters Media Foundation.

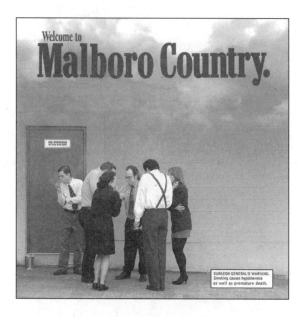

Camel Spoof Ad—Adbusters

Reprinted with permission from Adbusters Media Foundation.

SECTION THREE
Readings

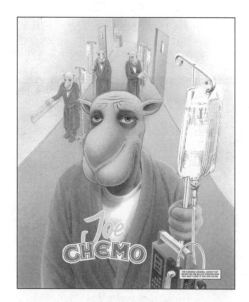

Thomas Frank—Why Johnny Can't Dissent

The public be damned! I work for my stockholders.
                                        —William H. Vanderbilt, 1879

Break the rules. Stand apart. Keep your head. Go with your heart.
                            —TV commercial for Vanderbilt perfume, 1994

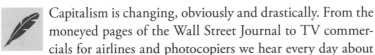 Capitalism is changing, obviously and drastically. From the moneyed pages of the Wall Street Journal to TV commercials for airlines and photocopiers we hear every day about the new order's globe-spanning, cyber-accumulating ways. But our notion about what's wrong with American life and how the figures responsible are to be confronted haven't changed much in thirty years. Call it, for convenience, the "countercultural idea." It holds that the paramount ailment of our society is conformity, a malady that has variously been described as over-organization, bureaucracy, homogeneity, hierarchy, logocentrism, technocracy, the Combine, the Apollonian. We all know what it is and what it does. It transforms humanity into "organization man," into "the man in the gray flannel suit." It is "Moloch whose mind is pure machinery," the "incomprehensible prison" that consumes "brains and imagination." It is artifice, starched shirts, tailfins, carefully mowed lawns, and always, always, the consciousness of impending nuclear destruction. It is a stiff, militaristic order that seeks to suppress instinct, to forbid sex and pleasure, to deny basic human impulses and individuality, to enforce through a rigid uniformity a meaningless plastic consumerism.

As this half of the countercultural idea originated during the 1950s, it is appropriate that the evils of conformity are most conveniently summarized with images of 1950s suburban correctness. You know, that land of sedate music, sexual repression, deference to authority, Red Scares, and smiling white people standing politely in line to go to church. Constantly appearing as a symbol of archbackwardness in advertising and movies, it is an image we find easy to evoke.

SECTION THREE
Readings

The ways in which this system are to be resisted are equally well understood and agreed-upon. The Establishment demands homogeneity; we revolt by embracing diverse, individual lifestyles. It demands self-denial and rigid adherence to convention; we revolt through immediate gratification, instinct uninhibited, and liberation of the libido and the appetites. Few have put it more bluntly than Jerry Rubin did in 1970: "Amerika says: Don't! The yippies say: Do It!" The countercultural idea is hostile to any law and every establishment. "Whenever we see a rule, we must break it," Rubin continued. "Only by breaking rules do we discover who we are." Above all rebellion consists of a sort of Nietzschean antinomianism, an automatic questioning of rules, a rejection of whatever social prescriptions we've happened to inherit. Just Do It is the whole of the law.

The patron saints of the countercultural idea are, of course, the Beats, whose frenzied style and merry alienation still maintain a powerful grip on the American imagination. Even forty years after the publication of *On the Road*, the works of Kerouac, Ginsberg, and Burroughs remain the sine qua non of dissidence, the model for aspiring poets, rock stars, or indeed anyone who feels vaguely artistic or alienated. That frenzied sensibility of pure experience, life on the edge, immediate gratification, and total freedom from moral restraint, which the Beats first propounded back in those heady days when suddenly everyone could have their own TV and powerful V-8, has stuck with us through all the intervening years and become something of a permanent American style. Go to any poetry reading and you can see a string of junior Kerouacs go through the routine, upsetting cultural hierarchies by pushing themselves to the limit, straining for that gorgeous moment of original vice when Allen Ginsberg first read "Howl" in 1955 and the patriarchs of our fantasies recoiled in shock. *The Gap* may have since claimed Ginsberg and *USA Today* may run feature stories about the brilliance of the beloved Kerouac, but the rebel race continues today regardless, with ever-heightening shit-references calculated to scare Jesse Helms, talk about sex and smack that is supposed to bring the electricity of real life, and ever-more determined defiance of the repressive rules and mores of the American 1950s—rules and mores that by now we know only from movies.

But one hardly has to go to a poetry reading to see the counter-cultural idea acted out. Its frenzied ecstasies have long since become an official aesthetic of consumer society, a monotheme of mass as well as adversarial culture. Turn on the TV and there it is instantly: the unending drama of consumer unbound and in search of an ever-heightened good time, the inescapable rock 'n' roll soundtrack, dreadlocks and ponytails bounding into Taco Bells, a drunken, swinging-camera epiphany of tennis shoes, outlaw soda pops, and mind-bending dandruff shampoos. Corporate America, it turns out, no longer speaks in the voice of oppressive order that it did when Ginsberg moaned in 1956 that *Time* magazine was "…always telling me about responsibility. Businessmen are serious. Movie producers are serious. Everybody's serious but me."

Nobody wants you to think they're serious today, least of all Time Warner. On the contrary: the Culture Trust is now our leader in the Ginsbergian search for kicks upon kicks. Corporate America is not an oppressor but a sponsor of fun, provider of lifestyle accoutrements, facilitator of carnival, our slang-speaking partner in the quest for that ever-more apocalyptic orgasm. The countercultural idea has become capitalist orthodoxy, its hunger for transgression upon transgression now perfectly suited to an economic-cultural regime that runs on ever-faster cyclings of the new; its taste for self-fulfillment and its intolerance for the confines of tradition now permitting vast latitude in consuming practices and lifestyle experimentation.

Consumerism is no longer about "conformity" but about "difference." Advertising teaches us not in the ways of puritanical self-denial (a bizarre notion on the face of it), but in orgiastic, never-ending self-fulfillment. It counsels not rigid adherence to the tastes of the herd but vigilant and constantly updated individualism. We consume not to fit in, but to prove, on the surface at least, that we are rock 'n' roll rebels, each one of us as rule-breaking and hierarchy-defying as our heroes of the 60s, who now pitch cars, shoes, and beer. This imperative of endless difference is today the genius at the heart of American capitalism, an eternal fleeing from "sameness" that satiates our thirst for the New with such achievements of civilization as the infinite brands of identical cola, the myriad colors and irrepressible variety of the cigarette rack at 7-Eleven.

SECTION THREE
Readings

As existential rebellion has become a more or less official style of Information Age capitalism, so has the countercultural notion of a static, repressive Establishment grown hopelessly obsolete. However the basic impulses of the countercultural idea may have disturbed a nation lost in Cold War darkness, they are today in fundamental agreement with the basic tenets of Information Age business theory. So close are they, in fact, that it has become difficult to understand the countercultural idea as anything more than the self-justifying ideology of the new bourgeoisie that has arisen since the 1960s, the cultural means by which this group has proven itself ever so much better skilled than its slow-moving, security-minded forebears at adapting to the accelerated, always-changing consumerism of today. The anointed cultural opponents of capitalism are now capitalism's ideologues.

The two come together in perfect synchronization in a figure like Camille Paglia, whose ravings are grounded in the absolutely noncontroversial ideas of the golden sixties. According to Paglia, American business is still exactly what it was believed to have been in that beloved decade, that is, "puritanical and desensualized." Its great opponents are, of course, liberated figures like "the beatniks," Bob Dylan, and the Beatles. Culture is, quite simply, a binary battle between the repressive Apollonian order of capitalism and the Dionysian impulses of the counterculture. Rebellion makes no sense without repression; we must remain forever convinced of capitalism's fundamental hostility to pleasure in order to consume capitalism's rebel products as avidly as we do. It comes as little surprise when, after criticizing the "Apollonian capitalist machine" (in her book, *Vamps & Tramps*), Paglia applauds American mass culture (in Utne Reader), the preeminent product of that "capitalist machine," as a "third great eruption" of a Dionysian "paganism." For her, as for most other designated dissidents, there is no contradiction between replaying the standard critique of capitalist conformity and repressiveness and then endorsing its rebel products—for Paglia the car culture and Madonna—as the obvious solution: the Culture Trust offers both Establishment and Resistance in one convenient package. The only question that remains is why Paglia has not yet landed an endorsement contract from a soda pop or automobile manufacturer.

Other legendary exponents of the countercultural idea have been more fortunate—William S. Burroughs, for example, who appears in a television spot for the Nike corporation. But so openly does the commercial flaunt the confluence of capital and counterculture that it has brought considerable criticism down on the head of the aging beat. Writing in the *Village Voice*, Leslie Savan marvels at the contradiction between Burroughs' writings and the faceless corporate entity for which he is now pushing product. "Now the realization that nothing threatens the system has freed advertising to exploit even the most marginal elements of society," Savan observes. "In fact, being hip is no longer quite enough—better the pitchman be 'underground.'" Meanwhile Burroughs' manager insists, as all future Cultural Studies treatments of the ad will no doubt also insist, that Burroughs' presence actually makes the commercial "deeply subversive"—"I hate to repeat the usual mantra, but you know, homosexual drug addict, manslaughter, accidental homicide." But Savan wonders whether, in fact, it is Burroughs who has been assimilated by corporate America. "The problem comes," she writes, "in how easily any idea, deed, or image can become part of the sponsored world."

The most startling revelation to emerge from the Burroughs/Nike partnership is not that corporate America has overwhelmed its cultural foes or that Burroughs can somehow remain "subversive" through it all, but the complete lack of dissonance between the two sides. Of course Burroughs is not "subversive," but neither has he "sold out": His ravings are no longer appreciably different from the official folklore of American capitalism. What's changed is not Burroughs, but business itself. As expertly as Burroughs once bayoneted American proprieties, as stridently as he once proclaimed himself beyond the laws of man and God, he is today a respected ideologue of the Information Age, occupying roughly the position in the pantheon of corporate-cultural thought once reserved strictly for Notre Dame football coaches and positive-thinking Methodist ministers. His inspirational writings are boardroom favorites, his dark nihilistic burpings the happy homilies of the new corporate faith.

For with the assumption of power by Drucker's and Reich's new class has come an entirely new ideology of business, a way of justifying and exercising power that has little to do with the "conformity" and the "establishment" so vilified by the countercultural idea. The management theorists and "leadership" charlatans of the Information Age don't waste their time prattling about hierarchy and regulation, but about disorder, chaos, and the meaninglessness of

SECTION THREE
Readings

443

convention. With its reorganization around information, capitalism has developed a new mythology, a sort of corporate antinomianism according to which the breaking of rules and the elimination of rigid corporate structure have become the central article of faith for millions of aspiring executives.

Dropping *Naked Lunch* and picking up *Thriving on Chaos*, the groundbreaking 1987 management text by Tom Peters, the most popular business writer of the past decade, one finds more philosophical similarities than one would expect from two manifestos of, respectively, dissident culture and business culture. If anything, Peters' celebration of disorder is, by virtue of its hard statistics, bleaker and more nightmarish than Burroughs'. For this popular lecturer on such once-blithe topics as competitiveness and pop psychology there is nothing, absolutely nothing, that is certain. His world is one in which the corporate wisdom of the past is meaningless, established customs are ridiculous, and "rules" are some sort of curse, a remnant of the foolish fifties that exist to be defied, not obeyed. We live in what Peters calls "A World Turned Upside Down," in which whirl is king and, in order to survive, businesses must eventually embrace Peters' universal solution: "Revolution!" "To meet the demands of the fast-changing competitive scene," he counsels, "we must simply learn to love change as much as we have hated it in the past." He advises businessmen to become Robespierres of routine, to demand of their underlings, "'What have you changed lately?' 'How fast are you changing?' and 'Are you pursuing bold enough change goals?'" "Revolution," of course, means for Peters the same thing it did to Burroughs and Ginsberg, Presley and the Stones in their heyday: breaking rules, pissing off the suits, shocking the bean-counters: "Actively and publicly hail defiance of the rules, many of which you doubtless labored mightily to construct in the first place." Peters even suggests that his readers implement this hostility to logocentrism in a carnivalesque celebration, drinking beer out in "the woods" and destroying "all the forms and rules and discontinued reports" and, "if you've got real nerve," a photocopier as well.

Today corporate antinomianism is the emphatic message of nearly every new business text, continually escalating the corporate insurrection begun by Peters. Capitalism, at least as it is envisioned by the best-selling management handbooks, is no longer about enforcing Order, but destroying it. "Revolution," once the totemic catchphrase of the counterculture, has become the totemic catchphrase of boomer-as-capitalist. The Information Age businessman holds inherited ideas and traditional practices not in reverence, but in high suspicion. Even reason itself is now found to be an enemy of true competitiveness, an out-of-date faculty to be scrupulously avoided by conscientious managers. A 1990 book by Charles Handy entitled *The Age of Unreason* agrees with Peters that we inhabit a time in which "there can be no certainty" and suggests that readers engage in full-fledged epistemological revolution: "Thinking Upside Down," using new ways of "learning which can ... be seen as disrespectful if not downright rebellious," methods of approaching problems that have "never been popular with the upholders of continuity and of the status quo." Three years later the authors of *Reengineering the Corporation* ("A Manifesto for Business Revolution," as its subtitle declares) are ready to push this doctrine even farther. Not only should we be suspicious of traditional practices, but we should cast out virtually everything learned over the past two centuries!

Business reengineering means putting aside much of the received wisdom of two hundred years of industrial management. It means forgetting how work was done in the age of the mass market and deciding how it can best be done now. In business reengineering, old job titles and old organizational arrangements—departments, divisions, groups, and so on—cease to matter. They are artifacts of another age.

As countercultural rebellion becomes corporate ideology, even the beloved Buddhism of the Beats wins a place on the executive bookshelf. In *The Leader as Martial Artist* (1993), Arnold Mindell advises men of commerce in the ways of the Tao, mastery of which he likens, of course, to surfing. For Mindell's Zen businessman, as for the followers of Tom Peters, the world is a wildly chaotic place of opportunity, navigable only to an enlightened "leader" who can discern the "timespirits" at work behind the scenes. In terms Peters himself might use were he a more more meditative sort of inspiration professional, Mindell explains that "the wise facilitator" doesn't seek to prevent the inevitable and random clashes between "conflicting field spirits," but to anticipate such bouts of disorder and profit thereby.

Contemporary corporate fantasy imagines a world of ceaseless, turbulent change, of centers that ecstatically fail to hold, of joyous extinction for the craven gray-flannel creature of the past.

SECTION THREE
Readings

445

Businessmen today decorate the walls of their offices not with portraits of President Eisenhower and emblems of suburban order, but with images of extreme athletic daring, with sayings about "diversity" and "empowerment" and "thinking outside the box." They theorize their world not in the bar car of the commuter train, but in weepy corporate retreats at which they beat their tom-toms and envision themselves as part of the great avant-garde tradition of edge-livers, risktakers, and ass-kickers. Their world is a place not of sublimation and conformity, but of "leadership" and bold talk about defying the herd. And there is nothing this new enlightened species of businessman despises more than "rules" and "reason." The prominent culture-warriors of the right may believe that the counterculture was capitalism's undoing, but the antinomian businessmen know better. "One of the t-shirt slogans of the sixties read, 'Question authority,'" the authors of *Reengineering the Corporation* write. "Process owners might buy their reengineering team members the nineties version: 'Question assumptions.'"

The new businessman quite naturally gravitates to the slogans and sensibility of the rebel sixties to express his understanding of the new Information World. He is led in what one magazine calls "the business revolution" by the office-park subversives it hails as "business activists," "change agents," and "corporate radicals." He speaks to his comrades through commercials like the one for "Warp," a type of IBM computer operating system, in which an electric guitar soundtrack and psychedelic video effects surround hip executives with earrings and hairdos who are visibly stunned by the product's gnarly 'tude (It's a "totally cool way to run your computer," read the product's print ads). He understands the world through *Fast Company*, a successful new magazine whose editors take their inspiration from Hunter S. Thompson and whose stories describe such things as a "dis-organization" that inhabits an "anti-office" where "all vestiges of hierarchy have disappeared" or a computer scientist who is also "a rabble rouser, an agent provocateur, a product of the 1960s who never lost his activist fire or democratic values." He is what sociologists Paul Leinberger and Bruce Tucker have called "The New Individualist," the new and improved manager whose arty worldview and creative hip derive directly from his formative sixties days. The one thing this new executive is definitely not is Organization Man, the hyper-rational counter of beans, attender of church, and wearer of stiff hats. In television commercials, through which the new American businessman presents his visions and self-understanding to the public, perpetual revolution and the gospel of rule-breaking are the orthodoxy of the day. You only need to watch for a few minutes before you see one of these slogans and understand the grip of antinomianism over the corporate mind:

> Sometimes You Gotta Break the Rules—Burger King
> If You Don't Like the Rules, Change Them—WXRT-FM
> The Rules Have Changed—Dodge
> The Art of Changing—Swatch
> There's no one way to do it.—Levi's
> This is different. Different is good—Arby's
> Just Different From the Rest—Special Export beer
> The Line Has Been Crossed: The Revolutionary New Supra
>   —Toyota
> Resist the Usual—the slogan of both Clash Clear Malt and
>   Young & Rubicam
> Innovate Don't Imitate—Hugo Boss
> Chart Your Own Course—Navigator Cologne
> It separates you from the crowd—Vision Cologne

In most, the commercial message is driven home with the vanguard iconography of the rebel: screaming guitars, whirling cameras, and startled old timers who, we predict, will become an increasingly indispensable prop as consumers require ever-greater assurances that, Yes! You are a rebel! Just look at how offended they are!

Our businessmen imagine themselves rebels, and our rebels sound more and more like ideologists of business. Henry Rollins, for example, the maker of loutish, overbearing music and composer of high-school-grade poetry, straddles both worlds unproblematically. Rollins' writing and lyrics strike all the standard alienated literary poses: He rails against overcivilization and yearns to "disconnect." He veers back and forth between vague threats toward "weak" people who "bring me down" and blustery declarations of his weightlifting ability and physical prowess. As a result he ruled for several years as the preeminent darling of *Details* magazine, a periodical handbook for the young executive on the rise, where rebellion has achieved a perfect synthesis with corporate ideology. In 1992 *Details* named

SECTION THREE
Readings

447

Rollins a "rock 'n' roll samurai," an "emblem ... of a new masculinity" whose "enlightened honesty" is "a way of being that seems to flesh out many of the ideas expressed in contemporary culture and fashion." In 1994 the magazine consummated its relationship with Rollins by naming him "Man of the Year," printing a fawning story about his muscular worldview and decorating its cover with a photo in which Rollins displays his tattoos and rubs his chin in a thoughtful manner.

Details found Rollins to be such an appropriate role model for the struggling young businessman not only because of his music-product, but because of his excellent "selfstyled identity," which the magazine describes in terms normally reserved for the breast-beating and soul-searching variety of motivational seminars. Although he derives it from the quality-maximizing wisdom of the East rather than the unfashionable doctrines of Calvin, Rollins' rebel posture is identical to that fabled ethic of the small capitalist whose regimen of positive thinking and hard work will one day pay off. Details describes one of Rollins' songs, quite seriously, as "a self-motivational superforce, an anthem of empowerment," teaching lessons that any aspiring middle-manager must internalize. Elsewhere, Iggy Pop, that great chronicler of the ambitionless life, praises Rollins as a "high achiever" who "wants to go somewhere." Rollins himself even seems to invite such an interpretation. His recent spoken-word account of touring with Black Flag, delivered in an unrelenting two-hour drill instructor staccato, begins with the timeless bourgeois story of opportunity taken, of young Henry leaving the security of a "straight job," enlisting with a group of visionaries who were "the hardest working people I have ever seen," and learning "what hard work is all about." In the liner notes he speaks proudly of his Demingesque dedication to quality, of how his bandmates "Delivered under pressure at incredible odds." When describing his relationship with his parents for the readers of *Details*, Rollins quickly cuts to the critical matter, the results that such dedication has brought: "Mom, Dad, I outgross both of you put together," a happy observation he repeats in his interview with the *New York Times* Magazine.

Despite the extreme hostility of punk rockers with which Rollins had to contend all through the 1980s, it is he who has been chosen by the commercial media as the godfather of rock 'n' roll revolt. It is not difficult to see why. For Rollins the punk rock decade was but a lengthy seminar on leadership skills, thriving on chaos, and total quality management. Rollins' much-celebrated anger is indistinguishable from the anger of the frustrated junior executive who finds obstacles on the way to the top. His discipline and determination are the automatic catechism of any small entrepreneur who's just finished brainwashing himself with the latest leadership and positive-thinking tracts; his poetry is the inspired verse of *21 Days to Unlimited Power* or *Let's Get Results, Not Excuses.* Henry Rollins is no more a threat to established power in America than was Dale Carnegie. And yet Rollins as king of the rebels—peerless and ultimate—is the message hammered home wherever photos of his growling visage appears. If you're unhappy with your lot, the Culture Trust tells us with each new tale of Rollins, if you feel you must rebel, take your cue from the most disgruntled guy of all: Lift weights! Work hard! Meditate in your back yard! Root out the weaknesses deep down inside yourself! But whatever you do, don't think about who controls power or how it is wielded.

The structure and thinking of American business have changed enormously in the years since our popular conceptions of its problems and abuses were formulated. In the meantime the mad frothings and jolly apolitical revolt of Beat, despite their vast popularity and insurgent air, have become powerless against a new regime that, one suspects, few of Beat's present-day admirers and practitioners feel any need to study or understand. Today that beautiful countercultural idea, endorsed now by everyone from the surviving Beats to shampoo manufacturers, is more the official doctrine of corporate America than it is a program of resistance. What we understand as "dissent" does not subvert, does not challenge, does not even question the cultural faiths of Western business. What David Rieff wrote of the revolutionary pretensions of multiculturalism is equally true of the countercultural idea: "The more one reads in academic multiculturalist journals and in business publications, and the more one contrasts the speeches of CEOs and the speeches of noted multiculturalist academics, the more one is struck by the similarities in the way they view the world." What's happened is not co-optation or appropriation, but a simple and direct confluence of interest.

The problem with cultural dissent in America isn't that it's been co-opted, absorbed, or ripped-off. Of course it's been all of these things. But it has proven so hopelessly susceptible to such assaults for the same reason it has become so harmless in the first place, so toothless even before Mr. Geffen's boys discover it angsting away in some bar in Lawrence, Kansas: It is no longer any different from the official culture it's supposed to be subverting. The basic impulses of the countercultural idea, as descended from the holy Beats, are about as threatening to the new breed of antinomian businessmen as Anthony Robbins, selling success and how to achieve it on a late-night infomercial.

The people who staff the *Combine* aren't like Nurse Ratched. They aren't Frank Burns, they aren't the Church Lady, they aren't Dean Wormer from "Animal House," they aren't those repressed old folks in the commercials who want to ban Tropicana Fruit Twisters. They're hipper than you can ever hope to be because hip is their official ideology, and they're always going to be there at the poetry reading to encourage your "rebellion" with a hearty "right on, man!" before you even know they're in the auditorium. You can't outrun them, or even stay ahead of them for very long: it's their racetrack, and that's them waiting at the finish line to congratulate you on how outrageous your new style is, on how you shocked those stuffy prudes out in the heartland.

SECTION THREE
Readings

Public Arguments on Food

Warwick Sabin—The Rich Get Thinner, The Poor Get Fatter: Is Fresh, Local Food Becoming a Luxury Item?

The Oxford American, *March 8, 2010. Reprinted with permission.*

 Our appreciation of Southern cuisine has a dark side. We usually acknowledge it with a laugh, or a devil-may-care sense of recklessness.

That fried chicken leg may kill you; that pork rib is going to take a year off your life. But it's worth it, you say. You are willing to live on the edge.

This apparent choice between good health and good eating is made even starker with every new report issued by the U.S. Centers for Disease Control and Prevention. The latest, issued in November 2009, was titled "Highest Rates of Obesity, Diabetes in the South," and it included some sobering statistics. Most Southern states have obesity rates hovering near, or above, the thirty-percent mark, and projections indicate that the problem is going to get much worse in the years ahead.

Of course, it doesn't take long for the researchers to trace the expanding waistlines back to the biscuits and gravy.

"Southern culture plays a role in the rising obesity rates in the region," reports a 2008 article in the *Chattanooga Times Free Press*. "Traditional Southern foods—even vegetables such as fried green tomatoes and fried okra—can be land mines for the weight-conscious, health experts said."

Intuitively, that may seem true, but it does not explain why our nation's skyrocketing obesity problem is a relatively recent phenomenon that is not confined to the South. The CDC data indicates that no state had an obesity rate higher than fifteen percent in 1990. By 1998, no state had a prevalence of obesity less than ten percent. As our lives become less physically demanding (with fewer jobs in agriculture and blue-collar trades), and our diets become less wholesome (with more sugar and artificial ingredients), all Americans are at risk of becoming ensnared in the obesity trap.

Still, there is a particularly sad irony in the South disproportionally suffering from an obesity epidemic that could be attributable to its regional cuisine. Many of what are now considered traditional

SECTION THREE
Readings

Southern dishes were to a large degree designed to fill empty stomachs and provide essential energy when work was hard and food was scarce.

Then, like now, the South had a higher rate of poverty than almost anywhere else in the nation. So what has changed?

Take a walk through the aisles of your grocery store and compare the prices of fresh fruits, vegetables, and meats to those of the mass-produced processed foods. It will quickly become clear that the poor people of the South are making the exact same decisions they made during the time of James Agee and Walker Evans—they are opting for the affordable calories.

The cruel fact is that fewer than one hundred years ago being poor meant you were painfully thin. Now, it means you are dangerously fat.

But this time, it's probably not the biscuits and gravy that are to blame so much as candy bars, soft drinks, and fast food.

In fact, our favorite Southern foods actually have become indulgences because an increasing number of Southerners cannot afford them. By an extraordinary twist of economics, the fresh, local produce once available cheaply at the back-road farm stand has become the preserve of the elites, available in gourmet-food shops at inflated prices.

It used to be that keeping a few free-range chickens, tending some grain-fed hogs, and raising a small vegetable garden was how people simply survived. Now these are often vanity projects for young hipsters and retired hedge-fund executives who have discovered the forgotten pleasures of "heirloom" tomatoes and artisanal sausage. Incredibly, we've reached a point in our society where things that humans have done for thousands of years—grow a vegetable, smoke or cure a piece of meat—now provide the grounds for smug satisfaction. (Think of Marie Antoinette at Versailles, playing shepherdess and milking the cows.)

In a region where farming is still a dominant industry, how can food that is fresh, local, and organic be beyond the reach of so many Southerners? Our states are among the nation's leaders in the cultivation of fruits, vegetables, rice, peanuts, poultry, and other agricultural products. Yet schoolchildren in poor, rural districts, surrounded by fields and chicken houses, eat processed lunches

SECTION THREE
Readings

delivered by food-service tractor-trailers from facilities that are thousands of miles away.

In the end, this paradox can be traced back to those fields and chicken houses, which are now incorporated elements of the devastatingly efficient agribusiness giants. Mechanization, genetic engineering, herbicides, pesticides, growth hormones, and massive economies of scale ensure that anything grown in the next town over is as likely to end up in a grocery store in Maine as in your neighborhood supermarket. In this environment, running a small farm according to organic principles and traditional methods requires greater commitment and investment, which explains why fresh produce is rarer and more expensive.

It is therefore easy to understand how the local food movement also has become another form of social protest against the forces that are corporatizing and homogenizing our society. Fair enough, but it should not make wholesome food so precious and inaccessible that it becomes a luxury item.

Already there has been a noticeable elevation of familiar Southern cuisine from the dairy bar to the martini bar; from the checkered tablecloth to the white tablecloth; from the blue plate to fine china. We're getting used to exclusive restaurants offering their interpretations of fried chicken, greens, pork rinds, and grits—with the requisite menu credit of the nearby organic farm where the meat and produce was raised.

In a bizarre reversal, now it is the wealthy who are rail-thin and eating beans and cornbread. And the poor? The message seems to be: Let them eat (Little Debbie) cake.

SECTION THREE
Readings

Eric Schlosser—Cheap Food Nation

Americans spend a smaller percentage of their income on food than anyone else, but it costs us dearly

Whenever a well-known athlete gets caught using anabolic steroids to run faster, pedal harder, or hit a baseball farther, there's a universal chorus of disapproval. Most Americans regard steroid use in sports as an unhealthy form of cheating. Under federal law, all performance-enhancing synthetic hormones are class III controlled substances; obtaining them without a prescription is a felony. Steroid users may suffer from a wide variety of physical and mental ailments, some of them irreversible"—and the long-term effects of the drugs are unknown.

Meanwhile, for the past two decades, a number of the same steroids abused by athletes have been given to U.S. cattle on a massive scale. Without much publicity or government concern, growth hormones like testosterone are routinely administered to about 80 percent of the nation's feedlot cattle, accelerating their weight gain and making them profitable to slaughter at a younger age. The practice is legal in the United States but banned throughout the European Union, due to concerns about its effect on human health. A recent study by Danish scientists suggested that hormone residues in U.S. beef may be linked to high rates of breast and prostate cancer, as well as to early-onset puberty in girls. Hormone residues excreted in manure also wind up in rivers and streams. A 2003 study of male minnows downstream from one Nebraska feedlot found that many of them had unusually small testes. When female minnows in a laboratory were exposed to trenbolone—a synthetic hormone widely administered to cattle—they developed male sex organs.

The whole idea of bulking up cattle with growth hormones symbolizes how the country's food system has gone wrong. Within a single generation, fundamental changes have occurred not only in how cattle are raised but also in how hogs and chicken are reared, fish are farmed, crops are grown, and most food is processed and distributed. The driving force behind all these changes has been the desire to make food cheaper and produce it faster. The industrialization of agriculture and livestock has made it possible for Americans

SECTION THREE
Readings

to spend less of their annual income on food than anyone else in the world. But the true cost of this system can't be measured by the low prices at Wal-Mart and McDonald's. When you consider the harm being done to animals, the land, ranchers, farmers, and our national health, this fast and cheap food is much too expensive.

A narrow and ruthless vision of efficiency now extends throughout the U.S. livestock industry, transforming sentient creatures into industrial commodities. Giving steroids to cattle doesn't improve the taste of beef. It doesn't make it more nutritious. It just makes beef cheaper by causing cattle to grow faster. The same pursuit of cheapness also removes livestock from their natural settings. Some feedlots now hold more than 100,000 animals. They live in each other's manure, eating grain from concrete troughs. Poultry houses typically contain tens of thousands of birds that see the outdoors only twice in their lives—on the day they're born and on the day they're taken to the slaughterhouse. Pigs are sensitive, affectionate animals, perhaps more intelligent than dogs. At modern hog farms, they often spend their entire lives crammed into small crates, becoming anxious, hostile, and depressed.

On the prairie, cattle manure serves as a natural fertilizer, scattered intermittently for miles. At U.S. feedlots and factory farms, more than a trillion pounds of manure are deposited every year. On that scale and at such concentrations, a perfectly natural substance can become a toxic one. When the two cattle feedlots outside Greeley, Colorado, operate at full capacity, they produce more excrement than Atlanta, Boston, Denver, and St. Louis combined. But unlike those cities, factory farms don't have elaborate waste-treatment facilities. They either spray the manure on nearby fields or dump it into giant pits, euphemistically known as "lagoons." Runoff from these lagoons and fields is one of the leading causes of water pollution in the United States. The manure also pollutes the air with dangerous chemicals like hydrogen sulfide, causing respiratory and neurological illnesses. And it poisons the land with heavy metals like cadmium, selenium, zinc, copper, and arsenic, which are frequently added to livestock feed. When not fully digested, these mineral additives wind up in manure, then in the soil—and eventually in the animals and people who eat the crops grown in that soil.

SECTION THREE
Readings

455

For years, U.S. farmers and ranchers have been told that the latest chemical and technological advances—hormones, pesticides, genetically modified crops, concentrated animal feeding operations—would increase their income. Instead, farmers and ranchers are steadily being driven off the land. Nine out of ten hog farmers have left the business since 1979. Those who remain are essentially employees of big processors like Smithfield Foods. Poultry growers have lost their independence in much the same way, investing large amounts of their own capital while obeying the directives of Tyson Foods. This concentration has been exacerbated by the lax enforcement of antitrust laws. In 1970, the top four meatpacking companies controlled 21 percent of the beef market. Today they control nearly 85 percent. The industry is more concentrated than it was in 1906, when Upton Sinclair attacked the unchecked power of the beef trust in *The Jungle*.

Such systemic changes might be justifiable if all this fast, cheap food greatly benefited the people who eat it. During the past 30 years, however, industrialized agriculture has posed grave new threats to human health. The incidence of food-borne illness has risen, as gigantic processing facilities serve as an ideal vector for spreading pathogens far and wide. The emergence of mad cow disease and E. coli O157:H7 has been linked to changes in how cattle are raised. The indiscriminate use of antibiotics in livestock feed has helped to create new superbugs that can sicken people. And the mass marketing of inexpensive, fatty, high-calorie foods has fueled epidemics of obesity and diabetes. The cost of a 99-cent hamburger doesn't include the dialysis you may need years later.

SECTION THREE

Readings

None of this was inevitable. Nor was it the result of the invisible hand or free-market forces. Despite a fondness for free-market rhetoric, the country's large food companies—ConAgra, Archer Daniels Midland, McDonald's, Kraft—have benefited enormously from the absence of real competition. They receive, directly and indirectly, huge subsidies from the federal government. About half of the annual income earned by U.S. corn farmers now comes from government crop-support programs. Cheap corn is turned into cheap fats, oils, sweeteners, and animal feed. Nearly three-quarters of the corn grown in the United States is fed to livestock, providing taxpayer support for inexpensive hamburgers and chicken nuggets. On the other hand, farmers who grow fresh fruits and vegetables receive few direct subsidies. The farm bills Congress enacts every year, with strong backing from agribusiness, help determine what Americans eat, promoting unhealthy foods and making wholesome ones relatively more expensive.

Throughout the European Union, laws have been passed to guarantee food safety and animal welfare, restrict the use of antibiotics among livestock, ban genetically engineered foods, encourage organic production, and begin the deindustrialization of agriculture. These laws do not mean a return to the 19th century. On the contrary, they encourage the wise, careful application of 21st-century technology, along with a sense of humility before nature.

U.S. fast-food and agribusiness companies aren't deliberately trying to mistreat animals, poison the land, or sicken their customers. But their relentless pursuit of the fast and the cheap is doing those very things. Like the chemical companies a generation ago that dumped toxic waste in streams without a second thought, they're imposing external costs on the rest of society. And nobody is stopping them—yet.

It would be wonderful if our government cared more about public safety and environmental health than about the profits of a handful of corporations. It would be terrific if the passage of new laws solved every one of these problems. Meaningful change, however, isn't going to come from the top. It's going to come from people who realize that there's a direct link between the food they eat and the society they inhabit. Changing your eating habits can send ripples far and wide in support of agricultural practices that are humane, diverse, and sustainable. "The condition of the passive consumer of food is not a democratic condition," Wendell Berry writes. "One reason to eat responsibly is to live free."

SECTION THREE
Readings

Eric Schlosser is the author of Fast Food Nation: The Dark Side of the All-American Meal *(Houghton Mifflin, 2001).*

Eric Schlosser, et al.—One Thing to Do About Food: A Forum

The Nation, *September 11, 2006. Copyright © 2009* The Nation. *Reprinted with permission from the September 11, 2006 issue of* The Nation.

Eric Schlosser

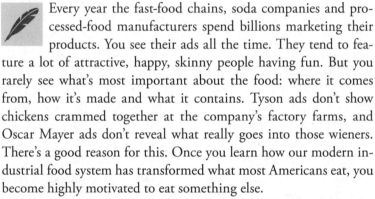 Every year the fast-food chains, soda companies and processed-food manufacturers spend billions marketing their products. You see their ads all the time. They tend to feature a lot of attractive, happy, skinny people having fun. But you rarely see what's most important about the food: where it comes from, how it's made and what it contains. Tyson ads don't show chickens crammed together at the company's factory farms, and Oscar Mayer ads don't reveal what really goes into those wieners. There's a good reason for this. Once you learn how our modern industrial food system has transformed what most Americans eat, you become highly motivated to eat something else.

The National Uniformity for Food Act of 2005, passed by the House and now before the Senate, is a fine example of how food companies and their allies work hard to keep consumers in the dark. Backed by the American Beverage Association, the American Frozen Food Association, the Coca-Cola Company, ConAgra Foods, the National Restaurant Association, the International Food Additives Council, Kraft Foods, the National Cattlemen's Beef Association and the US Chamber of Commerce, among many others, the new law would prevent states from having food safety or labeling requirements stricter than those of the federal government. In the name of "uniformity," it would impose rules that are uniformly bad. State laws that keep lead out of children's candy and warn pregnant women about dangerous ingredients would be wiped off the books.

What single thing could change the US food system, practically overnight? Widespread public awareness—of how this system operates and whom it benefits, how it harms consumers, how it mistreats animals and pollutes the land, how it corrupts public officials and intimidates the press, and most of all, how its power ultimately depends on a series of cheerful and ingenious lies. The modern environmental movement began forty-four years ago when *Silent Spring* exposed the deceptions behind the idea of "better living through chemistry." A similar movement is now gaining momentum on behalf of sustainable agriculture and real food. We must not allow the fast-food industry, agribusiness and Congress to deceive us. "We urgently need an end to these false assurances, to the sugar-coating of unpalatable facts," Rachel Carson famously argued. "In the words of Jean Rostand, 'The obligation to endure gives us the right to know.'"

Eric Schlosser is the author of the bestseller Fast Food Nation: The Dark Side of the All-American Meal, *and, with Charles Wilson,* Chew on This: Everything You Don't Want to Know About Fast Food *(both Houghton Mifflin).*

Marion Nestle

From a public health perspective, obesity is the most serious nutrition problem among children as well as adults in the United States. The roots of this problem can be traced to farm policies and Wall Street. Farm subsidies, tariffs and trade agreements support a food supply that provides 3,900 calories per day per capita, roughly twice the average need, and 700 calories a day higher than in 1980, at the dawn of the obesity epidemic. In this overabundant food economy, companies must compete fiercely for sales, not least because of Wall Street's expectations for quarterly growth. These pressures induce companies to make highly profitable "junk" foods, market them directly to children and advertise such foods as appropriate for consumption at all times, in large amounts, by children of all ages. In this business environment, childhood obesity is just collateral damage.

Adults may be fair game for marketers, but children are not. Children cannot distinguish sales pitches from information unless taught to do so. Food companies spend at least $10 billion annually enticing children to desire food brands and to pester parents to buy them. The result: American children consume more than one-third of their daily calories from soft drinks, sweets, salty snacks and fast food. Worse, food marketing subverts parental authority by making children believe they are supposed to be eating such foods and they—not their parents—know what is best for them to eat.

Today's marketing methods extend beyond television to include Internet games, product placements, character licensing and word-of-mouth campaigns—stealth methods likely to be invisible to

SECTION THREE
Readings

parents. When restrictions have been called for, the food industry has resisted, invoking parental responsibility and First Amendment rights, and proposing self-regulation instead. But because companies cannot be expected to act against corporate self-interest, government regulations are essential. Industry pressures killed attempts to regulate television advertising to children in the late 1970s, but obesity is a more serious problem now.

It is time to try again, this time to stop all forms of marketing foods to kids—both visible and stealth. Countries in Europe and elsewhere are taking such actions, and we could too. Controls on marketing may not be sufficient to prevent childhood obesity, but they would make it easier for parents to help children to eat more healthfully.

Marion Nestle, Paulette Goddard professor of nutrition, food studies and public health at New York University, is the author of Food Politics *(California) and* What to Eat *(North Point).*

Michael Pollan

Every five years or so the President of the United States signs an obscure piece of legislation that determines what happens on a couple of hundred million acres of private land in America, what sort of food Americans eat (and how much it costs) and, as a result, the health of our population. In a nation consecrated to the idea of private property and free enterprise, you would not think any piece of legislation could have such far-reaching effects, especially one about which so few of us—even the most politically aware—know anything. But in fact the American food system is a game played according to a precise set of rules that are written by the federal government with virtually no input from anyone beyond a handful of farm-state legislators. Nothing could do more to reform America's food system–and by doing so improve the condition of America's environment and public health–than if the rest of us were suddenly to weigh in.

The farm bill determines what our kids eat for lunch in school every day. Right now, the school lunch program is designed not around the goal of children's health but to help dispose of surplus agricultural commodities, especially cheap feedlot beef and dairy products, both high in fat.

The farm bill writes the regulatory rules governing the production of meat in this country, determining whether the meat we eat comes from sprawling, brutal, polluting factory farms and the big four meatpackers (which control 80 percent of the market) or from local farms.

Most important, the farm bill determines what crops the government will support—and in turn what kinds of foods will be plentiful and cheap. Today that means, by and large, corn and soybeans. These two crops are the building blocks of the fast-food nation: A McDonald's meal (and most of the processed food in your supermarket) consists of clever arrangements of corn and soybeans–the corn providing the added sugars, the soy providing the added fat, and both providing the feed for the animals. These crop subsidies (which are designed to encourage overproduction rather than to help farmers by supporting prices) are the reason that the cheapest calories in an American supermarket are precisely the unhealthiest. An American shopping for food on a budget soon discovers that a dollar buys hundreds more calories in the snack food or soda aisle than it does in the produce section. Why? Because the farm bill supports the growing of corn but not the growing of fresh carrots. In the midst of a national epidemic of diabetes and obesity our government is, in effect, subsidizing the production of high-fructose corn syrup.

This absurdity would not persist if more voters realized that the farm bill is not a parochial piece of legislation concerning only the interests of farmers. Today, because so few of us realize we have a dog in this fight, our legislators feel free to leave deliberations over the farm bill to the farm states, very often trading away their votes on agricultural policy for votes on issues that matter more to their constituents. But what could matter more than the health of our children and the health of our land?

Perhaps the problem begins with the fact that this legislation is commonly called "the farm bill—how many people these days even know a farmer or care about agriculture? Yet we all eat. So perhaps that's where we should start, now that the debate over the 2007 farm bill is about to be joined. This time around let's call it "the food bill" and put our legislators on notice that this is about us and we're paying attention.

Michael Pollan is the author, most recently, of In Defense of Food: An Eater's Manifesto. *He teaches journalism at UC, Berkeley.*

SECTION THREE

Readings

Wendell Berry

Alice Waters has asked me if I will propose one thing that could change the way Americans think about food. I will nominate two: hunger and knowledge.

Hunger causes people to think about food, as everybody knows. But in the present world this thinking is shallow. If you wish to solve the problem of hunger, and if you have money, you buy whatever food you like. For many years there has always been an abundance of food to buy and of money to buy it with, and so we have learned to take it for granted. Few of us have considered the possibility that someday we might go with money to buy food and find little or none to buy. And yet most of our food is now produced by industrial agriculture, which has proved to be immensely productive, but at the cost of destroying the means of production. It is enormously destructive of farmland, farm communities and farmers. It wastes soil, water, energy and life. It is highly centralized, genetically impoverished and dependent on cheap fossil fuels, on long-distance hauling and on consumers' ignorance. Its characteristic byproducts are erosion, pollution and financial despair. This is an agriculture with a short future.

Knowledge, a lot more knowledge in the minds of a lot more people, will be required to secure a long future for agriculture. Knowing how to grow food leads to food. Knowing how to grow food in the best ways leads to a dependable supply of food for a long time. At present our society and economy do not encourage or respect the best ways of food production. This is owing to the ignorance that is endemic to our society and economy. Most of our people, who have become notorious for the bulk of their food consumption, in fact know little about food and nothing about agriculture. Despite this ignorance, in which our politicians and intellectuals participate fully, some urban consumers are venturing into an authentic knowledge of food and food production, and they are demanding better food and, necessarily, better farming. When this demand grows large enough, our use of agricultural lands will change for the better. Under the best conditions, our land and farm population being so depleted, this change cannot come quickly. Whether or not it can come soon enough to avert hunger proportionate to our present ignorance, I do not know.

Wendell Berry, author of more than forty books of fiction, poetry and essays, has farmed a hillside in his native Henry County, Kentucky, for forty years. He has received numerous awards for his work, including the T.S. Eliot Award, the Aiken Taylor Award for poetry and the John Hay Award of the Orion Society.

Troy Duster and Elizabeth Ransom

Strong preferences for the kinds of food we eat are deeply rooted in the unexamined practices of the families, communities and cultural groups in which we grow up. From more than a half-century of social science research, we know that changing people's habitual behavior—from smoking to alcohol consumption, from drugs to junk food—is a mighty task. Individuals rarely listen to health messages and then change their ways.

If we as a nation are to alter our eating habits so that we make a notable dent in the coming health crisis around the pandemic of childhood obesity and Type II diabetes, it will be the result of long-term planning that will include going into the schools to change the way we learn about food. With less than 2 percent of the US population engaged with agriculture, a whole generation of people has lost valuable knowledge that comes from growing, preserving and preparing one's own food. A recent initiative by the City of Berkeley, California, represents a promising national model to fill this void. The city's Unified School District has approved a school lunch program that is far more than just a project to change what students eat at the noon hour. It is a daring attempt to change the institutional environment in which children learn about food at an early age, a comprehensive approach that has them planting and growing the food in a garden, learning biology through an engaged process, with some then cooking the food that they grow. If all goes well, they will learn about the complex relationship between nutrition and physiology so that it is an integrated experience—not a decontextualized, abstract, rote process.

But this is a major undertaking, and it will need close monitoring and fine-tuning. Rather than assuming that one size fits all in the school, we will need to find out what menu resonates with schools that are embedded within local cultures and climatic conditions"—

SECTION THREE
Readings

for example, teaching a health-mindful approach to Mexican, Chinese, Italian, Puerto Rican, Caribbean and Midwestern cuisine. Finally, we need to regulate the kinds of food sold in and around the school site"—much as we now do with smoking, alcohol and drugs. The transition from agrarian to modern society has created unforeseen health challenges. Adopting an engaged learning approach through agricultural production and consumption will help future generations learn what it means to eat healthy food and live healthy lives.

Troy Duster, director of the Institute for the History of Production of Knowledge at New York University, holds an appointment as Chancellor's Professor at the University of California, Berkeley. Elizabeth Ransom is a sociologist at the University of Richmond whose work focuses on globalization, food and the changing structure of agriculture.

Winona LaDuke

It's Manoominike Giizis, or the Wild Rice Making Moon, here on the White Earth reservation in northern Minnesota. The sound of a canoe moving through the wild rice beds on the Crow Wing or Rice lakes, the sound of laughter, the smell of wood-parched wild rice and the sound of a traditional drum at the celebration for the wild rice harvest links a traditional Anishinaabeg or Ojibwe people to a thousand years of culture and the ecosystem of a lake in a new millennium. This cultural relationship to food—manoomin, or wild rice—represents an essential part of what we need to do to repair the food system: We need to recover relationship.

Wild rice is the only North American grain, and today the Ojibwe are in a pitched battle to keep it from getting genetically engineered and patented. A similar battle is under way in Hawaii between Native Hawaiians and the University of Hawaii, which recently agreed to tear up patents on taro, a food sacred to Native Hawaiians. At one point "agriculture" was about the culture of food. Losing that culture—in favor of an American cultural monocrop, joined with an agricultural monocrop—puts us in a perilous state, threatening sustainability and our relationship to the natural world.

In the Ojibwe struggle to "keep it wild," we have found ourselves in an international movement of Slow Food and food sovereignty activists and communities who are seeking the same—the recovery or sustaining of relationship as a basic element of our humanity and as a critical strategy. In the Wild Rice Making Moon of the North Country, we will continue our traditions, and we will look across our lakes to the rice farmers of the rest of the world, to the taro farmers of the Pacific and to other communities working to protect their seeds for future generations, and we will know that this is how we insure that those generations will have what they need to be human, to be Anishinaabeg.

Winona LaDuke directs the White Earth Land Recovery Project and works on issues of bio-piracy, indigenous rights and renewable energy. Her five books include, most recently, Recovering the Sacred *(South End), and she is a two-time Green Party vice-presidential candidate. She lives on the White Earth Reservation in Minnesota. Her parents met when her father was selling wild rice.*

Peter Singer

There is one very simple thing that everyone can do to fix the food system. Don't buy factory-farm products.

Once, the animals we raised went out and gathered things we could not or would not eat. Cows ate grass, chickens pecked at worms or seeds. Now the animals are brought together and we grow food for them. We use synthetic fertilizers and oil-powered tractors to grow corn or soybeans. Then we truck it to the animals so they can eat it.

When we feed grains and soybeans to animals, we lose most of their nutritional value. The animals use it to keep their bodies warm and to develop bones and other body parts that we cannot eat. Pig farms use six pounds of grain for every pound of boneless meat we get from them. For cattle in feedlots, the ratio is 13:1. Even for chickens, the least inefficient factory-farmed meat, the ratio is 3:1.

Most Americans think the best thing they could do to cut their personal contributions to global warming is to swap their family car for a fuel-efficient hybrid like the Toyota Prius. Gidon Eshel and

SECTION THREE
Readings

465

Pamela Martin of the University of Chicago have calculated that typical meat-eating Americans would reduce their emissions even more if they switched to a vegan diet. Factory farming is not sustainable. It is also the biggest system of cruelty to animals ever devised. In the United States alone, every year nearly 10 billion animals live out their entire lives confined indoors. Hens are jammed into wire cages, five or six of them in a space that would be too small for even one hen to be able to spread her wings. Twenty thousand chickens are raised in a single shed, completely covering its floor. Pregnant sows are kept in crates too narrow for them to turn around, and too small for them to walk a few steps. Veal calves are similarly confined, and deliberately kept anemic.

This is not an ethically defensible system of food production. But in the United States—unlike in Europe—the political process seems powerless to constrain it. The best way to fight back is to stop buying its products. Going vegetarian is a good option, and going vegan, better still. But if you continue to eat animal products, at least boycott factory farms.

Peter Singer is professor of bioethics at Princeton University. His most recent book, co-authored with Jim Mason, is The Way We Eat: Why Our Food Choices Matter.

Vandana Shiva

Humanity has eaten more than 80,000 plant species through its evolution. More than 3,000 have been used consistently. However, we now rely on just eight crops to provide 75 percent of the world's food. With genetic engineering, production has narrowed to three crops: corn, soya, canola. Monocultures are destroying biodiversity, our health and the quality and diversity of food.

In 1998 India's indigenous edible oils made from mustard, coconut, sesame, linseed and groundnut processed in artisanal cold-press mills were banned, using "food safety" as an excuse. The restrictions on import of soya oil were simultaneously removed. Ten million farmers' livelihoods were threatened. One million oil mills in villages were closed. And millions of tons of artificially cheap GMO soya oil continue to be dumped on India. Women from the slums of

SECTION THREE

Readings

Delhi came out in a movement to reject soya and bring back mustard oil. "Sarson bachao, soyabean bhagao" (save the mustard, drive away the soyabean) was the women's call from the streets of Delhi. We did succeed in bringing back mustard through our "sarson satyagraha" (non-cooperation with the ban on mustard oil).

I was recently in the Amazon, where the same companies that dumped soya on India—Cargill and ADM—are destroying the Amazon to grow soya. Millions of acres of the Amazon rainforest—the lung, liver and heart of the global climate system—are being burned to grow soya for export. Cargill has built an illegal port at Santarém in Brazil and is driving the expansion of soya in the Amazon rainforest. Armed gangs take over the forest and use slaves to cultivate soya. When people like Sister Dorothy Stang oppose the destruction of the forests and the violence against people, they are assassinated.

People in Brazil and India are being threatened to promote a monoculture that benefits agribusiness. A billion people are without food because industrial monocultures robbed them of their livelihoods in agriculture and their food entitlements. Another 1.7 billion are suffering from obesity and food-related diseases. Monocultures lead to malnutrition—for those who are underfed as well as those who are overfed. In depending on monocultures, the food system is being made increasingly dependent on fossil fuels—for synthetic fertilizers, for running giant machinery and for long-distance transport, which adds "food miles."

Moving beyond monocultures has become an imperative for repairing the food system. Biodiverse small farms have higher productivity and generate higher incomes for farmers. And biodiverse diets provide more nutrition and better taste. Bringing back biodiversity to our farms goes hand in hand with bringing back small farmers on the land. Corporate control thrives on monocultures. Citizens' food freedom depends on biodiversity.

SECTION THREE
Readings

Dr. Vandana Shiva is a physicist, ecologist, activist, editor and author. She is the founder of the Research Foundation for Science, Technology and Ecology, a public interest research organization.

Carlo Petrini

By now it's practically a given that most people who produce food know nothing about gastronomy. In the past sixty years even the word "food" has been slowly emptied of its cultural meaning—of all the know-how and wisdom that should be naturally bound up with it. Industry and the production ethos have robbed people of the knowledge of food and reduced it to pure merchandise—a good to be consumed like any other.

So now gastronomy is seen as little more than folklore: diverting, yes (and nothing wrong with that), but vacuous, detached from our everyday lives. In fact, gastronomy is much more complex and profound. Gastronomy is a science, the science of "all that relates to man as a feeding animal," as Brillat-Savarin wrote in *The Physiology of Taste* (1825). It is a different kind of science, an interdisciplinary one that wants nothing to do with the ghettoization of knowledge or balkanization by specialty.

With its historical, anthropological, agricultural, economic, social and philosophical aspects, the science of gastronomy asks us to open our minds to the complexity of food systems, to think again about our own approach to our daily bread. It asks us to give food back its central role in our lives and the political agendas of those who govern. This also means returning to a respect for the earth, the source of all sustenance.

And it means a return to a sense of community that seems almost lost. We are always members of at least three communities at once: local, national and global. As global citizens, yes, we are destroying the planet—its equilibrium, its ecosystems and its biodiversity. As local citizens, though, we can make our own choices—choices that influence everyone's future. By producing, distributing, choosing and eating food of real quality we can save the world.

Gastronomic science tells us that the quality of food results from three fundamental and inseparable elements that I call the good, the clean and the just. This means paying attention to the taste and smell of food, because pleasure and happiness in food are a universal right (the good); making it sustainably, so that it does not consume more resources than it produces (the clean); and making it so that it creates no inequities and respects every person involved in its production (the just). By bringing food back to the center of our lives we commit ourselves to the future of the planet—and to our own happiness.

Carlo Petrini is the founder of the University of Gastronomic Sciences in Piedmont and Emilia Romagna, Italy. This article was translated from the Italian by Corby Kummer.

Eliot Coleman

Farmers may have strayed down a wrong path, but it isn't just agriculture's mistake. An addiction to treating the symptoms of problems rather than correcting their causes is an unwise choice made by our society as a whole. But the attitude that makes organic agriculture work could be the impetus for re-forming society.

The best organic farmers follow a pattern at odds with the pattern of chemical agriculture. As they become more proficient at working with the biology of the natural world, they purchase fewer and fewer inputs. Many purchase almost none at all. They use the natural fertility-improving resources of the farm by employing the benefits of deep-rooting legumes, green manures, crop and livestock rotations and so forth to correct the cause of soil fertility problems rather than attempting to treat the symptoms (poor yields, low quality) by purchasing chemical fertilizers. The same pattern applies to pest problems. By improving soil fertility, avoiding mineral imbalance, providing for adequate water drainage and air flow, growing suitable varieties and avoiding plant stress, organic farmers correct the causes of pest problems, thus preventing them, rather than treating the symptoms—insects and diseases—with toxic pesticides. Their aim is to cultivate ease and order rather than battle futilely against disease and disorder.

Like chemical agriculture, our economy is based on selling symptom treatments rather than trying to correct causes. For example, the medical profession peddles pills, potions and operations rather than stressing alternatives to destructive Twinkie nutrition, overstressed lifestyles and toxic pollution. Governments spend billions on armaments to prepare for wars or wage them (symptom treatment) instead of committing themselves to diplomacy and cooperation (cause correction). Although successful organic farmers demonstrate daily why correcting causes makes so much more sense than treating symptoms, this is not widely appreciated. If its implications were fully understood, organic farming would certainly

SECTION THREE
Readings

be suppressed. Its success exposes the artificiality of our symptom-focused economy and shows why society's most intractable problems never seem to get solved.

Eliot Coleman, who has been a farmer for almost forty years, is the author of Four Season Harvest *and* The New Organic Grower *(both Chelsea Green).*

Jim Hightower

In the very short span of about fifty years, we've allowed our politicians to do something remarkably stupid: turn America's food-policy decisions over to corporate lobbyists, lawyers and economists. These are people who could not run a watermelon stand if we gave them the melons and had the Highway Patrol flag down the customers for them—yet, they have taken charge of the decisions that direct everything from how and where food is grown to what our children eat in school.

As a result, America's food system (and much of the world's) has been industrialized, conglomeratized and globalized. This is food we're talking about, not widgets! Food, by its very nature, is meant to be agrarian, small-scale and local.

But the Powers That Be have turned the production of our edibles away from the high art of cooperating with nature into a high-cost system of always trying to overwhelm nature. They actually torture food—applying massive doses of pesticides, sex hormones, antibiotics, genetically manipulated organisms, artificial flavorings and color, chemical preservatives, ripening gas, irradiation...and so awfully much more. The attitude of agribusiness is that if brute force isn't working, you're probably just not using enough of it.

More fundamentally, these short-cut con artists have perverted the very concept of food. Rather than being both a process and product that nurtures us (in body and spirit) and nurtures our communities, food is approached by agribusiness as just another commodity that has no higher purpose than to fatten corporate profits.

There's our challenge. It's not a particular policy or agency that must be changed but the most basic attitude of policy-makers. And the only way we're going to get that done is for you and me to become the policy-makers, taking charge of every aspect of our food system—from farm to fork.

The good news is that this "good food" movement is already well under way and gaining strength every day. It receives little media coverage, but consumers in practically every city, town and neighborhood across America are reconnecting with local farmers and artisans to de industrialize, deconglomeratize, de-globalize—de-Wal-Martize—their food systems.

Of course, the Powers That Be sneer at these efforts, saying they can't succeed. But, as a friend of mine who is one of the successful pioneers in this burgeoning movement puts it: "Those who say it can't be done should not interrupt those who are doing it."

Look around wherever you are and you'll find local farmers, consumers, chefs, marketers, gardeners, environmentalists, workers, churches, co-ops, community organizers and just plain folks who are doing it. These are the Powers That Ought to Be—and I think they will be. Join them!

Jim Hightower (www.jimhightower.com) is a syndicated newspaper columnist, a radio commentor, and the author of six books, including Thieves in High Places *(Plume).*

SECTION THREE
Readings

Public Arguments about Human Dignity

Yuval Levin—Indignity and Bioethics

National Review Online, *May 14, 2008. Copyright © 2008 National Review, Inc. 215 Lexington Avenue, New York, NY 10016. Reprinted by permission.*

Human dignity has long been a contentious subject in American bioethics. A frequently employed if ill-defined concept in European political life, in international law, and in the ethical tradition of the West, dignity has had a particularly hard time finding its precise meaning and place in the Anglo-American sphere. Is it just a synonym for equality or autonomy, or does it describe something else—a concept foreign to our political vocabulary? And either way, does it belong in an American bioethics, or is it best left safely across the pond? Different scholars and observers through the years have taken for granted quite different definitions of the term, while others have simply denied its utility altogether.

To try to organize the dispute and help to make sense of the term, the President's Council on Bioethics—established by President Bush in 2001 to, among other things, "provide a forum for a national discussion of bioethical issues"—recently produced a collection of essays laying out the range of views on human dignity for public examination. The council (which I served as executive director during part of the president's first term) invited two dozen experts, including members of the council itself as well as outside academics and writers, to offer their thoughts on human dignity and bioethics.

The volume has so far drawn a modest response from bioethicists and others, some applauding the effort to lay out the range of opinions, and some bemoaning the lack of agreement on so seemingly basic a concept. But this week, in the latest issue of *The New Republic*, the volume has also elicited a bizarre and astonishing display of paranoid vitriol from an academic celebrity. Steven Pinker, the Harvard psychologist and best-selling author of books on language, cognition, and evolutionary biology, seems to have decided that the concept of human dignity is not only "stupid" but is a weapon of aggression in the arsenal of a religious crusade intent on crushing American liberty and "imposing a Catholic agenda on a secular democracy."

Pinker's essay is a striking exhibit of a set of attitudes toward religion and the West's moral tradition that has become surprisingly common among America's intellectual elite. It is a mix of fear, suspicion, and disgust that has a lot to do, for instance, with the Left's intense paranoia about the Bush administration, and with the peculiar notion that American conservatives have declared a "war on science"; and it involves more generally an inclination to reject any idea drawn in any way from a religiously inspired tradition—which unfortunately includes just about everything in the humanities.

These elements are all powerfully evident in Pinker's screed. After briefly introducing the subject, his essay manages almost entirely to ignore the substance of the volume under consideration (taking up no particular essay in the book, for instance) and addresses itself instead to what the author imagines is a sinister Catholic conspiracy to subject the nation to a papist theology of death. With deep alarm Pinker informs his readers that some of the contributors to the volume make their living at such "Christian institutions" as Georgetown University and that some of the essays even mention the Bible, which leads him to conclude that the work of the bioethics council, in this book and in general, "springs from a movement to impose a radical political agenda, fed by fervent religious impulses, onto American biomedicine."

This is, to begin with, patent nonsense. Even a cursory review of the council's reports and deliberations will demonstrate it has spent significantly less time than even its Clinton administration predecessor considering any explicitly religious views or discussing religious issues, and has in no way sought to ground any positions, arguments, or recommendations in religion. Huffing in his panicked flight from an imaginary inquisition, Pinker seems unable to distinguish between an openness to learning from the insights of the Western tradition and an assertion of sectarian theology. He even rejects the pedagogical value of literature (hectoring one contributor to the volume who has dared mention a novel), and seems to treat as a noxious pollutant any artifact of our civilization that has not been peer-reviewed by a committee of tenured biologists.

This leaves Pinker in the peculiar position of denying the grounds for even his own standards of ethics, though he is blissfully blind to the difficulty. Rather than human dignity, he wants to lean for support upon "personal autonomy—the idea that, because all

SECTION THREE
Readings

humans have the same minimum capacity to suffer, prosper, reason, and choose, no human has the right to impinge on the life, body, or freedom of another." But why not? Why should minimum capacities demand maximal protections if not for reasons rooted in the very traditions and sources he declares out of bounds, or a Popish cabal?

But Pinker will not wait to hear the answer. He rushes on to paint the bioethics council as a committee of pious executioners, arguing that "this government-sponsored bioethics does not want medical practice to maximize health and flourishing; it considers that quest to be a bad thing, not a good thing," and asserting without basis that the council (which, more than all of its predecessors in previous administrations, was designed to provide a diversity of opinion and not merely support for the positions of the president who appointed it) was "packed" with "conservative scholars and pundits, advocates of religious (particularly Catholic) principles in the public sphere, and writers with a paper trail of skittishness toward biomedical advances, together with a smattering of scientists (mostly with a reputation for being religious or politically conservative)." Pinker might have examined the record of the council's discussions (including its devastating grilling of him in 2003, which may help explain some of his vehemence), its reports, and the backgrounds of its members, especially the scientist members, for a sense of how absurdly misinformed is this diatribe.

He is not much better informed about the book he claims to have read, asserting, for instance, that no one was given an opportunity to defend the view that dignity means essentially nothing more than autonomy or is a useless or pernicious concept, though several of the essays in the volume (most notably Patricia Churchland's contribution, and elements of Daniel Dennett's, among others) do just that.

But Pinker saves his most brazenly venomous and disingenuous assault for one of the volume's contributors in particular: Leon Kass, the council's former chairman. He begins with a sweepingly inaccurate survey of Kass's views and works, and misleadingly implies that a passage he quotes from Kass's 1994 book about eating is from Kass's essay on dignity in the volume being reviewed, later referring again to the passage while never offering any context. He says Kass has "pro-death anti-freedom views," and asserts that Kass is a "vociferous advocate of a central role for religion in morality and public life." A vociferous person is publicly insistent—can Pinker point to a single instance of Kass calling for a central role for religion in public life? Pinker concludes by repeating the scurrilous lie that Kass "fired" two members of the bioethics council who disagreed with him "on embryonic stem-cell research, on therapeutic cloning (which Kass was in favor of criminalizing), and on the distortions of science that kept finding their way into Council reports." Disagreement on stem cell research and therapeutic cloning were an intentional function of the original design of the council's membership, as about half its members disagreed with President Bush's views on one or another of those issues, and were chosen with that disagreement in mind. Neither of the two members Pinker has in mind was by any means the most vocal or active of these opponents, their departures had nothing to do with their substantive views, and several of the members named to the council since their departure have also opposed the President's views on these issues. Scientific content in all of the council's reports, meanwhile, was carefully vetted with outside experts before publication, and it is no surprise that Pinker offers no specific instances of "distortions of science" — there are none he could offer.

Loath to rest easy with religious bigotry and slander, however, Pinker concludes with a stunning display of confusion, managing to mystify himself with simple questions and to dismiss centuries of debate with a shrug. He then informs us that dignity is relative and fungible, and—at last, the punch line—that it is in any case just a phenomenon of human perception. He says those who disagree with him have blood on their hands ("even if progress were delayed a mere decade by moratoria, red tape, and funding taboos (to say nothing of the threat of criminal prosecution), millions of people with degenerative diseases and failing organs would needlessly suffer and die") and so, by implication, that no limit on scientific research could be justified on any grounds other than safety.

It would be hard to answer the bioethics council's thoughtful and varied collection with a less appropriate rejoinder than Pinker's insulting, ill-informed, and anti-intellectual tirade. He misrepresents the most elementary facts about the council's work and intentions, repeating baseless charges and engaging in crude character assassination; and his assertion that the council is intolerant of dissenting opinion is belied by the fact that his rant is based on remarks he actually delivered at a council meeting, by invitation. His

SECTION THREE
Readings

475

fears of a religious, and especially a Catholic, plot to overthrow democracy are absurd. And his insistence on filtering out of American life any hint of religious influence is badly misguided.

Even if dignity remains difficult to define, undignified public discourse is easy to discern, and Pinker has offered an obvious example.

Yuval Levin is a fellow at the Ethics and Public Policy Center and senior editor of The New Atlantis *magazine. He is a former executive director of the President's Council on Bioethics.*

SECTION THREE
Readings

Steven Pinker—The Stupidity of Dignity

Conservative bioethics' latest, most dangerous ploy.

The New Republic, *May 28, 2008. Reprinted by permission of* The New Republic. *Copyright © 2008.*

 This spring, the President's Council on Bioethics released a 555-page report, titled *Human Dignity and Bioethics*. The Council, created in 2001 by George W. Bush, is a panel of scholars charged with advising the president and exploring policy issues related to the ethics of biomedical innovation, including drugs that would enhance cognition, genetic manipulation of animals or humans, therapies that could extend the lifespan, and embryonic stem cells and so-called "therapeutic cloning" that could furnish replacements for diseased tissue and organs. Advances like these, if translated into freely undertaken treatments, could make millions of people better off and no one worse off. So what's not to like? The advances do not raise the traditional concerns of bioethics, which focuses on potential harm and coercion of patients or research subjects. What, then, are the ethical concerns that call for a presidential council?

Many people are vaguely disquieted by developments (real or imagined) that could alter minds and bodies in novel ways. Romantics and Greens tend to idealize the natural and demonize technology. Traditionalists and conservatives by temperament distrust radical change. Egalitarians worry about an arms race in enhancement techniques. And anyone is likely to have a "yuck" response when contemplating unprecedented manipulations of our biology. The President's Council has become a forum for the airing of this disquiet, and the concept of "dignity" a rubric for expounding on it. This collection of essays is the culmination of a long effort by the Council to place dignity at the center of bioethics. The general feeling is that, even if a new technology would improve life and health and decrease suffering and waste, it might have to be rejected, or even outlawed, if it affronted human dignity.

Whatever that is. The problem is that "dignity" is a squishy, subjective notion, hardly up to the heavyweight moral demands assigned to it. The bioethicist Ruth Macklin, who had been fed up with loose talk about dignity intended to squelch research and therapy, threw down the gauntlet in a 2003 editorial, "Dignity Is a Useless Concept." Macklin argued that bioethics has done just fine

SECTION THREE
Readings

with the principle of "personal autonomy"—the idea that, because all humans have the same minimum capacity to suffer, prosper, reason, and choose, no human has the right to impinge on the life, body, or freedom of another. This is why informed consent serves as the bedrock of ethical research and practice, and it clearly rules out the kinds of abuses that led to the birth of bioethics in the first place, such as Mengele's sadistic pseudoexperiments in Nazi Germany and the withholding of treatment to indigent black patients in the infamous Tuskegee syphilis study. Once you recognize the principle of autonomy, Macklin argued, "dignity" adds nothing.

Goaded by Macklin's essay, the Council acknowledged the need to put dignity on a firmer conceptual foundation. This volume of 28 essays and commentaries by Council members and invited contributors is their deliverable, addressed directly to President Bush. The report does not, the editors admit, settle the question of what dignity is or how it should guide our policies. It does, however, reveal a great deal about the approach to bioethics represented by the Council. And what it reveals should alarm anyone concerned with American biomedicine and its promise to improve human welfare. For this government-sponsored bioethics does not want medical practice to maximize health and flourishing; it considers that quest to be a bad thing, not a good thing.

To understand the source of this topsy-turvy value system, one has to look more deeply at the currents that underlie the Council. Although the *Dignity* report presents itself as a scholarly deliberation of universal moral concerns, it springs from a movement to impose a radical political agenda, fed by fervent religious impulses, onto American biomedicine.

The report's oddness begins with its list of contributors. Two (Adam Schulman and Daniel Davis) are Council staffers, and wrote superb introductory pieces. Of the remaining 21, four (Leon R. Kass, David Gelernter, Robert George, and Robert Kraynak) are vociferous advocates of a central role for religion in morality and public life, and another eleven work for Christian institutions (all but two of the institutions Catholic). Of course, institutional affiliation does not entail partiality, but, with three-quarters of the invited contributors having religious entanglements, one gets a sense that the fix is in. A deeper look confirms it.

Conspicuous by their absence are several fields of expertise that one might have thought would have something to offer any discussion of dignity and biomedicine. None of the contributors is a life scientist"—or a psychologist, an anthropologist, a sociologist, or a historian. According to one of the introductory chapters, the Council takes a "critical view of contemporary academic bioethics and of the way bioethical questions are debated in the public square"—so critical, it seems, that Macklin (the villain of almost every piece) was not invited to expand on her argument, nor were mainstream bioethicists (who tend to be sympathetic to Macklin's viewpoint) given an opportunity to defend it.

Despite these exclusions, the volume finds room for seven essays that align their arguments with Judeo-Christian doctrine. We read passages that assume the divine authorship of the Bible, that accept the literal truth of the miracles narrated in Genesis (such as the notion that the biblical patriarchs lived up to 900 years), that claim that divine revelation is a source of truth, that argue for the existence of an immaterial soul separate from the physiology of the brain, and that assert that the Old Testament is the only grounds for morality (for example, the article by Kass claims that respect for human life is rooted in Genesis 9:6, in which God instructs the survivors of his Flood in the code of vendetta: "Whoso sheddeth man's blood, by man shall his blood be shed, for in the image of God was man made").

The Judeo-Christian—in some cases, explicitly biblical"—arguments found in essay after essay in this volume are quite extraordinary. Yet, aside from two paragraphs in a commentary by Daniel Dennett, the volume contains no critical examination of any of its religious claims.

SECTION THREE

Readings

How did the United States, the world's scientific powerhouse, reach a point at which it grapples with the ethical challenges of twenty-first-century biomedicine using Bible stories, Catholic doctrine, and woolly rabbinical allegory? Part of the answer lies with the outsize influence of Kass, the Council's founding director (and an occasional contributor to TNR), who came to prominence in the 1970s with his moralistic condemnation of in vitro fertilization, then popularly known as "test-tube babies." As soon as the procedure became feasible, the country swiftly left Kass behind, and, for most people today, it is an ethical no-brainer. That did not stop Kass from subsequently assailing a broad swath of other medical practices as ethically troubling, including organ transplants, autopsies, contraception, antidepressants, even the dissection of cadavers.

Kass frequently makes his case using appeals to "human dignity" (and related expressions like "fundamental aspects of human existence" and "the central core of our humanity"). In an essay with the revealing title "L'Chaim and Its Limits, " Kass voiced his frustration that the rabbis he spoke with just couldn't see what was so terrible about technologies that would extend life, health, and fertility. "The desire to prolong youthfulness," he wrote in reply, is "an expression of a childish and narcissistic wish incompatible with devotion to posterity." The years that would be added to other people's lives, he judged, were not worth living: "Would professional tennis players really enjoy playing 25 percent more games of tennis?" And, as empirical evidence that "mortality makes life matter," he notes that the Greek gods lived "shallow and frivolous lives"—an example of his disconcerting habit of treating fiction as fact. (Kass cites *Brave New World* five times in his *Dignity* essay.)

Kass has a problem not just with longevity and health but with the modern conception of freedom. There is a "mortal danger," he writes, in the notion "that a person has a right over his body, a right that allows him to do whatever he wants to do with it." He is troubled by cosmetic surgery, by gender reassignment, and by women who postpone motherhood or choose to remain single in their twenties. Sometimes his fixation on dignity takes him right off the deep end:

> Worst of all from this point of view are those more uncivilized forms of eating, like licking an ice cream cone"—a catlike activity that has been made acceptable in informal America but that still offends those who know eating in public is offensive. ... Eating on the street"—even when undertaken, say, because one is between appointments and has no other time to eat"—displays [a] lack of self-control: It beckons enslavement to the belly. ... Lacking utensils for cutting and lifting to mouth, he will often be seen using his teeth for tearing off chewable portions, just like any animal. ... This doglike feeding, if one must engage in it, ought to be kept from public view, where, even if we feel no shame, others are compelled to witness our shameful behavior.

And, in 2001, this man, whose pro-death, anti-freedom views put him well outside the American mainstream, became the President's adviser on bioethics"—a position from which he convinced the president to outlaw federally funded research that used new stem-cell lines. In his speech announcing the stem-cell policy, Bush invited Kass to form the Council. Kass packed it with conservative scholars and pundits, advocates of religious (particularly Catholic) principles in the public sphere, and writers with a paper trail of skittishness toward biomedical advances, together with a smattering of scientists (mostly with a reputation for being religious or politically conservative). After several members opposed Kass on embryonic stem-cell research, on therapeutic cloning (which Kass was in favor of criminalizing), and on the distortions of science that kept finding their way into Council reports, Kass fired two of them (biologist Elizabeth Blackburn and philosopher William May) and replaced them with Christian-affiliated scholars.

Though Kass has jawboned his version of bioethics into governmental deliberation and policy, it is not just a personal obsession of his but part of a larger movement, one that is increasingly associated with Catholic institutions. (In 2005, Kass relinquished the Council chairmanship to Edmund Pellegrino, an 85-year-old medical ethicist and former president of the Catholic University of America.) Everyone knows about the Bush administration's alliance with evangelical Protestantism. But the pervasive Catholic flavoring of the Council, particularly its *Dignity* report, is at first glance puzzling. In fact, it is part of a powerful but little-known development in American politics, recently documented by Damon Linker in his book *The Theocons*.

SECTION THREE
Readings

For two decades, a group of intellectual activists, many of whom had jumped from the radical left to the radical right, has urged that we rethink the Enlightenment roots of the American social order. The recognition of a right to life, liberty, and the pursuit of happiness and the mandate of government to secure these rights are too tepid, they argue, for a morally worthy society. This impoverished vision has only led to anomie, hedonism, and rampant immoral behavior such as illegitimacy, pornography, and abortion. Society should aim higher than this bare-bones individualism and promote conformity to more rigorous moral standards, ones that could be applied to our behavior by an authority larger than ourselves.

Since episodes of divine revelation seem to have decreased in recent millennia, the problem becomes who will formulate and interpret these standards. Most of today's denominations are not up to the task: Evangelical Protestantism is too anti-intellectual, and mainstream Protestantism and Judaism too humanistic. The Catholic Church, with its long tradition of scholarship and its rock-solid moral precepts, became the natural home for this movement, and the journal *First Things*, under the leadership of Father Richard John Neuhaus, its mouthpiece. Catholicism now provides the intellectual muscle behind a movement that embraces socially conservative Jewish and Protestant intellectuals as well. When Neuhaus met with Bush in 1998 as he was planning his run for the presidency, they immediately hit it off.

Three of the original Council members (including Kass) are board members of First Things, and Neuhaus himself contributed an essay to the *Dignity* volume. In addition, five other members have contributed articles to *First Things* over the years. The concept of dignity is natural ground on which to build an obstructionist bioethics. An alleged breach of dignity provides a way for third parties to pass judgment on actions that are knowingly and willingly chosen by the affected individuals. It thus offers a moralistic justification for expanded government regulation of science, medicine, and private life. And the Church's franchise to guide people in the most profound events of their lives"—birth, death, and reproduction"—is in danger of being undermined when biomedicine scrambles the rules. It's not surprising, then, that "dignity" is a recurring theme in Catholic doctrine: The word appears more than 100 times in the 1997 edition of the Catechism and is a leitmotif in the Vatican's recent pronouncements on biomedicine.

To be fair, most of the chapters in the *Dignity* volume don't appeal directly to Catholic doctrine, and of course the validity of an argument cannot be judged from the motives or affiliations of its champions. Judged solely on the merits of their arguments, how well do the essayists clarify the concept of dignity?

By their own admission, not very well. Almost every essayist concedes that the concept remains slippery and ambiguous. In fact, it spawns outright contradictions at every turn. We read that slavery and degradation are morally wrong because they take someone's dignity away. But we also read that nothing you can do to a person, including enslaving or degrading him, can take his dignity away. We read that dignity reflects excellence, striving, and conscience, so that only some people achieve it by dint of effort and character. We also read that everyone, no matter how lazy, evil, or mentally impaired, has dignity in full measure. Several essayists play the genocide card and claim that the horrors of the twentieth century are what you get when you fail to hold dignity sacrosanct. But one hardly needs the notion of "dignity" to say why it's wrong to gas six million Jews or to send Russian dissidents to the gulag.

So, despite the best efforts of the contributors, the concept of dignity remains a mess. The reason, I think, is that dignity has three features that undermine any possibility of using it as a foundation for bioethics.

First, *dignity is relative.* One doesn't have to be a scientific or moral relativist to notice that ascriptions of dignity vary radically with the time, place, and beholder. In olden days, a glimpse of stocking was looked on as something shocking. We chuckle at the photographs of Victorians in starched collars and wool suits hiking in the woods on a sweltering day, or at the Brahmins and patriarchs of countless societies who consider it beneath their dignity to pick up a dish or play with a child. Thorstein Veblen wrote of a French king who considered it beneath his dignity to move his throne back from the fireplace, and one night roasted to death when his attendant failed to show up. Kass finds other people licking an ice-cream cone to be shamefully undignified; I have no problem with it.

Second, *dignity is fungible.* The Council and Vatican treat dignity as a sacred value, never to be compromised. In fact, every one of us voluntarily and repeatedly relinquishes dignity for other goods in life. Getting out of a small car is undignified. Having sex is undignified. Doffing your belt and spread-eagling to allow a security guard to slide a wand up your crotch is undignified. Most pointedly, modern medicine is a gantlet of indignities. Most readers of this article have undergone a pelvic or rectal examination, and many have had the pleasure of a colonoscopy as well. We repeatedly vote with our feet (and other body parts) that dignity is a trivial value, well worth trading off for life, health, and safety.

SECTION THREE
Readings

Third, *dignity can be harmful.* In her comments on the *Dignity* volume, Jean Bethke Elshtain rhetorically asked, "Has anything good ever come from denying or constricting human dignity?" The answer is an emphatic "yes." Every sashed and be-medaled despot reviewing his troops from a lofty platform seeks to command respect through ostentatious displays of dignity. Political and religious repressions are often rationalized as a defense of the dignity of a state, leader, or creed: Just think of the Salman Rushdie fatwa, the Danish cartoon riots, or the British schoolteacher in Sudan who faced flogging and a lynch mob because her class named a teddy bear Mohammed. Indeed, totalitarianism is often the imposition of a leader's conception of dignity on a population, such as the identical uniforms in Maoist China or the burqas of the Taliban.

A free society disempowers the state from enforcing a conception of dignity on its citizens. Democratic governments allow satirists to poke fun at their leaders, institutions, and social mores. And they abjure any mandate to define "some vision of 'the good life'" or the "dignity of using [freedom] well" (two quotes from the Council's volume). The price of freedom is tolerating behavior by others that may be undignified by our own lights. I would be happy if Britney Spears and "American Idol" would go away, but I put up with them in return for not having to worry about being arrested by the ice-cream police. This trade-off is very much in America's DNA and is one of its great contributions to civilization: my country 'tis of thee, sweet land of liberty.

SECTION THREE

Readings

So is dignity a useless concept? Almost. The word does have an identifiable sense, which gives it a claim, though a limited one, on our moral consideration.

Dignity is a phenomenon of human perception. Certain signals from the world trigger an attribution in the mind of a perceiver. Just as converging lines in a drawing are a cue for the perception of depth, and differences in loudness between the two ears cue us to the position of a sound, certain features in another human being trigger ascriptions of worth. These features include signs of composure, cleanliness, maturity, attractiveness, and control of the body. The perception of dignity in turn elicits a response in the perceiver.

Just as the smell of baking bread triggers a desire to eat it, and the sight of a baby's face triggers a desire to protect it, the appearance of dignity triggers a desire to esteem and respect the dignified person.

This explains why dignity is morally significant: We should not ignore a phenomenon that causes one person to respect the rights and interests of another. But it also explains why dignity is relative, fungible, and often harmful. Dignity is skin-deep: it's the sizzle, not the steak; the cover, not the book. What ultimately matters is respect for the person, not the perceptual signals that typically trigger it. Indeed, the gap between perception and reality makes us vulnerable to dignity illusions. We may be impressed by signs of dignity without underlying merit, as in the tin-pot dictator, and fail to recognize merit in a person who has been stripped of the signs of dignity, such as a pauper or refugee.

Exactly what aspects of dignity should we respect? For one thing, people generally want to be seen as dignified. Dignity is thus one of the interests of a person, alongside bodily integrity and personal property, that other people are obligated to respect. We don't want anyone to stomp on our toes; we don't want anyone to steal our hubcaps; and we don't want anyone to open the bathroom door when we're sitting on the john. A value on dignity in this precise sense does have an application to biomedicine, namely greater attention to the dignity of patients when it does not compromise their medical treatment. The volume contains fine discussions by Pellegrino and by Rebecca Dresser on the avoidable humiliations that today's patients are often forced to endure (like those hideous hospital smocks that are open at the back). No one could object to valuing dignity in this sense, and that's the point. When the concept of dignity is precisely specified, it becomes a mundane matter of thoughtfulness pushing against callousness and bureaucratic inertia, not a contentious moral conundrum. And, because it amounts to treating people in the way that they wish to be treated, ultimately it's just another application of the principle of autonomy.

There is a second reason to give dignity a measure of cautious respect. Reductions in dignity may harden the perceiver's heart and loosen his inhibitions against mistreating the person. When people are degraded and humiliated, such as Jews in Nazi Germany being forced to wear yellow armbands or dissidents in the Cultural Revolution being forced to wear grotesque haircuts and costumes,

SECTION THREE
Readings

onlookers find it easier to despise them. Similarly, when refugees, prisoners, and other pariahs are forced to live in squalor, it can set off a spiral of dehumanization and mistreatment. This was demonstrated in the famous Stanford prison experiment, in which volunteers assigned to be "prisoners" had to wear smocks and leg irons and were referred to by serial numbers instead of names. The volunteers assigned to be "guards" spontaneously began to brutalize them. Note, though, that all these cases involve coercion, so once again they are ruled out by autonomy and respect for persons. So, even when breaches of dignity lead to an identifiable harm, it's ultimately autonomy and respect for persons that gives us the grounds for condemning it.

Could there be cases in which a *voluntary* relinquishing of dignity leads to callousness in onlookers and harm to third parties"— what economists call negative externalities? In theory, yes. Perhaps if people allowed their corpses to be publicly desecrated, it would encourage violence against the bodies of the living. Perhaps the sport of dwarf-tossing encourages people to mistreat all dwarves. Perhaps violent pornography encourages violence against women. But, for such hypotheses to justify restrictive laws, they need empirical support. In one's imagination, anything can lead to anything else: Allowing people to skip church can lead to indolence; letting women drive can lead to sexual licentiousness. In a free society, one cannot empower the government to outlaw any behavior that offends someone just because the offendee can pull a hypothetical future injury out of the air. No doubt Mao, Savonarola, and Cotton Mather could provide plenty of reasons why letting people do what they wanted would lead to the breakdown of society.

The sickness in theocon bioethics goes beyond imposing a Catholic agenda on a secular democracy and using "dignity" to condemn anything that gives someone the creeps. Ever since the cloning of Dolly the sheep a decade ago, the panic sown by conservative bioethicists, amplified by a sensationalist press, has turned the public discussion of bioethics into a miasma of scientific illiteracy. *Brave New World*, a work of fiction, is treated as inerrant prophesy. Cloning is confused with resurrecting the dead or mass-producing babies.

Longevity becomes "immortality," improvement becomes "perfection," the screening for disease genes becomes "designer babies" or even "reshaping the species." The reality is that biomedical research is a Sisyphean struggle to eke small increments in health from a staggeringly complex, entropy-beset human body. It is not, and probably never will be, a runaway train.

A major sin of theocon bioethics is exactly the one that it sees in biomedical research: overweening hubris. In every age, prophets foresee dystopias that never materialize, while failing to anticipate the real revolutions. Had there been a President's Council on Cyberethics in the 1960s, no doubt it would have decried the threat of the Internet, since it would inexorably lead to 1984, or to computers "taking over" like HAL in *2001*. Conservative bioethicists presume to soothsay the outcome of the quintessentially unpredictable endeavor called scientific research. And they would stage-manage the kinds of social change that, in a free society, only emerge as hundreds of millions of people weigh the costs and benefits of new developments for themselves, adjusting their mores and dealing with specific harms as they arise, as they did with in vitro fertilization and the Internet.

Worst of all, theocon bioethics flaunts a callousness toward the billions of non-geriatric people, born and unborn, whose lives or health could be saved by biomedical advances. Even if progress were delayed a mere decade by moratoria, red tape, and funding taboos (to say nothing of the threat of criminal prosecution), millions of people with degenerative diseases and failing organs would needlessly suffer and die. And that would be the biggest affront to human dignity of all.

SECTION THREE
Readings

Steven Pinker is Johnstone Professor of Psychology at Harvard and the author of The Stuff of Thought.

SECTION THREE
Readings

Section Four

Revision and Reflection

INTRODUCTION: WE DARE TO TALK ABOUT ELOQUENCE

By Carol Nowotny-Young

Why Revise? Why Reflect? Why Not Just Be Done with It?

In the course of reading and working through assignments based on the concepts of this book, you may have lost sight of the fact that all of it—the book, your assignments, what you have learned during this course—is about writing, first and foremost. True, you have been working on particular genres of writing, especially those most used in academic and public spheres, but the same principles that hold for writing good short stories, novels, poems, plays, and creative essays hold true for these genres of writing as well. Writing is a craft—which means that regardless of the genre you are writing in and the topic you are writing about, you need to make sure it skillfully, clearly, and maybe even eloquently communicates to its audience.

Although it may seem as though most writing that occurs in academia or in various workplaces is anything but pleasurable to read, it nonetheless is true that the more pleasurable you make the reading experience for your audience, the more likely they are to read closely and carefully, not only grasping what you have to say but better understanding and remembering it. How often has it happened to you that you have read through a few pages of a reading assignment for a class, only to realize that you remember nothing of what you just read? Of course, it could be that you were tired and distracted or that the material was overly complex, but more than likely you didn't grasp what you were reading because the writer didn't make it easy for you to pay attention to it. This is not to say that eloquent writing is entertaining, even though sometimes it definitely is. Eloquent writing may not be entertaining in the least, but it holds your attention.

You may have guessed by now that by "eloquent," I am referring to writing that keeps a reader engaged in the text, absorbed by what the writing says. You may be used to thinking of eloquence as a clever or especially moving use and arrangement of words, and in some definitions and uses of the word, it may mean exactly that. However, that type of eloquence is usually the province of the professional writer, one who has dedicated her life to using and arranging words in clever or moving ways. I want you to think of eloquence as something achievable for the person who just needs to communicate clearly. And since communication is a two-way dynamic—that is, it involves not only someone putting words out for others to hear or read, but also someone else hearing or reading and trying to comprehend the words—the writer needs to give some thought to his accomplice in this act of communication: the reader. According to William Zinsser, a writer who has spent a great deal of effort making his writing eloquent and writing books to help others make their writing eloquent, a reader is defined as "someone with an attention span of about sixty seconds—a person assailed by forces competing for the minutes that might otherwise be spent on a magazine or a book" (9). Most readers don't have to read your writing; that means you have to make them *want* to read your writing. And you might as well include your teacher in this reader category. Yes, your teacher is paid to read your writing, and he will slog through it no matter what. But while you're at it, why not make your writing eloquent, so instead of getting grouchy and impatient while he slogs through that essay, your teacher becomes absorbed in it, maybe even too absorbed to give much attention to the inevitable errors that escaped your proofreading eye. Did you say you wanted an A on your paper? Making it eloquent (as well as conforming to the assignment, by the way) is more than half the battle toward getting that A. As William Zinsser also wrote, "The person snoozing in a chair, holding a magazine or a book, is a person who was being given too much unnecessary trouble by the writer" (9). If you give your teacher "too much unnecessary trouble" in reading your essay, you are not likely to get the grade you want. If, later, when you have graduated and are working in your field, you give your readers (in this case, co-workers, colleagues, superiors, customers) "too much unnecessary trouble," the consequences could be even graver—loss of a project, loss of respect by your colleagues, loss of opportunities for advancement, even loss of your job.

What Does it Take to Become Eloquent?

Okay, so now that you're feeling a bit stressed about all those "losses" I just piled on top of you, let's look at the remedy: revision and reflection. Although those are two separate words, the process of each goes hand-in-hand with the process of the other. You begin revising when you begin reflecting upon what you have written. As you will hear from me as well as others, nobody is born an accomplished writer; nobody is born with eloquence at their fingertips. Some people are born with the ability to process language well and to think easily in metaphoric ways. But, like the person with the talent to become a virtuoso violinist, the talented writer first has to learn how to use the tools of the craft, has to look at how others have accomplished certain effects, has to practice, practice, and practice AND be corrected by someone who knows the craft and is proficient in it herself. Yes, even though you hate getting your papers back full of red ink, this feedback is part of the process of learning to write.

Let me tell you a story. I decided when I was of a certain age (not childhood, adolescence, or young adulthood) that I was going to learn how to play the violin. I had always loved the sound of the violin, and now I was going to learn to make that sound myself. Now, I wasn't coming to this undertaking as a complete novice; I had learned to play the piano, clarinet, and guitar when I was a child, and I had even majored in music as an undergraduate. I had a trained ear, knew how to read music, and was well aware of the discipline it would take to become even moderately proficient at the violin. I went into my lessons with eyes wide open. At first, my trained ear couldn't bear to hear the only sounds I was capable of producing on my violin. I spent my practice sessions and my lessons wincing at how I played. I knew very well how the music was supposed to sound; I just didn't know how to make it sound that way. But I listened to the advice of my teachers, and gradually I improved. After I got to the point where I could occasionally play something that didn't sound too bad, I expected to start getting a good word or two from my teacher. Praise, however, was not forthcoming. The best I could get out of him was "Well, now that's sounding more like what it should sound like." Once in a great while, I would even play something that sounded halfway good to my ear. Invariably, when that happened, I would assume that my teacher would say, "Wow, that sounded good!" And, invariably, instead of saying that, he would point out some areas that I hadn't played quite right.

The lesson I was learning as a student of the violin was not lost on me in my own classroom. Even though the feedback I was giving my students was on writing, not music, it didn't differ markedly in intent and spirit from the feedback my violin teacher was giving me.

I was reminded of how much it hurts to think I had done something especially well, only to be told about what I didn't do well. Whenever one of my students handed me an essay and said, "I think that's the best writing I've ever done," I would wince inwardly, knowing that I would have to point out mistakes and assess the weaknesses of the writing. When I looked at the essay, I would hope against hope that it really WAS superior writing, that I could just say, "You're right. I've never seen such amazing writing from you! Bravo!" But that usually didn't happen. And even though I knew how my student would feel when she got her paper back with my comments all over it, I also knew that she needed those comments if she was ever going to produce the best writing she had ever done. Because just as I had found out from being a student of the violin that the remedy for not playing perfectly was to go back and practice some more, I already knew from being a teacher of writing that the only remedy for not writing perfectly (and I use this term loosely, by the way, as there is no such thing as "perfection" in any art or craft) is to go back and practice writing some more.

This is the way to become eloquent: heed the feedback you are given; go back and practice with this feedback in mind. Although you wouldn't want to continuously revise the same piece of writing over and over (just as in learning to play the violin, I haven't played the same piece of music over and over), think about the fact that every time you write, you are practicing your writing. This includes letters and e-mails, blogs, notes you take in class, journals or diaries you write in, even annotations you write in textbooks. Every one of these activities requires that you write in a way that accounts for what your audience will need or expect, fulfills the purpose for the writing, and is as clear as you can make it. This includes writing you do only for yourself. Have you ever written a note to yourself and then later wondered what you meant by it? And I'm not talking about just being able to read your own handwriting. Whenever I write myself notes, I try to think of words that will jog my memory for what I'm trying to remember or write in such a way that I will immediately know what I was trying to tell myself. When you write to others, you even more need to use language and methods that will tell them what you meant to say. While this may seem self-evident and simple, it's much harder than it seems and takes much more effort than one might think.

Revising and Reflecting in this Section

By this time in your class, you have done lots of revising. You may have even done some reflecting (actually, if you've revised, you've also reflected—that is, thought about how you could change something in your essay and why it might be better than what you originally wrote).

But now your instructor may ask you to do a different kind of revising, one that you may be used to thinking of as rewriting. What if you've written an essay, only to discover that you wrote it for the wrong audience or in the wrong genre? At this point in the semester, your instructor may ask you to take your public argument essay and cast it in another form or write it to a different audience (or both). This involves reflecting. If you write to a different audience, what will have to change? Will you have to use a different voice, explain some things you didn't explain in the original, take out some explanations you included in the original, use different examples, highlight different sources, or even create a different thesis? If you change the genre—say, from a newspaper op-ed piece to a magazine article—how will you have to change the writing? Will one require a different paragraphing or sentence style than the other? Will you have to go into more depth in one than in the other? Will you have to include more examples or facts in one than in the other? Will you have to change the way you organize the material? Before you make any changes in genre or audience, you will need to think deeply about all the changes in the writing that will have to accompany any change in the rhetorical situation.

To complicate matters further, your instructor may even ask you to change your public argument essay into a visual/spatial piece, a presentation you could give in class or even in a more public venue for a wider audience. Now you really have to think about everything you will need to revise. A presentation means your audience is in front of you, not reading your essay in the privacy of their own homes. They might ask questions; they might even start falling asleep or rolling their eyes. In order to understand what you present to them, they will need you to provide some visual prompts, to speak clearly in an organized manner, to move through the argument a little more slowly than you may want to so that they can more easily follow and digest what you are presenting. They really will want you to be interesting.

Now it really sounds intimidating. But if you reflect carefully on the feedback you were given on your written public argument, think about who your audience will be and what they will need and expect from you, and consider various methods of expressing the points of your argument in a visual/spatial way, you can be very successful with this project.

Where Do You Go from Here?

It will happen often in your future career that you will be asked to turn a report into a presentation or proposal into a speech. You might be asked to expand an initial inquiry into a full-blown article or report. This section will help you do that. All of it is based on revision skills. If you know how to take a piece of writing and make it better, you will be able to turn a piece of writing into something different from its original form. Both processes require lots of reflection and revising and differ only in the direction you take to get to your finished product.

In Chapter 18, "Reflection and the Art of Revision," I'll go into more depth about what reflection is and how it can help you revise. In Chapter 19, "Global Revision," Faith Kurtyka describes what global revision is and how to go about it to not only improve your writing but also to turn a piece into a different kind of writing. In Chapter 20, "Revising for Style," Star Medzerian shows you how manipulating point of view, use of sources, and word choice may change a lackluster piece of writing into a, well, more eloquent argument that engages your audience and better serves your purposes. In Chapter 21, "Reflecting on the Revision Process," Erica Cirillo-McCarthy shows you some methods of reflection that will help you think more productively about how to revise. Following these chapters are some readings by authors who discuss the writing process and how they go about it. As you read through them, think about the advice they are passing on to you and how you can use what they tell you in your own writing.

You don't have to be a great writer to engage your audience and communicate your ideas. But you do have to work at it—remember, practice, practice, and practice some more. Take the feedback you are given, and reflect upon how it may guide you to making better rhetorical choices in your revision. Don't be afraid to try different forms and methods. The truth is, anyone can be eloquent if they work at it. And eloquence will ultimately make your writing successful.

Work Cited

Zinsser, William. *On Writing Well.* 4th ed. New York: Harper Perennial, 1990.

Process and Techniques of Revision and Reflection

Preface

Revision and reflection are often treated as afterthoughts to the writing process. We tend to think of revision as the last step of writing a paper and reflection as something we do to justify our writing choices to a teacher. Revision, however, should occur throughout all stages of the writing process. As you'll learn in this chapter, revision is about much more than simply making your writing better: revision helps you think about making changes to your writing for different occasions and audiences. Reflection allows you to better understand your choices as a writer, to think consciously about those choices, and to explain them to people who are invested in your work. Because you make choices every time you type a word on the page, revision and reflection are always happening. The following chapters will explain how revision and reflection can be useful when repurposing writing from a classroom context to a public audience.

Chapter 18

Reflection and the Art of Revision

By Carol Nowotny-Young

What exactly is reflection? What does it mean to reflect? For some people, the word reflection calls up images of sitting quietly in a summer forest with shafts of sunlight falling between the foliage of full-leafed trees, the air slightly hazy and warm, and the sounds of birdsong and humming insects filling the silence, while their thoughts roam freely inside their heads. For others, the word means looking into a mirror or a body of still water and considering the image that gazes back at them. For still others, reflection means something they should have done before doing something else, so now they have to reflect with the hard clarity of hindsight on the disaster that could have been avoided if only they had reflected first and acted later. Reflection: free-roaming thoughts, visions of the self, or punishing afterthought? Maybe all of them or even none of them.

Nancy Sommers, a writer and teacher of writing, asks in her essay "Between the Drafts," "Where does revision come from? Or, as I think about it now, what happens between the drafts? Something has to happen or else we are stuck doing mop and broom work, the janitorial work of polishing, cleaning, and fixing what is and always has been" (317). Eventually she concludes that what happens is a whole lot of thinking—thinking that rightly could be called "reflection."

Nothing much changes or improves without reflection. But it is also true that human beings are invariably dissatisfied by the status quo, no matter how comfortable or gratifying it may be. We are always in a state of change, even if the changes are so subtle it may appear that we are standing still. I am not talking about the inevitable changes of nature, aging, or time and chance. I am talking about the changes we seek out. "I could do that better," we think, or "I know what's here. I want to see what's there." So we're always on the move, even if it's just in our heads, nomads of the mind.

For those who want to do a job well—whether it's constructing a building, writing a proposal, or even just digging a hole—we know there are always ways the job can be done better. And pondering how the job could be done better is reflection. For those who create art of any kind, reflection according to this definition is essential to the process of creation. There is no such thing as the perfect performance, the perfect painting, or the perfect poem. Art by definition is always in the process of becoming. This is especially true of writers. No matter how good the short story or novel or essay is, a writer can look at it later and see how it could have been done better.

Of course, there is no point in endlessly revising the same piece of writing. At some point, the writer has to call it done and move on. But it's also true that a piece of writing is rarely done in one draft, with just a little of what Sommers calls "mop and broom work" to clean up the misspellings and grammatical errors, straighten out the confused sentence structures, and rearrange the paragraphs into a more coherent order. For many of us, maybe even all of us on some level, this is bad news; we suffered so much just composing that draft that we can't bear to think about it any further. Nevertheless, if we really allow ourselves to think about it, we realize that much of that draft is lame or clumsy or even just plain stupid. And if we've thought that far, we will begin to think about how to make it better.

Just as revising is an essential part of the writing process, so is reflection. But reflection can occur at many points in the writing process: between drafts, during the writing, after the writing, or even long after the writing has been graded, distributed, or even published. Reflection is an important part of the revision process, but it can also be an important act even if you have no plans to revise any further. Reflection on one piece of writing can help you when you write another piece, even writing that is substantially different in form or purpose.

The question then becomes, is there a right way to reflect on your writing? Several points come to mind:

- For reflection to be truly helpful to the writer, he must reflect with a mind open to all possible insights, even the realization that the piece is a total failure. Realizing that your writing has failed miserably is hard to accept, as is failure in any task you take on, but if your writing is to ever improve, accepting failures is essential. Once you accept the failure, you can take a closer look at how and why it failed and learn to recognize what you need to work on. But it's equally important to recognize when your writing has succeeded. You need to know what you've done well and why it is good in order to do it again.

- Reflection is also more productive when it is conducted with a humble spirit. In fact, writing is rarely either a total failure or a total success but falls somewhere in between. In fact, your writing may be quite good, but it can always be better, right? A humble spirit allows you to reflect on how your writing is progressing and consider ways and directions that it can move. A humble spirit also helps you accept the need to revise again, even when you just want to consider it good enough and move on. A humble spirit helps you remember that something was a problem in a previous piece of writing and that you need to rethink your approaches to this new piece of writing. A humble spirit reminds you that your writing is not perfect, but is in the process of becoming so.

- Reflection is best undertaken when you can give it your full attention. If you are distracted by something else, reflection may not go deep enough to provide any insights about your writing. It can even occur while you are writing, so if you are writing with only half your attention, you might miss opportunities to discover some new idea that your writing could bring you to.

- Reflection doesn't always occur when you are sitting in front of your computer and staring at a piece of writing. It can happen anywhere—while you are showering or eating, washing dishes or digging in your garden, working out at the gym or taking a walk—anywhere and anytime that your attention isn't focused elsewhere. Take note of how you are reflecting. Write down some ideas that come to you, if you can. If you can't, at least try to store them in your memory to write down later.

You don't even need to reflect purely in your mind. You can also reflect on paper by focusing on a particular aspect of your writing and then freewriting on it for a particular period of time. The freewriting helps your mind focus and stay connected to a point long enough to allow you to explore it in more depth. It also gives you a record of your reflection.

Reflection is an essential part of the writing process, as essential as invention, drafting, and revision. Any time you are reflecting on your writing, you are changing, progressing in the depth of your thinking, sharpening your perception and critical faculties, and improving the quality of your writing. Even if the changes don't seem very profound or even apparent, they are occurring and will manifest in your writing sooner or later. So make it a habit to reflect on your writing. It is one of the surest ways to improve your work.

Work Cited

Sommers, Nancy. "Between the Drafts." *On Writing Research: The Braddock Essays 1975–1998*. Ed. Lisa Ede. Boston: Bedford/St. Martin's, 1999. 312–320.

Chapter 19

Global Revision

By Faith Kurtyka

Once we move out of the classroom and into the "real world" beyond, our writing goals change. We may no longer be focused only on getting a solid thesis statement or incorporating the right amount of quotes into a research paper. This does not mean that we abandon everything we learned in college; instead, we translate similar principles into texts with different goals. In writing for the general public, the responsibility falls on you to captivate their interest and attention. It is all the more important, then, to know your audience. The most important principle for writing in "the real world" is analyzing your audience and revising with that audience in mind.

An audience's understanding of a text is filtered through the prism of their experience, emotions, and concerns at any given moment. To successfully write and revise for different audiences, you must be able to imagine that audience.

Questions of Audience Awareness

- Why would my audience read my text? Why would they ignore it?

- What do I want my audience to do/think/feel as a result of reading my text?

- What will be interesting and important to them? What don't they need to know?

- What information will they believe in and what will they be skeptical of?

- Will they already believe my information is credible or will I have to prove myself?

- Will they have time to read my text or will they only give it a quick glance?

- How much of what I'm telling them will they already know? What will be new?

- Where will my text be located? How will that determine its audience?

You always knew that your friend Lucy was destined for greatness. Lucy was president of the student government in college, volunteered every week at the homeless shelter, and was always hitting you up for a donation to her favorite charity. After your college graduation, she tells you that her career goal is to be President of the United States, but she's starting small by running for city council. "You were always good with writing," she says. "Will you help me with some of the publicity for my campaign?" She shows you the poster she's designed so far:

Vote for Lucy Bellamy! She's AWESOME!
- 3.5 GPA
- President of MUSB
- Volunteer in the Community

You interview Lucy with your list of audience awareness questions. In your interview, you learn that Lucy wants to hang up posters on campus because that's where the city council district is. She has a large group of friends and supporters on campus, and she is hoping to propel their support into the city council race. Many people on campus already know her name, and they know that "MUSB" is "My University Student Board." They probably don't know anything about city council. You scout out some locations to see what kind of people are there and what they are doing—it is primarily students rushing to classes.

Exercise 1: Based on these answers (and your own knowledge of college campuses and students), fill in the rest of the chart. Each answer leads you to a decision about how the poster should look.

Audience Awareness Question	Answer	Implication for the Poster
Why would my audience read my text?	Because they see Lucy's name and she is popular on campus	Make Lucy's name big!
What will be interesting and important to them? What don't they need to know?	Need to know Lucy's credentials as a student, what she'll do as a city council person; Don't need to know anything else	Stress what she's done as a student, say what she will do on city council
Why would my audience ignore my text?		
How much of what I'm telling them will they already know? What will be new?		

When you revise for the public sphere, it's likely that someone will ask you to defend your choices. In this instance, Lucy will want to know why you think your poster is better than hers. Having solid answers to the questions above will allow you to justify your decisions.

"Great!" Lucy says, after you turn in the finished poster. "Now I'm holding a press conference. Can you help me with my speech?" The first thing to do is revisit your list of questions. A press conference means that Lucy will reach a wider audience who probably doesn't know her. You cannot rely on name recognition to attract your audience. Consider that Lucy is only 22 years old, and may not look how people expect a city councilperson to look. Lucy gives you the following first draft of the speech she's begun writing herself:

> Hello Ladies and Gentlemen. My name is Lucy Bellamy, and I am running for Eighth Ward City Council. I am qualified for this position because I have a 3.5 GPA, was president of MUSB, and I volunteer a lot.

Exercise 2: Based on the **Questions of Audience Awareness**, what problems can you identify with Lucy's speech? How should Lucy address her audience? How should she introduce herself? Will her audience know that "MUSB" stands for My University Student Board? What does it matter that she volunteers "a lot"? How does that qualify her for the position on city council?

Aristotle's concept of the **enthymeme** is useful for trying to figure out how to make your case. An enthymeme is a syllogism, or three-step reasoning scheme. One of the steps of an enthymeme is missing because it is assumed. Using your audience's assumptions is an effective way to argue because they fill in the missing step for you —the argument becomes theirs and feels like common sense. Here's the syllogism that Lucy set up in her speech:

> Lucy was president of MUSB
> People who are Presidents of MUSB are qualified to run for city council.
> Therefore, Lucy is qualified to be on city council.

As you can see, the effectiveness of this argument rests on the audience assuming that the **second premise** is true. Some audiences will think it is; some will think it is not. A more effective argument would revise to make the syllogism truer for a wider audience. In essence, you need to find something else to qualify Lucy. To find a different premise, you ask Lucy some questions about what she did as MUSB president. She says she planned an all-campus party with free pizza and a bouncy castle, re-organized the student government to save money while improving student programs, and campaigned to get the library open 24 hours during finals week. Your job now is to figure out which of these things your audience will find most persuasive to get to the conclusion that "Lucy is qualified to be on city council." This requires, again, learning about your audience and learning what Lucy will have to do on the city council (as well as what your audience *believes* about what people do on the city council). Do city council members need to plan pizza parties? Not really. Do they need to organize budgets? Absolutely. Consider building an enthymeme around this premise for Lucy's campaign speech, remembering that her audience will likely have no idea what an "MUSB" is: "As president of the student government at My University, I re-organized the student government to increase effectiveness and cut spending."

Let's consider a different example. Say you feel passionately about the 8-page research paper you wrote for your English class about women in the workplace. Recently, Desert Wind Plastics, a company that is a major employer in your community, cut funding for a childcare center for its employees. You want your research paper to reach a wider audience, so you decide to write a letter to the editor of your local newspaper. Begin by comparing the assignment sheet your teacher gave you for your English paper and the editorial policy for letters to the editor of the *Arizona Daily Star*.

Research Paper Assignment	Editorial Policy for the *Arizona Daily Star*
Your topic should address some current issue in your major and advance your knowledge. You should have a thesis, generally at the end of the introductory material that states your main argument. The body of your paper should provide evidence to support your thesis, using 7–10 scholarly sources (no internet except for library databases) Page length: 5–8 double-spaced pages	Maximum length is 150 words. Letters more likely to be selected: • Are short and clear. Short means two to three paragraphs. Clear means you quickly explain what prompted you to comment, giving appropriate background, and then make your point. • Are about a current event. • Are about something that others might be interested in. • Add to the public debate. • Are written and argued in a responsible way. • Tell how the news has touched an individual. • Do not include inflammatory statements or name calling. • Include facts and figures that are annotated and verifiable.

Here are the first two paragraphs of your research paper:

Women in the workforce face challenges in progressing to higher-paying positions. One of the causes of this situation is the stereotypes that are present about what women are capable of. Women are judged on their looks, not their abilities, and they are seen to be too emotional and too sensitive to make logical decisions. Men are intimidated by powerful and strong women, and they think women don't belong in positions of power. In this essay, I will argue that inequality in the workplace still exists even today.

According to Alice Kessler-Harris, "Feminist lawyers have disagreed sharply about whether to struggle for special treatment for women in the workforce or to opt for equal treatment with men" (477). This quote shows that women have not achieved equality in the workplace. Women don't know if they want extra privileges or to be treated equally. Extra privileges would entail maternity leave, flexible hours, childcare options, and the opportunity to work from home. Equal treatment would mean being considered for promotion not taking into account gender. However because women struggle with their responsibilities at home and in their jobs, employers should take this into account.

Refer to the **Questions of Audience Awareness**. The *Arizona Daily Star* editorial policy provides you with some answers to these questions. For example, the newspaper wants letters that "add to the public debate." Think about how you can frame the argument above to speak to the issue of Desert Wind Plastics. Also consider the way you will have to simplify and scale down your research paper. Your audience will not need to know all the information you have in your full research paper.

To the Editor: Even in this day and age, women in the workforce face challenges in progressing to higher-paying positions. I was sad to read that Desert Wind Plastics was considering cutting its childcare program because women struggle with their responsibilities at home and in their jobs.

What other evidence or support might you need? What else would you need to find out about the situation of Desert Wind Plastics, and how might you link it to the arguments in the research paper above? What else could you adapt and how?

Globally Revising Your Own Writing

The example above of changing your research paper into a letter to the editor is an example of revising for "the public sphere," which means an audience outside of your classroom. Revising for the public sphere typically requires "global revision," or large-scale changes to your paper, often meaning you must re-write the entire piece. If you revise for the public sphere, consider the following questions:

1. What was the purpose and audience of your original paper? How successfully did it achieve that purpose and reach that audience?

2. Why are you revising this paper?

3. Whom are you revising for? Get solid answers to the **Questions of Audience Awareness**.

4. How will the following aspects of your paper change?

   • Length
   • Format
   • Appearance
   • Use of evidence
   • Introduction and conclusion
   • Structure of your argument
   • Depth of your argument

Chapter 20

Revising for Style

By Star Medzerian

You may have heard the word "style" mentioned in previous writing classes. "Style" has many definitions, but most commonly it refers to how you express your ideas in writing. Think of an author's style you admire. Maybe it is Hemingway or Faulkner; maybe it is the person sitting next to you in class. Have you ever thought about why you enjoy this person's style? There are particular qualities that distinguish one writer from another and make some more or less enjoyable to read. Together, these qualities form the writer's style.

While it makes sense to consider style at all stages of your writing process, considering style when you revise allows you to focus your attention on the craft of your writing. Often, we are so concerned with *what* we are writing we do not consider *how* we are writing it. But, when you revise aspects of your style, you may find that your ideas change as well. Revising for style, then, is not simply polishing up your draft with "better" language, but it is also a process of bringing your ideas as they exist on the page closer to what you intended them to mean.

Before you can begin revising for style, you will want to familiarize yourself with some key concepts associated with style. Once you can recognize these aspects of your style, you will be able to think more consciously about them as choices. You have probably heard of some of these before but may not have thought of them as stylistic features of your writing. Knowing what makes up an author's style can help you revise your own style and figure out what you admire in others' styles.

Let's explore these key concepts by referring back to the revision scenario presented earlier, in which you are revising a research essay into a letter to the editor. When your revision involves changing genres, as this one does, it will also involve stylistic changes. After all, academic essays and letters to the editor are vastly different types of writing with different audiences, contexts, and purposes. So, let's consider some of the stylistic differences between these two genres.

Point of View

One aspect to consider when revising for style is point of view. Typically, research essays are written in third-person to create a more neutral tone that highlights the argument over the arguer. While many instructors will allow you to bring personal experience into a research essay, third-person can make you appear less biased and more credible. Compare, for instance, the following sentences:

> However, because women struggle with their responsibilities at home and in their jobs, employers should take this into account.

> I was sad to read that Desert Wind Plastics was considering cutting its childcare program because women struggle with their responsibilities at home and in their jobs.

The first is from the sample research essay and the second is from the letter to the editor. While both sentences convey the same basic idea, they present that idea in different ways. The first sentence seems much more distanced from the reader, because it is using the point that women struggle with work and home life to argue for a particular action—that employers should consider this situation. The second sentence, however, brings the author's own feelings about a local situation into the argument. The phrase "I was sad" shortens the distance between the writer and the reader, making the writing more personal, biased, and emotional.

Use of Sources

In a research essay for class, such as the sample essay here on inequality in the workplace, you will be expected to cite outside sources. These citations may be in the form of direct quotations or paraphrases and should include information about where they were found, such as the author's name and/or page number. Integrating outside sources into your argument can build your credibility by showing that you have read what others have written about your topic.

In a letter to the editor, however, your purpose is quite different. Most often, letters to the editor are written to express an opinion or persuade others regarding a news item or community issue. While student essays will have formal ways of referring to the ideas of others, letters to the editor will emphasize the author's own perspective on the issue and will not include citations. The following examples illustrate this idea:

According to Alice Kessler-Harris, "Feminist lawyers have disagreed sharply about whether to struggle for special treatment for women in the workforce or to opt for equal treatment with men" (477).

Even in this day and age, women in the workforce face challenges in progressing to higher-paying positions.

You will probably notice right away that the first example, taken from the sample research essay, includes quotation marks, a page number in parentheses, and an introductory phrase that acknowledges the source of the information. The second sentence, from the letter to the editor, does not include these citation conventions, which is considered acceptable for this particular genre. However, if you were to write this same sentence in a research paper, your teacher would probably ask you to support your idea with a source.

Word Choice

Like other aspects of style, word choice is dependent on the genre and audience of your writing assignment. You may choose to call someone "curvy" instead of "fat," knowing that they would be less likely to be offended by the word curvy. Likewise, you may choose to tell a prospective employer why you "left" your last job, as opposed to using the word "quit." These examples point out the importance of connotation when choosing words for your writing.

Another issue related to word choice is jargon, or words specific to a particular group or topic. For example, a doctor in an operating room may say one thing to her nurse when diagnosing a patient's condition but use different words to describe the same condition to the patient. The specialized language, or jargon, that is used between the doctor and nurse may not make sense to the patient. So the doctor must adjust her words accordingly. The same is true when revising from one form of writing to another. Your classmates and instructor will have a shared vocabulary that has developed over the semester. The general public who would read your letter to the editor, however, has not been sitting in the same classroom as you and may not be familiar with your terminology.

Word choices should always consider audience, and the audience for a newspaper is much broader than the audience for a class research paper. That is, more people read local newspapers than will read your class research essay. However, because letters to the editor are intended to address local concerns, you may find that they are more specific. When we compare excerpts from both pieces of writing, we can see how the word choices were chosen for particular audiences. Pay careful attention to the italicized words:

> However because women struggle with their responsibilities at home and in their jobs, *employers* should take this into account.

> I was sad to read that *Desert Wind Plastics* was considering cutting its childcare program because women struggle with their responsibilities at home and in their jobs.

Because the first example is from a research paper about inequality in the workplace in general, the word "employers" is used to refer to everyone who employs women. This could include thousands of businesses. However, in the second sentence, the word "employers" is narrowed to "Desert Wind Plastics," a local business that would probably be known to the audience reading the *Arizona Daily Star*. The argument has been revised from a general observation to a specific call for action.

Concision

Usually, teachers will recommend that you use as few words as possible to communicate your ideas to an audience. You may be tempted at times to add in extra descriptor words, to meet a page limit or to make your writing sound "smarter." Eliminating words where they are not needed may actually make your writing more direct and easier to read. The opposite of concision is wordiness. Wordiness does not mean using a lot of words; rather, it means using more words than are needed to make your point. The easiest way to make wordy writing concise is to look for redundancy. Phrases like "few in number," "first and foremost," and "unite together" are wordy; they use more words than are needed. "Few in number" could become "few;" "first and foremost" could become "first;" and "unite together" could be just "unite."

While concision is always an important part of your style, it is especially useful to consider when revising. Changing genres from an essay to a letter to the editor means that expectations for length change as well. Your research essay may be 8 pages long, but your letter to the editor will only be 150 words, about the length of the previous paragraph. This means you must choose your words wisely. Consider the following sentence from the research essay:

Equal treatment would mean being considered for promotion not taking into account gender.

One way to make this sentence more concise is to change "not taking into account" to "regardless of." The sentence then becomes:

Equal treatment would mean being considered for promotion regardless of gender.

Another example from the letter to the editor could be made more concise by replacing a clichéd phrase with a single word:

Even in this day and age, women in the workforce face challenges in progressing to higher-paying positions.

Here, the phrase "in this day and age" could be replaced with "today," leaving us with four fewer words and a more original claim. When you omit the words you do not need, you can add words that will make your ideas more specific and easier to read. In both research essays and letters to the editor, every word matters.

Exercise: Analyzing and Revising Your Own Style

Considering style when you revise can make your writing more persuasive and engaging. Use the following questions to analyze and begin revising a piece of your own writing.

1. Read over your essay. How would you describe your style? What is the tone of your writing?

2. From what point of view is your essay written? How do you think this point of view affects your style? How might changing your point of view affect your argument?

3. How you cite your sources is just as important as whom you cite. How do you integrate outside sources into your own writing (paraphrases, direct quotations, etc.)? What types of sources do you use to support your points? Why did you choose these sources and how do they affect your credibility?

4. Look through your essay for words that might be known only to the audience of your essay. How would you change these words to make them understandable to a larger or smaller audience? What words do you need to further define or explain?

5. Underline all the long sentences in your essay. Then, look through these sentences for words that can be omitted or phrases that can be shortened. Even short sentences can be made more concise, but long sentences can be a good starting point until you know what to look for. Compare the original sentences to the more concise ones. What was gained or lost in the process of revision?

Chapter 21

Reflecting on the Revision Process

By Erica Cirillo-McCarthy

Many people do not understand the importance of reflecting on the writing process. However, reflection has the potential to improve our writing and help us envision ourselves in regards to the topic and the audience. People do not become better writers by just writing; they become better writers through the act of reflection. Many published writers know the power of reflection. By making reflection an important part of the writing process and part of your assignments, your instructors hope that you will continue to reflect on your writing throughout your academic career and beyond.

Consider this: you want to start cooking more for yourself because the student union offers greasy fried foods that begin to become boring by the third week of the semester. However, you have never really ventured into the realm of real cooking, sticking to ramen noodles and microwave meals. Now, you want to start cooking for yourself and have checked out some recipes online. You start with something basic, like pasta primavera. As you eat it, you reflect on what worked and what did not work. Did you use too much pepper? Not enough? Did you cook your veggies too long, making them mushy? In other words, you reflect on what you can improve upon for next time. The second time you make pasta primavera for your roommates, it is better than the first attempt, and they love it. Then, you cook it for your finicky sister, who does not like too much pepper, so you leave it out. In this reflection and consideration of audience, you become a stronger cook and more confident at the same time.

Reflection can and should be done at the *global* and *local* level. Consider the larger issues you tackled in moving your research paper into a letter to the editor. Larger issues would include reconsideration of audience or a revision of the thesis. Organization and presentation of sources would also fall under the *global* umbrella. *Local* issues would include stylistic changes which occurred after a reconsideration of audience. Making the sentences shorter and clearer and economically using sources to back up claims falls into the realm of local revision.

Let's revisit our research paper and the process of revising it into a letter to the editor. When reflecting on writing, take a look at the larger changes you made. Why did you make them? How effective were the changes? Take a step back and consider how these changes took into account audience and purpose. How does this awareness affect your perception of yourself as a writer?

Original Draft	Revised Draft	Reflection on Revision
Women in the workforce face challenges in progressing to higher-paying positions. One of the causes of this situation is the stereotypes that are present about what women are capable of. Women are judged on their looks and not their abilities, and they are seen to be too emotional and too sensitive to make logical decisions. Men are intimidated by powerful and strong women, and they think women don't belong in positions of power. In this essay, I will argue that inequality in the workplace still exists even today.	To the Editor: Even today, women in the workforce face challenges in progressing to higher-paying positions. I was sad to read that Desert Wind Plastics was considering cutting its childcare program because women struggle with their responsibilities at home and in their jobs.	In the original draft, I was working within the conventions of academic writing—meaning, I needed to write an introduction that set the stage for my topic, and I needed to contextualize my argument. I think I did a good job of detailing the specifics for my audience, especially when I discuss the three stereotypes women face in the workforce. However, I had to reconsider the introduction when I revised for the letter to the editor because I had to get right to the point. My entire intro had to be reduced to two sentences. It was a tough process, but I figured out the most important things I needed to say and said it with the least number of words. Understanding my audience helped me realize I needed to cut my intro to better suit the situation.

Now let's take a look at the stylistic changes made in the different drafts. How did these stylistic reconsiderations change your writing? How did they make you reconsider the meaning and the necessity of each word? How did audience awareness function in your stylistic changes?

Original Draft	Revised Draft	Reflection on Revision
"According to Alice Kessler-Harris, 'Feminist lawyers have disagreed sharply about whether to struggle for special treatment for women in the workforce or to opt for equal treatment with men' (477)."	"Even today, women in the workforce face challenges in progressing to higher-paying positions."	Writing a research paper implies using credible sources and citing them correctly. When I went to write the letter to the editor, I had to cut out many of the sources, but still find a way to state my claim. This was challenging because I became used to using sources on this topic; the move to making claims on my own in short sentences not only clarified my writing, but also my ideas.
"However, because women struggle with their responsibilities at home and in their jobs, employers should take this into account."	"I was sad to read that Desert Wind Plastics was considering cutting its childcare program because women struggle with their responsibilities at home and in their jobs."	In the letter to the editor, I had to be as specific as possible; otherwise, this could have turned into a general rant. So I replaced the word *employers* with *Desert Wind Plastics*. In addition to moving the sentence around, I reconsidered my tone and tried to reach out to those who would read the letters to the editor. I did not feel comfortable using my emotion in my research paper, but in the letter to the editor, I knew it would only help persuade people if they knew exactly how I felt on the issue and why I was writing the letter.

The process of reflection looks not only at the larger changes in your writing, but even the sentence-level issues. It is not about looking at editing changes, i.e., looking at a misplaced comma and talking about why you took that out in the second draft. It is looking at the changes and considering why the changes took place and the potential impacts these changes will have on the audience. The practice of reflection on the writing process as a whole can improve your writing and your sense of yourself as a writer.

Exercise: Reflecting on Your Own Revisiosn Process

1. What was specifically revised from one draft to another?

2. Point to global changes: how did you reconsider your thesis or organization?

3. What led you to these changes? A reconsideration of audience? A shift in purpose?

4. How do these changes affect your credibility as an author?

5. How will these changes better address the audience or venue?

6. Point to local changes: how did you reconsider sentence structure and style?

7. How will these changes assist your audience in understanding your purpose?

8. Did you have to reconsider the conventions of the particular genre in which you are writing?

9. Finally, how does the process of reflection help you reconsider your identity as a writer?

As you can see, writing, through revision and reflection, is a recursive process. Writers continue to return to the writing, return to the rhetorical choices made, return to a reconsideration of audience. It is through this process that writers realize what needs work and what works really well. No one is born with natural writing abilities. True, some people enjoy writing more than others, but anyone can become a strong writer. It takes awareness, and it is through the revision and reflection process that writers become more aware of themselves and the rhetorical situation.

Readings on Revision and Reflection

Erec Toso—Into the Words

This essay was written especially for Writing Public Lives *by Erec Toso, author of the acclaimed* Zero to the Bone: Rewriting Life After a Snakebite.

"I went to the woods because I wished to live deliberately."
—Henry David Thoreau

I am standing in "no man's land," the space between two walls of razor wire fifteen feet high. I am waiting for the electric lock to snap open the latch that will free the locked gate leading to the guard house. Winter wind bites through my jacket and prison pants. They are prison pants because I wear them only for this task. The Arizona Department of Corrections does not allow blue jeans. I have to dress up in khakis. My costume is part of the ritual, of setting aside this time to do my work, my real work.

Rare fresh snow shines on the mountains around the Tucson valley. That brilliant white comes all the way down to the foothills, about 4,000 feet I estimate. The day is astonishingly clear, the desert air having been rinsed by the winter storm. I can see the mountains through the screen of concertina wire in the space between gray block buildings. One of the many ravens rides the wind above me, the rasp of his wings audible as he adjusts his glide toward the roosting murder already in the yard. They look like ornaments in the bare cottonwood, a kind of gallows Christmas tree. They will be my company when I get into the yard and walk to the Programs Room.

I carry a plastic tub full of books, pens, pads of paper, and folders. This stuff is golden to the guys I am going to work with today. We will convene the writing workshop and go over poems, essays, and short stories in the Programs Room. We don't have any high tech screens, Elmos, teaching stations, DVDs, YouTube, or other media. We are lucky to have decrepit desks, cracked plastic chairs, a chalkboard, the few lights that have working bulbs in them, and a few hours to talk about writing.

I am going into the words, and I will soon be listening more intently than I do at any other time in my week. Inmates will read. We will talk about the work, the words, and we will consider choices. If they are willing to listen, to consider options, and to do the work, their writing may be published. Many have gone before them. Some have won national awards for their writing, been featured on interviews on radio and national news television. Some have gone on to teach. Most just pay more attention to how it is they speak to others, whether guards or family.

The words can be a scary place to go and I do not underestimate the fear of going there. We are "made of words" as Scott Momaday says, and some of those words, which form the basis of beliefs, assumption, values—nothing less that a framework for viewing the world, are held under guard, behind barbed wires of defense. Words form stories which can serve as a guide through life or be a kind of poison that leads to self-destruction or places like prison. I know that I have to tread carefully here. Words, like the woods, can be a dangerous place to wander. It helps to be awake and careful, full of care, alert, ready to respond.

Our conversations are not unlike those I have in university classes. In some ways, these two settings are connected. The decrease in state funding for the university has closely paralleled the increase in funding for prisons, and numbers of prison beds are predicted using numbers of students not reading at grade level in elementary school. Literacy and incarceration are two sides of the same coin.

Here is a funny thing about writing. It is best when the writer seems to care about the subject and to take the time to craft the presentation so that readers can care about it too. I would go so far as to say a writer has to cultivate powers of observation, of self-awareness, of—and here is a big one—of *feeling*. Men in prison learn not to feel. It is part of a survival strategy. In the workshops, to write well, they have to learn to feel again, even if it is in limited doses of two hours at a time.

They also have to learn to listen to other points of view. The workshops are likely the only place inside the fences where men of different races can sit down and talk to one another. Those walls do not come down easily.

One of the guys, let's call him James, tested me for months. If I said yes he said no. If I liked a piece, he dissed it. He looked at me hard through his rimmed reading glasses, a tear tattooed to his right cheek, below his blazing blue eyes. Like most of the inmates, his arms wore "sleeves," the ink of tattoos from wrist to shoulder.

"I like to use the word 'love' in my poem," he says one time while we discuss the merits of concrete telling detail.

Every man in the workshop has his eyes on me, waiting.

"'Love' is fine," I say, "as long as you show what you mean by it. Right now it's too loose. Readers won't see what love looks like to you unless you help them out. What are some of the words, specific words—things, places, people, actions—that define that for you?"

He looks at me again, this time, with some recognition.

"One time, I noticed this bird. It was a different kind of bird than we usually see around here. It wasn't a pigeon or a raven. It was blue, and it flew into and out of the yard. It was just as happy here as it was outside. It did not have to change when it went through the razor wire. It was free. It made me mad and jealous."

A couple of the guys nodded approving comments. We went around the circle and spoke in terms other than love, choosing from the repertoire of experience. No generality or cliché or Hallmark card moments.

James still bristles sometimes at criticism, but he takes it in. He begins to do the hard work of choosing. Doing time and doing work. He has begun to move into words as well and his poetry shows it. His work has made it into the *Walking Rain Review* as published, quality work. This from a man who admits that he never learned to write in school, but faked it. He claimed to have a photographic memory and would listen to what others said or read when reading. He would pretend he couldn't see the words without glasses and then absorb what others read aloud. I can only imagine the shame he felt.

Of course, there are others: J., the San Francisco heroin addict turned literary scholar, M. the armed robber who writes sonnets and villanelles, and W. the skinhead and spiritual philosopher. All of them have stories, have a voice that rises out of the disasters of their lives. And they are much better writers than my students at the university. My students, sons and daughters of privilege for the most part, can't find time to read required material, much less expend effort at serious consideration of how best to express a thought. They

SECTION FOUR
Readings

523

hesitate at the edge of the words, a little afraid of what they might find if they entered. One has to be a bit desperate or confined or courageous to go into the words. And, for a while, he or she might get lost. Identity has a way of dissolving when examined beneath the bright, unflinching light of critical thought and choice.

What I ask of the inmates, students, and myself is hard work. A while back I wanted to give up residence here in the words, to stop thinking about them, to stop actively assembling them into a story that would guide my life, a story that would make sense of the disparate craziness that life is sometimes. But I went back to the university with all of its contradictions, bureaucracy and webs of abstraction. Yes, the promise of finding better words, the right ones, has pulled me back to the campus. Why should I go to the words? What lies there that might mean, might serve as some piece of flotsam to cling to? Is there some way to use words to get here, to get closer to the live wire of sensate and sentient moments?

Sometimes when I collect student papers, I find it hard to engage with them, to pose questions about how choices are made, how communication is most effective. But I have to confess that I find the work a strain. I wonder if it is my fault. Those papers, some of them so tortured that they assault my sensibilities of written language. So many words, so few meaningful stories. Are we writing the wrong things? I love my students, but their writing bothers me and my low grade stress becomes the stress of low grades. It is not their fault. Is it mine? Have I connected my own story with my teaching? Have I found a way to blend patience and care, coming from the patient who has been cared for, with the needs of a large university? Again, I don't know but keep asking.

Still some of the papers weigh on me. I carry them everywhere and everywhere avoid them. They hunker down in my book bag, weighty and resentful at them for trying to be something else, someplace other than here. They speak in beefy, self-inflated importance on subjects they know only through distant dreams. They parrot the voices of their parents, blindly, deliberately undoing themselves in the repetition. Yet, despite the odds, a voice emerges, occasionally, and it shocks me with its simple honesty.

But in the continual contact I begin again to see the architecture of language. In the same way that I used to read the pitch of roof, the drainage patterns, the cracks in the tar, the age and quality of the materials, I now read papers for leaks, do triage, provide estimates for repair, recommendations for replacement of conceptual structures. I read the grids and trusses of text. But there is more, something ineffable, something intangible in the potential for expression: the choosing. The choosing and honing and music making of language. With a moment of deliberation before speaking or writing, I am discovering, anyone can alter his or her perception, creating harmony rather than dissonance, art rather than cliché, wonder rather than ennui. This heady wine of potential possesses and consumes me.

I know through long contact how to go into the words, into the silence of choice, of suspension of impulse, into the no-man's land of reflection and listening for the right sounds, the right surprise. But, like climbing mountains, it is a hard place to live, and no one can stay at those altitudes for long. Trying on different ways of seeing things, of new words, can feel foreign, uncomfortable. The change turns me inside out. What was it James Baldwin had written? "We look forward to change about as much we look forward to being born." He was right.

I need empathy and reason and quiet compassion to woo these words out of myself, the inmates, and students. I need to find the right words and build them, one by one, like adobe blocks in a house fit for desert living, into a story in which I find meaning, energy, life force, and my truth.

A story can be revised in times of crisis. Now is just such a time. We need to get out, to wake up, to un-plug, to slow down, to stop long enough to realize that some of the old stories no longer work. The stories of a desert that will support massive, water-hungry cities no longer work. The stories that we don't need a wild nature to define us as civilized no longer work. The stories that we do have to pay attention and to do the hard work of actively taking responsibility for this time, this place, our communities no longer serve us. It is time to re-write, re-think, re-see our stories. It is in that rewriting that the experience of being alive can shift from fear to awe, from subjugation to co-existence, from apathy to agency, from poison to medicine.

In a similar manner, each of us has the opportunity to "go to the words" when we consider what story we will tell about this time of

SECTION FOUR
Readings

our lives. This time, of course, is the here and now, whenever we stop to consider what it is we will write, when deliberate for a moment to consider the path words will take, and choose the telling that best serves our purposes.

Too soon, the two hours of workshop are over, and it's time for "count." The inmates have to get back to the units, their cells. We gather up the loose books and poems to be copied for the next workshop and talk.

James asks "Are you coming back next week?"

I answer that I will.

He says "Good." Then he nods, about to say something else. But then declines. The connections are always incomplete, unresolved, needing work.

We walk out together. He pauses to light a cigarette at the electric lighter that is mounted on a steel pipe at the corner of the sidewalk, a crossroad in the yard. "Well, take care," he says and turns toward his unit. He knows how to survive and he tells me he is learning how to live.

I take the bus back to the Main Gate and pass through the sally port. The prison recedes in the mirror as I drive back up toward the interstate and then toward Tucson and home. I feel more alive than any other time in my weekly routine. I have touched something and know that I am one of the most selfish men on Earth. I do this for me. I need a push to go into the words, need confinement, need prompting, but most of all need care, and dare I say it—love—for life, my place in this moment, this forbidding desert, this open sky.

The reverie fades and I am immersed in the business of livelihood and needing to eat—back down to the bottom of Maslow's hierarchy. At Paco's, my favorite Mexican taco shop, I try not to spill salsa on my prison pants. Here in re-entry after the writing workshops at the prison, it is quiet enough to sit and let the prison voices lift off and away from me. Those voices dim soon after passing back into the "free world." There is so much noise here that I have to listen hard to remember what they said, how they said it, and let those voices settle into my mind before I forget them, voices in search of the words born of patient selection, of answering the right questions, of a desire to be true.

Stephen King—And Furthermore, Part 1: Door Shut, Door Open

Earlier in this book, when writing about my brief career as a sports reporter for the *Lisbon Weekly Enterprise* (I was, in fact, the entire sports department; a small-town Howard Cosell), I offered an example of how the editing process works. That example was necessarily brief, and dealt with nonfiction. The passage that follows is fiction. It is completely raw, the sort of thing I feel free to do with the door shut—it's the story undressed, standing up in nothing but its socks and undershorts. I suggest that you look at it closely before going on to the edited version.

The Hotel Story

Mike Enslin was still in the revolving door when he saw Ostermeyer, the manager of the Hotel Dolphin, sitting in one of the overstuffed lobby chairs. Mike's heart sank a little. *Maybe should have brought the damned lawyer along again, after all*, he thought. Well, too late now. And even if Ostermeyer had decided to throw up another roadblock or two between Mike and room 1408, that wasn't all bad; it would simply add to the story when he finally told it.

Ostermeyer saw him, got up, and was crossing the room with one pudgy hand held out as Mike left the revolving door. The Dolphin was on Sixty-first Street, around the corner from Fifth Avenue; small but smart. A man and woman dressed in evening clothes passed Mike as he reached, out and took Ostermeyer's hand switching his small overnight case to his left hand in order to do it. The woman was blonde, dressed in black, of course, and the light, flowery smell of her perfume seemed to summarize New York. On the mezzanine level, someone was playing "Night and Day" in the bar, as to underline the summary.

"Mr. Enslin. Good evening."

"Mr. Ostermeyer. Is there a problem?"

Ostermeyer looked pained. For a moment he glanced around the small, smart lobby, as if for help. At the concierge's stand, a man was discussing theater tickets with his wife while the concierge himself watched them with a small, patient smile. At the front desk, a man with the rumpled look one only got after long hours in Business Class was discussing his reservation with a woman in a smart black suit that could itself have doubled for evening wear. It was business as usual at the Hotel Dolphin. There was help for everyone except poor Mr. Ostermeyer, who had fallen into the writer's clutches.

"Mr. Ostermeyer?" Mike repeated, feeling a little sorry for the man.

"No," Ostermeyer said at last. "No problem. But, Mr. Enslin... could I speak to you for a moment in my office?"

So, Mike thought. *He wants to try one more time.*

Under other circumstances he might have been impatient. Now he was not. It would help the section on room 1408, offer the proper ominous tone the readers of his books seemed to crave—it was to be One Final Warning—but that wasn't all. Mike Enslin hadn't been sure until now, in spite of all the backing and filling; now he was. Ostermeyer wasn't playing a part. Ostermeyer was really afraid of room 1408, and what might happen to Mike there tonight.

"Of course, Mr. Ostermeyer. Should I leave my bag at the desk, or bring it?"

"Oh, we'll bring it along, shall we?" Ostermeyer, the good host, reached for it. Yes, he still held out some hope of persuading Mike not to stay in the room. Otherwise, he would have directed Mike to the desk...or taken it there himself. "Allow me."

"I'm fine with it," Mike said. "Nothing but a change of clothes and a toothbrush."

"Are you sure?"

"Yes," Mike said, holding his eyes. "I'm afraid I am." For a moment Mike thought Ostermeyer was going to give up. He sighed, a little round man in a dark cutaway coat and a neatly knotted tie, and then he squared his shoulders again. "Very good, Mr. Enslin. Follow me."

The hotel manager had seemed tentative in the lobby, depressed, almost beaten. In his oak-paneled office, with the pictures of the hotel on the walls (the Dolphin had opened in October of 1910—Mike might publish without the benefit of reviews in the journals or the big-city papers, but he did his research), Ostermeyer; seemed to gain assurance again. There was a Persian carpet on the floor. Two standing lamps cast a mild yellow light. A desk-lamp with a green lozenge-shaped shade stood on the desk, next to a humidor. And next to the humidor were

Mike Enslin's last three books. Paperback editions, of course; there had been no hardbacks. Yet he did quite well. *Mine host has been doing a little research of his own*, Mike thought.

Mike sat down in one of the chairs in front of the desk. He expected Ostermeyer to sit behind the desk, where he could draw authority from it, but Ostermeyer surprised him. He sat in the other chair on what he probably thought of as the employees' side of the desk, crossed his legs, then leaned forward over his tidy little belly to touch the humidor.

"Cigar, Mr. Enslin? They're not Cuban, but they're quite good."

"No, thank you. I don't smoke."

Ostermeyer's eyes shifted to the cigarette behind Mike's right ear—parked there on a jaunty jut the way an oldtime wisecracking New York reporter might have parked his next smoke just below his fedora with the PRESS tag stuck in the band. The cigarette had become so much a part of him that for a moment Mike honestly didn't know what Ostermeyer was looking at. Then he remembered, laughed, took it down, looked at it himself, then looked back at Ostermeyer.

"Haven't had a cigarette in nine years," he said. "I had an older brother who died of lung cancer. I quit shortly after he died. The cigarette behind the ear…" He shrugged. "Part affectation, part superstition, I guess. Kind of like the ones you sometimes see on people's desks or walls, mounted in a little box with a sign saying BREAK GLASS IN CASE OF EMERGENCY. I sometimes tell people I'll light up in case of nuclear war. Is 1408 a smoking room, Mr. Ostermeyer? Just in case nuclear war breaks out?"

"As a matter of fact, it is."

"Well," Mike said heartily, "that's one less worry in the watches of the night."

Mr. Ostermeyer sighed again, unamused, but this one didn't have the disconsolate quality of his lobby-sigh. Yes, it was the room, Mike reckoned. His room. Even this afternoon, when Mike had come accompanied by Robertson, the lawyer, Ostermeyer had seemed less flustered once they were in here. At the time Mike had thought it was partly because they were no longer drawing stares from the passing public, partly because Ostermeyer had given up. Now he knew better. It was the room. And why not? It was a room with good pictures on the walls, a good rug on the floor, and good cigars— although not Cuban—in the humidor. A lot of managers had no doubt conducted a lot of business in here since October of 1910; in its own way it was as New York as the blonde woman in her black off-the-shoulder dress, her smell of perfume and her unarticulated promise of sleek sex in the small hours of the morning—New York sex. Mike himself was from Omaha, although he hadn't been back there in a lot of years.

"You still don't think I can talk you out of this idea of yours, do you?" Ostermeyer asked.

"I know you can't," Mike said, replacing the cigarette behind his ear.

What follows is revised copy of this same opening passage—it's the story putting on its clothes, combing its hair, maybe adding just a small dash of cologne. Once these changes are incorporated into my document, I'm ready to open the door and face the world.

~~The Hotel Story~~ **1408** ①

By Stephen King

② Mike Enslin was still in the revolving door when he

Olin

saw ~~Ostermeyer,~~ the manager of the Hotel Dolphin,

sitting in one of the overstuffed lobby chairs. Mike's

heart sank ~~a little~~. *Maybe should have brought the*

damned lawyer along again, after all, he thought.

Olin

Well, too late now. And even if ~~Ostermeyer~~ had

decided to throw up another roadblock or two

between Mike and room 1408, that wasn't all bad; ~~it~~

there were compensations.

~~would simply add to the story when he finally told it~~

Olin

~~↳ Ostermeyer saw him, got up, and~~ was crossing

the room with one pudgy hand held out as Mike left

the revolving door. The Dolphin was on Sixty-first

Street, around the corner from Fifth Avenue, small

but smart. A man and woman dressed in evening

clothes passed Mike as he reached out and took

Olin's

~~Ostermeyer's~~ hand, switching his small overnight

On Writing

case to his left hand in order to do it. The woman was blonde, dressed in black, of course, and the light, flowery smell of her perfume seemed to summarize New York. On the mezzanine level, someone was playing "Night and Day" in the bar, as if to underline the summary.

"Mr. Enslin. Good evening."

"Mr. ~~Ostermeyer~~ *Olin.* Is there a problem?"

~~Ostermeyer~~ *Olin* looked pained. For a moment he glanced around the small, smart lobby, as if for help. At the concierge's stand, a man was discussing theater tickets with his wife while the concierge himself watched ~~them~~ with a small, patient smile. At the front desk, a man with the rumpled look one only got after long hours in Business Class was discussing his reservation with a woman in a smart black suit that could itself have doubled for evening wear. It was business as usual at the Hotel Dolphin. There was help for everyone except poor Mr. ~~Ostermeyer~~ *Olin,* who had fallen into the writer's clutches.

"Mr. ~~Ostermeyer~~ *Olin*?" Mike repeated, ~~feeling a little sorry for the man.~~

Stephen King

"No," Ostermeyer said at last. "No problem. But, Mr. Enslin . . . could I speak to you for a moment in my office?"

~~So,~~ Mike thought. ~~He wants to try one more time~~ *And well, and why not?* ~~Under other circumstances he might have been impatient. Now he was not.~~ It would help the section on room 1408, ~~offer~~ *add to* the ~~proper~~ ominous tone the readers of his books seemed to crave. *and that wasn't all,* ~~it was to be One Final Warning—but that wasn't all,~~ Mike Enslin hadn't been sure until now, in spite of all the backing and filling; now he was. ~~Ostermeyer~~ *Olin* wasn't playing a part. ~~Ostermeyer~~ *Olin* was really afraid of room 1408, and what might happen to Mike there tonight.

④ "Of course, Mr. ~~Ostermeyer~~ *Olin.*" ~~Should I leave my bag at the desk, or bring it?"~~

"Olin," "Oh, we'll bring it along, shall we?" Ostermeyer, the good host, reached for ~~it. Yes, he still held out~~ *Mike's bag.* ~~some hope of persuading Mike not to stay in the room. Otherwise, he would have directed Mike to the desk . . . or taken it there himself.~~ "Allow me."

"I'm fine with it," Mike said. "Nothing but a change of clothes and a toothbrush."

"Are you sure?"

On Writing

(5) "Yes," Mike said, holding his eyes. "I'm ~~afraid I~~ already wearing my lucky Hawaiian shirt." He smiled. "It's the one with ~~on~~ the ghost repellent."

~~For a moment Mike thought Ostermeyer was~~ 9 Olin ~~going to give up. He~~ sighed, a little round man in a dark cutaway coat and a neatly knotted tie, ~~and then he squared his shoulders again.~~ "Very good, Mr. Enslin. Follow me."

The hotel manager had seemed tentative in the lobby, ~~depressed,~~ almost beaten. In his oak-paneled office, with the pictures of the hotel on the walls (the Dolphin had opened in October of 1910—Mike might publish without the benefit of reviews in the journals or the big-city papers, but he did his research), ~~Ostermeyer~~ Olin seemed to gain assurance again. There was a Persian carpet on the floor. Two standing lamps cast a mild yellow light. A desk-lamp with a green lozenge-shaped shade stood on the desk, next to a humidor. And next to the humidor were Mike Enslin's last three books. Paperback editions, of course; there had been no hardbacks. ~~Yet he did quite well.~~ *Mine host has been doing a little research of his own,* Mike thought.

Stephen King

(6) Mike sat down ~~in one of the chairs~~ in front of the

desk. He expected ~~Ostermeyer~~ Olin to sit behind the

desk, ~~where he could draw authority from it,~~ but

~~Ostermeyer~~ Olin surprised him. He ~~sat in the other chair~~ took the chair

~~on what he probably thought of as the employees'~~ beside Mike,

~~side of the desk,~~ crossed his legs, then leaned for-

ward over his tidy little belly to touch the humidor.

"Cigar, Mr. Enslin? ~~They're not Cuban, but~~ o

~~they're quite good."~~

"No, thank you. I don't smoke."

~~Ostermeyer~~ Olin's 's eyes shifted to the cigarette behind

Mike's right ear—parked ~~there~~ on a jaunty jut the

way an oldtime wisecracking New York reporter

might have parked his next smoke just below ~~his~~

~~fedora with~~ the PRESS tag stuck in the band. of his fedora. The cig-

arette had become so much a part of him that for a

moment Mike honestly didn't know what ~~Oster~~ Olin

~~meyer~~ was looking at. Then he ~~remembered,~~ e

laughed, took it down, looked at it himself, then

looked back at ~~Ostermeyer~~ Olin.

"Haven't had ~~a cigarette~~ one in nine years," he said.

"I had an older brother who died of lung cancer. I

(7) quit ~~shortly~~ after he died. The cigarette behind the

On Writing

ear . . ." He shrugged. "Part affectation, part super- ~~Like the Hawaiian shirt. Or the cigarettes~~ stition, I guess. ~~Kind of like the ones~~ you some-

times see on people's desks or walls, mounted in a

little box with a sign saying BREAK GLASS IN CASE OF

EMERGENCY. ~~I sometimes tell people I'll light up in~~

~~case of nuclear war.~~ Is 1408 a smoking room, Mr.
Olin
~~Ostermeyer?~~ Just in case nuclear war breaks out?"

"As a matter of fact, it is."

"Well," Mike said heartily, "that's one less worry
Ⓔ
in the watches of the night."
Olin
Mr. ~~Ostermeyer~~ sighed again, ~~unamused~~ but
sigh
this ~~one~~ didn't have the disconsolate quality of his
office,
lobby-sigh. Yes, it was the ~~room,~~ Mike reckoned.
office
His ~~room.~~ Even this afternoon, when Mike had

come accompanied by Robertson, the lawyer,
Olin
~~Ostermeyer~~ had seemed less flustered once they

were in here. ~~At the time Mike had thought it was~~
⑨
~~partly because they were no longer drawing stares~~

~~from the passing public, partly because Oster-~~

~~meyer had given up. Now he knew better. It was~~
Where else could you feel in charge, if not in your special place? Olin's
~~the room. And why not?~~ ~~It~~ was a room with good ⌐office

pictures on the walls, a good rug on the floor, and

good cigars ~~although not Cuban~~ in the humi-

Stephen King

dor. A lot of managers had no doubt conducted a
lot of business in here since ~~October of~~ 1910; in its
own way it was as New York as the blonde ~~woman~~
in her black off-the-shoulder dress, her smell of
perfume and her unarticulated promise of sleek (New York)
sex in the small hours of the morning. ~~New York~~
~~sex.~~ Mike himself was from Omaha, although he
hadn't been back there in ~~a lot of~~ 5 years.

"You still don't think I can talk you out of this
                                    Olin
idea of yours, do you?" ~~Ostermeyer~~ asked.

"I know you can't," Mike said, replacing the cigarette behind his ear.

The reasons for the majority of the changes are self-evident; if
you flip back and forth between the two versions, I'm confident that
you'll understand almost all of them, and I'm hopeful that you'll see
how raw the first-draft work of even a so-called "professional writer"
is once you really examine it.

Most of the changes are cuts, intended to speed the story. I have
cut with Struck [editor's note: William Strunk, co-author of *The
Elements of Style*] in mind—"Omit needless words"—and also to
satisfy the formula stated earlier [in King's book, from which this
excerpt is taken]: 2nd Draft = 1st Draft – 10%.

I have keyed a few changes for brief explanation:

1. Obviously, "The Hotel Story" is never going to replace "Kill-
   dozer!" or *Norma Jean, the Termite Queen* as a title. I simply slot-
   ted it into the first draft, knowing a better one would occur as I
   went along. (If a better title doesn't occur, an editor will usually
   supply his or her idea of a better one, and the results are usually
   ugly.) I like "1408" because this is a "thirteenth floor" story, and
   the numbers add up to thirteen.

2. Ostermeyer is a long and gallumphing name. By changing it to
   Olin via global replace, I was able to shorten my story by about
   fifteen lines at a single stroke. Also, by the time I finished "1408,"

I had realized it was probably going to be part of an audio collection. I would read the stories myself, and didn't want to sit there in the little recording booth, saying Ostermeyer, Ostermeyer, Ostermeyer all day long. So I changed it.

3. I'm doing a lot of the reader's thinking for him here. Since most readers can think for themselves, I felt free to cut this from five lines to just two.

4. Too much stage direction, too much belaboring of the obvious, and too much clumsy back story. Out it goes.

5. Ah, here is the lucky Hawaiian shirt. It shows up in the first draft, but not until about page thirty. That's too late for an important prop, so I stuck it up front. There's an old rule of theater that goes, "If there's a gun on the mantel in Act I, it must go off in Act III." The reverse is also true; if the main character's lucky Hawaiian shirt plays a part at the end of a story, it must be introduced early. Otherwise it looks like a *deus ex machina* (which of course it is).

6. The first-draft copy reads "Mike sat down in one of the chairs in front of the desk." Well, duh—where else is he going to sit? On the floor? I don't think so, and out it goes. Also out is the business of the Cuban cigars. This is not only trite, it's the sort of thing bad guys are always saying in bad movies. "Have a cigar! They're Cuban!" Fuhgeddaboudit!

7. The first- and second-draft ideas and basic information are the same, but in the second draft, things have been cut to the bone. And look! See that wretched adverb, that "shortly"? Stomped it, didn't I? No mercy!

8. And here's one I didn't cut...not just an adverb but a Swiftie: "Well," Mike said heartily... But I stand behind my choice not to cut in this case, would argue that it's the exception which proves the rule. "Heartily" has been allowed to stand because I want the reader to understand that Mike is making fun of poor Mr. Olin. Just a little, but yes, he's making fun.

9. This passage not only belabors the obvious but repeats it. Out it goes. The concept of a person's feeling comfortable in one's own special place, however, seemed to clarify Olin's character, and so I added it.

SECTION FOUR
Readings

537

I toyed with the idea of including the entire finished text of "1408" in this book, but the idea ran counter to my determination to be brief, for once in my life. If you would like to listen to the entire thing, it's available as part of a three-story audio collection, *Blood and Smoke*. You may access a sample on the Simon and Schuster Web site, http://www.SimonSays.com. And remember, for our purposes here, you don't need to finish the story. This is about engine maintenance, not joyriding.

SECTION FOUR
Readings

Mary Kennan Herbert—Poetry and Comment

Journal of the Medical Humanities, Vol. 22, 1, March 2001, 83–86.
Reprinted with permission obtained via RightsLink.

Skin Man

Skin Man Seven

A dermatologist must be the world's
best lover: those hands hold my face
in the intensity of a gaze unmatched
by any other visual suitor. My face,
my face. Fingers walk across brows,
a magnifying glass exhumes secrets
that I hid from everyone on eyelids
now naked to the eye, revealed by
plows turning over epidermis, furrows
made visible, friable, according to farmers
who can see right through solid soil,
who can see how to make earth yield
and comply. My eyes, eyelids, brow,
bone, cheek, chin. Skin Man looks
harder at my soul's mask than anyone,
peeling off layers, cornices, shades,
showing off the real me, now rid of
the public facade, one foolish face
undressed by one wise face who knows
what the skull confesses, easy pickings.

Skin Man Seventeen

Most of my patients are AIDS victims,
said the doctor gayly. I don't get too many
cases of adolescent acne any more, or
even ordinary basal cells.
Well, I must be a nice change of pace,
with my cancer-flecked face. Almost as frisky
as freckles, a light-hearted carcinoma,
bless my soul, it's like tinkling bells.

SECTION FOUR
Readings

No Karposi Sarcoma, just this cute
crusty crater trying to hide and then exposing
itself, flinging open an epidermis raincoat
to show off flesh fighting itself in Hell.

This is an unusual type, the physician
enthusiastically explained. It grows heartily
under the surface of the skin, not like the
pearly bumps. This one rarely tells
you what it's up to (no good, right?), it's
secretive, hiding. A poet's cheek it's stealing.
Ah, you have that famous Irish skin,
the M.D. cheerfully said. He knows what sells.

Skin Man Nineteen

Hey, pizza face. No, you have it all wrong. Behind this mask
is a beautiful poet. Look, I will be happy to peel it off. Just ask.
We will just roll up this skin like an old rug, an easy task,
and then look at me, look at me, a radiant wordsmith, a gift so true,
eye candy, the one you see in the mirror, the one who loves you.
Ah, that smile will knock your socks off, and those eyes, those eyes
so blue,
okay, gray. It doesn't matter, the face is your ticket to Paradise.
You don't have to worry about losing a breast, or whatever. Gray
skies—
well, you know the rest. No problem can get you down—get wise,
nothing stands in your way when you see God or me in the mirror,
either one will do, either one cures acne, the blues, the terror.

Commentary

Everything is fair game for a poet. Mockingbirds, a flash of feathers,
flesh, the Inferno, a foundry, bordello, belladonna, pubic hair, police, lice, poultry, cold waves of the North Atlantic splashing against
the rocky coast of Maine, sunrise, sloth, Thoth. This stream of consciousness, Doc, is what I rely on to get me over a creative hump or
through a slump or a swamp.

Hmmm, a case of skin cancer was the triggering device for a
series of poems? Yes, I confess.

No drugs or booze? Some poets rely on the bottle or the cigarette, but in this case I think it's the box of memories that does it. It's the memories of very focused episodes: the good doctor slicing away at my face. "It's bigger than I would like," he said casually, referring to the naughty bit of tissue, his cheerful voice carved into my slate. His voice was destined to trigger a poem. Images and words jam-packed into a little box, and they've just got to come out. They've just got to, or else the visual and verbal suppressed memories feed neurotic behavior, noncreative behavior. The poetry is a healthier outlet than developing shingles or a stuttering problem.

Why the series of Skin Man poems? When I was in my twenties, I spent lots of time on the beach, roasting, toasting my fair skin. I paid the price for such vanity, for about 25 years later I developed skin cancers on my face. Interestingly, at about the same time, I began to write poetry once again after a hiatus of about three decades. I had written poetry as a college undergraduate, but then wrote nothing until after a midlife divorce and career change. I developed my poetry along with some basal cell and squamous cell carcinomas.

A neighbor, a fine surgeon, looked at my face and commented, yeah, that took about 25 years of incubation. So I was incubating the good and the bad, together. I have developed six cases of carcinomas on my face. Maybe there are still more, waiting to come on stage, like ideas for poems eventually taking form, stepping forth to take a bow. I got pretty good at diagnosing myself. I learned how to tell a good bump from a bad bump.

I began to write poems about many things in my middle years. The skin cancer episodes did not trigger poems at first, but after a while they did, and these poems had to be written. I wrote several of them to take my mind off of my face. The skin cancer poems were a way to express my anger and my interest in "facing" a medical problem. It wasn't like the horror of dealing with breast cancer or colon cancer, but skin cancer is a very visible attack on one's persona. For example, I was embarrassed to mention my skin cancer to a psychiatrist, because it seemed like a trivial complaint, not a serious issue like AIDS or incest. But it is an attack on one's sense of self all the same, and a reminder of mortality every time one faces a mirror.

A student of mine came up to me after class one day and said, "Professor Herbert, you have chalk on your face." It was not chalk, it was the scar tissue of one of the skin cancers, a permanent re-

SECTION FOUR
Readings

minder of my folly in romping in the sun. So I tried to deal with these ideas in my poems, and the poems are the best way to share my concerns.

The language of cancer and medicine became part of my poetic language. The methodology of physicians and their affect became part of my thinking as a poet. I wanted to defuse the depressive aspects and also incorporate some humor. No matter how awful the diagnosis or the disease, there is always a bit of humor to be found. Laughter and poetry play a role in therapy; poetry can bring a touch of wit to uncomfortable situations. Poems can alleviate sorrow if they can elicit a smile, even a half-smile. The therapy is in the language. I did not want to portray my own dermatological problems as dramatizations of a major life-threatening illness but, at the same time, it was important to convey my emotional distress and possible feelings, of others in the same boat.

Writing a series of poems about skin cancer became an interesting and unusual creative challenge. I eventually wrote twenty poems in the "Skin Man" group. Then I stopped. I had other fish to fry. Twenty seemed to be enough, but I might go back to them again. I could add more. The muse will tell me when and if I should. Or my flesh will speak out, and then I will record what the skin wants to say.

SECTION FOUR
Readings